MASTERING THE OLD TESTAMENT

MASTERING THE OLD TESTAMENT

EZRA, NEHEMIAH, ESTHER

MARK ROBERTS

LLOYD J. OGILVIE, GENERAL EDITOR

WORD PUBLISHING
Dallas•London•Vancouver•Melbourne

MASTERING THE OLD TESTAMENT, Volume 11: *Ezra, Nehemiah, Esther*.
Copyright © 1993 by Word, Inc. All rights reserved. No portion of this book may be
reproduced in any form whatsoever, except for brief quotations in reviews, without
written permission from the publisher.

[Formerly, *The Communicator's Commentary Series, Old Testament*]

Library of Congress Cataloging in Publication Data
Main entry under title:

Mastering the Old Testament
[The Communicator's commentary.]
   Bibliography: p.
   Contents: OT11. Ezra, Nehemiah, Esther/by Mark D. Roberts
   1. Bible. O.T.—Commentaries. I. Ogilvie, Lloyd
John. II. Roberts, Mark D.,
BS1151.2.C66   1993   221.7'7   93-39330
ISBN 0–8499–3550–4 (v. OT11) [pbk]
ISBN 0–8499–0416–1 (v. OT11) [hd]

Printed in the United States of America

349   AGF   987654321

To my grandmother, Martha Williams,
and to the memory of my grandfather,
Donald Williams.
Thanks for everything!

Contents

Section Two: The Book of Esther

Editor's Preface

God has called all of His people to be communicators. Everyone who is in Christ is called into ministry. As ministers of "the manifold grace of God," all of us—clergy and laity—are commissioned with a challenge to communicate our faith to individuals and groups, classes and congregations.

The Bible, God's Word, is the objective basis of the truth of His love and power that we seek to communicate. In response to urgent, unexpressed needs of pastors, teachers, Bible study leaders, church school teachers, small group enablers, and individual Christians, the Communicator's Commentary is offered as a penetrating search of the Scriptures of the Old and New Testament to enable vital personal and practical communication of the abundant life.

Many current commentaries and Bible study guides provide only some aspects of a communicator's needs. Some offer in-depth scholarship but no application to daily life. Others are so popular in approach that biblical roots are left unexplained. Few offer impelling illustrations that open windows for the reader to see the exciting application for today's struggles. And most of all, seldom have the expositors given the valuable outlines of passages so needed to help the preacher or teacher in his or her busy life to prepare for communicating the Word to congregations or classes.

This Communicator's Commentary series brings all of these elements together. The authors are scholar-preachers and teachers outstanding in their ability to make the Scriptures come alive for individuals and groups. They are noted for bringing together excellence in biblical scholarship, knowledge of the original Hebrew and Greek, sensitivity to people's needs, vivid illustrative material from biblical, classical, and contemporary sources, and lucid communication by the use of clear outlines of thought. Each has been selected to contribute to this series because of his Spirit-empowered ability to help people live in the skins of biblical characters and provide a "you-are-there" intensity to the drama of events of the Bible which have so much to say about our relationships and responsibilities today.

The design for the Communicator's Commentary gives the reader an overall outline of each book of the Bible. Following the introduction, which reveals the author's approach and salient background on the book, each chapter of the commentary provides the Scripture to be exposited. The New King James Bible has been chosen for the Communicator's Commentary because it combines with integrity the beauty of language, underlying Hebrew and Greek textual basis, and thought-flow of the 1611 King James Version, while replacing obsolete verb forms and other archaisms with their everyday contemporary counterparts for greater readability. Reverence for God is preserved in the capitalization of all pronouns referring to the Father, Son, or Holy Spirit. Readers who are more comfortable with another translation can readily find the parallel passage by means of the chapter and verse reference at the end of each passage being exposited. The paragraphs of exposition combine fresh insights to the Scripture, application, rich illustrative material, and innovative ways of utilizing the vibrant truth for his or her own life and for the challenge of communicating it with vigor and vitality.

It has been gratifying to me as editor of this series to receive enthusiastic progress reports from each contributor. As they worked, all were gripped with new truths from Scripture—God-given insights into passages, previously not written in the literature of biblical explanation. A prime objective of this series is for each user to find the same awareness: that God speaks with newness through the Scriptures when we approach them with a ready mind and a willingness to communicate what He has given; that God delights to give communicators of His Word "I-never-saw-that-in-that-verse-before" intellectual insights so that our listeners and readers can have "I-never-realized-all-that-was-in-that-verse" spiritual experiences.

The thrust of the commentary series unequivocally affirms that God speaks through the Scriptures today to engender faith, enable adventuresome living of the abundant life, and establish the basis of obedient discipleship. The Bible, the unique Word of God, is unlimited as a resource for Christians in communicating our hope to others. It is our weapon in the battle for truth, the guide for ministry, and the irresistible force for introducing others to God.

A biblically rooted communication of the Gospel holds in unity and oneness what divergent movements have wrought asunder. This commentary series courageously presents personal faith, caring for individuals, and social responsibility as essential, inseparable dimensions of biblical Christianity. It seeks to present the quadrilateral Gospel in its fulness which calls us to unreserved commitment to Christ, unrestricted self-esteem in His grace, unqualified love for others in personal evangelism, and undying efforts to work for justice and righteousness in a sick and suffering world.

A growing renaissance in the church today is being led by clergy and laity who are biblically rooted, Christ-centered, and Holy Spirit-empowered. They have dared to listen to people's most urgent questions and deepest needs and then to God as He speaks throughout the Bible. Biblical preaching is the secret of growing churches. Bible study classes and small groups are equipping the laity for ministry in the world. Dynamic Christians are finding that daily study of God's Word allows the Spirit to do in them what He wishes to communicate through them to others. These days are the most exciting time since Pentecost. The Communicator's Commentary is offered to be a primary resource of new life for this renaissance.

It has been very encouraging to receive the enthusiastic responses of pastors and teachers to the twelve New Testament volumes of the Communicator's Commentary series. The letters from communicators on the firing line in pulpits, classes, study groups, and Bible fellowship clusters across the nation, as well as the reviews of scholars and publication analysts, have indicated that we have been on target meeting a need for a distinctly different kind of commentary on the Scriptures, a commentary that is primarily aimed at helping interpreters of the Bible to equip the laity for ministry.

This positive response has led the publisher to press on with an additional twenty-one volumes covering the books of the Old Testament. These new volumes rest upon the same goals and guidelines that undergird the New Testament volumes. Scholar-preachers with facility in Hebrew as well as vivid contemporary exposition have been selected as authors. The purpose throughout is to aid the preacher and teacher in the challenge and adventure of Old Testament exposition in communication. In each volume you will meet Yahweh, the "I AM" Lord who is Creator, Sustainer, and Redeemer in the unfolding drama of His call and care of Israel. He is the Lord who acts, intervenes, judges, and presses His people into the immense challenges and privileges of being a chosen people, a holy nation. And in the descriptive exposition of each passage, the implications of the ultimate revelation of Yahweh in Jesus Christ, His Son, our Lord, are carefully spelled out to maintain unity and oneness in the preaching and teaching of the Gospel.

It is a distinct pleasure to introduce the author of this outstanding commentary on Ezra, Nehemiah, and Esther, the Reverend Doctor Mark Roberts, Pastor of the Irvine Presbyterian Church, Irvine, California. Over the past twenty-one years, I have been privileged to know Mark Roberts as a personal friend, member of the First Presbyterian Church of Hollywood and then as an esteemed colleague in ministry on the church staff, from 1984 to 1991. He served as Director of College Ministries and subsequently as Associate Pastor of Educational Ministries of the church before moving to the Irvine church where he has become a revered preacher.

Dr. Roberts pursued his education at Harvard University, where he received his Bachelor of Arts, magna cum laude, in Philosophy, his Master of Arts in the Study of Religion, and his Doctor of Philosophy in New Testament and Christian Origins.

As you will soon discover in reading this volume, Dr. Roberts is a first-rate scholar, is highly skilled in Hebrew, Greek, and Aramaic, and is an excellent biblical expositor. He is also a very lucid writer, an impelling preacher and teacher, and a visionary pastor. Mark exemplifies the finest of a new and emerging generation of scholar-preachers in America today.

As the author of this volume, Dr. Roberts is no stranger to the vision and development of the Communicator's Commentary series. He has been my close working assistant in the editing and final preparation for publication of the Old Testament volumes of the series. His contribution to the project has been invaluable. Therefore, I was delighted when he agreed to invest his experience, scholarship, and communication skills in the writing of this significant volume. As you will soon discern, the result is one of the most penetrating and inspiring commentaries on these three crucial books of the Old Testament available to preachers and teachers today.

Mark Roberts has faithfully and intentionally written this commentary for communicators. Each discussion of the biblical text in every chapter anticipates the needs and questions of today's preachers and teachers. Dr. Roberts' experience of preaching and teaching these books of the Old Testament on several occasions has greatly contributed to his ability to know what communicators need.

This commentary has two main strengths, among many others. First, Dr. Roberts has done in-depth study of the text. His goal to help the reader understand the text is achieved by his working knowledge of Hebrew and Aramaic. This provides the reader with deep insight and fresh inspiration for his or her own communication of the material.

The second major strength of this commentary is that it is full of useful applications and illustration. Commenting on this, Dr. Roberts says, "As a preacher, my most difficult challenge is to find good illustrative material, especially stories. Since my goal is to assist communicators, I have filled these pages with useful illustrations that will help communicators to think of similar situations from their own lives."

You will not have read far into this commentary before you are impressed with the way Dr. Roberts has achieved the focused purpose of the Communicator's Commentary series: illuminating exposition of the Scriptures and inspiring application for contemporary preaching and teaching.

Another stunning aspect of this commentary is the author's strong effort to engage our culture. Although he includes quotations from classic sources—hymns, biographies, and literature—many of the illustrations come from newspapers, popular movies, television programs, and secular books on leadership. His interaction with pop culture reflects his passion to communicate with persons often ignored by preachers and teachers: young people, inquirers, and secular unbelievers. Without ever compromising God's truth, he strives to communicate it in a way that engages people in our world today.

In a period of history like ours that cries out for decisive and compelling leaders in the church, Dr. Roberts' commentary of Ezra-Nehemiah (one book in the Hebrew and treated as such in this commentary) provides rich resources for understanding and implementation of the biblical principles of leadership. These principles are spelled out utilizing the best of the contemporary literature on the effective leader's style and strengths. This commentary of Ezra-Nehemiah should be required reading for pastors and church officers. Here again the author's scholarship helps us live in the tumultuous world of Ezra and Nehemiah while at the same time enabling us to discover God's strategy for the church in our turbulent world today.

The interpretation of Esther will provide preachers and teachers a fresh approach to this often misinterpreted and neglected book of the Bible. He proposes an explanation of the secularism of Esther and brilliantly connects this explanation with the book's literary purpose, theological significance, and contemporary relevance. Throughout, Dr. Roberts' treatment of Esther encourages us to grapple with the soul-sized moral issues of our lives in the light of God's wisdom. It raises and confronts the problems of racism and ethnic conflict that dog our steps today. Most important of all, this commentary on Esther challenges us to consider what it means to live as God's people in an alien, secular culture.

As communicators we all long for those magnificent moments in our preparation when we are gripped with an inspired insight into a passage of Scripture that prompts us to exclaim, "That will preach!" We are filled with excitement and enthusiasm to share what we've discovered. This is exactly what will happen as you study this commentary. It is power-packed and brimming over with new insight into familiar passages and with keys to unlock the preaching and teaching values of passages seldom utilized by communicators of the Word.

This commentary is so rich with personal and practical inspiration and application for daily living that many will want to use it for devotional reading as a part of their own daily discipline of Bible study and prayer.

Mark Roberts' profound faith and dynamic adventure as a man in Christ shines through on each page of this commentary. He is vulnerable, open, and honest about how the Scriptures he explains have impacted his own life as a person, preacher, and leader.

I commend this commentary to you with gratitude to the author for all he has meant to me as my friend and for all he has done in helping me put the Old Testament volumes of this Communicator's Commentary series into your hands.

LLOYD OGILVIE

Author's Preface

This is a commentary for communicators. At every step in the process of researching and writing I have kept in mind the needs and concerns of teachers and preachers who seek to understand the Scriptures and to communicate their timeless truths in today's world. Of course that is exactly what I seek to do each week as I preach to the congregation at Irvine Presbyterian Church. I have worked through most of the material in this book with the Irvine church, as well as with various groups at the First Presbyterian Church of Hollywood. These experiences have helped to make this commentary more useful for those who labor alongside me "in the trenches" of Bible teaching and preaching.

Throughout my writing I have kept in mind three questions that challenge everyone who teaches the Bible:

1. What did the text mean in its original context?

2. What does the text mean for us?

3. How can we illustrate the text so that it will come alive today?

The first question demands careful exegesis. I have done my best to understand each passage in its historical and literary context, paying attention to issues of language, form, and style. I have approached exegesis of the text from the perspective of the communicator who needs to understand the basic meaning of a passage without solving every academic puzzle.

The second question—What does the text mean for us?—challenges us to interpret and to apply Old Testament narratives in our contemporary world. Whereas in exegesis one can make some definitive judgments about meaning, interpretation and application allow for greater freedom and creativity. In the commentary I have tried to keep exegetical and hermeneutical concerns somewhat distinct, although they always mesh in practice. Exegetical comments are followed by separate sections for interpretation, which I call "Reflections" or "From a Christian Perspective." These titles suggest that other reflections or perspectives may be equally valid and worthy of communication. I hope that my suggestions serve as a catalyst for the reader's own creative process of interpretation and application.

As a preacher, I find the third question, the question of *illustration*, to be the most challenging. Using the tools of exegesis I can usually discover the original meaning of the passage on which I am preaching. In most cases, worthwhile interpretations come through prayerful reflection on what the text originally meant. But illustration . . . now there's a pesky chore! I often struggle to find stories that convey the meaning of a text with clarity and emotion. Yet gripping illustrations have never been more important for effective communication. They give life to difficult concepts and power to applications. If a picture is worth a thousand words, then a perfect illustration is worth a whole sermon!

In order to help communicators, I have filled this commentary with illustrations. I begin each chapter with a story that introduces the passage under examination. (I have in fact used most of these stories to begin sermons, so I can vouch for their usefulness.) The interpretive material at the end of each chapter also contains one or more stories that entertain while they instruct. I have often included anecdotes from my personal experiences. I do this as an example for other communicators, since I have found that my congregation responds most favorably to stories of my life, my struggles, and my victories. Of course the reader is free to tell my stories in the third person, "A certain man was walking along the road . . . ," etc. I hope, however, that my reminiscences will remind the reader of applicable personal experiences from his or her own life, for nothing adds to the power and personality of communication like personal anecdotes.

The reader will find a broad range of illustrative materials in this commentary: from Calvin's *Institutes* to the recent best-seller *In Search of Excellence*; from Shakespeare's *Julius Caesar* to Peter Benchley's *Jaws*. My illustrations run the gamut from the sublime to the ridiculous. I recognize that some of the stories will be more useful to some readers than to others. I have tried to include something for the wide spectrum of communicators who will use this commentary: youth ministers, preachers, women's Bible-study leaders, those who teach lunchtime Bible studies for business people, and so on.

Also, I must confess my particular passion for communicating with youth and with the unchurched. Each Sunday the junior highers at Irvine Presbyterian Church sit in the front rows of the sanctuary. Their presence continually reminds me of my need to communicate with youth through my illustrations, especially in a time of history when millions of Christian young people are leaving the church. I also find among my listeners a growing group of unchurched people who are looking to the church for meaning and community. These secular people, who do not understand Christian jargon and find it difficult to relate to church-specific illustrations, desperately need to hear and to grasp the gospel of Jesus Christ. We can stand back and lament the growing secularism of our society, but when we stand up in the pulpit or lectern we are called to communicate God's truth to worldly people, many of whom do not know the first thing about God. Illustrations from "their world" draw them in to hear God's truth, while making that truth understandable. I hope this commentary will challenge you and equip you to communicate God's timeless truth in the temporal forms of this secular generation.

I am grateful to Lloyd Ogilvie and Word, Inc. for the privilege of writing this commentary. It has been a pleasure to work closely with David Pigg, manager of academic and pastoral publishing at Word, and with my editor, Terri Gibbs. She has made this book immensely more readable and beneficial for the readers.

Many others have offered their prayers and support. I am particularly thankful for: the congregations in Irvine and Hollywood whose input has enriched my work; my staff colleagues, Friday morning prayer group, and Saturday evening prayer group, who have regularly prayed for this project; Fred Bush and Tod Bolsinger, who have been valuable sounding boards for my work; and Dorothy Larson, who has helped with copying, mailing, and communicating with Word, Inc. I owe special thanks to my wonderfully patient family. Linda has been more than gracious in allowing me the time to finish this project. Nathan, in his entire three months of life, has yet to know a Saturday when his Dad had nothing else to do but play with him. Next Saturday begins a new chapter in our life together!

I have dedicated this volume to my grandparents, Donald and Martha Williams, who have given me a lifetime of love, encouragement, and prayer—not to mention ham sandwiches and Doritos. I wish my grandfather were still alive to enjoy the dedication of this book. His love for God's truth and my grandmother's love for communicating God's truth have impacted my life—and therefore this commentary—beyond measure.

MARK ROBERTS

Why Study Ezra and Nehemiah?

Our first question as we embark upon a study of Ezra and Nehemiah should be: *Why study these books at all?* Indeed, if we do not ask this question ourselves, our students and parishioners will ask it of us! Twice in my ministry I have preached through Ezra and Nehemiah, both at Hollywood Presbyterian Church and at Irvine Presbyterian Church. And each time the people wanted to know why I had chosen to preach on such relatively obscure biblical texts. (The fact that I was writing a commentary on the books did not seem to be an adequate answer.)

As we studied through Ezra and Nehemiah, however, my church members began to see and to experience the contemporary relevance of these biblical books, which, on the surface, seem so far removed from our experiences today. The fact is, the stories and themes contained within these books speak profoundly to our deepest longings and questions. Ezra and Nehemiah address issues that make the front pages of our newspapers—and they speak to the yearnings of our hearts. Specifically, I would offer four reasons why Ezra and Nehemiah deserve careful study today:

1. They address our need, both personal and corporate, for restoration and renewal.
2. They provide models of leadership that we should imitate.
3. They tell stories of real people just like us.
4. They help us to avoid the dire "Wawona Syndrome."

Our Need for Restoration and Renewal

We yearn for restoration and renewal on all levels of life. As I listen to members of my congregation, I sense a yearning for spiritual restoration. People long to recover a fresh, intimate relationship with God because years of busyness and spiritual neglect have led many of us to a wasteland of distance from God. Like the psalmist we pray,

Create in me a clean heart, O God,
And renew a steadfast spirit within me.
Do not cast me away from Your presence,
And to not take Your Holy Spirit from me.
Restore to me the joy of Your salvation,
And uphold me by Your generous Spirit.
Psalm 51:10–12

In addition to the need for spiritual renewal, millions of people today ache for emotional healing. We know too well the deep wounds that come from having alcoholic parents, or from childhood sexual abuse. Many of us pray to have our emotional lives restored to what God has intended for us all along. As a pastor, I am both amazed and distressed at the large number of men and women who have experienced horrible things from their own family members, and who yearn to know the healing, renewing power of God.

Our need for restoration also touches upon relationships. Broken marriages and splintered families fill our communities—and our churches. Families, former business partners, and neighbors seek to rebuild shattered relationships. And all too often these days I find myself sitting down with a Christian couple who ask me in desperation: "How can God restore our marriage when it feels so dead?"

Brokenness touches us not only in personal and relational ways, but within our social order as well. Hate rules the day in our world. We read about ethnic cleansing in Bosnia or racial divisions within our own cities. Our memories continue to play back the vivid pictures of rioting in Los Angeles in April of 1992. And where I live, in Orange County, California, people are stunned these days by an outbreak of senseless violence among our young people—not the inner city poor, but the suburban rich who are on their way to our finest colleges. In his inaugural address, President Bill Clinton spoke passionately of the need for renewal in America, and regardless of our political leanings, we must certainly agree.

Throughout the Western World churches are closing their doors, unable to pay the bills. Others continue to stay afloat, but only as dwindling, aging congregations. I come from a denomination that, like most of the major denominations in America, loses members by the thousands each year. Church leaders and members are asking: "How can restoration happen in our church? How can we recover our zeal?"

On virtually every level of life we yearn for restoration, and that is exactly why we need to study Ezra and Nehemiah. These books narrate the story of how God restored his fallen nation after it had been destroyed by the Babylonians. As we will see, God's restoration deals with practical matters, such as rebuilding the Dung Gate of a city wall, and with deeply spiritual matters, such as the confession of national sin. *Ezra and Nehemiah will help us to be renewed in our own lives and to become leaders of renewal in our churches and throughout our world.*

I experienced the power of God to use these books early in my ministry. When I first began as the College Director at Hollywood Presbyterian Church I thought I knew exactly how to succeed in my job. But after five dismal months I saw the group shrink to half its original size, and those who remained complained about everything. I felt drained, discouraged, and full of doubt about my fitness to pastor. On a two-day personal retreat, the Lord led me to study Ezra and Nehemiah. There I discovered principles that sparked personal renewal and a transformation of my ministry. As I led the college group through a study of these books, our relationship began to change for the better. God used Ezra and Nehemiah to renew my life and my ministry, and I trust that he will do the same for you and your church!

MODELS OF LEADERSHIP FOR TODAY

It has become commonplace to decry the absence of leadership in America. Whereas other nations have their heroes, such as Lech Walesa or Nelson Mandela, we seem to live without leaders of stature and moral fortitude. Leaders to whom we once looked have fallen in disgrace, while others have simply been eclipsed by a changing world in which they have become increasingly impotent. Two years ago the nation hailed President Bush as a miraculous coalition-builder and a brilliant strategist. Recently we watched as he turned over the reigns of power to a relatively untried Governor from Arkansas. What ever happened to Mikhail Gorbachev, Margaret Thatcher, and Ronald Reagan?

The crisis of leadership affects the church in America and throughout the world. We all know the infamous pastors who have fallen in disgrace. But it seems that hardly a week goes by but that we hear of some other pastor or Christian leader who has resigned because of sexual immorality. This lack of strong leadership is a worldwide concern for the Church. In 1988, the Lausanne Committee for World Evangelization sponsored "Leadership '88" in Washington D.C. It was an event designed for older leaders to encourage and to "pass on the torch" to younger leaders. Yet the conference accomplished less than its organizers and participants had hoped. Nagging questions remain: Who will lead the Church into the next millennium? What will Christian leadership look like in the year 2000?

Ezra and Nehemiah provide models for leaders of today and tomorrow. Although they led God's people more than 2400 years ago, their priorities and practices continue to be relevant in our world. In fact, as we will see, both Ezra and Nehemiah illustrate principles found in today's best sellers on leadership. Anyone who has been given authority to lead—in church, in business, in schools, in the family, anywhere—should study the examples of Ezra and Nehemiah carefully. My own pastoral practice has benefited and been significantly shaped by a study of these men.

STORIES ABOUT PEOPLE JUST LIKE US

We certainly need to know the straightforward theological sections of the Bible—the Law, the Prophets, and the letters of Paul—for they provide the bedrock for our understanding of God and our faith. But good theology also comes to life in the narratives of Scripture. As we read stories about the patriarchs, the kings, the disciples, and the earliest Christians, we learn from those who have gone before us. We laud their victories and mourn their failures; we relate to their vain efforts, their fears, and their utterly familiar humanness.

People who are just like us fill the pages of Ezra and Nehemiah. As we study, we will encounter people rejoicing over God's miraculous blessings; mourning because the "good ol' days" are gone; becoming discouraged and failing to obey God; facing impossibly difficult ethical decisions; asking the boss for a special favor; confronting the mockery of enemies and the treachery of friends; delighting in success; and reeling with failure. Even though a gulf of 2400 years stands between us and those who star in Ezra and Nehemiah, we will find our lives and our struggles vividly portrayed in these ancient pages.

22

AVOIDING THE "WAWONA SYNDROME"

As a child, I loved the Wawona tree in Yosemite National Park. It was a Giant Sequoia redwood that had been carved out as a tunnel—while still standing as a living tree. I can still remember the thrill of being in my parents' car as we drove through the middle of that awesome tree. But several years ago the Wawona tree fell to the ground and died. Naturalists investigated why the tree had fallen when it appeared to be thriving. They discovered that although nutriment continued to flow to the high branches the root system had been irreparably damaged. The weak roots finally could support the giant tree no longer, and it fell with a ponderous thud.

Many Christians today suffer from what I call the "Wawona Syndrome"—they have been cut off from their theological roots. Let me give just one example. A highly touted preacher in California recently confronted a difficult social issue in his church. After weeks of careful study, he confidently announced one Sunday: "I've found God's answer for us. I'm quite sure of it because I went back to the source of all truth and read it cover to cover. Last week I re-read the entire New Testament!" He went on to propose his solution to the problem, which, I believe, was sorely lacking. Why had he missed the mark? Possibly because he did not go back to the complete truth of God. He completely omitted the Old Testament from his consideration! He read the New Testament, not in its proper historical and theological context, but rather in light of his own presuppositions and prejudices. He missed God's direction, in my opinion, because he ignored the strategic theological roots of the Old Testament.

The "Wawona Syndrome" occurs whenever Christians disregard the Old Testament. The second-century heretic Marcion blatantly rejected the Jewish Scriptures as inspired by an inferior deity. Now while most of us would disagree with Marcion's position, we regularly imitate his practice by failing to study the Old Testament. And it is easy to understand how this can happen. The Old Testament feels distant and foreign. It was written long ago about people who lived in a different world. Many Old Testament practices seem distasteful—animal sacrifices, for example. So, most of us limit our Old Testament reading to a few Psalms, especially the ones we like, or we might enjoy a smattering of prophetic passages, especially those in Händel's *Messiah*. But, by and large, we ignore the rest of our Old Testament roots.

Yet if we are to take the New Testament seriously, we must realize how utterly dependent it is upon the Old. Moreover, the New Testament itself teaches us to regard the Hebrew Scriptures as "inspired by God" and "profitable" (2 Tim. 3:16). If we want a faith that lasts, a theology that is true, and a Christian life deeply rooted within God's revelation, then we need to study the Old Testament, including Ezra and Nehemiah. Indeed, for persons unfamiliar with the Hebrew Scriptures, these books provide a particularly easy point of introduction.

A LITERARY AND HISTORICAL INTRODUCTION TO EZRA AND NEHEMIAH

Ezra-Nehemiah: One Book

Although English translations of the Bible regard Ezra and Nehemiah as two separate books, in actuality they were written as one continuous work. In the earliest versions of the Hebrew Bible, Ezra-Nehemiah appeared as a unit.[1] This is also true for the ancient Greek translation of the Old Testament, the Septuagint, in which Ezra-Nehemiah stands as one book called Esdras B (or Esdras II). The textual history of Ezra-Nehemiah seems confusing at first, with the ancient Greek and Latin versions of the Bible employing a variety of names and textual variants.[2] However, the modern interpreter may trust the authenticity of the text as it stands in English Bibles but should regard Ezra-Nehemiah as a single book with two parts.

Ezra-Nehemiah: A Collection of Sources

The reader of Ezra-Nehemiah will quickly notice diverse literary elements, including autobiographical stories, extensive lists, letters, and third-person descriptions. One may be surprised to discover that the book includes both Hebrew and Aramaic languages. Ezra 4:8–6:18 and 7:12–26 were written in Aramaic while the rest was written in Hebrew. The author of Ezra-Nehemiah did not compose his work out of completely original material, but, rather, collected many older sources and edited them into a continuous and well-ordered account. The sources found in Ezra-Nehemiah include:

1. Royal decree(s) (Ezra 1:2–4; 6:3–5)
2. Lists of people (Ezra 2; Neh. 7, 11, 12)

3. Aramaic letters (Ezra 4:8–6:12; 7:12–26)
4. Ezra's memoirs (portions of Ezra 7–10, perhaps Neh. 8)
5. Nehemiah's memoirs (most of Neh. 1–7 and 13, perhaps other sections of Nehemiah).

The fact that the editor of Ezra-Nehemiah used sources like these strengthens the historical reliability of the work. It also prepares the reader to interpret the text with sensitivity to its components and overall structure. The person who penned the collection that we read as Ezra-Nehemiah did not simply paste things together in a random or even chronologically-rigid way. Rather, he carefully wove the strands together to produce a coherent and theologically-textured literary fabric—one that also tells a good story.

The Author of Ezra-Nehemiah

We do not know exactly who edited the disparate sources that make up Ezra-Nehemiah. Scholars have often identified him with the person who composed 1 and 2 Chronicles, known as "The Chronicler."[3] This conclusion is based on theological similarities between the books of Chronicles and Ezra-Nehemiah and upon a telling overlap between the last verses of 2 Chronicles and the first verses of Ezra. (Ezra 1:1–3 reproduces 2 Chronicles 36:22–23 almost verbatim.) Stylistic and theological variations between Chronicles and Ezra-Nehemiah suggest, however, that the author of the later work was closely related to the Chronicler but was not the same person.[4] In the end, we are left with a variety of ingenious theories about the author or authors of Ezra-Nehemiah but without any indubitable choice. We do know, however, that he was a careful scholar who affirmed the sovereignty of God and longed for the full restoration of Israel.

The Date of Composition

As in the case of authorship, we cannot achieve certainty about when the unidentified editor collected sources and composed Ezra-Nehemiah. Of course this must have happened after the events described, which could establish the earliest possible date at around 430 B.C. Most scholars agree that the final editing of the book happened no later than 300 B.C. Many of the sources in Ezra-Nehemiah, however, are earlier than 430 B.C.; the decree of Cyrus (Ezra 1:2–4; 6:3–5), for example, was given in 538 B.C.

The Genre and Purpose of Ezra-Nehemiah

Commentaries and Old Testament introductions rarely consider the nature of Ezra-Nehemiah. Conservative scholars simply assume that it is a work of history, and critical scholars become so wrapped up in questions of sources and composition that they easily overlook the nature of the finished work. To be sure, Ezra-Nehemiah should be considered a work of history along the lines of 1 and 2 Chronicles. Thus, in English Bibles Ezra-Nehemiah joins the "historical" books. The Hebrew canon, however, places it among the "Writings" (the third section of the Scriptures, following the Law and the Prophets). To identify Ezra-Nehemiah as history, however, does not mean that it was composed according to modern standards of historiography. For example, a basic chronological sequence gives order to the book, but Ezra 4:6–23 intentionally disrupts the chronological flow. The author wanted to tell what happened, but not as a listing of mere facts. Rather, he recounted the facts according to his theological commitments, and, I might add, according to divine inspiration.

Ezra-Nehemiah was written, therefore, not simply to recount what happened. If we read only to find out what went on 2400 years ago, then we will miss the point. The author wanted to instruct and to edify by telling a story of restoration through Ezra and Nehemiah. He selected certain primary sources and carefully crafted his account in order to illustrate something profound about God and God's restoration of his people.

Chronological Puzzles in Ezra-Nehemiah

As mentioned above, the author of Ezra-Nehemiah structured his work by an overarching chronological schema. He does not, however, tell his story in a strictly chronological order. The text in Ezra 4:5 places the action within the reign of Darius, king of Persia from 522 to 486 B.C. Then chapters 5 and 6 continue telling the story of what happened during his reign, but 4:6–23 interrupts the sequence by describing what happened while Artaxerxes I was king (4:7–23; 465–423 B.C.). This shows that while the author values chronology he does not always describe events in the order in which they occurred. Of course this does not mean that he is either deceptive or a poor historian. The idea that history must always be recounted chronologically is ours, not his.

Because the author exercises literary freedom in his account, certain chronological puzzles plague those of us who look for the precise order in which things happened. One such puzzle concerns Sheshbazzar and Zerubbabel. Ezra 1:8 identifies Sheshbazzar as "the prince of Judah" who led the people from Babylon to Jerusalem, and Ezra 5:14–16 recognizes him as the "governor" who laid the foundation for the temple. But when chapter 2 lists those who returned from Babylon, Sheshbazzar is not mentioned. Chapter 3 pictures Zerubbabel as the one who superintended the founding of the temple, moreover, the prophet Haggai applies the title of "governor" to him (for example, Hag. 1:1). Yet Ezra-Nehemiah never spells out the relationship between Sheshbazzar and Zerubbabel, nor does it clarify the apparent confusion of their roles. While scholars have offered several theses to explain this oddity,[5] I regard it as a historical puzzle that may not have a definitive solution simply because the author chose to pay attention to other things in his writing.

The historical relationship between Ezra and Nehemiah has also vexed commentators. A cursory reading of the text seems at first to explain their relationship quite clearly: Ezra came to Jerusalem thirteen years before Nehemiah, who, upon arriving in Judah, served alongside Ezra for an unspecified duration of time. This may in fact be exactly what happened, but, upon closer inspection, the text causes us to wonder about this order of events. For example, King Artaxerxes sent Ezra to Judah to teach the Law in the seventh year of Artaxerxes (Ezra 7:7–10). According to the story, Ezra did not fulfill this assignment until after Nehemiah arrived, some 13 years later (Neh. 2:1; 8:1–12). How odd! Moreover, in the autobiographical source material from Ezra and Nehemiah, neither person mentions the other (except for Neh. 12:36). Finally, what Ezra did accomplish in his first year appears to have been forgotten completely by Nehemiah only a few years later. In fact, it seems never to have happened at all (Ezra 9–10; Neh. 13). Ezra ends up looking like a procrastinator who failed in significant aspects of his mission. Yet this certainly does not match his elevated status within Jewish tradition, where he stands as a second Moses. Could it be, scholars have wondered, that the author of Ezra-Nehemiah rearranged the order of events here, much as he did in Ezra 4? Did Ezra actually follow Nehemiah? Gallons of academic ink have been spilled in an attempt to offer solutions to this vexing problem.[6]

In this commentary I assume that Ezra preceded Nehemiah, just as the text states. Objections to this position have been answered by scholars, and I feel it provides the best perspective from which to understand Ezra-Nehemiah. At any rate, the author of Ezra-Nehemiah wanted his readers to view the ministries of Ezra and Nehemiah as concurrent and complementary. I do want to add, however, that holding a high view of scriptural authority does not compel one to place Ezra before Nehemiah. This would be true only if the author intended to provide a rigidly chronological order of events. But if the author wanted, instead, to tell a theologically-shaped story by a creative use of historical sources, then we could accept any number of historical theses and still uphold biblical inerrancy or infallibility. Generally speaking, advocates of either of these positions on biblical authority qualify their views in terms of the writer's intentions and rightly so! I believe that, in theory, the author of Ezra-Nehemiah could have altered the chronology of events without being deceptive or in any way untruthful since chronology was not his main intention. But I also believe that, in fact, he placed Ezra and Nehemiah in their actual order.

If these last sentences have confused you thoroughly, let me give an example to explain further. As a preacher I always try to tell the truth, especially in my illustrations. I know so many Christians who doubt the credibility of preachers because they have heard too many far-fetched stories. Unlike some preachers, I do not use "poetic license" as an excuse for exaggeration or fabrication. But sometimes I do change details in a story. Suppose I want to illustrate a sermon with a story that someone has shared with me in strictest confidence. I will ask that person for permission to share "a version" of his or her story. I promise to change enough relevant details, including names, so that no one will be able to identify the individual involved. My congregation understands and supports this practice. Therefore, since I do not intend or pretend to reveal privileged information in preaching, one would scarcely accuse me of being untruthful. Analogously, if the author of Ezra-Nehemiah intended to present a theological painting rather than a factual photograph, then only one who ignored his intentions would accuse him of being errant or fallible.

Overview of the Contents of Ezra-Nehemiah

Ezra-Nehemiah tells the story of the restoration of Judah after the Babylonian exile. It focuses on events that happened between 538 B.C. and 430 B.C. (or so). The time-line chart at the end of this introduction places the major events of Ezra-Nehemiah in a helpful chronological framework.

Ezra-Nehemiah can be divided into four major sections:

  I.   Restoration of the Temple   Ezra 1:1–6:22

  II. Restoration of Covenant Life, Phase One: The Work of Ezra
       Ezra 7:1–10:44

  III. Restoration of the Wall through Nehemiah
       Nehemiah 1:1–6:19

  IV. Restoration of Covenant Life, Phase Two: Ezra and Nehemiah
       Work Together   Nehemiah 7:1–13:31

The theme of restoration ties the whole book together. Somewhat surprisingly, Ezra himself does not appear until the last four chapters of the book bearing his name. Nehemiah, on the other hand, dominates the first six chapters of the book of Nehemiah. For a more detailed overview of the contents of Ezra-Nehemiah, see the outline that appears at the end of this introduction.

The Place of Ezra-Nehemiah Within the History of Israel

The story of Ezra-Nehemiah can best be understood within the context of Israelite history, which begins with God's *covenant with Abraham* in Genesis 12. God told Abram (soon to be called Abraham) to go from his country to a new land in which God would make from Abram's seed a great and blessed nation (Gen. 12:1–3). Abraham trusted God and entered into a covenantal relationship with him (Gen. 12:4; 15:6).

Although Abraham settled in the land of promise, his great-grandchildren were driven to Egypt by famine. There they spent more than 400 years in bondage to the Pharaohs until God delivered them

29

through the leadership of Moses. In that context God *made another covenant with Israel,* as found in Exodus:

> And Moses went up to God, and the Lord called to him from the mountain, saying, "Thus you shall say to the house of Jacob, and tell the children of Israel: 'You have seen what I did to the Egyptians and how I bore you on eagles' wings and brought you to Myself. Now therefore, if you will indeed obey My voice and *keep My covenant,* then you shall be a special treasure to Me above all people; for all the earth is Mine. And you shall be to Me a kingdom of priests and a holy nation.' These are the words which you shall speak to the children of Israel." So Moses came and called for the elders of the people, and laid before them all these words which the Lord commanded him. Then all the people answered together and said, "All that the Lord has spoken we will do."
>
> *Exodus 19:3–8 (emphasis added)*

Israel would be God's "special treasure" and "holy nation" if the people obeyed his voice and kept his covenant: the Law revealed on Mt. Sinai.

After a series of missteps, Israel conquered the land of promise and became God's holy nation. Unlike other nations, Israel had no human king. God was their only sovereign, who ruled through human judges. But the people were not satisfied with a divine king. They wanted to be just like the other nations, so they clamored for a human king. In spite of their rejection of God as king, God nevertheless heeded their wishes in anointing King Saul over Israel.

Once the human kingship had been established, *God again updated his covenant with Israel, this time through King David.* As Psalm 89 records, God said:

> I have made a covenant with My chosen,
> I have sworn to My servant David;
> "Your seed I will establish forever,
> And build up your throne to all generations."
> *Psalm 89:3–4*

If the descendants of David disobeyed God, then he would punish them, but he would not remove David's line from the kingship of Israel, which would last forever (Ps. 89:30–37).

In the following years, David's kingdom deteriorated, falling from glory into ruin. His grandchildren divided Israel into two kingdoms: the Northern Kingdom of Israel and the Southern Kingdom of Judah. Because the kings of the north led the people to reject God and worship the Baals, in 722 B.C. God raised up Assyria to destroy the Northern Kingdom.

Matters in Judah appeared to be better for a while, as the people occasionally listened to the prophets who called them back to God. But, increasingly, Judah also rejected God. Meanwhile, the once mighty Assyrian empire fell to the Babylonians in 612 B.C. Seven years later the infamous dictator Nebuchadnezzer ascended to the throne of Babylon, with his sights set upon Judah, and in 587 B.C. Jerusalem fell to the Babylonians. Nebuchadnezzar's men killed the leaders of Judah, burned the temple in Jerusalem to the ground after pillaging its sacred contents, and took the best and brightest citizens of Judah back to Babylon as prisoners.

The year 587 B.C. appeared to be the end of the dream for the Children of Israel. The nation promised to Abraham had completely collapsed. God's special people, named in the Mosaic covenant, were special no more. The Davidic kingdom had been completely ruined, along with the temple, the center of Jewish worship. The multifaceted covenant between God and his people appeared to have been decimated through the unfaithfulness of Israel.

In exile the people yearned for the day when God would rebuild the nation. The prophet Ezekiel looked forward to spiritual restoration, when "dry bones" would come to life again (Ezek. 37:4 ff.). Jeremiah had prophesied the defeat of Babylon and the reestablishment of Israel (Jer. 50:1–5). Isaiah was even more specific about how this would happen:

> Thus says the LORD to His anointed,
> To Cyrus, whose right hand I have held—
> To subdue nations before him
> And loose the armor of kings,
> To open before him the double doors,
> So that the gates will not be shut:
> 'I will go before you
> And make the crooked places straight;
> I will break in pieces the gates of bronze
> And cut the bars of iron.

> I will give you the treasures of darkness
> And hidden riches of secret places,
> That you may know that I, the LORD,
> Who call you by your name,
> Am the God of Israel.
> For Jacob My servant's sake,
> And Israel My elect,
> I have even called you by our name;
> I have named you, though you have not known Me. . . .'
> I have raised him up in righteousness,
> And I will direct all his ways;
> He shall build My city
> And let My exiles go free
> Not for price nor reward,"
> Says the LORD of hosts.
>
> *Isaiah 45:1–4, 13*

As the people in exile yearned for God's restoration, Jeremiah and Isaiah promised deliverance from the Babylonians through God's anointed, Cyrus, who would restore Israel.

In the context of the history of Israel through the Exile, then, we read Ezra 1:1:

> Now in the first year of Cyrus king of Persia, that the word of the LORD by the mouth of Jeremiah might be fulfilled, the LORD stirred up the spirit of Cyrus king of Persia, so that he made a proclamation throughout all his kingdom. . . .

The appointed time had come—restoration was at hand.

RESOURCES FOR STUDYING EZRA-NEHEMIAH

Teachers and preachers of Ezra-Nehemiah are blessed with a wealth of resources for studying this ancient document. Although I know that taste in commentaries varies widely, nonetheless I would make a few suggestions. I believe that one who embarks upon the serious study of a biblical book should, if at all possible, have access to at least two commentaries on that book. Since you have this commentary already, I will suggest other options.

The Word Biblical Commentary volume on *Ezra, Nehemiah* by H.G.M. Williamson is detailed, innovative, and clear. This is an academic commentary, to be sure, full of scholarly arguments, extensive references, and plenty of Hebrew. It demands time and thought, but rewards those who are willing to invest what is required.

A third commentary I would recommend is Derek Kidner's volume in the Tyndale Old Testament Commentary series. This text is solidly conservative and persuasive in its arguments. Since this commentary is quite short, it gets to the point quickly. After Kidner, evangelical communicators would appreciate the New International Commentary on the Old Testament volume by F. Charles Fensham. I have found it particularly useful when looking for biblical cross-references. Additional commentaries will be cited in the bibliography.

In addition to having two solid commentaries, students of the Old Testament should have a detailed Bible atlas and at least one quality Bible encyclopedia or dictionary. Several years ago I decided to spend most of my "book allowance" on volumes like these for my personal research library. These usually cost more than popular books, but they pay off handsomely in years of regular use.

NOTES

1. H. G. M. Williamson, *Ezra, Nehemiah,* Word Biblical Commentary (Waco, TX: Word Books, 1985), p. xxi.

2. See the helpful chart in W. S. LaSor, D. A. Hubbard, and F. W. Bush, *Old Testament Survey,* (Grand Rapids: Eerdmans, 1982), p. 639; and R. W. Klein, "The Books of Ezra-Nehemiah," *The Anchor Bible Dictionary,* 6 vols. (New York: Doubleday, 1992).

3. For example, R. H. Pfeiffer, "The Books of Ezra and Nehemiah," *The Interpreter's Dictionary of the Bible,* 4 vols. (Nashville: Abingdon Press, 1962). Myers not only attributes authorship of Ezra-Nehemiah to the Chronicler, but also identifies the Chronicler as Ezra himself (J. M. Myers, *Ezra • Nehemiah,* The Anchor Bible [Garden City, NY: Doubleday, 1965], pp. lxviii–lxxx). This is possible, but widely rejected by scholars. Williamson has proposed two stages of composition in Ezra-Nehemiah. If he is correct, then we would more accurately refer to "editors" or "authors" of the work. I use the singular because

it is sufficient for one who teaches or preaches. Scholars enjoy the challenge of greater complexity. See H. G. M. Williamson, *Ezra and Nehemiah*, Old Testament Guides (Sheffield, England, JSOT, 1987), pp. 37–45.

4. Klein, "Ezra-Nehemiah." See also B. S. Childs, *Introduction to the Old Testament as Scripture* (Philadelphia: Fortress, 1979), p. 639.

5. See the discussions in Lasor, Hubbard, and Bush, *Old Testament Survey*, pp. 648–49 and D. Kidner, *Ezra & Nehemiah*, Tyndale Old Testament Commentaries (Downers Grove: InterVarsity, 1979), pp. 139–42.

6. See the discussions in: Klein, " Ezra-Nehemiah"; LaSor, et. al., *Old Testament Survey*, pp. 649–52; Williamson, *Ezra, Nehemiah*, pp. 55–76; and Kidner, *Ezra & Nehemiah*, pp. 146–58.

An Outline of Ezra-Nehemiah

I. Restoration of the Temple   (Ezra 1:1–6:22)

  A. God Begins to Restore Through Cyrus   (1:1–11)
    1. The Proclamation of Cyrus   (1:1–4)
    2. Response to the Proclamation   (1:5–11)
  B. The People Who Returned to Jerusalem   (2:1–70)
    1. Introduction to the List   (2:1–2)
    2. The List of People   (2:3–63)
    3. Conclusion to the List   (2:64–70)
  C. Establishing the Foundations   (3:1–13)
    1. Laying the Spiritual Foundation   (3:1–7)
    2. Laying the Material Foundation   (3:8–13)
  D. Opposition to Restoration   (4:1–24)
    1. The Opposition Begins   (4:1–5)
    2. Other Examples of Opposition   (4:6–23)
    3. The Opposition Succeeds   (4:24)
  E. Resumption of Restoration   (5:1–6:12)
    1. Help from God's Prophets   (5:1–2)
    2. Official Inquiry and Response   (5:3–6:12)
      a. Questions from Officials   (5:3–5)
      b. Letter from Tattenai to Darius   (5:6–17)
      c. Response of Darius   (6:1–12)
  F. Completion and Celebration   (6:13–22)
    1. Completion of the Temple   (6:13–15)
    2. The People Celebrate the Dedication   (6:16–18)
    3. The People Celebrate the Passover   (6:19–22)

II. Restoration of Covenant Life, Phase One: The Work of Ezra   (7:1–10:44)

  A. The King Commissions Ezra   (7:1–28)
    1. Introduction to Ezra   (7:1–10)
    2. Ezra's Commission   (7:11–26)
    3. Ezra's Response to the Commission   (7:27–28)
  B. Ezra Returns to Jerusalem   (8:1–36)
    1. Those Who Accompany Ezra   (8:1–14)
    2. Ezra Recruits Levites and Temple Servants   (8:15–20)

Historical Time-Line Chart for Ezra-Nehemiah

Dates	Key Rulers	Key Events and People	References
		Babylonian Empire	
		Prophets: Jeremiah, Zephaniah, Nahum, Habbakuk	Ezra 1:1
600 B.C.	Nebuchadnezzar (Babylon, 605–562)	Fall of Nineveh/Assyria (612)	
		Fall of Jerusalem (587) *Prophet: Ezekiel*	
550 B.C.	Cyrus (Persia, 550–530)	Cyrus overthrows the Medes (550)	
		Persian Empire	
		Cyrus overthrows Babylon (539)	
		Cyrus issues Edict for Restoration (538)	
	Cambyses (530–522)	Rebuilding of temple begins	Ezra 1:1
	Darius I (522–486)	*Prophets: Haggai, Zechariah*	Ezra 5:1
500 B.C.		Temple is finished (516/515)	Ezra 6:15
	Xerxes (486–465)		Ezra 4:6
		Prophet: Malachi (?)	
	Artaxerxes I (465–423)		
450 B.C.		Ezra comes to Jerusalem (458)	Ezra 7:7
		Nehemiah comes to Jerusalem (445)	Neh. 1:1
		Wall rebuilt under Nehemiah (445)	Neh. 2:1
	Xerxes II (423)	Joint ministry of Ezra and Nehemiah (445 through ?)	Neh. 8–12
	Darius II (423–404)	Nehemiah's second stay in Jerusalem (after 433)	Neh. 13:6
400 B.C.			

Restoration of the Temple

Ezra 1:1–6:22

The first part of Ezra-Nehemiah is a narration of the rebuilding of the temple in Jerusalem after its destruction by the Babylonians in 587 B.C. The story begins in 538 B.C. when Cyrus, king of Persia, issued a royal decree calling for the rebuilding of the Jewish temple. The section concludes with the dedication of the completed temple in 516 or 515 B.C. During the twenty-two years after Cyrus' proclamation and before the dedication, the people struggled to complete the task set before them; they confronted not only opposition but also personal discouragement.

The first six chapters of Ezra combine a variety of source materials, including:

- the decree of Cyrus (1:2–4; 6:3–5)
- a list of implements for the temple (1:9–11)
- a list of people (2:3–67)
- accounts of events in Jerusalem (3:1–4:5; 6:13–22)
- Aramaic letters (4:8–22; 5:6–17; 6:3–12).

The theme of restoration ties the diverse elements of this section together. In the pattern of Ezra-Nehemiah, physical restoration (of the temple) occurs before spiritual restoration (through Ezra). But, as the story will show, even rebuilding the temple required the providence and intervention of God.

CHAPTER ONE

God Begins to Restore Through Cyrus

Ezra 1:1–11

WHO'S IN CHARGE HERE?

While on a retreat, a group from my church went bowling in a small mountain village. These folks went to have fun, not to demonstrate their minimal talent for bowling. They accidentally dropped balls, rather than rolling them, and laughed boisterously at themselves. In all of their hilarity, however, they failed to notice how much they were disturbing the other bowlers, who took the game far more seriously. Finally, the manager of the alley stormed over to the group and demanded: "Who's in charge here?" My friend, who happened to be responsible for the group, tried desperately to shrink away at that point but to no avail. Indeed, he was in charge—and soon had a new challenge: to keep the group quiet, or leave!

And who is in charge of our lives? Usually we like to pretend that we are. We value financial security, stable jobs, and a predictable schedule. We carry "Daytimers" or "Day Runners" to guarantee order throughout the day. But inevitably we discover the truth: we are not in control after all. One day the boss calls us into his office and announces that our division has been terminated—and so have we. Or the doctor utters those dreaded words: "I'm sorry, but you have cancer."

Sometimes delightful additions to our lives reveal the limits of our power. This happened to me recently when my wife gave birth to our first son. I have to admit that in all of my joy as a father I have also discovered a new sense of helplessness. How do I comfort a crying baby at 3:30 in the morning? My life seems even more out of control today than it did two months ago!

And we certainly wonder these days who is in charge of the world. One moment we rejoice as the Berlin Wall crumbles, democracy comes to Russia, and justice begins to dawn in South Africa; but the next moment Saddam Hussein invades Kuwait and we go to war. As soon as we have celebrated our victory over Iraq, troops ship out to Somalia, and civil war wreaks havoc in Bosnia. We wonder about our world: "Who is in charge here?"

The first chapter of Ezra answers this question as it begins to unfold the story of the restoration of the temple in Jerusalem.

THE PROCLAMATION OF CYRUS (1:1–4)

1:1 Now in the first year of Cyrus king of Persia, that the word of the LORD by the mouth of Jeremiah might be fulfilled, the LORD stirred up the spirit of Cyrus king of Persia, so that he made a proclamation throughout all his kingdom, and also put it in writing, saying,

2 Thus says Cyrus king of Persia: All the kingdoms of the earth the LORD God of heaven has given me. And He has commanded me to build Him a house at Jerusalem which is in Judah.

3 Who is among you of all His people? May his God be with him, and let him go up to Jerusalem which is in Judah, and build the house of the LORD God of Israel (He is God), which is in Jerusalem.

4 And whoever is left in any place where he dwells, let the men of his place help him with silver and gold, with goods and livestock, besides the freewill offerings for the house of God which is in Jerusalem.

Ezra 1:1–4

The story begins *"in the first year of Cyrus king of Persia."* Actually, this date should be identified with the first year Cyrus had authority over Babylon and Judah (539 B.C.). Cyrus ruled only a small region of the Median Empire (in modern Iran) until 550 B.C. when he took control of the larger empire, later known as the Persian Empire. Under his effective leadership the empire expanded in all directions.

Cyrus waited for several years before moving against Babylon (modern Iraq). In 539 B.C., life in Babylon was so terrible and the king of Babylon so intensely disliked that when Cyrus entered the city to capture it, no one opposed him. From that point onward, the Persian Empire included all of what we now know as Syria and Israel, in addition to Iran.

We know about Cyrus from various ancient sources besides Ezra-Nehemiah, but one of these in particular offers valuable background for the passage under consideration—the "Cyrus Cylinder." This is a small clay cylinder that was found by archaeologists, on which writing about Cyrus appears, including portions of his own memoirs. He recounts that the Babylonian god, Marduk, was displeased with how he had been worshipped. So,

> he scanned and looked (through) all the countries, searching for a righteous ruler willing to lead him (i.e. Marduk) (in the annual procession). (Then) he pronounced the name of Cyrus (*Ku-ra-aš*), king of Anshan, declared him . . . to be(come) the ruler of all the world.[1]

The Cylinder further relates how Marduk helped Cyrus become successful and ultimately helped him overthrow Babylon without any resistance. Then Cyrus speaks, introducing himself in this way: "I am Cyrus, king of the world, great king, legitimate king, king of Babylon, king of Sumer and Akkad, king of the four rims (of the earth). . . ."[2]

Although Cyrus worshiped the Persian gods, when he entered Babylon he began to worship the local gods there, especially Marduk: "When I entered Babylon . . . as a friend . . . Marduk, the great lord, [induced] the magnanimous inhabitants of Babylon . . . [to love me], and I was daily endeavoring to worship him."[3] The Babylonians had indeed welcomed Cyrus "as a friend," so he repaid Marduk with worship.

Rather than tyrannize his subjects as the Babylonian rulers had done, Cyrus sought good for the people under his reign. Concerning the inhabitants of Babylon he says: "I brought relief to their dilapidated housing, putting (thus) an end to their (main) complaints."[4] Moreover, Cyrus sought to reestablish religions devastated by Babylon, and he highly regarded sacred cities such as Jerusalem (which, however, Cyrus does not mention by name):

> I returned to (these) sacred cities on the other side of the Tigris, the sanctuaries of which have been ruins for a long time, the images which (used) to live therein and established for them

permanent sanctuaries. I (also) gathered all their (former) inhabitants and returned (to them) their habitations.[5]

Notice what Cyrus claims to have done: (1) he returned religious images stolen by the Babylonians to their rightful places; (2) he rebuilt temples for those images; and (3) he resettled the displaced peoples in their proper homelands.

Why would Cyrus choose such an enlightened and magnanimous course? He may have done so to rally popular support for his regime, but it is interesting to note what he writes about his respect for the gods: "May all the gods whom I have resettled in their sacred cities ask daily Bel and Nebo for a long life for me and may they recommend me (to him); to Marduk, my lord. . . ."[6] Cyrus seems to have believed that by returning idols to former locations he had in fact returned the gods themselves. In other words, he sought to gain divine favor by restoring indigenous religions and peoples.

Curiously, this strategy seems to have worked with the God of Israel, or at least from Cyrus' point of view, for Isaiah 45 proclaims:

Thus says the LORD to His anointed,
To Cyrus, whose right hand I have held—
To subdue nations before him
And loose the armor of kings,
To open before him the double doors,
So that the gates will not be shut: . . .
I have raised him up in righteousness,
And I will direct all his ways;
He shall build My city
And let My exiles go free,
Not for price nor reward,"
Says the LORD of hosts.

Isaiah 45:1, 13

Amazingly, Isaiah's prophecies name Cyrus as God's "anointed"— his "messiah" (in Anglicized Hebrew)—who has been raised up by God to do his bidding.

Ezra 1:1 announces that *"the LORD"* of Israel, not Marduk, *"stirred up the spirit of Cyrus king of Persia. . . ."* This fulfills God's own prophecy, which verse 1 attributes to *"Jeremiah."* Although, unlike Isaiah, he did not identify Cyrus by name, Jeremiah did prophesy the downfall of Babylon and the restoration of Judah:

And this whole land [Judah] shall be a desolation and an aston-
ishment, and these nations shall serve the king of Babylon
seventy years. Then it will come to pass, when seventy years are
completed, that I will punish the king of Babylon and that nation,
the land of the Chaldeans, for their iniquity, says the LORD.

Jeremiah 25:11–12

For thus says the LORD: After seventy years are completed at
Babylon, I will visit you and perform My good word toward you,
and cause you to return to this place.

Jeremiah 29:10

Ezra 1:2–4 provides a Hebrew translation of the proclamation
Cyrus issued by the Lord's inspiration. In this brief statement, Cyrus,
who claimed to be king of the whole earth (v. 2), ordered the rebuilding of the temple in Jerusalem and allowed displaced Judeans to
return there (v. 3). Moreover, he encouraged those Jews who did not
return to offer financial support to those who did (v. 4). These aspects
of the decree in 1:2–4 fit precisely with what we already know about
Cyrus from his own memoirs.

This decree, especially in the NKJV translation, makes Cyrus sound as if
he were a "closet Jew." From the Cyrus Cylinder, however, we know
that he recognized every regional god. Verse 3, therefore, should be
translated a bit differently than the NKJV: "Who is among you of all his
[not "*His*"] people? May his god [not "*God*"] be with him, and let him go
up to Jerusalem which is in Judah, and build the house of the LORD God
of Israel, he is the god who is in Jerusalem [not "(*He is God*), *which is
in Jerusalem*"]." The Cylinder shows that Cyrus was a polytheist who
recognized regional gods and their limited authority. Unlike Ezra-
Nehemiah, he did not affirm the ultimate sovereignty of the one true
God, the LORD of Abraham, Isaac, and Jacob. Nevertheless, this one
God did choose and use Cyrus to accomplish his purposes. Through
Cyrus, the Persian "messiah" (Isa. 45:1), God began to restore Judah.

RESPONSE TO THE PROCLAMATION (1:5–11)

5 Then the heads of the fathers' houses of Judah
and Benjamin, and the priests and the Levites, with all
whose spirits God had moved, arose to go up and
build the house of the LORD which is in Jerusalem.

6 And all those who were around them encouraged them with articles of silver and gold, with goods
and livestock, and with precious things, besides all
that was willingly offered.

7 King Cyrus also brought out the articles of the
house of the LORD, which Nebuchadnezzar had taken
from Jerusalem and put in the temple of his gods;

8 and Cyrus king of Persia brought them out by
the hand of Mithredath the treasurer, and counted
them out to Sheshbazzar the prince of Judah.

9 This is the number of them: thirty gold platters,
one thousand silver platters, twenty-nine knives,

10 thirty gold basins, four hundred and ten silver
basins of a similar kind, and one thousand other
articles.

11 All the articles of gold and silver were five
thousand four hundred. All these Sheshbazzar took
with the captives who were brought from Babylon to
Jerusalem.

Ezra 1:5–11

The Jewish leaders who responded to the call of Cyrus are identified in verse 5. The *"heads of the fathers' houses"* indicate leaders of
small groups of people. The nation of Israel had been divided into
tribes, tribes into families, and families in "the fathers' houses."[7]
"Judah and Benjamin" are the two tribes of the Southern Kingdom
from which Nebuchadnezzar took exiles back to Babylon. The decree
of Cyrus, therefore, applies primarily to persons from these tribes.
"The priests and the Levites" deserve specific mention because not only
are they the religious leaders of Israel, but a rebuilt temple could not
function properly without priestly and Levitical personnel.

The NKJV of 1:5 misses the nuance of the Hebrew by translating:
"with all those whose spirits God had moved." A better rendering might
be: "among which groups, all whose spirits God had moved." In
other words, all of those who returned from Babylon to Jerusalem,
both lay people and leaders, were people motivated by God. The Hebrew expression *"whose spirits God had moved"* uses the same verb
found in 1:1, "the LORD stirred up the spirit of Cyrus." Both verses
depict God alone as the author of restoration, as the one who stirred
up Cyrus to proclaim liberation and who stirred up the people to embrace their new freedom.

Note in verse 6 that *"all those who were around"* the returning people *"encouraged them with articles of silver and gold." "All"* here includes not only the Jews who chose to stay in Babylon but the gentiles as well. The expression *"articles of silver and gold"* echoes Exodus 12:35–36, which reads:

> Now the children of Israel had done according to the word of Moses, and they had asked from the Egyptians articles of silver, articles of gold, and clothing. And the LORD had given the people favor in the sight of the Egyptians, so that they granted them what they requested. Thus they plundered the Egyptians.

In Jewish tradition, accepting the offerings of silver and gold would remind the people of God's previous blessings. The Psalmist refers to this symbol in Psalm 105:36–37:

> He also destroyed all the firstborn in their land [Egypt],
> The first of all their strength.
> He also brought them [the Jews] out with silver and gold,
> And there was none feeble among His tribes.

By mentioning "silver and gold" in verse 6, and repeating the phrase in verse 11, the author would be reminding his Jewish readers of the first exodus from Egypt. The departure from Babylon represented a second exodus, another time when God delivered his people from foreign tyranny.

The phrase *"all that was willingly offered"* (v. 6) is a technical phrase that refers to freewill offerings for the temple (see 1:4). If someone wanted to thank God for something unusual, that person would make a special offering, one that was not required, out of his or her own free will.

In verse 7, we see that Cyrus went one step further in his support for Jewish restoration. He brought *"out the articles of the house of the LORD, which Nebuchadnezzar had taken from Jerusalem and put in the temple of his gods."* This desecration by Nebuchadnezzar is described in 2 Chronicles 36:18. Ezra-Nehemiah names *"Mithredath"* as the treasurer who turned the sacred implements over to *"Sheshbazzar the prince of Judah"* (v. 8).

The mystery of Sheshbazzar's identity was discussed in the "Introduction to Ezra-Nehemiah: Chronological Puzzles in Ezra-Nehemiah." We do not know exactly who Sheshbazzar was or how he related to Zerubbabel. All we know for certain is that Sheshbazzar was a leader of Judah (1:8 calls him "prince;" 5:14 calls him "governor") who had some initial role in the rebuilding process. Soon, however, he appears to have turned the assignment over to Zerubbabel, or at least to have shared it with him.

In this passage, the short list of items returned to the temple offers a few conundrums (vv. 9–10). For one, the items listed total 2499, whereas verse 11 mentions a total of 5400 gold and silver pieces. It is possible that the list was incomplete, or perhaps the numbering was a bit inaccurate. Another oddity is the phrase *"twenty-nine knives,"* which is likely an attempt to translate an obscure Persian word that probably did not mean "knife." Scholars do not know what the word actually means, but this does not present a great difficulty because widespread opinion is held that the term is not significant to the main point of this passage. By including this list, Ezra-Nehemiah reiterated what had already been seen in verses 7–8: the exact items that were once removed from the temple would be returned. Thus, even though a new building had to be constructed from new materials, the silver and gold pieces would provide a physical continuity between the old and the new. This would enable the people to sense a relationship between their new experiences and the previous experiences of their forebears.

For us too, physical objects can produce emotional connections with the past. I remember my college roommate, Henry, who carried around one of the fattest wallets I have ever seen. I don't know how he managed to feel comfortable with that monstrous thing in his pocket. One day I asked him why he didn't put his wallet on a diet. He opened it up and showed me what contributed to its girth. It was full of reminders of his father: dog tags from Army service in World War II, a driver's license, and pictures. Henry's father had died several years earlier, but the tangible items in that oversized wallet connected him with his dad—like the temple implements connected the people of Israel with their past.

The final sentence of chapter 1 reads: *"All these [articles] Sheshbazzar took with the captives who were brought from Babylon to Jerusalem"* (v. 11). In college I learned never to use a passive construction without specifying "by whom" an action had been done. The editor of Ezra-Nehemiah, without input from my writing teacher, simply states that the captives "were brought from Babylon to Jerusalem." By whom? Clearly, it was not by Sheshbazzar, since he brought up the articles of silver and gold. The text would seem to imply that God brought the Israelites from Babylon to Jerusalem. If so, this would fulfill Jeremiah's prophecy:

> I will be found by you, says the LORD, and I will bring you back from your captivity; I will gather you from all the nations and from all the places where I have driven you, says the LORD, and I will bring you to the place from which I cause you to be carried away captive.
>
> *Jeremiah 29:14*

Once again we hear an echo of the first exodus, when God "brought up" the people from Egypt (Exod. 3:8; 1 Sam. 10:18; 2 Sam. 7:6; Amos 3:1). By stirring up Cyrus and the leaders who respond to his proclamation, God brought the people into the land from the exile, just as he had brought them into the land initially through Moses' leadership.

REFLECTIONS ON EZRA 1:1–11

Who's in charge here? Who's in charge of the world? Ezra 1 answers these questions simply and repeatedly: *God is in charge.* This passage vividly illustrates God's sovereignty over his people—indeed, over all peoples, and over all of human history. It provokes us to reflect upon the *scope, security,* and *scandal* of God's sovereignty.

The Scope of God's Sovereignty

In Ezra 1, God is described as having the power to move a king who himself claimed to be "king of the world, great king, . . . king of the four rims (of the earth)." Moreover, God did this in order to fulfill the prophetic word that he had spoken through Jeremiah (v. 1). God also moved in the spirits of the Jews who decided to return to Jerusalem (v. 5). Finally, Ezra-Nehemiah implies that the LORD brought the people up from Babylon to Judah.

Certainly, the God of the Bible holds sway over all of human history. Not only human hearts, but political processes, also, stand under the sovereign rule of God. And as Ezra-Nehemiah shows,

God's reign is not limited to his own people—he can raise up even a foreign king to fulfill his prophecies.

However, the fact of God's sovereignty does not obliterate human freedom and responsibility. Later portions of Ezra-Nehemiah (such as the confession in Nehemiah 1) show that human beings may act contrary to God's will and may be held accountable for their wrong choices. The issue of God's sovereignty in the world becomes even more complex in the New Testament, where Satan is identified as the ruler of this world (for example, John 12:31). Yet Christians affirm that, ultimately, God is in charge of all creation and that everything will eventually be subject to God's direct rule (1 Cor. 15:25; Eph. 1:22).

Biblical teaching on the scope of God's sovereignty opposes the American tendency to limit God's interest and authority to the personal realm.[8] Religious belief and practice belong, we believe, within the confines of family, friendship, and private life. Recently, a public official in Los Angeles was accused of allowing his Christian faith to impact his professional decisions. His opponents and the media attacked him on the basis of their assumption that "religion" belongs only in one's private world. Yet biblical teaching proclaims God's sovereignty over all of life, including politics and business.

As we take the fullness of God's sovereignty seriously, our ways of thinking and acting will change. We will begin to see our "secular" jobs as "spiritual" turf, as places where God's standards still apply. We will also think differently about national affairs. Too many Christians today limit God's interest to matters of prayer in schools, abortion, family values, and sexual behavior. Undoubtedly these issues do stand under God's sovereignty and within his care, but so do such crises as hunger, poverty, racism, health care, and education. Embracing God's sovereignty will also affect our prayers. We will stop and consider whether we pray for the world as if God had anything to say about it, or whether we simply pray for our personal needs.

The Security of God's Sovereignty

Because God's rule extends to every aspect of life, we can feel secure. In Paul's words, "We know that all things work together for good to those who love God, to those who are the called according to His purpose" (Rom. 8:28). Likewise, we may trust in God with the assurance that he will guide us:

Trust in the Lord with all your heart,
And lean not on your own understanding;
In all your ways acknowledge Him,
And He shall direct your paths.

Proverbs 3:5–6

Our yearning for security will be found not in the size of our bank accounts, nor in the amount of insurance we have, nor in our tenure at work, nor in our friends, but in God and God alone.

I confess, however, it is difficult for me to find my security in God's sovereignty alone. It is something I continually work at. My first experience of truly trusting God came when I was in junior high school. My father had worked in the aerospace industry for many years. Then, like most in his profession, in the early 1970's he faced an extended time of unemployment. I worried endlessly about our future as a family. Would we lose our home? Would we be forced to move far away?

One evening as I prayed about these fears I sensed God's presence and care as never before. Though my mind lacked specific answers, I sensed in my heart that God would watch over our family. My habitual worrying stopped, and I found security, not in any specific promise of God, but in God's trustworthy love. How I wish I could sustain this sense of security! Don't you?

The Scandal of God's Sovereignty

But here is the problem: If God is indeed sovereign over everything, then why are things so bad? A man in my church stood by helplessly as his daughter almost starved herself to death through anorexia (a compulsive eating disorder). In deep anguish he asked me: "Where is God in all of this?" He reminded me that we who preach on the sovereignty of God cannot do so glibly, as if everything in life were hunky-dory, for we proclaim God's authority over all circumstances and situations to people in real pain.

I was preaching on Ezra chapter 1 at Hollywood Presbyterian Church during the Fall of 1990. In the week prior to my sermon, two of the young people involved in our church's urban ministry were shot in a drive-by gang shooting. One boy, Ernie, who had been specially loved, was killed. The next Sunday night I stood up to proclaim

God's sovereignty over all creation, including the neighborhoods of Hollywood. Before me sat the youth leaders who had worked with Ernie. Their eyes seemed to cry out in unison: Where is God in all of this?

Ezra 1 does not address this "scandal" of God's sovereignty directly, but the people of Israel certainly had lived the scandal as they languished during the Babylonian exile. Remember how shortly before Babylon invaded Judah, the prophet Habbakuk had cried out to God:

> O LORD, how long shall I cry,
> And You will not hear?
> Even cry out to You, "Violence!"
> And You will not save.
> Why do You show me iniquity,
> And cause me to see trouble?
> For plundering and violence are before me;
> There is strife, and contention arises.
>
> *Habakkuk 1:2–3*

Similarly, the Psalmist does not refrain from lamenting the scandal of God's inaction:

> My God, My God, why have You forsaken Me?
> Why are You so far from helping Me,
> And from the words of My groaning?
> O My God, I cry in the daytime,
> but You do not hear;
> And in the night season,
> and am not silent.
>
> *Psalm 22:1–2*

One could quote dozens of other biblical passages that ask basically the same question: *Where is God in all of this?*

Scripture does not solve the problem of God's inaction or soothe the scandal of God's sovereignty. In fact, rather than downplaying this scandal, the Bible teaches us to live in the tension by confessing God's sovereignty in a world full of pain. The Scriptures encourage us to wrestle with God, to cry out in our frustration. We run a great and terrible risk as Christians if we smile and say, "Oh, God's in charge and everything is fine," when deep inside we are being torn apart by the scandal of a sovereign God who does not appear to act.

Can you and I echo the voice of the Psalmist when we hurt: "My God, My God, why have You forsaken me?"(Ps. 22:1). Jesus did— from the Cross (Mark 15:34). If the Son of God could be so honest in his hour of desperation, cannot we be as honest and bold before God? Openly wrestling with the scandal of God's sovereignty leads us down the road to a deeper, truer intimacy with God. As we travel that road, Jesus walks with us as one who understands, for perhaps the most scandalous aspect of God's sovereignty is the fact that he allowed his own Son to suffer and die. When we let our hearts cry out to God, the Holy Spirit moves us ever closer to the heart of God—a heart revealed most intensely in the Cross of Christ.

Psalm 22 contains more than an honest lament about God's absence. Note what line of thought the psalmist develops after he has cried out to God:

> But You are holy,
> Enthroned in the praises of Israel.
> Our fathers trusted in You;
> They trusted, and You delivered them.
>
> *Psalm 22:3–4*

From openly sorrowing, the Psalmist moves to confessing God's greatness and faithfulness to deliver. Likewise, when we struggle with God's slowness to deliver us, we need to worship him, to proclaim who he is, and to remember his grace in times past. We join our broken world in "groaning" while we wait for God to set all things right again (Rom. 8:22–23). We know that, meanwhile, no matter how dire our situation, nothing in all the universe "shall be able to separate us from the love of God which is in Christ Jesus our Lord" (Rom. 8:39).

NOTES

1. Translation from J. B. Pritchard, ed., *The Ancient Near East: An Anthology of Texts and Pictures*, 2 vols. (Princeton: Princeton University Press, 1958), 1:206.

2. Pritchard, *Ancient Near East,* 1:207.

3. Pritchard, *Ancient Near East,* 1:207.

4. Pritchard, *Ancient Near East,* 1:207.

5. Pritchard, *Ancient Near East,* 1:208.

6. Pritchard, *Ancient Near East,* 1:208.

7. J. Blenkinsopp, *Ezra-Nehemiah,* Old Testament Library (Philadelphia: The Westminster Press, 1981), p. 77.

8. See the excellent analysis of American religion in R. N. Bellah, et al., *Habits of the Heart: Individualism and Commitment in American Life* (New York: Harper and Row, 1985), pp. 219–49.

CHAPTER TWO

The People Who Returned to Jerusalem

Ezra 2:1–70

A LIST OF HIDDEN TREASURES

Moving ahead to Ezra chapter 2, we see a long list of names and may likely be tempted to skip the chapter altogether. It makes us wonder what lessons could possibly emerge from a protracted list of people? We might also wonder what preacher would be foolish enough to read this text in Sunday morning worship.

When I preached on Ezra 2, the Sunday morning bulletin noted the Scripture reading as: Ezra 2:1–70. I had planned to read only sections from this chapter—about fifteen verses. That Sunday, my ordinary schedule was changed, however, and I had to miss the opening minutes of worship in order to visit some Sunday school classes. I thought I had carefully timed events to make sure I would arrive back in worship in plenty of time to read the verses, but, unfortunately, things did not go as I had planned (naturally!). When the time came for the Scripture to be read, I was still busy in the classrooms. One of my associates, Mike, realized that someone had to read the Scripture lesson in my place, so he stood up and proceeded to read Ezra chapter 2—all seventy verses!

While I would not recommend that you read all seventy verses when you teach or preach on this text, I would urge you not to skip the chapter. For, as we will see, this passage contains hidden treasures for the careful interpreter, and it raises issues that must be considered by all Christians and Christian communities.

INTRODUCTION TO THE LIST (2:1–2)

> 2:1 Now these are the people of the province who
> came back from the captivity, of those who had been
> carried away, whom Nebuchadnezzar the king of
> Babylon had carried away to Babylon, and who
> returned to Jerusalem and Judah, everyone to his
> own city.
> 2 Those who came with Zerubbabel were Jeshua,
> Nehemiah, Seraiah, Reelaiah, Mordecai, Bilshan,
> Mispar, Bigvai, Rehum, and Baanah. The number of
> the men of the people of Israel:
>
> *Ezra 2:1–2*

Verses 1 and 2 introduce the list of names that follows. It explains
that those included in the list are *"the people of the province who came
back from the captivity,"* of those whose ancestors had been carried
away by Nebuchadnezzar to Babylon (v. 1). Verse 2 mentions specific
leaders of Judah. For example, *"Zerubbabel"* was to oversee the rebuilding of the temple, and *"Jeshua"* was designated as the High
Priest at the time (5:2; see Zech. 3:1). (Note here that *"Nehemiah"* identifies someone other than the main character of the book of
Nehemiah.)

Strangely, the list in Ezra 2, along with its foreword in 2:1–2, appears almost identically in Nehemiah (7:6–72). (A few minor
differences reflect the cumbersome Hebrew numbering system.) The
passage in Nehemiah 7 provides more information about the origin
of this list:

> Then my God put it into my heart to gather the nobles, the rulers,
> and the people, that they might be registered by genealogy. And I
> found a register of the genealogy of those who had come up in
> the first return, and found written in it. . . .
>
> *Nehemiah 7:5*

The editor of Ezra-Nehemiah reprinted this genealogical record early
in his composition. The list purportedly includes "those who had
come up in the first return," although it does not list all of the people
individually, but rather by groups. We do not know exactly why the
list was originally compiled or who compiled it.

THE LIST OF PEOPLE (2:3–63)

3 the people of Parosh, two thousand one hundred and seventy-two;

4 the people of Shephatiah, three hundred and seventy-two;

5 the people of Arah, seven hundred and seventy-five;

6 the people of Pahath-Moab, of the people of Jeshua and Joab, two thousand eight hundred and twelve;

7 the people of Elam, one thousand two hundred and fifty-four;

8 the people of Zattu, nine hundred and forty-five;

9 the people of Zaccai, seven hundred and sixty;

10 the people of Bani, six hundred and forty-two;

11 the people of Bebai, six hundred and twenty-three;

12 the people of Azgad, one thousand two hundred and twenty-two;

13 the people of Adonikam, six hundred and sixty-six;

14 the people of Bigvai, two thousand and fifty-six;

15 the people of Adin, four hundred and fifty-four;

16 the people of Ater of Hezekiah, ninety-eight;

17 the people of Bezai, three hundred and twenty-three;

18 the people of Jorah, one hundred and twelve;

19 the people of Hashum, two hundred and twenty-three;

20 the people of Gibbar, ninety-five;

21 the people of Bethlehem, one hundred and twenty-three;

22 the men of Netophah, fifty-six;

23 the men of Anathoth, one hundred and twenty-eight;

24 the people of Azmaveth, forty-two;

25 the people of Kirjath Arim, Chephirah, and Beeroth, seven hundred and forty-three;

26 the people of Ramah and Geba, six hundred and twenty-one;

27 the men of Michmas, one hundred and twenty-two;

28 the men of Bethel and Ai, two hundred and twenty-three;

29 the people of Nebo, fifty-two;

30 the people of Magbish, one hundred and fifty-six;

31 the people of the other Elam, one thousand two hundred and fifty-four;

32 the people of Harim, three hundred and twenty;

33 the people of Lod, Hadid, and Ono, seven hundred and twenty-five;

34 the people of Jericho, three hundred and forty-five;

35 the people of Senaah, three thousand six hundred and thirty.

36 The priests: the sons of Jedaiah, of the house of Jeshua, nine hundred and seventy-three;

37 the sons of Immer, one thousand and fifty-two;

38 the sons of Pashhur, one thousand two hundred and forty-seven;

39 the sons of Harim, one thousand and seventeen.

40 The Levites: the sons of Jeshua and Kadmiel, of the sons of Hodaviah, seventy-four.

41 The singers: the sons of Asaph, one hundred and twenty-eight.

42 The sons of the gatekeepers: the sons of Shallum, the sons of Ater, the sons of Talmon, the sons of Akkub, the sons of Hatita, and the sons of Shobai, one hundred and thirty-nine in all.

43 The Nethinim: the sons of Ziha, the sons of Hasupha, the sons of Tabbaoth,

44 the sons of Keros, the sons of Siaha, the sons of Padon,

45 the sons of Lebanah, the sons of Hagabah, the sons of Akkub,

46 the sons of Hagab, the sons of Shalmai, the sons of Hanan,

47 the sons of Giddel, the sons of Gahar, the sons of Reaiah,

48 the sons of Rezin, the sons of Nekoda, the sons of Gazzam,

49 the sons of Uzza, the sons of Paseah, the sons of Besai,

50 the sons of Asnah, the sons of Meunim, the sons of Nephusim,

51 the sons of Bakbuk, the sons of Hakupha, the sons of Harhur,

52 the sons of Bazluth, the sons of Mehida, the sons of Harsha,

53 the sons of Barkos, the sons of Sisera, the sons of Tamah,

54 the sons of Neziah, and the sons of Hatipha.

55 The sons of Solomon's servants: the sons of Sotai, the sons of Sophereth, the sons of Peruda,

56 the sons of Jaala, the sons of Darkon, the sons of Giddel,

57 the sons of Shephatiah, the sons of Hattil, the sons of Pochereth of Zebaim, and the sons of Ami.

58 All the Nethinim and the children of Solomon's servants were three hundred and ninety-two.

59 And these were the ones who came up from Tel Melah, Tel Harsha, Cherub, Addan, and Immer; but they could not identify their father's house or their genealogy, whether they were of Israel:

60 the sons of Delaiah, the sons of Tobiah, and the sons of Nekoda, six hundred and fifty-two;

61 and of the sons of the priests: the sons of Habaiah, the sons of Koz, and the sons of Barzillai, who took a wife of the daughters of Barzillai the Gileadite, and was called by their name.

62 These sought their listing among those who were registered by genealogy, but they were not found; therefore they were excluded from the priesthood as defiled.

63 And the governor said to them that they should not eat of the most holy things till a priest could consult with the Urim and Thummim.

Ezra 2:3–63

This list spells out groups of people in the following categories:

2:3–20	Lay people (according to their ancestry)
2:21–35	Lay people (according to their ancestral home town)
2:36–39	Priests (according to ancestry)
2:40	Levis (according to ancestry)
2:41	Singers (according to ancestry)
2:42	Gatekeepers (according to ancestry)
2:43–58	Servants: Nethinim and Solomon's servants (according to ancestry)
2:59–63	Those who could not demonstrate their ancestry

The *"Nethinim"* appear in verses 43–54. The word is Hebrew, meaning "those given." It is an abbreviation of a longer phrase: "those given to the service of the sanctuary."[1] Later Ezra clarifies their precise role and origin: ". . . the Nethinim, whom David and the leaders had appointed for the service of the Levites" (8:20). Thus, as the Levites assisted the priests (Num. 3:5–13) so the Nethinim assisted the Levites. Many English versions translate the Hebrew word *"nĕtînîm"* as "temple servants" (for example, NIV or NRSV).[2]

The structure of this list reveals fundamental values in the Jewish community of the time. First of all, it shows the centrality of the temple. Priests, Levites, and others who worked in the temple receive special mention. Second, the list shows the importance of an individual's place of birth. A significant group of people are known by their city of origin rather than by their family of origin (2:21–35). Third, and foremost, the list displays how much Israel valued ancestry. Those who could prove their genealogical roots, belonged in the community; they had a place in the restored nation.

This was not true of those who could not identify their family backgrounds. Verses 59 and 60 specifically call out those who *"could not identify their father's house or their genealogy, whether they were of Israel"* (v. 59). The text does not say what happened to these people, though they were probably treated as outsiders. The situation was worse for priests who could not demonstrate their parentage: they were *"excluded from the priesthood as defiled"* (v. 62). Even more, *"the governor said to them that they should not eat of the most holy things till a priest could consult with the Urim and Thummim"* (v. 63). The most holy things were the parts of the sacrifices given by the people that the priests were allowed to eat for food (Lev. 7:28–36). Unfortunately, these priests were not only excluded from the priesthood but also from their means of support. The *"Urim and Thummim"* mentioned here elude exact identification by scholars, but, apparently, they formed part of the priestly apparatus that enabled the high priest to determine God's will (Num. 27:21; 1 Sam. 28:6). Therefore, the "fatherless" priests were excluded until the high priest could make a definitive determination of their fate.

Categorizing those with indeterminate ancestry and excluding priests with this problem grates against our notion of inclusivity. Moreover, it sounds frightfully close to the "ethnic cleansing" practiced so vilely in Bosnia. In fairness to Israel, however, we should remember that God's covenant with Abraham included the blessing of his descendants (Gen. 12:2). Moreover, intermixing pure Jewish stock with pagan families consistently had led Israel into serious trouble. Invariably, every time they compromised the sacredness of ancestry, God's people quickly compromised the holiness of their religion. In this light, we can understand why a people who were seeking to be restored to God would want to be ethnically pure.

The exclusion of priests as "defiled" seems particularly mean-spirited, but, again, we must remember that the priesthood was hereditary. Only the descendants of Aaron were to serve as priests. If purported priests could not demonstrate their family background, then they could very well be impostors. Undoubtedly, the people who had just suffered through years of exile would be particularly sensitive to anything that might endanger their national renewal. It would be like someone asking me to officiate as the minister at their wedding, and my response being something like this: "Sure, I'll marry you. But my ordination papers have been lost, so I can't prove that I am a licensed minister. But I really am, so there should be no problem. Right?" Wrong! Anyone who needed a legal minister would certainly go elsewhere. Analogously, at this strategic time of restoration, Israel needed priests that conformed to God's exact standard, so the questionable priests were excluded.

CONCLUSION TO THE LIST (2:64–70)

64 The whole assembly together was forty-two thousand three hundred and sixty,
65 besides their male and female servants, of whom there were seven thousand three hundred and

thirty-seven; and they had two hundred men and women singers.

66 Their horses were seven hundred and thirty-six, their mules two hundred and forty-five,

67 their camels four hundred and thirty-five, and their donkeys six thousand seven hundred and twenty.

68 Some of the heads of the fathers' houses, when they came to the house of the LORD which is in Jerusalem, offered freely for the house of God, to erect it in its place:

69 According to their ability, they gave to the treasury for the work sixty-one thousand gold drachmas, five thousand minas of silver, and one hundred priestly garments.

70 So the priests and the Levites, some of the people, the singers, the gatekeepers, and the Nethinim, dwelt in their cities, and all Israel in their cities.

Ezra 2:64–70

The total of 42,360 appears also in Nehemiah 7:66. Unfortunately, it does not sum up the actual numbers of the list (Ezra = 29,818; Nehemiah = 31,089). Although commentators have proposed many solutions to this dilemma, in all likelihood it reflects the awkward Hebrew numbering system along with possible copying inconsistencies.[3] It may also mean that women were included in the total, but not in the constituent numbers indicated above.[4]

Verses 68–69 mention special gifts for the rebuilding effort. The people gave freely, "according to their ability" (v. 69), and they also gave generously, as the large totals testify.

The chapter ends with the resettlement of those who came up from Babylon to Judah in their respective towns and cities (v. 70).

REFLECTIONS ON EZRA 2:1–70

Count Me In . . . Or Count Me Out!

The list in Ezra 2 shows who rightly belonged to the restored community and who did not belong. It registers who is counted in and who is counted out.

We all desire to be counted in, to belong to a group. We hate feeling excluded. While I was a graduate student at Harvard, Professor Krister Stendahl invited me to a dinner of theological faculty in the Boston area because he knew I would be interested in the discussion topic for the evening. When we arrived for hors d'oeuvres at the faculty lounge of Weston Seminary, rather than welcoming me with friendly smiles, a couple of my other professors greeted me with puzzled looks. Finally, one of them asked: "Why are you here?" His tone of voice let me know that I had broken in on a "closed" club. After I explained that Professor Stendahl had invited me, he appeared to be satisfied, but I spent most of the evening feeling like an unwelcome outsider. Because I was a student, not a faculty member, I was not accepted as one of the group.

Do you know that feeling? Have you ever felt like a fifth-wheel at a party or in a group of exclusive friends? Have you ever been the victim of prejudice because of your race or your gender? If you have ever felt the sting of exclusion then you will be particularly sensitive to those Jews in our story who could not prove their parentage. I hope we oppose such forms of exclusion, especially those that are based upon race or family privilege. In the discussion above I have attempted to explain the rationale for Israel's exclusionary policies, but that does not mean I support such measures today. Even if understandable, it seems sad that the very quality that included some people within Israel (ancestry) resulted in excluding others.

Yet, before we point a self-righteous finger at Israel, we must consider our own ways. Are we really any better than they were? Could it be that the very categories by which we feel included actually exclude other people? As Christians we affirm that membership in the Body of Christ depends simply upon faith in Jesus Christ as Lord and Savior. We also accept our calling to draw outsiders to Christ by welcoming them into our gatherings. But our attitudes and actions often contradict these theological convictions. Let me suggest several examples.

A Church Full of "My Kind of People"

There is something wonderful about being in a group of church people. We share common values; we speak the same language; in sum, we feel included because we share a similar subculture. Often we are sociologically homogeneous as well. The church I pastor in

Irvine, California, for example, comprises mostly white, middle-class, well-educated people with traditional values: my kind of people!

But the very things that give us a sense of belonging can exclude others. When I began as pastor at the church, we followed a cherished tradition for welcoming visitors. During each worship service we would ask visitors to stand and introduce themselves to the congregation. To us this seemed like a friendly, welcoming gesture. But I soon noticed that the majority of visitors never stood. In fact, they preferred not to introduce themselves to a room full of strangers and felt uncomfortable being asked to do so. What seemed warm and friendly to us actually seemed rude to many visitors!

I mentioned that the ethnic makeup of Irvine Presbyterian Church is primarily white. Now while this may seem normal to many of us who are white, Anglo-Saxon protestants, it actually excludes a significant percentage of our community. Currently, 17 percent of Irvine is Asian, especially Chinese, Japanese, or Korean. When Asians visit our church they quickly notice our racial narrowness, and many look for a church more inclusive of their culture. Should our church make a more concerted effort to reflect the ethnic mix of our community? I am encouraged by the InterVarsity chapter at the University of California, Irvine. This group reflects the ethnic diversity on campus more than any other campus organization. Persons from diverse races and cultures gather for worship, prayer, and teaching. It is a wonderful example of the Church as it is meant to be, with neither Jew nor Greek, slave nor free, male nor female, but all one in Jesus Christ (Gal. 3:28).

Speaking the Right Language

Have you ever noticed that we Christians have a distinct way of speaking? We use words and phrases that have meaning for us as a unique group. Knowing and using these bits of language help us to feel included. We can walk into churches throughout the country and be asked, "Are you born again?" The response, "Yes, I'm born again" will immediately provoke a responsive recognition and an enthusiastic handshake. We could offer dozens of similar examples.

But have you ever taken a non-Christian friend to a Christian fellowship group, only to realize that your friend does not have the slightest idea what anyone is talking about? Someone may say, "I feel really blessed because the Lord spoke to me this week during my quiet time as I spent an hour in the Word." And your friend is thinking, "What in the world is that person talking about?" How sad that the very ones who need to know the Lord may be put off by our exclusive words and mannerisms that say, inadvertently: "You don't belong here, but we do."

Not long ago, a friend of mine attended a prayer meeting as a brand new Christian. He had never prayed out loud with other Christians, so he did not know the familiar prayer jargon. When he prayed, he talked to God in such a direct and open way that some members of the group became uncomfortable. They scolded him later, saying: "You don't pray in the right way." What a tragic experience for my friend—and for the Church!

It is also time that we Christians became sensitive to the way our language tends to exclude women. We find ourselves comfortable referring to all Christians as "sons of God" or "brothers in Christ," because we have grown accustomed to a subculture that uses male nouns in an inclusive way to refer to men and women. But many segments of our society no longer hear such phrases inoffensively. If I were to say to my congregation, "We are all sons of God," some of my listeners (both male and female) would be put off—especially visitors who are not familiar with Christian jargon. I might lose a hearing with the very people who most need to hear the gospel.

Ironically, even in our efforts to be inclusive of all people we can unintentionally alienate some. I remember worshiping with a group that had worked hard to embrace a breadth of races. In celebration we sang the great hymn of inclusivity, "In Christ There is No East or West." But then, as a congregation of men and women, we sang this verse:

> Join hands, then, *brothers* of the faith,
> Whate'er your race may be;
> Who serves my Father as a son
> Is surely kin to me.[5]

No one meant to exclude the sisters—the daughters of God—and the women were good sports about the hymn, but it made me realize how easy it is for us to exclude people even when celebrating our inclusiveness.

Now, whenever I bring up the topic of gender-inclusive language, I inevitably hear two objections. First of all, people fear that I am advocating the abolition of male names for God, such as "Father." Although Scripture teaches that God transcends any gender (Gen. 1:27; Hos. 11:9), it also leads us to refer to God as Father and King. I affirm and employ this usage. But I work hard to use gender inclusive language when talking about people. I refer to "human beings" rather than to "men," or "humankind" rather than "man." Second, people say to me, "Oh, come on, we all know what the words mean. When we say 'brothers,' I hear 'brothers and sisters.' Why make such a big deal about this?" I agree that many of us who have been raised in the church can hear male language inclusively, but we are called to communicate the gospel to those who are outside the church, who might be uncomfortable with our language patterns. How sad it would be if my unwillingness to alter word usage kept someone from hearing and accepting the Good News!

Is Exclusion from Christian Fellowship Ever Right?

We may, on some occasions, draw lines that keep folks from sharing in the fullness of Christian fellowship. When we do this, we must be clear and intentional, and we must be certain we stand upon solid biblical ground. For example, Presbyterians invite all Christians to participate in communion. People who have not confessed faith in Christ may attend worship with us but may not receive communion. Similarly, we at Irvine Presbyterian welcome all Christians to join our church. A potential new member who says, "I like your church but I don't believe in Jesus" would be advised to wait to join until he or she confessed faith in Christ.

Sometimes Christians must exclude a brother or a sister from fellowship. Scriptural teaching in Matthew 18:15–17 and 1 Corinthians 5:1–5 contradicts principles of "niceness," for when a Christian continues to sin without repentance and rejects restorative care from the church, then the church has grounds to exclude him or her from fellowship for a season. Yet Jesus reminds us to regard that person "as a heathen and a tax collector" (Matthew 18:17)—someone for whom Christ died, whom we hope to draw back into the church.

Church discipline in the Presbyterian Church (U.S.A.) is governed by the "Rules of Discipline," a section in our *Book of Order*. The preamble to the "Rules" reminds us why we would prohibit a Christian from fellowship:

> The power that Jesus Christ has vested in his Church, a power manifested in the exercise of church discipline, is one for building up the body of Christ, not for destroying it, for redeeming, not for punishing. It should be exercised as a dispensation of mercy and not of wrath, so that the great ends of the Church may be achieved, that all children of God may be presented faultless in the day of Christ.[6]

Whereas those excluded from Israel for want of ancestry were excluded for life, we separate Christians out of fellowship only until they are reconciled with God and the community of faith.

Finally, as Israel prevented some proclaimed Priests and Levites from ministering in that role, so we may need to prevent some individuals from performing certain ministerial functions. Although all Christians are called to minister (Eph. 4:12), not every Christian has a right to serve in a leadership role. For instance, a young man who was a member at Hollywood Presbyterian Church, came by my office there because he "felt called to the ordained ministry." I quickly discovered that this young man had never served as a lay person in any role that demonstrated his pastoral abilities. Moreover, he had recently punched another member of the church over a petty argument. I sensed that, if, indeed, God were calling him to be a pastor, he would need time to grow in his ministry skills and to mature in his faith before he would be prepared to lead. But this young man would not be slowed down. He demanded my full and immediate support, requesting a positive recommendation for seminary. In good faith as a steward of Christ's ministry, I could not encourage him until he had demonstrated fitness for pastoral ministry, so he stormed out of my office in a rage because "I had been unsupportive."

Yes, there is a time to exclude someone from Christian fellowship and perhaps also from ministry. When we take this difficult step, however, we do so with the hope of redemption and reconciliation. We remember that God invites sinners into his fellowship and calls all Christians to maturity and to service.

NOTES

1. F. Brown, S. Driver, and C. Briggs, *A Hebrew and English Lexicon of the Old Testament* (Oxford: Clarendon Press, 1975), s.v. *"nĕtînîm."*

2. For more information on the Nethinim, see: J. P. Healey, "Nethinim," *The Anchor Bible Dictionary*, 6 vols., ed. D. N. Freedman (New York: Doubleday, 1992), hereafter *ABD*.

3. See D. Kidner, *Ezra and Nehemiah*, Tyndale Old Testament Commentaries, ed., D. J. Wiseman (Downers Grove: InterVarsity, 1979), pp. 43–44.

4. H. G. M. Williamson, *Ezra, Nehemiah,* Word Biblical Commentaries (Waco, TX: Word Books, 1985), pp. 37–38.

5. John Oxenham, "In Christ There Is No East or West."

6. "Rules of Discipline," Preamble, part b, in *The Constitution of the Presbyterian Church (U.S.A.), Part II: Book of Order* (Louisville: The Office of the General Assembly, 1992).

CHAPTER THREE

Establishing the Foundations

Ezra 3:1–13

STARTING WITH THE FOUNDATIONS

During the 1930s, in the midst of the Great Depression, the Farmers and Merchants Bank of Long Beach had accumulated dozens of homes because owners could not pay their mortgages. Then a major earthquake rocked Long Beach, badly damaging many of the bank's properties. My grandfather, a civil engineer by training, went to work for the bank with one primary task: to restore the ruined homes. As he began to investigate, he found that most of the buildings had simply fallen off of their foundations. The inadequate foundations were not able to support the weight of houses being rattled by the earthquake. In the next year my grandfather oversaw the restoration of these homes, primarily through rebuilding their foundations.

Restoration of many kinds begins with laying a solid foundation, for only upon a secure base may one build a secure structure—a home, a temple, a marriage, a nation. As Ezra 3 illustrates this principle, it challenges us to lay solid foundations for our lives.

LAYING THE SPIRITUAL FOUNDATION (3:1–7)

3:1 And when the seventh month had come, and the children of Israel were in the cities, the people gathered together as one man to Jerusalem.
2 Then Jeshua the son of Jozadak and his brethren the priests, and Zerubbabel the son of Shealtiel and his brethren, arose and built the altar of

the God of Israel, to offer burnt offerings on it, as it is written in the Law of Moses the man of God.

3 Though fear had come upon them because of the people of those countries, they set the altar on its bases; and they offered burnt offerings on it to the LORD, both the morning and evening burnt offerings.

4 They also kept the Feast of Tabernacles, as it is written, and offered the daily burnt offerings in the number required by ordinance for each day.

5 Afterwards they offered the regular burnt offering, and those for New Moons and for all the appointed feasts of the LORD that were consecrated, and those of everyone who willingly offered a freewill offering to the LORD.

6 From the first day of the seventh month they began to offer burnt offerings to the LORD, although the foundation of the temple of the LORD had not been laid.

7 They also gave money to the masons and the carpenters, and food, drink, and oil to the people of Sidon and Tyre to bring cedar logs from Lebanon to the sea, to Joppa, according to the permission which they had from Cyrus king of Persia.

Ezra 3:1–7

By *"the seventh month,"* the people who had returned from Babylon were settled *"in the cities"* (v. 1). The seventh month, for Jews, signifies a season of intense piety since it contains such major holidays as The Day of Atonement and the Feast of Tabernacles. During this time the people gathered together in Jerusalem *"as one man,"* which means, "with common purpose"[1] or "unanimously."[2]

"Jeshua the son of Jozadak" was the High Priest, and his *"brethren"* were also *"priests"*(v. 2).[3] *"Zerubbabel"* was the governor of Judah.[4] By mentioning these names, verse 2 emphasizes that both religious and civic leaders rose up to build *"the altar of the God of Israel, to offer burnt offerings on it."* They did this in obedience to the *"Law of Moses,"* which had commanded that the people make sacrifices to God.

They positioned the rebuilt altar *"on its bases,"* that is, upon its original foundations. Thus the new altar was placed exactly where the old one had been before it was destroyed by the Babylonians.[5]

Even though an interval of decades stood between these people and the last time Jews had sacrificed to God, nevertheless the continuity of place connected the new with the old. Today we can still see a Jewish commitment to keep the temple in its original location by their devoted regard for the temple mount in Jerusalem.

Verse 3 adds a strange qualification to their restoration of the altar: *"Though fear had come upon them because of the people of those countries, they set the altar. . . ."* The Hebrew literally reads: "They built the altar on its foundations *because* [*kî*] of their fear of the people of the lands." Perhaps a fear of neighboring peoples encouraged the Jews to focus on the priority of reestablishing their relationship with God. Restoring worship of God might ward off danger, because God's presence would protect the people.[6] So the people began to offer *"both the morning and evening burnt offerings"* as prescribed in the Law (Exod. 29:38–46). These sacrifices would remind the people of God's daily presence with them.

With the reestablishment of the altar, the people were able to offer the elaborate sacrifices required in the *"Feast of Tabernacles"* (4:4).[7] This Feast was also known as the Feast of Booths or Sukkoth (the Hebrew word for "booths" is *"sūkkôt"*). It was one of Israel's three great festivals and was celebrated in the fall. The Feast of Tabernacles combined a harvest festival (similar to our Thanksgiving) with a reminder of the Exodus, when Israel had to live in booths (tents) after being set free from Egypt.

Verses 5 and 6 list several of the required sacrifices that were made on the altar. We might paraphrase these verses as follows: "From then on they offered all of the prescribed and voluntary sacrifices." Then verse 6 adds a small surprise: *"although the foundation of the temple of the LORD had not been laid."* Even before the restoration of the temple began, the people worshiped as if they had a temple. They did not wait until they had a building to worship God as the Law prescribed. No, even before they laid the physical foundation for the temple, they laid a spiritual foundation of worship.

Continuing on to verse 7 we read of the initial preparations for the restoration of the temple itself. The officials of Judah hired laborers (*"masons and the carpenters"*) and arranged for the necessary building supplies. *"Joppa"* was a port city about fifty miles northwest of Jerusalem. Actually, verse 7 serves as a transition between verses 1–6 and what follows in the next section.

70

LAYING THE MATERIAL FOUNDATION (3:8–13)

8 Now in the second month of the second year of
their coming to the house of God at Jerusalem,
Zerubbabel the son of Shealtiel, Jeshua the son of
Jozadak, and the rest of their brethren the priests and
the Levites, and all those who had come out of the
captivity to Jerusalem, began work and appointed the
Levites from twenty years old and above to oversee
the work of the house of the LORD.

9 Then Jeshua with his sons and brothers,
Kadmiel with his sons, and the sons of Judah, arose as
one to oversee those working on the house of God:
the sons of Henadad with their sons and their
brethren the Levites.

10 When the builders laid the foundation of the
temple of the LORD, the priests stood in their apparel
with trumpets, and the Levites, the sons of Asaph,
with cymbals, to praise the LORD, according to the
ordinance of David king of Israel.

11 And they sang responsively, praising and
giving thanks to the LORD: "For He is good, For His
mercy endures forever toward Israel." Then all the
people shouted with a great shout, when they praised
the LORD, because the foundation of the house of the
LORD was laid.

12 But many of the priests and Levites and heads
of the fathers' houses, old men who had seen the first
temple, wept with a loud voice when the foundation
of this temple was laid before their eyes. Yet many
shouted aloud for joy,

13 so that the people could not discern the noise
of the shout of joy from the noise of the weeping of
the people, for the people shouted with a loud shout,
and the sound was heard afar off.

Ezra 3:8–13

Verse 8 describes the beginning of the physical restoration of the
temple. *"Zerubbabel,"* the government authority, *"Jeshua,"* the religious authority, and the other religious officials, *"the priests and the
Levites,"* led the nation in this project. Moreover, *"all those who had
come out of the captivity"* joined in the effort for that was why they had

come (see 1:3, 5). Notice that the leaders appointed mature *"Levites . . . to oversee the work."* This fits broadly within the job description of a Levite: to assist the priests and to take care of the temple and its contents. Verse 9 identifies by name the leading Levite families who oversaw the workers.

In verse 10 we find the second surprise of Ezra 3. Just as soon as the builders completed the foundation, everyone stopped working to celebrate. Both the priests, arrayed *"in their apparel,"* and the Levites, who grabbed their *"cymbals,"* began to *"praise the LORD, according to the ordinance of David king of Israel."* (David was credited with establishing musical worship within the temple.)[9] We find the emphasis here, once again, on the continuity in Israel's worship between the past and the present.

The priests and Levites sang *"responsively,"* drawing *"all the people"* into worship (v. 11). The song found in this verse repeats a familiar refrain, found throughout the Psalms (for example, Ps. 106:1):

> For He is good,
> For His mercy endures forever toward Israel.

It celebrates God's goodness and, especially, his covenant faithfulness towards Israel. The NKJV uses *"mercy"* to translate the Hebrew word *"ḥesed"*, which is often used to describe God's faithful care for Israel in light of his everlasting covenant.[10] (This term plays a significant role throughout Ezra-Nehemiah. See, for example, the discussion of Nehemiah 1:5 and 13:22). In joyous song, the people gave credit to God for their progress in restoration; they worshiped *"with a great shout."*

Suddenly, verses 12-13 reveal the third surprise of Ezra 3: in the midst of such a clamorous celebration, *"many"* of the older priests, Levites, and family leaders *"wept with a loud voice when the foundation of this temple was laid before their eyes; yet many shouted aloud for joy"* (v. 12). The noise they created was so loud that people far away could hear it but could not distinguish the weeping from the rejoicing (v. 13).

Why did the older people weep? Out of joy? Or out of sorrow? The text attributes the weeping to those *"old men who had seen the first temple"* (v. 12). But were they happy or sad to see the new foundation? It seems to me that verse 12 provides a clue when it says: *"Yet many shouted aloud for joy."* By implication, those who wept did not express joy. The Hebrew word "to weep" ("*bākâ*") usually connotes the expression of sadness.[11] Besides 3:12, it always functions this way in Ezra-Nehemiah (see 10:1; Neh. 1:4; 8:9). The prophecies of Haggai and Zechariah also suggest that the weeping in Ezra 3:12 was due to sadness. God spoke through Haggai to the people during the restoration process, saying: "Who is left among you who saw this temple in its former glory? And how do you see it now? In comparison with it, is this not in your eyes as nothing?" (Hag. 2:3). Those who remembered the glorious temple of Solomon "despised the day of small things" (Zech. 4:10). The Jewish historian Josephus (first century A.D.) offers this interpretation of events:

> But the priests and the Levites and the elders of the families, recalling to mind the former temple which had been very great and costly, and seeing that the one recently constructed fell short of the old one because of their poverty, and considering how far they had fallen below their ancient prosperity and a state worthy of the temple, were downcast, and being unable to master their grief at this thought, were moved to laments and weeping.[12]

Chapter 3 closes with a bizarre yet moving scene. Multitudes praised God with loud thanksgivings while others wept with almost equal fervor.

REFLECTIONS ON EZRA 3:1–13

The Appropriateness of Mourning

Can you relate to the experience of the elders who mourned while others celebrated? Do you know what it is like to feel sad because things are not like they used to be, or because your life has not turned out as you had hoped? Have you ever wept because of change—even change you wanted?

A friend of mine, John, works as a developer. He builds condominium complexes, often in places where homes once stood. A few years ago he bought a home from some of his friends who knew when they sold it to him that he intended to tear it down. On the day John's company razed the home, the original owners came to watch. With memories of life in that home filling their hearts, they stood at a distance and wept. Poor John, there he stood, watching his good friends cry as he destroyed their family home.

Admittedly mourning is a normal, healthy part of life. As Ecclesiastes reminds us, there is "A time to weep, and a time to laugh; A time to mourn, and a time to dance" (Eccl. 3:4–5).[13] The American tendency to deny sadness and avoid grief leads to emotional and physical disease. We must learn that it is right to feel sad when we experience loss.

So, on one level we empathize with those Jewish elders who wept when they realized that the rebuilt temple would not match the glory of the former temple. Their response shows an understandable sadness about change and the loss of "the good ol' days." But something seems wrong about their display of emotion in the setting of Ezra 3. After all, they chose to demonstrate their sadness right in the middle of a worship service of praise and thanksgiving. They did not weep discreetly but in overwhelmingly loud wails. Furthermore, from the book of Haggai we learn that the negative response among these Jewish elders actually discouraged the workers from completing the rebuilding project (Hag. 2:3–4). So while we sympathize with their sadness over change, we rightfully question the appropriateness of their expression in this setting.

Without doubt, anyone who has attempted to bring about change within the church knows how debilitating it can be to have people vociferously share their sadness and misgivings. Such "grief" can easily become manipulative foot-dragging. For example, we have intended to build a sanctuary at Irvine Presbyterian for several years. Early in the process an architect designed a magnificent building, but one that exceeded our budget by several million dollars. Obviously we could not even think of following through with such an expensive design. Yet, even now, some members speak wistfully about what "could have been." Perhaps they do not realize how easily they discourage those who are trying to work with more realistic designs.

We must find ways in the church, and in our personal lives, to grieve over losses without becoming mired in the past. Seven years ago my father died. My mother continued to live in the house they shared together for thirty years, and recently she has made necessary and beautiful changes in the house: she has replaced curtains she and my father picked out together and has removed the wallpaper they hung together. While my mother weeps again over the loss of her husband each time she makes such changes, she does not allow her healthy grief to keep her in a house with dilapidated furnishings. In contrast to the inappropriate display of grief by the elders of Jerusalem, we need to find, like my mother, right ways to grieve even as we move ahead with our lives.

First Things First!

Ezra 3 tells a story about foundations—both literal and figurative. On the one hand, the people laid the foundations for the temple, yet before they began, they laid spiritual foundations by offering sacrifices to God upon the rebuilt altar. Ezra 3 reminds us to put first things first, to establish right priorities for our lives.

As we observed, this chapter contains several surprises. First, the people sacrificed to God before they had a temple (v. 6). Although they came up to Jerusalem for the explicit purpose of rebuilding the temple, they placed the highest priority upon the worship of God, not on the building in which that worship would occur. We can imagine that dissenting voices said, "Oh, let's wait to sacrifice until we have a real temple." But the leaders of Judah knew that worship could and should begin right away. First things first!

The second surprise in Ezra is that as soon as the workers finished the foundation they stopped everything for an extended service of praise and thanksgiving. Again, we can imagine what the pragmatists in the crowd must have said, "Why are we stopping now? We'll lose our momentum. Let's build now, and worship later." But again the priests and the Levites insisted upon the appropriate spiritual priorities. Once again, worship came before building. First things first!

Ezra 3 challenges us to put first things first in our lives and to make worship one of those first things. The Westminster Shorter Catechism (A.D. 1647) proclaims that our chief purpose in life is "to glorify God, and to enjoy him forever."[14] Worshiping and glorifying God need to be a top priority. So it should not surprise us that many Christians lack vitality in their relationship with God because they neglect worship. They view worship in church as the warm-up for the main event, the sermon. Sadly, many pastors seem to think the same thing! But true worship stands at the center of a living faith in God. Worship puts our focus in the right place for it reminds us who deserves all the glory. Truly, worship is a sure foundation upon which we can build our lives.

This chapter from Ezra should also provide encouragement for smaller or newer churches. Increasingly, American Christianity is dominated by the "megachurch": the massive church with membership in the 1000's, complete with magnificent campus and outstanding facilities. Pastors and other Christian leaders read books by megachurch pastors hoping to discover the key to their "success." We imitate their ways and long for their resources. Now I am not criticizing megachurches because those I have visited encourage genuine Christian commitment and true worship of God. But those of us who do not have the large buildings and phenomenal facilities can take heart from Ezra 3. Regardless of size, we can major in the majors; we can worship God whether we have impressive facilities or not. In fact, some of the most vibrant and authentic worship I have experienced took place at the Vineyard Christian Fellowship in Anaheim when it met in a massive and thoroughly unattractive warehouse. In many cities across America one might find better worship in simple school gymnasiums than in ornate church sanctuaries!

An implicit warning in Ezra 3 calls us not to let buildings distract us from what really matters. As I write this chapter, our church has just increased activities regarding our building project. We hope to begin construction of our sanctuary within a year. As the pastor, I rejoice in God's vision for this congregation, yet I also feel a strong responsibility to keep everyone focused on what really matters: God and his glory! We can worship *now* in our fellowship hall in spirit and in truth; we don't have to wait until we have "a real sanctuary." Moreover, as we move ahead with the trials of a major building project, my task as pastor will be to keep our eyes focused in the right direction—not upon ourselves and our building, but upon God and his call to reach our community with the gospel. May we always remember to keep first things first!

NOTES

1. C. F. Fensham, *The Books of Ezra and Nehemiah,* The New International Commentary on the Old Testament (Grand Rapids: Eerdmans, 1982), p. 59.

2. C. F. Keil and F. Delitzsch, *Ezra, Nehemiah, Esther,* Commentary on the Old Testament, vol. 3 (Peabody, MA: Hendrickson, 1989), p. 50.

3. See also 5:2. *"Jeshua"* is Aramaic. The prophets Haggai and Zechariah refer to Jeshua by his Hebrew name, Joshua, and identify him as the High Priest (Hag. 1:1; Zech. 3:1).

4. Haggai 1:1. We do not know when or how Zerubbabel took over from Sheshbazzar. See comments in: "Introduction to Ezra-Nehemiah: Chronological Puzzles in Ezra-Nehemiah."

5. Blenkinsopp, *Ezra-Nehemiah,* p. 97.

6. Kidner, *Ezra & Nehemiah,* pp. 45–46, Blenkinsopp, *Ezra-Nehemiah,* p. 98. Other interpretations are found in Fensham, *Ezra and Nehemiah,* p. 59; Williamson, *Ezra, Nehemiah,* p. 46.

7. These sacrifices are spelled out in Numbers 29:12–38.

8. See J. D. Rylaarsdam, "The Feast of Booths," *The Interpreter's Dictionary of the Bible,* ed. G. A. Buttrick, 4 vols. (Nashville: Abingdon, 1962), hereafter *IDB.*

9. Fensham, *Ezra and Nehemiah,* p. 64.

10. See R. L. Harris, *"hesed,"* *Theological Wordbook of the Old Testament,* ed., R. L. Harris (Chicago: Moody, 1980); and K. D. Sakenfeld, "Love: Old Testament: E: hesed, *ABD* (New York: Doubleday, 1992).

11. J. N. Oswalt, *"bākâ",* *Theological Wordbook of the Old Testament,* ed., R. L. Harris (Chicago: Moody, 1980) hereafter *TWOT.*

12. Josephus, *Jewish Antiquities,* 11:81. Translation by R. Marcus in Josephus, 10 vols., Loeb Classical Library (Cambridge: Harvard University Press, 1978). The footnote to this section adds: "Josephus here amplifies somewhat" (6:353).

13. See my "Reflections on Nehemiah 1:1–11" below.

14. "The Westminster Shorter Catechism," Question 1, in P. Schaff, ed., *The Creeds of Christendom,* 3 vols., 6th edition revised by D. S. Schaff (Grand Rapids: Baker, 1983), 3: 676.

CHAPTER FOUR

Opposition to Restoration

Ezra 4:1–24

THE EMPIRE STRIKES BACK

In 1977, millions of Americans enjoyed George Lucas' film, *Star Wars*. In the movie a small, ragged band of rebels opposes the Empire: an evil regime personified by the devilish Darth Vader. After a series of exploits, the good guys seem to be in desperate straits. But in the closing moments of the film, the hero, Luke Skywalker, trusts the Force, blows up the Death Star, and escapes sure destruction. Good has triumphed over evil, and Hollywood has made a bundle of money!

Then just three years later, millions flocked again to the theaters to see *The Empire Strikes Back*, the sequel to *Star Wars*. In that film, Darth Vader and his evil Empire sought revenge against the rebels. By the end of the film, the future once more seemed bleak for the good guys. But a glimmer of hope remained, at least enough to entice filmgoers back to the movies for the final installment of the *Star Wars* trilogy, *Return of the Jedi*.

Anyone who is familiar with drama (or with Hollywood's ability to capitalize on a good thing) is not surprised by these sequels to *Star Wars*. Like all good stories, each film depended upon conflict. Just when things seemed to be going well, then everything began to unravel. The apparent triumph of good over evil did not last for long, because the conflict, and thus the emotional momentum, had to continue. This makes for good drama—but complicated living.

In Ezra 3, the people of Judah began to rebuild the temple. Working industriously, they laid the foundations; then they paused for a time in order to praise and to thank God for his faithfulness. Everything was progressing according to plan. But as we approach Ezra 4 we find that opposition to the rebuilding project had developed. Conflict reared its ugly head, stalling a project that seemed to be going so well. This chapter can serve as preparation for the opposition that will inevitably come in our lives.

OPPOSITION BEGINS (4:1–5)

> 4:1 Now when the adversaries of Judah and Ben-
> jamin heard that the descendants of the captivity were
> building the temple of the LORD God of Israel,
> 2 they came to Zerubbabel and the heads of the
> fathers' houses, and said to them, "Let us build with
> you, for we seek your God as you do; and we have
> sacrificed to Him since the days of Esarhaddon king
> of Assyria, who brought us here."
> 3 But Zerubbabel and Jeshua and the rest of the
> heads of the fathers' houses of Israel said to them,
> "You may do nothing with us to build a house for our
> God; but we alone will build to the LORD God of
> Israel, as King Cyrus the king of Persia has com-
> manded us."
> 4 Then the people of the land tried to discourage
> the people of Judah. They troubled them in building,
> 5 and hired counselors against them to frustrate
> their purpose all the days of Cyrus king of Persia,
> even until the reign of Darius king of Persia.
>
> *Ezra 4:1–5*

Those who came to the leaders in Jerusalem made a simple offer: *"Let us build with you"* (v. 2). They explained their apparent friendliness on the basis of a common religious faith: *"for we seek your God as you do; and we have sacrificed to Him since the days of Esarhaddon king of Assyria, who brought us here"* (v. 2). Although the Bible identifies Esarhaddon as an Assyrian king (2 Kgs. 19:37; Isa. 37:38), only here does it mention his resettling of people. His predecessors, however, had resettled foreign people in the province of Samaria while it was under Assyrian rule (2 Kgs. 17:24–41). Information in 2 Kings 17 indicates that while these transplanted pagans worshiped the God of Israel, they did not do so exclusively. The claim in 4:2, "we seek your God *as you do*," misrepresents the truth. Those who offered to help may have sought the God of Israel, but they did so syncretistically, along with a pantheon of other gods.

The Jewish reaction to this offer of help (v. 3) does not seem related to theological concerns. Apparently, *"Zerubbabel and Jeshua"* rejected the offer because their commission from King Cyrus allowed the temple to be rebuilt only by those who had returned from exile (1:3). It is possible they worried that accepting local help might jeopardize royal support. But, even so, the harsh rejection in verse 3 seems to be an overreaction.

To understand why the Jews reacted so strongly, we need to note verse 1, which identifies those coming to help as *"the adversaries of Judah and Benjamin"*. On the surface, the gesture in verse 2 seems innocent, but in reality it reflects the attempts of opponents to derail the rebuilding project. Plan A in the opposition involved infiltrating the ranks of the Jews, thus causing Judah to compromise its integrity. But the plan failed because the astute Judean leaders rejected this counterfeit offer of "help."

Verses 4–5 confirm the validity of the leaders' skepticism. Notice that once *"the people of the land"* realized they could not infiltrate the work, they moved on to Plan B: a strategy that involved various attempts *"to discourage the people of Judah"* (v. 4), or literally, *"to weaken their hands"*.[1] The adversaries (4:1) and perhaps others,[2] *"troubled them in building"* and even *"hired counselors"* to frustrate the people of Judah. In this context, hiring counselors means bribing Persian officials to harass the Jews.[3]

Unfortunately, verse 5 concludes with an unhappy note: the people of the land succeeded in their efforts to obstruct the building project. They impeded the progress on the temple from the time of Cyrus, when the foundation had been laid, *"even until the reign of Darius king of Persia,"* a period of about sixteen years.

OTHER EXAMPLES OF OPPOSITION (4:6–23)

6 In the reign of Ahasuerus, in the beginning of his reign, they wrote an accusation against the inhabitants of Judah and Jerusalem.

7 In the days of Artaxerxes also, Bishlam, Mithredath, Tabel, and the rest of their companions wrote to Artaxerxes king of Persia; and the letter was

written in Aramaic script, and translated into the
Aramaic language.

8 Rehum the commander and Shimshai the scribe
wrote a letter against Jerusalem to King Artaxerxes in
this fashion:

9 From Rehum the commander, Shimshai the scribe,
and the rest of their companions—representatives of
the Dinaites, the Apharsathchites, the Tarpelites, the
people of Persia and Erech and Babylon and Shushan,
the Dehavites, the Elamites,

10 and the rest of the nations whom the great and
noble Osnapper took captive and settled in the cities
of Samaria and the remainder beyond the River—and
so forth.

11 This is a copy of the letter that they sent him—
To King Artaxerxes from your servants, the men of
the region beyond the River, and so forth:

12 Let it be known to the king that the Jews who
came up from you have come to us at Jerusalem, and
are building the rebellious and evil city, and are
finishing its walls and repairing the foundations.

13 Let it now be known to the king that, if this city
is built and the walls completed, they will not pay tax,
tribute, or custom, and the king's treasury will be
diminished.

14 Now because we receive support from the
palace, it was not proper for us to see the king's
dishonor; therefore we have sent and informed the
king,

15 that search may be made in the book of the
records of your fathers. And you will find in the book
of the records and know that this city is a rebellious
city, harmful to kings and provinces, and that they
have incited sedition within the city in former times,
for which cause this city was destroyed.

16 We inform the king that if this city is rebuilt and
its walls are completed, the result will be that you will
have no dominion beyond the River.

17 The king sent an answer: To Rehum the commander, to Shimshai the scribe, to the rest of their
companions who dwell in Samaria, and to the remainder beyond the River: Peace, and so forth.

18 The letter which you sent to us has been clearly read before me.

19 And I gave the command, and a search has been made, and it was found that this city in former times has revolted against kings, and rebellion and sedition have been fostered in it.

20 There have also been mighty kings over Jerusalem, who have ruled over all the region beyond the River; and tax, tribute, and custom were paid to them.

21 Now give the command to make these men cease, that this city may not be built until the command is given by me.

22 Take heed now that you do not fail to do this. Why should damage increase to the hurt of the kings?

23 Now when the copy of King Artaxerxes' letter was read before Rehum, Shimshai the scribe, and their companions, they went up in haste to Jerusalem against the Jews, and by force of arms made them cease.

Ezra 4:6–23

Somewhat surprisingly, the next section of Ezra moves quickly through time to another historical era, after the temple had been rebuilt. Verse 6 mentions *"an accusation against the inhabitants of Judah and Jerusalem"* that was raised in the beginning of *"the reign of Ahasuerus,"* but we are given no further details about this instance of opposition. "Ahasuerus" is the Hebrew form of the Persian name that was better known in its Greek form, "Xerxes." Xerxes I ruled over the Persian empire from 486 through 465 B.C., or about thirty years after the temple had been rebuilt (see the time-line on page 38).

The following verses (4:7–23) recount another instance of opposition to Judah, this time during the reign of "Artaxerxes" (v. 7). If, as seems likely, this refers to Artaxerxes I, then this incident occured between 465 and 423 B.C., during which time he ruled the Persian Empire. It must also have happened before Nehemiah's successful rebuilding of the Jerusalem wall in 445 B.C.

Sometime during the reign of Artaxerxes I, Jews who had recently returned from Babylon to Judah (with Ezra?) began to rebuild Jerusalem and especially its broken walls (v. 12). This caused concern for those who lived outside of Judah, probably because they enjoyed their positions of power over the Jews. So the residents from the lands and their leaders wrote a letter of complaint to Artaxerxes with the intention of stopping the rebuilding project (v. 16). Verse 7 identifies some of those who wrote the letter and clarifies that it was written in Aramaic, a Semitic language closely related to Hebrew. This was the official language of the Persian Empire (and also the primary language of Jesus). Beginning with 4:8, Ezra utilized Aramaic for 52 verses, through 6:18. It was the original language of the letters copied into the text, and the author of Ezra-Nehemiah chose to compose in Aramaic as well, perhaps for stylistic reasons.

The letter was sent officially from *"Rehum the commander"* and his scribe *"Shimshai"* (vv. 8–9). Rehum, who served some function in the Persian government, claimed to have written on behalf of a cluster of people who lived near Judah (vv. 9–10), including especially those who had been settled in *"Samaria"* by *"Osnapper"* (v. 10). Osnapper refers to King Ashurbanipal of Assyria (669–626 B.C.) who followed the practice of his predecessors by resettling people in new lands.[4] He is called, *"great and noble"* in this letter to illustrate how the writers honored their kings.

Verse 10 refers to *"the remainder beyond the River."* The phrase "beyond the River," which appears often throughout Ezra-Nehemiah, is the Persian name for the region that extended from the Euphrates River to the Mediterranean Sea and included all of Judah and Samaria.[5]

The opponents carefully crafted their letter to slander the Jews and to worry the king. The threat they purported was simple: The Jews have a history of independence and rebellion (vv. 12, 15), therefore, if they are allowed to rebuild the wall of Jerusalem they will not pay the tax owed to the king (v. 13). As a result, not only would *"the king's treasury . . . be diminished"* (v. 13), but he would lose his authority over the entire region (v. 16). The creators of the letter motivated Artaxerxes through fear of losing money and power—a classic and effective strategy!

What was the king's response? At his request (v. 15), a search was made of Persia's historical archives, in which Jewish independence and sedition were documented (v. 19). Verse 20 may refer to ancient Jewish kings (David, Solomon), but it probably alludes instead to Artaxerxes' own predecessors.[6] His point was: I also deserve to receive *"tax, tribute, and custom"* (v. 20). Verse 21 records the stop-work order that was issued, although Artaxerxes reserved the right to change his mind at a later date (as he did in Nehemiah 2).

With the king's endorsement, the local officials went up to Jerusalem and *"by force of arms"* made the Jews stop rebuilding the wall. We do not know exactly when this situation occured during the reign of Artaxerxes, but it may have been a significant factor in motivating Nehemiah to intercede on behalf of his native land (Nehemiah 1–2).

Why did the editor of Ezra-Nehemiah interrupt his story of the rebuilding of the temple with events from later decades? I would propose that he did not have sources to document exactly how the opponents "frustrated their purpose all the days of Cyrus king of Persia, even until the reign of Darius king of Persia" (v. 5). But, rather than allow his summary in verses 5 and 24 to stand alone, the editor used a later event to serve two purposes: (1) to illustrate the kind of opposition that occurred while Cyrus and Darius ruled, and (2) to supply a background to the story of Nehemiah, thus prefiguring what was to come.

OPPOSITION SUCCEEDS (4:24)

24 Thus the work of the house of God which is at Jerusalem ceased, and it was discontinued until the second year of the reign of Darius king of Persia.
Ezra 4:24

The opposition succeeded in its plan to halt reconstruction of the temple. A sixteen year interval separates the initiation of rebuilding in chapter 3 and the later resumption of rebuilding in chapter 5. Verse 24 repeats the sad note already mentioned in verse 5. By returning to the earlier era of kings Cyrus and Darius, the editor of Ezra-Nehemiah employed a familiar literary device called "repetitive resumption." The final phrase, *"until the second year of the reign of Darius king of Persia,"* foreshadows Ezra 5.

But Ezra-Nehemiah does not tell the whole story of why work on the temple stopped, so we need to turn to the prophet Haggai to fill in the blanks. He tells us that God rebuked the people for not building his "house" (Hag. 1:3). They had put off construction of the temple in order to build their own "paneled houses" (Hag. 1:4), and, as a result, God chastised them with economic hardships (Hag. 1:6) and a drought (Hag. 1:11). These difficulties, of course, further hindered work on the temple. Although not stated specifically, we can imagine how the people of Judah, faced with threats and harassment from outsiders, turned away from God's work to meet their personal needs. Then, as the years passed, it became easier and easier to procrastinate at resuming work on the temple. By the reign of Darius, only God could motivate the people to rebuild again, and, indeed, that is precisely what he did (Ezra 5).

REFLECTIONS ON EZRA 4:1–24

Anticipating Opposition

It goes without saying that we who labor in God's kingdom will encounter opposition. Like the people of Judah, our work will not proceed without hassles and frustrations. In fact, chapter 4 of Ezra exemplifies some of the kinds of opposition that we may encounter.

We noted that the adversaries of Judah first attempted to infiltrate the ranks of God's people. On the surface, they appeared to offer a friendly gesture of support, but beneath the façade lay an attempt to compromise the integrity of God's work force. As Christians who serve God, we may also receive offers of "help" from "wolves in sheep's clothing." Occasionally this may come from religious cultists who pretend to be orthodox Christians, but more often the help that threatens our integrity takes a different form. It comes as "techniques" from our culture that promise "success" for the church. For example, Christians who seek God's healing may import New Age techniques of prayer that deny God's sovereignty over the healing process. Rather than ask in faith for God to heal, these well-intentioned folk use manipulative strategies to force God's hand. In these situations the integrity of faith and ministry is compromised through a partnership with a false "friend"—New Age methodology.

There is another adversary that has invaded modern Christianity. Within the past twenty years a biblical church-growth movement has brought new life to old churches and has resulted in thousands of new fellowships being established. But, in the midst of all this, some Christian leaders have fallen into the bigger-is-better trap, against the counsel of wise church-growth experts. These leaders have introduced Madison Avenue values into the church. Slickness has taken the place of integrity; adding members has become the new bottom line, even in the face of compromising the gospel; and the ends of "growth" have come to justify almost any means of attaining that growth. Once again, the integrity of God's work has become infected by a theologically-bogus strategy for growing larger churches. Disciple-making has gotten lost in the shuffle. Let me reiterate that I am not criticizing the church-growth movement founded by Donald McGavran and led by C. Peter Wagner and others. I am thinking, rather, of undiscerning Christian leaders who have abandoned the authentic gospel, and who have failed to measure their methods by the plumb line of the Scriptures.

What did the opponents of Judah do once they realized they could not infiltrate as false friends? They adopted a second strategy. They tried to "discourage" the workers by bothering them and bribing government officials to trip them up. Unfortunately, this strategy succeeded for many years.

We who labor in the Lord's work also face discouragement. Some-times this comes from people outside the church. For example, throughout Southern California today many churches have been straightjacketed in their development by neighbors who do not want a church nearby. "We don't want the noise or the traffic," they say. So civic officials, looking ahead to the next election, deny building per-mits to churches or place impossible demands upon them. Church leaders face endless meetings that prove to be fruitless, and the re-sult, of course, is discouragement.

But I find it particularly tragic that the most common source of dis-couragement for Christian leaders today comes from within the body of Christ. Those who attempt to bring renewal to the church almost inevitably hear the "seven last words of the church": We never did it that way before! I know of one church that appears to be heading for imminent dissolution because of this very problem. Some of its key members have said publicly that they would rather see their church close down than experience renewal. Now that is discouraging!

Unmasking the Opposition

Ezra identified the people of the land as Judah's adversaries, and, indeed, they were, on one level. Similarly, I have just mentioned the opposition that can come from neighbors and church members. But in order to oppose the enemy effectively as Christians, we must un-mask our true opposition. We must realize that people who resist God's work are simply pawns in a game played by our true Enemy. In Ephesians, Paul describes the real nature of our opposition:

> Put on the whole armor of God, that you may be able to stand against the wiles of the devil. For we do not wrestle against flesh and blood, but against principalities, against powers, against the rulers of the darkness of this age, against spiritual hosts of wick-edness in the heavenly places.
>
> *Ephesians 6:11–12*

Human agents often unwittingly serve as "front men" for Satan and his spiritual forces. We must look beyond these "pawns" and realize that Satan is our true enemy; or perhaps more accurately stated, Sa-tan is God's true enemy.

Recognizing the source of our opposition provides three benefits for us. First, when we have to confront human opponents, we see them as pawns in a larger game. *We can be set free from disliking the people who stand in the way of God's work*, whether they are in the church or in the world. We will find it easier to love them and to pray for them.

Second, *we can be empowered to fight proficiently.* Instead of focusing our efforts upon people, we can focus on spiritual warfare and weap-ons. As Paul writes to the Corinthians:

> For though we walk in the flesh, we do not war according to the flesh. For the weapons of our warfare are not carnal but mighty in God for pulling down strongholds, casting down arguments and every high thing that exalts itself against the knowledge of God, bringing every thought into captivity to the obedience of Christ.
>
> *2 Corinthians 10:3–5*

Later we will discuss further how to fight with spiritual weapons (see below, "Reflections on Nehemiah 4:1–23"), but here we emphasize that spiritual opposition necessitates a spiritual response.

Third, when we know the actual identity of our opposition, *we can have confidence in our ultimate victory,* for on the cross Christ broke the power of sin—he vanquished Satan and his hold upon us. As 1 John 3:8 teaches, "For this purpose the Son of God was manifested, that He might destroy the works of the devil." He did this through his death

at Calvary. What remains is merely the mop-up effort until Christ returns to rule supreme over all creation. Christ, and we as his people,
will be victorious. As Paul encouraged the Romans with the inevita-
bility and imminence of God's victory through them, "And the God
of peace will crush Satan under your feet shortly" (Rom. 16:20), so
we, in times of discouragement, can be encouraged by the fact that as
God's people we will be victorious.

The reality of spiritual warfare, however, affronts our self-reliance.
If, indeed, we do not wrestle against flesh and blood, then we cannot
fight alone—we need God. We need divine power, and we need
God's weapons. When we unmask our opposition we are confronted
with the need for a new reliance upon God. We discover, as well,
new ways to experience God's faithfulness and power as he crushes
Satan under our feet.

NOTES

1. Brown, Driver, and Briggs, *Lexicon* (Oxford: Clarendon, 1975),
s.v. *"rāpâ."*

2. Williamson, *Ezra, Nehemiah,* p. 50.

3. Fensham, *Ezra and Nehemiah,* p. 68.

4. Fensham, *Ezra and Nehemiah,* p. 73. See also A. L. Oppenheim,
"Assyria and Babylonia," *IDB* (Nashville: Abingdon, 1962).

5. M. E. Hardwick, "Beyond the River," *ABD* (New York: Doubleday,
1992).

6. Williamson, *Ezra, Nehemiah,* p. 64.

7. Williamson, *Ezra, Nehemiah,* p. 57.

CHAPTER FIVE

Resumption of Restoration

Ezra 5:1–6:12

THE STIGMA OF A FALSE START

As the Barcelona sun beat down on the semifinalists for the Olympic 100-meter dash, they were instructed to "take their marks." Soon the second command came, "set." The sprinters rose in readiness for the gun. But before it fired, one of the runners jumped the gun. A quick double-firing of the gun informed everyone that someone had made a false start. Subsequently, the runners returned to their positions, and every eye in the stadium was focused on that unfortunate runner since another false start would eliminate him from further competition.

My heart went out to this sprinter as I remembered a similar experience of a false start. In high school I ran the high hurdles for our track team, and since I was not blessed with blazing speed, I needed every advantage I could get. My coach worked extensively on my start. If I could burst out of the blocks ahead of the other hurdlers, then I began with an advantage that could possibly carry me to the finish line in first place. But at the beginning of a race, sometimes my nervousness would get the best of me, and I would jump the gun. Then, creeping back to the blocks in embarrassment, I would try again. The second time, however, the stigma of having made a false start inevitably caused me to hesitate briefly after the starter's pistol fired. Because no matter how I finished the race, I did not want to make another false start!

I wonder if the people of Israel felt the stigma of a false start in 521 B.C. Although they had completed the foundations and had commenced work on the temple, the project remained untouched for sixteen years. For more than a decade the unbuilt temple reminded the residents of Jerusalem that they had failed—in spite of a splendid start. Perhaps some had tried to rally the others to build, but the fear of failing again overwhelmed their good intentions.

The prophet Haggai provides additional information about Judah during this period of history. He tells us that the people were procrastinating, saying, "The time has not come, the time that the LORD's house should be built" (Hag. 1:2). In the meantime, however, some had built their own homes complete with luxurious paneling (Hag. 1:4). Whereas the wealthy attended to their own conspicuous consumption, the majority of the Jews struggled to exist through drought, famine, and economic hardship (Hag. 1:6–9). Rampant self-interest and the necessity for self-preservation crushed any interest in rebuilding God's house.

How, then, would God's people get back on track? How would they overcome the stigma of a false start in order to complete the building project? How would their priorities be corrected so that God could once again take first place? Chapters 5 and 6 of Ezra show how God revived his people and helped them to start again to build his house.

HELP FROM GOD'S PROPHETS (5:1–2)

> 5:1 Then the prophet Haggai and Zechariah the
> son of Iddo, prophets, prophesied to the Jews who
> were in Judah and Jerusalem, in the name of the God
> of Israel, who was over them.
> 2 So Zerubbabel the son of Shealtiel and Jeshua
> the son of Jozadak rose up and began to build the
> house of God which is in Jerusalem; and the prophets
> of God were with them, helping them.
>
> *Ezra 5:1–2*

According to 5:1, *"the prophet Haggai and Zechariah the son of Iddo"* began to prophesy to the residents of Judah and Jerusalem. Because we have written records of their prophecies, we know exactly what God said through them. Through Haggai God rebuked the people for their failure to rebuild the temple and called them to a new beginning: "Go up to the mountains and bring wood and build the temple, that I may take pleasure in it and be glorified" (Hag. 1:8). Through Zechariah God declared, "I am returning to Jerusalem with mercy; My house shall be built in it . . ." (Zech 1:16). Both prophets distinguished Zerubbabel, "governor of Judah," and Joshua, "the high priest" (Hag. 1:1), as leaders who would oversee the work on the temple:

> "Yet now be strong, Zerubbabel," says the LORD ; "and be strong, Joshua, son of Jehozadak, the high priest; and be strong, all you people of the land," says the LORD , "and work; for I am with you," says the LORD of hosts.
>
> *Haggai 2:4*

> The hands of Zerubbabel
> Have laid the foundation of this temple;
> His hands shall also finish it.
> Then you will know
> That the LORD of hosts has sent Me to you."
>
> *Zechariah 4:9*

Ezra 5 shows that Haggai and Zechariah successfully inspired *"Zerubbabel the son of Shealtiel and Jeshua the son of Jozadak"* (5:2, "Jeshua" is the Aramaic form of the Hebrew name, "Joshua"), for they began to rebuild the temple after many years of delay.

Verse 2 adds that *"the prophets of God were with them, helping them."* Haggai and Zechariah did not sit far off, shouting their prophecies from a distance; rather, they stood shoulder to shoulder with those whom they had encouraged. The phrase "helping them" almost suggests that Haggai and Zechariah pitched in to build. While this is possible from the meaning of the Aramaic verb,[1] Ezra 6:14 implies that prophetic help came in the form of messages from God, not craftsmanship. This is how the first-century Jewish historian Josephus interprets these events:

> Haggai and Zechariah, two prophets who were among them at that time, urged them to take courage and not to be apprehensive of any untoward action by the Persians, for God, they said, foretold this to them. And so, having faith in the prophets, they applied themselves vigorously to the building, without relaxing for a single day.[2]

91

So the prophets of God successfully stirred up the people and their leaders. Finally, in the second year of Darius, rebuilding God's temple began again.

QUESTIONS FROM OFFICIALS (5:3–5)

> 3 At the same time Tattenai the governor of the region beyond the River and Shethar-Boznai and their companions came to them and spoke thus to them: "Who has commanded you to build this temple and finish this wall?"
> 4 Then, accordingly, we told them the names of the men who were constructing this building.
> 5 But the eye of their God was upon the elders of the Jews, so that they could not make them cease till a report could go to Darius. Then a written answer was returned concerning this matter.
>
> *Ezra 5:3–5*

Once the Jews began rebuilding the temple, leaders from the surrounding regions become concerned. *"Tattenai the governor of the region beyond the River and Shethar-Boznai and their companions"* came to Jerusalem to ask questions about the project (v. 3). An ancient tablet mentions Tattenai as governor of the province "Beyond the River."[3] Apparently he ruled over a region broader than Judah, of which Zerubbabel was governor. Shethar-Boznai may have been his assistant or ally.

Tattenai and those with him asked the Jews who had commanded them to build the temple *and finish this wall"* (v. 3). They may have been referring to the walls of the temple or to the city walls, we cannot be sure. The question does not necessarily indicate a meanness of spirit, for it would not have been out of line for a Persian official to ask the Jews if they had permission to undertake such a project. The NKJV translation of verse 5 implies a sense of hostility: *"But the eye of their God was upon the elders of the Jews, so that they could not make them cease till a report could go to Darius"* (5:5). According to this translation, Tattenai and his friends wanted to stop the building but could not do so. Yet the Aramaic of verse 5 reads simply: "and they did not stop them until the report could go to Darius." We do not know for certain whether the officials wanted to stop the Jews from building or simply wanted to make sure that they had the proper building permits.

Verse 4 in the NKJV also seems strange. The officials ask who gave the Jews permission to build. *"Then, accordingly, we told them the names of the men who were constructing this building"* (v. 4). Again, the original of this verse reads differently: "Also, accordingly, we asked them, 'What are the names of the men who are building this building?'" What verse 4 originally meant was: "Also, accordingly, they [Tattenai, etc.] asked them [the Jews], 'What are the names of the men who are building?'" This translation is supported by the letter from Tattenai to Darius, in which Tattenai states that he asked for the names of those in charge of the building project (v. 10). Several modern translations follow this line as well (NIV, NRSV).

Because *"the eye of their God was upon the elders of the Jews,"* the official inquiry from Tattenai and his companions did not halt the building project (v. 5). Admittedly this phrase is a bit unusual. We would expect something like, "Because the hand of their God was upon them . . . ," but according to Job 36:7, God "does not withdraw His eyes from the righteous." Psalm 33 further confesses:

> Behold, the eye of the LORD is on those who fear Him,
> On those who hope in His mercy,
> To deliver their soul from death,
> And to keep them alive in famine.
>
> *Psalm 33:18–19*

Putting the image in more familiar terms, English speakers would say, "God watches over those who fear him." This would be an apt description of what happened in Ezra 5. God watched over his people so they were able to keep on building. In fact, as 5:8 indicates, the people worked diligently and made significant progress.

LETTER FROM TATTENAI TO DARIUS (5:6–17)

6 This is a copy of the letter that Tattenai sent:
The governor of the region beyond the River, and
Shethar-Boznai, and his companions, the Persians
who were in the region beyond the River, to Darius
the king.

7 They sent a letter to him, in which was written thus—To Darius the king: All peace.

8 Let it be known to the king that we went into the province of Judea, to the temple of the great God, which is being built with heavy stones, and timber is being laid in the walls; and this work goes on diligently and prospers in their hands.

9 Then we asked those elders, and spoke thus to them: "Who commanded you to build this temple and to finish these walls?"

10 We also asked them their names to inform you, that we might write the names of the men who were chief among them.

11 And thus they returned us an answer, saying: "We are the servants of the God of heaven and earth, and we are rebuilding the temple that was built many years ago, which a great king of Israel built and completed.

12 But because our fathers provoked the God of heaven to wrath, He gave them into the hand of Nebuchadnezzar king of Babylon, the Chaldean, who destroyed this temple and carried the people away to Babylon.

13 However, in the first year of Cyrus king of Babylon, King Cyrus issued a decree to build this house of God.

14 Also, the gold and silver articles of the house of God, which Nebuchadnezzar had taken from the temple that was in Jerusalem and carried into the temple of Babylon—those King Cyrus took from the temple of Babylon, and they were given to one named Sheshbazzar, whom he had made governor.

15 And he said to him,' Take these articles; go, carry them to the temple site that is in Jerusalem, and let the house of God be rebuilt on its former site.'

16 Then the same Sheshbazzar came and laid the foundation of the house of God which is in Jerusalem; but from that time even until now it has been under construction, and it is not finished."

17 Now therefore, if it seems good to the king, let a search be made in the king's treasure house, which is there in Babylon, whether it is so that a decree was

issued by King Cyrus to build this house of God at
Jerusalem, and let the king send us his pleasure
concerning this matter.

Ezra 5:6–17

Verses 6 and 7 introduce the letter from Tattenai to Darius, which
the editor of Ezra-Nehemiah chose to include here. Verse 8 may explain why Tattenai and his companions thought the Jews were
building a wall in addition to the temple (v. 3) when it emphasizes
that the builders were using "heavy stones, and timber" (v. 8). The
letter repeats the Jewish response to the first of Tattenai's questions:
Who gave you permission to build? (v. 9). Then, after explaining why
the temple needed to be rebuilt in the first place (vv. 11–12), the Jews
recap the decree of Cyrus, as found in Ezra 1. This response answers
Tattenai's question. Then the Jews go on to explain a bit more about
the restoration project, especially with regard to the return of the sacred implements to the temple. Presumably their purpose was to
authenticate Cyrus' commitment to the project.

Once again the mysterious figure of Sheshbazzar appears on the
scene. He was introduced in chapter 1 as the leader who transported
the sacred implements from Babylon to Jerusalem (1:11; 5:14–15), but
here he also receives credit for laying the foundation of the temple (v.
16). Then why does Ezra 3 identify Zerubbabel as the secular leader
who oversaw the founding of the temple? Scholars have not fully explained this apparent contradiction. Perhaps "Sheshbazzar" and
"Zerubbabel" are two names for the same person; or perhaps two different men served concurrently; or perhaps Zerubbabel finished
what Sheshbazzar had begun.[4]

In addition, verse 16 also contains evidence of a Jewish exaggeration. The people tell Tattenai; *"and from that time [of Cyrus] even until
now it [the temple] has been under construction, and it is not yet finished"*
(v. 16). We know from Haggai and Zechariah that the people had
ceased building years ago. It is strange that the Jewish leaders
stretched the truth like this, but they probably wanted to make sure
that their laxity had not invalidated Cyrus' decree. They wanted to
operate under the authority of Cyrus, even though they had disobeyed his order to rebuild years ago by stopping the work.

Tattenai's letter ends with a recommendation that the king order a
search of his *"treasure house,"* in which ancient documents were kept

(v. 17). There, presumably, evidence for the Jewish claim of authorization by Cyrus would be found. (In fact, as 6:2 indicates, the evidence was not in Babylon.) Once more the letter contains no indication of hostile opposition to the temple restoration. Rather, Tattenai and the other officials seem to want to know only if the project has been authorized by the appropriate Persian officials. For a contrast, see the letter to King Artaxerxes found in Ezra 4:12–16.

RESPONSE OF DARIUS (6:1–12)

6:1 Then King Darius issued a decree, and a search was made in the archives, where the treasures were stored in Babylon.

2 And at Achmetha, in the palace that is in the province of Media, a scroll was found, and in it a record was written thus:

3 In the first year of King Cyrus, King Cyrus issued a decree concerning the house of God at Jerusalem: "Let the house be rebuilt, the place where they offered sacrifices; and let the foundations of it be firmly laid, its height sixty cubits and its width sixty cubits,

4 with three rows of heavy stones and one row of new timber. Let the expenses be paid from the king's treasury.

5 Also let the gold and silver articles of the house of God, which Nebuchadnezzar took from the temple which is in Jerusalem and brought to Babylon, be restored and taken back to the temple which is in Jerusalem, each to its place; and deposit them in the house of God"—

6 Now therefore, Tattenai, governor of the region beyond the River, and Shethar-Boznai, and your companions the Persians who are beyond the River, keep yourselves far from there.

7 Let the work of this house of God alone; let the governor of the Jews and the elders of the Jews build this house of God on its site.

8 Moreover I issue a decree as to what you shall do for the elders of these Jews, for the building of this house of God: Let the cost be paid at the king's

expense from taxes on the region beyond the River; this is to be given immediately to these men, so that they are not hindered.

9 And whatever they need—young bulls, rams, and lambs for the burnt offerings of the God of heaven, wheat, salt, wine, and oil, according to the request of the priests who are in Jerusalem—let it be given them day by day without fail,

10 that they may offer sacrifices of sweet aroma to the God of heaven, and pray for the life of the king and his sons.

11 Also I issue a decree that whoever alters this edict, let a timber be pulled from his house and erected, and let him be hanged on it; and let his house be made a refuse heap because of this.

12 And may the God who causes His name to dwell there destroy any king or people who put their hand to alter it, or to destroy this house of God which is in Jerusalem. I Darius issue a decree; let it be done diligently.

Ezra 6:1–12

It is obvious that Darius followed Tattenai's advice. When a search of the *"archives"* in Babylon proved fruitless, the search continued in the *"palace"* of *"Achmetha"* (vv. 1–2). Achmetha is an Aramaic term for the city usually known as Ecbatana, the capital of the former Median empire. Because of it's higher elevation (in modern Iran, about 175 miles southwest of Tehran), Persian kings often spent summers there. The fact that Darius went to such effort to find evidence of Cyrus' wishes seems to indicate his reverence for the past. Rather than issuing a new decree, Darius wanted to keep faith with the will of his predecessor.

The scroll found in Achmetha contained information similar to that in the decree of Ezra 1. Most important, it justified the Jewish claim to have been authorized by Cyrus (vv. 3–5). On this basis, then, Darius updated the decree of Cyrus with a new command for Tattenai and his companions. First of all, they were commanded to stay away from Jerusalem (v. 6). This would guarantee that they could not hinder the work (v. 7). Specifically, Darius ordered: *"let the governor of the Jews and the elders of the Jews build this house of God on its site"* (v. 7). Furthermore, Tattenai and his colleagues were ordered to assist the Jews in their endeavor (vv. 8–10). From the revenues collected for the Persian Empire, Tattenai had to pay the costs of the rebuilding project. In addition, he was obliged to supply sacrifices for the temple so that the priests would *"pray for the life of the king and his sons"* (vv. 9–10). It would appear that Darius followed the lead of Cyrus: by supporting the temple and its work he hoped that he would be blessed. As a conclusion, just in case Tattenai and his companions were unwilling to follow orders, Darius included a threat of death to anyone who did not follow his orders (vv. 11–12). Certainly the temple would be completed now.

REFLECTIONS ON EZRA 5:1–6:12

How to Get Started Again

After sixteen years of procrastination and delay, finally the Jews began to rebuild God's temple again. What enabled them to start again? What broke through their complacency and fear? This question is not merely academic but relates to our personal lives, for we all find ourselves like the Jews at times: worn out, preoccupied, and unwilling to do what God has called us to do. Perhaps we wander from intimacy with the Lord and prayer rarely proceeds from our mouths, not to mention from our hearts. How do we begin again? Or perhaps we realize that our marriages are lifeless. The stress of a busy life has taken its toll and years of neglect bring us to the brink of divorce. How can we start again?

I find it particularly difficult to begin anew when I feel the stigma of a false start. When I have started something before, only to fail, I approach new beginnings with wariness, even cynicism. A voice inside of me says: "Oh, don't even try to renew your prayer life. You've tried before, and failed. It just won't work." How can I find the hope to start again with the Lord?

We can find a helpful clue in Ezra 5. Notice the chain of events in the second year of Darius that caused the Jews to begin work on the temple project again. First, God called Haggai and Zechariah into prophetic service. They in turn called God's people to obedience and inspired the leaders of Judah, Zerubbabel and Jeshua, to oversee the activities. Once again we are reminded that restoration begins with

98

God, who is sovereign over all things and who inspires successful new beginnings.

Yet God did not rebuild the temple himself; rather, he raised up and used people who would respond to his initiative. He called Haggai and Zechariah who were ready to be used by God. Then, through these prophets he addressed and encouraged Zerubbabel and Jeshua, the leaders of Judah. Although they could have disregarded the word of the LORD, they chose to obey instead. Thus, God initiated a new beginning that continued as people responded to God's initiative. What would have happened if Haggai and Zechariah, or Zerubbabel and Jeshua, had been indifferent to God's leading? What if their response had been, No! We can only speculate, of course, but presumably the work on the temple would not have commenced anew.

Starting again begins with God, but it continues as we respond obediently to his initiative. For instance, a couple in my church were on the verge of divorce. They had filed all the necessary papers, and their divorce was scheduled to become final in a month or so. One Sunday morning they "happened" to attend church (separately, of course) when I spoke on the sanctity of marriage and the dreadfulness of divorce. By God's grace each of them heard his call to start anew. On Monday morning I received a phone call from the husband, who wanted to talk about a possible restoration of their marriage. Thus began a process of rebuilding that continues to this day. In fact, I recently had the privilege of leading them in a service renewing their wedding vows. What turned this couple around? What gave them the courage to start again? On the one hand, God used me to speak his truth prophetically; yet, more importantly, the Holy Spirit spoke to the hearts of this couple, and they responded with openness and obedience.

Ezra 5 speaks incisively to those of us who lead in the church. We are called to seek the Lord, to listen to his truth, and to respond with obedience. We who teach and preach have a distinctive opportunity and responsibility to lead God's people into renewal, into making a fresh start. Although our sovereign God can revive his people in any way he chooses, he usually works through leaders like you and me. In our freedom to start over again and in our willingness to call others to the same, God's church will be renewed continually by the Holy Spirit.

Living Under God's Eye

Ezra 5:5 attributes success in rebuilding to the fact that "the eye of God" was upon the Jews. We would say, "God was watching over them." If God's special attention is necessary for successful restoration, is there anything we can do to make sure God watches us? Or, to put it another way, if God stands behind every new start, can we do anything to bring about God's initiative?

Let's look again at Psalm 33:18–19:

> Behold, the eye of the LORD is on those who fear Him,
> On those who hope in His mercy,
> To deliver their soul from death,
> And to keep them alive in famine.

This Psalm teaches that God's "eye" will be upon "those who fear Him, on those who hope in His mercy." Therefore, if we want God to bless us with new beginnings, we can do something: We can fear God! We can hope in his mercy!

Fearing God means respecting his sovereignty. We fear God when we recognize his awesome majesty and power; when we submit our lives to him in humble worship; in short, when we realize that we are not in charge. We must look to God for direction, for sustenance, and for renewal. Scripture teaches that "the fear of the LORD is the beginning of wisdom (Ps. 111:10; Prov. 9:10). Reverence for God's divine wisdom places us in a position to receive wisdom from him. Psalm 33 promises that when we fear God, he will watch out for us.

It also states that the eye of the LORD is "on those who hope in His mercy" (Ps. 33:19). The word translated as mercy is *"ḥesed"* in Hebrew. It signifies God's covenant faithfulness or God's love within the context of relationship. In other words, God watches over those with whom he has a relationship.

If we are yearning for a fresh start or for God's blessing, we are not helpless. Although we cannot force God's sovereign hand, we can begin to fear God and to put our hope in him alone. When our internal priorities line up correctly, with God as our highest priority, then we are prepared for his eye to be upon us and for his renewal to be in our lives. We are ready to obey when he calls.

As a leader, I find it all too easy to put my respect and hope in something other than God. Sometimes I trust in my own cleverness and ability to persuade. Sometimes I trust market surveys and strategic planning. Sometimes I put my sole trust in people. But, inevitably these all prove to be disappointing. Then I am reminded once again that God alone is fully trustworthy. Only in the context of a preeminent respect for God will our trust in human ability find a proper balance.

These days the church I pastor is in much the same position as Judah in 521 B.C. Several years before I came as pastor, the church leaders attempted to go forward with plans to build a sanctuary, but the project stalled for several reasons, including my predecessor's departure to pastor a church in New Jersey. Since I came to the church eighteen months ago, many have wondered: "Will we try to build again?" Some have warned: "Now is not the time to build." Others have urged: "Let's build right now." Throughout the past year, the leaders and I have completed a thorough study of the situation. We have considered all aspects of our building plans. But, far more important, we have prayed and waited upon God. Even six months ago the twelve elders on our Board would not have agreed to start again with a building program. But in the last three months, God has moved in their hearts. Without any arm-twisting, the elders voted three weeks ago to go ahead with the project.

Why has this happened now? The answer has to do in part with our leaders. We have people like Haggai and Zechariah who have spoken prophetically of God's call to our church. We also have people like Zerubbabel and Jeshua who have expressed God's call in tangible ways. Even more significantly, the elders and I have attempted to fear God and to trust in his *hesed*. We have not done so perfectly, of course, but as I listen to our conversations and prayers, I believe that we sincerely want God's best for our church. And God, who always relates to us with *hesed*, has graciously kept his eye upon us. So we move ahead with confidence, not in ourselves and our careful planning, but in God, who alone will enable us to be the church he has called us to be.

NOTES

1. Brown, Driver, and Briggs, *Lexicon*, s.v. "*sĕᶜad*."

2. Josephus, *Jewish Antiquities*, 11:5. Translation by R. Marcus in *Josephus*, 10 vols., Loeb Classical Library (Cambridge: Harvard University Press, 1978).

3. D. E. Suiter, "Tattenai," *ABD* (New York: Doubleday, 1992).

4. See "Introduction to Ezra-Nehemiah: Chronological Puzzles in Ezra-Nehemiah."

CHAPTER SIX

Completion and Celebration

Ezra 6:13–22

No Time to Party

Jean is an amazing lady. Her energy for serving the Lord seems unending. And without exaggeration, many of our church programs depend upon her faithful, tireless service. But Jean has a problem: she has a hard time relaxing and an even harder time enjoying a party.

I realized this for the first time when I was serving on a committee with her. As it happened, the committee had to meet on her birthday. Of course that would not deter Jean. She would be at the meeting ready to work hard making decisions and taking notes regardless of her birthday. But when she showed up for the committee meeting we surprised her by throwing a birthday party in her honor. We decorated the wall with a large banner proclaiming: Happy Birthday, Jean! We served cake, ice cream, and punch.

When Jean arrived, she seemed flustered at first, then she promptly sat down and took out her notebook. When I told her that we had canceled the meeting to have a party instead she seemed even more uncomfortable. After a few moments of awkward silence she asked, "Well then may I go home?" "This party is for you," I laughed, "but we won't keep you here against your will. You may go home if you'd like to." At that Jean stood up, grabbed her notebook, and headed for home. The rest of us sat amazed, feeling sad for Jean, who obviously could not enjoy a party, even one thrown in her honor.

You probably know someone like Jean. Maybe you are like her. Frankly, I think there is a bit of Jean in many of us who serve Christ because we live in a religious environment where "celebrating" has a negative connotation, where being dour, serious, and overly focused upon getting things done is the epitome of Christianity. So we rarely take time out to celebrate. Others of us would like to celebrate, but we have grown too weary even to try. Our lives have been touched by tragedy: the death of a loved one, divorce, or unemployment. How can we celebrate when life is so imperfect?

Well, if we are never able to answer that question we will probably retreat into the dullness of a joyless existence. But the last half of Ezra 6 shows us a different way to live. It shows us how God's people celebrate—and how we can join in the celebration.

COMPLETION OF THE TEMPLE (6:13–15)

13 Then Tattenai, governor of the region beyond the River, Shethar-Boznai, and their companions diligently did according to what King Darius had sent.
14 So the elders of the Jews built, and they prospered through the prophesying of Haggai the prophet and Zechariah the son of Iddo. And they built and finished it, according to the commandment of the God of Israel, and according to the command of Cyrus, Darius, and Artaxerxes king of Persia.
15 Now the temple was finished on the third day of the month of Adar, which was in the sixth year of the reign of King Darius.

Ezra 6:13–15

The first portion of Ezra 6 contains a royal decree from Darius, king of Persia, to Tattenai, Shethar-Boznai, and their companions. These Persian leaders in the region near Judah had asked Darius if it was true, as the Jews claimed, that Cyrus had permitted them to rebuild the temple. A search disclosed the original decree of Cyrus, which, indeed, had commanded the Jews to rebuild. Darius reaffirmed that decree and added that Tattenai and company were to help the Jews with supplies and offerings. He ended the decree with a frightening threat: *"Whoever alters this edict, let a timber be pulled from his house and erected, and let him be hanged on it; and let his house be made a refuse heap because of this"* (v. 11). It comes as no surprise, therefore, to read that Tattenai and his companions *"diligently did according to what King Darius had sent"* (v. 13). Most subordinates would obey their king, especially when faced with the threat of impalement!

Verse 14 summarizes the story that began in 5:1. Not only did *"the elders of the Jews"* build, but they also *"prospered through the prophesying of Haggai the prophet and Zechariah the son of Iddo"* (v. 14). These prophets, whom God had raised up and who had encouraged Zerubbabel and Jeshua, enabled the Jews to overcome their hesitation and to build with zeal. Therefore, as verse 14 continues, *"they built and finished it."* The project that was initiated years earlier was finally completed.

The temple was completed *"according to the commandment of the God of Israel, and according to the command of Cyrus, Darius, and Artaxerxes king of Persia"* (v. 14). Ezra 1 and 6 reproduce the commands of Cyrus and Darius, but what about those of God and Artaxerxes? We know that God's command to complete the temple came through the prophecies of Haggai and Zechariah. Though these are not reproduced in Ezra-Nehemiah, they do appear in the biblical books of Haggai and Zechariah. (See the discussion of Ezra 5:1–2 above.) God is mentioned first on the list because, indeed, he is sovereign even over the great kings of Persia. Including Artaxerxes in this group of leaders seems strange for two reasons. First of all, Artaxerxes I did not begin to reign until 465 B.C., some fifty years after the temple had been completed. Second, in Ezra 4:17–22 a letter from Artaxerxes appears because it is thematically relevant, although chronologically out of place. (See above on Ezra 4:6–23.) However, in that letter Artaxerxes does not support Jewish rebuilding efforts (of the wall); only later did he support Jewish restoration (Ezra 7, Nehemiah 2), but the reader of Ezra-Nehemiah is not given that information yet. Undoubtedly then, the inclusion of Artaxerxes in 6:14 demonstrates, once again, the tendency of the editor to favor thematic or theological order rather than a strictly chronological presentation. (See the discussion of Ezra 4:6–23 above.)

Verse 15 identifies the precise day on which the temple was finished, *"the third day of the month of Adar, which was in the sixth year of the reign of King Darius."* Adar was the twelfth month of the Jewish year, which approximates our late February and early March. Since the rebuilding effort began again in the second year of Darius (5:24), the whole project required about four years to complete.

THE PEOPLE CELEBRATE THE DEDICATION (6:16–18)

16 Then the children of Israel, the priests and the
Levites and the rest of the descendants of the
captivity, celebrated the dedication of this house of
God with joy.
17 And they offered sacrifices at the dedication of
this house of God, one hundred bulls, two hundred
rams, four hundred lambs, and as a sin offering for all
Israel twelve male goats, according to the number of
the tribes of Israel.
18 They assigned the priests to their divisions and
the Levites to their divisions, over the service of God
in Jerusalem, as it is written in the Book of Moses.

Ezra 6:16–18

Verses 16–17 recount how the people celebrated the dedication of
their rebuilt temple. Notice how *"joy"* characterizes their celebration
(v. 16), which included a surfeit of sacrifices: *"one hundred bulls, two
hundred rams, four hundred lambs, and as a sin offering for all Israel twelve
male goats . . ."* (6:17).

Yet intermingled with the joyous celebrations are elements of disappointment. For one thing, what may seem to us an excessive
number of offerings actually pales in comparison with what had been
sacrificed during the dedication of the original temple. On that occasion King Solomon and the people "were sacrificing sheep and oxen
that could not be counted or numbered for multitude" (2 Chr. 5:6).
Moreover, in the first dedication, fire came down from heaven to consume the sacrifices, while the very glory of God filled the temple (2
Chr. 7:1–2). Then "King Solomon offered a sacrifice of twenty-two
thousand bulls and one hundred and twenty thousand sheep. So the
king and all the people dedicated the house of God" (2 Chr. 7:5). In
comparison to first temple dedication, Ezra 6 is definitely a meager
celebration.

Another element of disappointment is the *"sin offering,"* which was
rightly a part of the celebration and was appropriately sacrificed in
the new temple. Yet it certainly must have been a dismal reminder to
the people of their failure before God. In this line of thought, it is also
significant that the sin offering consisted of *"twelve male goats, according to the number of the tribes of Israel"* (v. 17). Yet at the time of the

offering, only two tribes remained intact: Judah and Benjamin. Wouldn't the people have felt a twinge of sadness while sacrificing for tribes that had been destroyed because of their disobedience? But the people did not allow these notes of sadness to dampen their celebration; they exalted with joy. Unlike the mixture of weeping and rejoicing in Ezra 3, here only rejoicing was heard.

In verse 18 we note that the leaders reestablished the *"divisions"* of the priests and Levites who labored in the temple. In other words, they made sure that the temple, now rebuilt, immediately began to function properly.

THE PEOPLE CELEBRATE THE PASSOVER (6:19–22)

19 And the descendants of the captivity kept the Passover on the fourteenth day of the first month.

20 For the priests and the Levites had purified themselves; all of them were ritually clean. And they slaughtered the Passover lambs for all the descendants of the captivity, for their brethren the priests, and for themselves.

21 Then the children of Israel who had returned from the captivity ate together with all who had separated themselves from the filth of the nations of the land in order to seek the LORD God of Israel.

22 And they kept the Feast of Unleavened Bread seven days with joy; for the LORD made them joyful, and turned the heart of the king of Assyria toward them, to strengthen their hands in the work of the house of God, the God of Israel.

Ezra 6:19–22

The temple was completed in the month of Adar, the last month of the Jewish calendar. The first month of the year, Nisan, was the month of the great festivals of Passover, Unleavened Bread, and Firstfruits. Ezra 6 concludes by noting that the people kept the festivals of Passover and Unleavened Bread.

How appropriate to celebrate these holidays in the environs of a new temple! In celebrating Passover, the Jews remembered God's deliverance from Egypt; the Feast of Unleavened Bread reminded them of their quick departure from Egypt. What an appropriate way to celebrate the completion of their deliverance from the Babylonians, who had destroyed the temple in 587 B.C. It is no wonder they celebrated with joy, not only because of God's historical deliverance, but also because *"the LORD made them joyful, and turned the heart of the king of Assyria toward them, to strengthen their hands in the work of the house of God, the God of Israel"* (v. 22).

Reference to the king of Assyria seems strange here, though it refers to Darius, who, as king of Persia ruled over Assyria.[1] However it serves to emphasize the main point: that God had made the people joyful by helping them to finish building the temple.

In contrast to the earlier acts of exclusiveness, verse 21 describes an unusual note of inclusiveness. You will recall that in Ezra 2 those who could not prove their ancestry were excluded from the community. But here, those who returned from the exile *"ate together with all who had separated themselves from the filth of the nations of the land in order to seek the LORD God of Israel"* (v. 21). Inclusion within Israel now depended, not upon ancestry, but upon the intention of one's heart to seek God. Perhaps the experience of God's gracious care had encouraged the "insiders" to open their hearts to the former "outsiders."

REFLECTIONS ON EZRA 6:13–22

Christians Can Celebrate

I live in a serious city—Irvine, California. Here the residents work hard. We strive for success; we worry about our kids (trying to give them every advantage); in short, we take ourselves and our lives very seriously. If we do take days off from work, we spend them improving our homes, our abilities, or our bodies. People in Irvine just do not like to relax and have fun. I think we need God to show us how.

And a good place to start is Ezra 6. It teaches us how to unwind and enjoy ourselves. It exemplifies what we see throughout the Scriptures: God created humankind to celebrate and to rejoice. Of course there are times for seriousness and sorrow, but the biblical balance weighs in favor of joy and feasting. Note these pertinent verses that are too frequently overlooked:

Afterward Moses and Aaron went in and told Pharaoh, "Thus says the LORD God of Israel: 'Let My people go, *that they may hold a feast to Me* in the wilderness.'"

Exodus 5:1 (emphasis added)

You will show me the path of life;
In Your presence is *fullness of joy;*
At Your right hand are *pleasures forevermore.*

Psalm 16:11 (emphasis added)

And in this mountain
The LORD of hosts will make for all people
A feast of choice pieces,
A feast of wines on the lees,
Of fat things full of marrow,
Of well-refined wines on the lees.

Isaiah 25:6 (emphasis added)

And the ransomed of the LORD shall return,
And come to Zion with singing,
With *everlasting joy* on their heads.
They shall obtain *joy and gladness,*
And sorrow and sighing shall flee away.

Isaiah 35:10 (emphasis added)

The LORD your God in your midst,
The Mighty One, will save;
He will rejoice over you with gladness,
He will quiet you with His love,
He will rejoice over you with singing.

Zephaniah 3:17 (emphasis added)

The kingdom of heaven may be compared to a king who gave a wedding banquet for his son.

Matthew 22:2 NRSV

Even as God rejoices with gladness (Zeph. 3:17), so we are called to delight in his presence. One form of expressing this delight is what the Old Testament calls "feasts." We might call them celebrations. God created humankind with a unique ability to celebrate. In fact, among all his creatures, he made us to be creatures of joy. Jesus came to bring the kingdom of heaven to earth, which he compares to a wedding reception. When he comes again, the earth will be transformed into one magnificent celebration.

Without doubt, the church offers the greatest potential for gladness in our increasingly serious world. While serving at Hollywood Presbyterian Church I participated in an event that approximated the kingdom of God more than any religious gathering I have seen. It was called the "Fall Family Fun Fair." On a Saturday morning in October, the church gathered to celebrate. There were activity booths for kids and adults (pastors had the "privilege" of sitting in the dunking booth); there were cake walks, hot dogs, sacks of popcorn—you name it, we had it. The most unusual aspect of the Fair, however, was the variety of people gathered there. Like the city of Los Angeles itself, the crowd was diverse in every way. Toddlers stumbled around with painted faces while grandmothers sold candied apples. Upper-middle class, suburban, white kids mixed wonderfully with inner-city children of every color. For a few hours that Saturday, we played and celebrated; we tasted a bit of the kingdom that is coming. And what a glorious and joyful way to communicate the gospel of Jesus Christ! In the midst of a city shattered by its diversity, at the Fall Family Fun Fair God's people gathered in all their variety to enjoy each other. For a short time, God's kingdom came and his will was done on earth as it is in heaven.

Joy Even in Sadness

Every time I preach about joy, I am aware of those in my congregation who suffer. I think of those who have lost loved ones recently; I remember those who have lost jobs; and I see the faces of people who are hurting. Nevertheless, I freely commend the way of joy.

Can we celebrate when life is not perfect? Can we rejoice even when life is filled with problems? The people of Israel teach us to celebrate even in the midst of a confused and broken world. They celebrated the dedication of the temple even though it was not nearly as magnificent as the first temple. They made offerings for the twelve tribes of Israel even though ten had been destroyed. Can we celebrate when life is not perfect? Should we? Ezra 6 answers, yes!

That is not to say, of course, that we should deny our sadness. In fact, we discover a greater freedom to celebrate when we acknowledge our true feelings, joy and sorrow alike. The Bible does not commend denial or pretense, rather, it commends energetic celebration alongside of honest sorrow. Yesterday I visited a family in my parish whose home had just burned down. A fire that began in a neighbor's garage soon engulfed their house and left it completely uninhabitable. Many of their prized possessions were destroyed. But even as they wept over what they had lost, David and Wendy rejoiced over God's loving protection. Their daughter could easily have lost her life in the blaze, but she was fine. And their friends have wrapped arms of love around them: helping them sort through the rubble, providing meals and hospitality, and simply being with them during a difficult time. Even in this time of loss, they are rejoicing over what truly matters. As Wendy said, "*Things* don't really count much after all."

Of course sometimes we lose, not things, but people. Several years ago my father, Dave, died of cancer. Just eighteen months later, my mother-in-law, Marion, died in exactly the same way. I will never forget the first family gathering after her death when my father-in-law offered to host our Easter dinner. As we came together, we felt the absence of Marion intensely. There we were in her home, using her dishes, only two months after she had died. We felt awkward, not quite knowing what to do or say. Then as we sat down to dinner my father-in-law, Bill, called us to pray. Before he prayed, he said: "I know this is a hard day. We miss Marion, and we miss Dave. But at the same time we are glad to know that because of Easter, they are with the Lord. So we feel sad and happy together."

With that introduction he prayed, thanking God for those whom we missed so powerfully and especially for Christ who died and rose again. When he said "Amen," I doubt that a dry eye remained. Bill's honest mix of celebration and sadness somehow set us free. We felt sad, but we rejoiced; even as we shared stories about our departed parents we looked ahead to the resurrection when we will be reunited with them.

As Christians, we rejoice in our mixed-up world because we know how the story ends; we know that Jesus will be triumphant, and we know that he will bind up the brokenhearted. Today we rejoice, but only in part—yet, we do rejoice. We used to sing a popular song that included this line: "And they'll know we are Christians by our love." Indeed, love does communicate the gospel of Christ, and so does joy. May it also be true of us: "And they'll know we are Christians by our joy!"

111

NOTES

1. See Fensham, *Ezra and Nehemiah*, pp. 96–7; Williamson, *Ezra, Nehemiah*, p. 85.

Restoration of Covenant Life, Phase One: The Work of Ezra

Ezra 7:1–10:44

More than fifty years pass between the last verse of Ezra 6 and the beginning of chapter 7. The temple had been completed in the year 516 B.C. (or 515 B.C.), the seventh year of King Darius I of Persia. He continued to reign for another thirty years before passing his rule to Xerxes I, who served as king from 486 B.C. to 465 B.C. Artaxerxes I, who followed Xerxes, began to rule in 465 B.C.. The action of Ezra 7 takes place in the seventh year of king Artaxerxes, or 458 B.C.

Here we are finally introduced to the man, Ezra, and to his work of restoration. Unlike those who rebuilt the temple, Ezra focused on the nonmaterial aspect of restoration. He labored so that God's people might once again know and obey the Torah, the Law of God revealed through Moses.

This section of Ezra begins with an introduction to the man Ezra (7:1–10), followed by a description of the king's commission that sent him to Judah (7:11–26). Chapter 8 describes certain aspects of his trip from Babylon to Jerusalem, and chapters 9 and 10 recount his confrontation with the people over the practice of Jewish intermarriage. The editor of Ezra-Nehemiah utilized several sources in composing chapters 7–10, including: first-person memoirs from Ezra and a letter from King Artaxerxes to Ezra.

CHAPTER SEVEN

The King Commissions Ezra

Ezra 7:1–28

FINDING THE KEY TO GOD'S BLESSING

As a preacher and teacher of the Bible, I watch other communicators carefully because I want to learn how to convey God's truth more faithfully and effectively. Motivating my observation is a desire for God to use and to bless my communication of his Word. As I scrutinize others, I have come to some interesting conclusions. Some preachers who demonstrate admirable elocution (vocal control, strong gestures, memorized scripts, poetic eloquence) seem to have limited success. Few people become Christians under their preaching, and their churches are mired in the doldrums of mediocrity. Conversely, other preachers who lack the technical skills often associated with good preaching have led hundreds of people to Christ while building dynamic, growing churches. Their sermons, which might not earn a passing grade in a seminary preaching class, move people into genuine relationships with God and with other Christians.

I have come to the conclusion, therefore, that effective communication of God's truth requires more than expertise in public speaking. Although I try to improve all aspects of my preaching, I am especially eager to focus on those elements that truly matter. So I wonder: If perfect elocution is not essential to effective preaching, what is? What is the key to God's blessing in the ministry of communication? Certainly a discussion of God's blessing must acknowledge his sovereignty, yet to a certain extent we are able to influence God in the matter of blessing. Ezra 7 shows us that "the good hand of God" was upon Ezra, guiding and favoring his ministry, but it also teaches us why God honored Ezra—it gives us the *kî* (key) to God's blessing.

INTRODUCTION TO EZRA (7:1–10)

7:1 Now after these things, in the reign of
Artaxerxes king of Persia, Ezra the son of Seraiah, the
son of Azariah, the son of Hilkiah,
    2 the son of Shallum, the son of Zadok, the son
of Ahitub,
    3 the son of Amariah, the son of Azariah, the son
of Meraioth,
    4 the son of Zerahiah, the son of Uzzi, the son of
Bukki,
    5 the son of Abishua, the son of Phinehas, the
son of Eleazar, the son of Aaron the chief priest—
    6 this Ezra came up from Babylon; and he was a
skilled scribe in the Law of Moses, which the LORD
God of Israel had given. The king granted him all his
request, according to the hand of the LORD his God
upon him.
    7 Some of the children of Israel, the priests, the
Levites, the singers, the gatekeepers, and the
Nethinim came up to Jerusalem in the seventh year of
King Artaxerxes.
    8 And Ezra came to Jerusalem in the fifth month,
which was in the seventh year of the king.
    9 On the first day of the first month he began his
journey from Babylon, and on the first day of the fifth
month he came to Jerusalem, according to the good
hand of his God upon him.
    10 For Ezra had prepared his heart to seek the
Law of the LORD, and to do it, and to teach statutes
and ordinances in Israel.

Ezra 7:1–10

Finally, after six chapters in the book of Ezra, we meet the man for
whom the book is named. Ezra 7 begins with the temporal phrase
"Now after these things" (v. 1), which connects this chapter with what
directly preceeded it. In fact, a fifty-year interval lies between 6:22
and 7:1.[1] Notice that verse 1 describes the events of the chapter as taking place during *"the reign of Artaxerxes king of Persia."* Verses 8 and 9
identify the time period more precisely: *"in the seventh year of King
Artaxerxes,"* or 458 B.C. At this point we know relatively little about

Jewish life during the fifty years between the completion of the temple and the time of Ezra.

After the temporal setting is noted, verses 1–5 introduce Ezra by giving his family tree. This long list of ancestors not only emphasizes his importance,[2] but also identifies Ezra as a priest, a direct descendant of *"Aaron the chief priest"* (v. 5).

We learn more about Ezra in verse 6 where he is portrayed as *"a skilled scribe in the Law of Moses."* The Hebrew states literally that he was a "quick" scribe, or a fast copier; however, the term implies not only speed, but proficiency in the Law of God as well. The word "scribe" denotes one who is learned, a Torah scholar. We would call him a "rabbi." It is likely, however, that "scribe" also designates Ezra as an official in the Persian government. Some have argued that he was, in fact, the "secretary of state for Jewish affairs," but this cannot be known with certainty.[3] As a whole, the chapter emphasizes Ezra's religious role.

Verse 6 also notes that *"the king granted him all his request, according to the hand of the LORD his God upon him."* Ezra-Nehemiah does not tell exactly what Ezra requested or how this occurred (contrast Nehemiah 2), but it is likely that he asked to return to Jerusalem and to function along the lines of his commission in 7:12–26. Without supplying all of the historical details, chapter 7 emphasizes God's hand of blessing upon Ezra. This is mentioned three times and without doubt explains his success (7:6, 9, 28).

Verses 7–9 provide an overview of Ezra's trip from Babylon to Jerusalem in *"the seventh year of King Artaxerxes"* (v. 7). Later, chapter 8 will offer additional details. (For a clarification of the titles in 7:7, see the commentary on chapter 8, to follow.)

Note here how verse 9 reiterates the explanation of Ezra's success: *"according to the good hand of the LORD his God upon him."* Then verse 10 continues to explain: *"For Ezra had prepared his heart to seek the Law of the LORD, and to do it, and to teach statutes and ordinances in Israel."* The word "for" is translated from the Hebrew term *"kî,"* which sounds like the English word "key." This Hebrew conjunction may also be translated as "because."[4] Here it explains why God's hand rested upon Ezra.[5] God blessed Ezra's ministry because Ezra prepared his heart. The phrase translated "prepared his heart" connotes a whole-hearted commitment of oneself to something. We would say, "Ezra committed himself completely to God."

Specifically, Ezra committed himself to three actions. First, he prepared his heart *"to seek the Law of the LORD."* The verb *"to seek"* is a literal translation of a Hebrew verb that also means "to study."[6] It implies an energetic effort to find God's truth as revealed in the Law, the Mosaic Torah. Second, Ezra committed himself *"to do"* the Law. Obedience followed the preparation of careful study. Third, he planned to *"teach statutes and ordinances in Israel."* The word "statutes" here may refer to the general principles of the Law, while "ordinances" refers to specific principles. Taken together, this phrase means that Ezra planned to teach the whole Law, not just parts of it.

The text introduces Ezra, therefore, as a priest, a religious scholar, a student of God's law who lived and taught what he studied, and a man blessed by God. Ezra led an expedition of Jews from Babylon to Jerusalem, where he intended to teach the Law of God.

We should note here that the figure of Ezra looms large in Jewish traditional lore. One section of the Jewish Talmud, a collection of ancient rabbinic teachings, comments that "Ezra would have been worthy of receiving the Torah had Moses not preceded him."[7] Other ancient Jews attributed the writing of Chronicles or Malachi to Ezra.[8] In some segments of Judaism, Ezra took on legendary qualities. The Apocryphal book called 2 Esdras ("Esdras" is the Greek name for Ezra) envisions Ezra as receiving a series of apocalyptic revelations. In the final chapter of 2 Esdras, God inspires Ezra to dictate the entire Hebrew Bible, as well as many esoteric religious writings, from memory, speaking forty days and nights without rest (2 Esd. 14:37–48). Although Ezra may have been a towering figure in Jewish tradition, Ezra-Nehemiah presents him in a more human and realistic light.[9]

EZRA'S COMMISSION (7:11–26)

11 This is a copy of the letter that King Artaxerxes gave Ezra the priest, the scribe, expert in the words of the commandments of the LORD, and of His statutes to Israel:

12 Artaxerxes, king of kings, To Ezra the priest, a scribe of the Law of the God of heaven: Perfect peace, and so forth.

13 I issue a decree that all those of the people of Israel and the priests and Levites in my realm, who volunteer to go up to Jerusalem, may go with you.

14 And whereas you are being sent by the king and his seven counselors to inquire concerning Judah and Jerusalem, with regard to the Law of your God which is in your hand;

15 and whereas you are to carry the silver and gold which the king and his counselors have freely offered to the God of Israel, whose dwelling is in Jerusalem;

16 and whereas all the silver and gold that you may find in all the province of Babylon, along with the freewill offering of the people and the priests, are to be freely offered for the house of their God in Jerusalem—

17 now therefore, be careful to buy with this money bulls, rams, and lambs, with their grain offerings and their drink offerings, and offer them on the altar of the house of your God in Jerusalem.

18 And whatever seems good to you and your brethren to do with the rest of the silver and the gold, do it according to the will of your God.

19 Also the articles that are given to you for the service of the house of your God, deliver in full before the God of Jerusalem.

20 And whatever more may be needed for the house of your God, which you may have occasion to provide, pay for it from the king's treasury.

21 And I, even I, Artaxerxes the king, issue a decree to all the treasurers who are in the region beyond the River, that whatever Ezra the priest, the scribe of the Law of the God of heaven, may require of you, let it be done diligently,

22 up to one hundred talents of silver, one hundred kors of wheat, one hundred baths of wine, one hundred baths of oil, and salt without prescribed limit.

23 Whatever is commanded by the God of heaven, let it diligently be done for the house of the God of heaven. For why should there be wrath against the realm of the king and his sons?

24 Also we inform you that it shall not be lawful to impose tax, tribute, or custom on any of the priests, Levites, singers, gatekeepers, Nethinim, or servants of this house of God.

25 And you, Ezra, according to your God-given
wisdom, set magistrates and judges who may judge
all the people who are in the region beyond the River,
all such as know the laws of your God; and teach
those who do not know them.
26 Whoever will not observe the law of your God
and the law of the king, let judgment be executed
speedily on him, whether it be death, or banishment,
or confiscation of goods, or imprisonment.

Ezra 7:11–26

The next section of the chapter contains Ezra's commission from King Artaxerxes. Verse 11 introduces what follows: *"the letter that King Artaxerxes gave Ezra."* Verse 6 hints that this letter followed Ezra's request, but the text does not tell that part of the story. The letter from the king is presented in its original language, Aramaic (vv. 12–26). This is the second instance of Aramaic material in what is otherwise a Hebrew document (see also 4:8–6:18). As we mentioned earlier, Persian officials used Aramaic for official correspondence as it was the lingua franca for their vast empire.

The letter is addressed from King Artaxerxes to *"Ezra the priest, a scribe of the Law of the God of heaven"* (v. 12). As mentioned above, the term "scribe" may have identified Ezra as an official in the Persian government. The editor of Ezra-Nehemiah, however, plays up the religious significance of the term. He presents Ezra as a scholar: an expert in God's law who will teach the people to obey.

The letter from Artaxerxes included several noteworthy factors. First, it permitted all Jews, including *"priests and Levites,"* to return to Jerusalem with Ezra, if they wished to do so (v. 13). By granting this permission, Artaxerxes reaffirmed the policy initially established by Cyrus (Ezra 1).

Second, the king sent Ezra *"to inquire concerning Judah and Jerusalem, with regard to the Law of your God which is in your hand"* (v. 14). Apparently Ezra had a copy of the Mosaic law, or a portion of it, that he carried from Babylon to Jerusalem. But what does it mean that he was "to inquire concerning Judah and Jerusalem, with regard to the Law"? A definitive answer cannot be offered, but the sense of the verse (and what follows) suggests that Ezra was sent, among other things, to find out if the people were following the Law. If not, then Ezra was given the authority to teach them and to enforce obedience (vv. 25–26).

119

Third, the king charged Ezra with the responsibility for carrying gifts and financial contributions for the temple in Jerusalem (vv. 15–19). Once more, like his predecessor Cyrus, Artaxerxes contributed generously to the worship of God in an effort to elicit God's blessing rather than his wrath (v. 23). He also offered to pay for whatever else Ezra required for the temple (v. 20), and he commanded Persian officials in the region near Judah to take care of Ezra's financial needs (vv. 21–22). In addition, the officials were forbidden to tax any of those who served in the temple (v. 24).

Fourth, verses 25 and 26 spell out in greater detail Ezra's duties as a scholar of God's Law. He was to appoint *"magistrates and judges who may judge all the people,"* as long as the people *"know the laws of your God"* (v. 25). Furthermore, those who did not know the Law were not to be held liable, but were to be taught. Thus Ezra's second task was to *"teach those who do not know them [the laws]"* (v. 25). Finally, the king granted Ezra permission to punish anyone who disobeyed the Law, by *"death, or banishment, or confiscation of goods, or imprisonment"* (v. 26). Accordingly, Ezra was sent not only to inquire into the state of legal knowledge and obedience in Judah (v. 14), but also to teach the Law, to judge by it, and to enforce it.

Ezra's commission almost seems too good to be true. Why would a Persian king care about the state of religious obedience in Judah? The answer may lie in the fact that Artaxerxes' behavior fits the strategy of his predecessor, Cyrus, to support indigenous religions. Through such nonpartisan support, Cyrus had hoped to earn the favor of all the gods within his empire. This would seem to be Artaxerxes' hope as well (v. 23). Moreover, the king's letter indicates his high regard for Ezra, who may have been one of his civic officials. Artaxerxes trusted Ezra with riches (vv. 15–22) and recognized his *"God-given wisdom"* (v. 25). Ezra may have asked the king to send him to Jerusalem for a sacred purpose that also supported Persian strategies. Undoubtedly, Artaxerxes knew he could rest assured that this wise priest and scholar would make sure the Jewish God received appropriate worship—worship that would presumably guarantee continued blessings for Artaxerxes.

EzRA'S RESPONSE TO THE COMMISSION (7:27–28)

27 Blessed be the LORD God of our fathers, who
has put such a thing as this in the king's heart, to
beautify the house of the LORD which is in Jerusalem,

28 and has extended mercy to me before the king
and his counselors, and before all the king's mighty
princes.
        So I was encouraged, as the hand of the LORD
my God was upon me; and I gathered leading men of
Israel to go up with me.

Ezra 7:27–28

The closing verses of chapter 7 show Ezra's delight in Artaxerxes' commission. The narrative now comes from the pen of Ezra, who wrote in the first person about his response to the king's letter. First of all he blessed God, *"who has put such a thing as this in the king's heart, to beautify the house of the LORD which is in Jerusalem"* (v. 27). In spite of the fact that Ezra had no doubt encouraged the king in his generosity, God alone received the credit for Artaxerxes' support of the Jewish temple. Moreover, he declared that God had *"extended mercy"* to him in the presence of the king and his court by sending him on a divine mission to Judah (v. 28). Emotionally, Ezra was *"encouraged"* by what had transpired, events which he attributed to the fact that *"the hand of the LORD my God was upon me"* (v. 28). He did not take credit for the king's actions, nor did he assign them to the king himself; rather, Ezra stated that he was blessed by God alone. The chapter closes with Ezra's first steps in fulfilling his commission.

REFLECTIONS ON EZRA 7:1–28

The *Kî* to God's Blessing

The General Editor of this commentary, Lloyd Ogilvie, is one of the most articulate and compelling communicators I have heard. Without a doubt, God has richly blessed Lloyd's ministry of preaching, teaching, and writing. Thousands of people have come to faith in Christ or have been renewed in their faith through his communication of the gospel. I have seen his preaching keep the First Presbyterian Church of Hollywood on the cutting edge of God's work in the world today.

For seven years I served on staff under Lloyd's leadership. I had the opportunity to watch him in action, not only in the spotlight, but also behind the scenes. And that is why I would suggest that Lloyd's ministry is not blessed simply because of his outstanding talent or resonant voice. Rather, I know with certainty that one of the reasons God has blessed Lloyd's ministry is because like Ezra, he has committed himself to study, to do, and to teach God's truth. In essence, he illustrates the *kî* to God's blessing, if you will pardon the play on words.

During my tenure at Hollywood Presbyterian, Lloyd would often phone me as he prepared for an upcoming sermon. Inevitably he would say something like this: "I'm working on a passage in Romans for next week's sermon. I'd like to talk to you about the meanings of several Greek words." So I would pull out my Greek lexicon and concordance and together we would discuss the meaning of Paul's words. I was continually impressed with Lloyd's commitment to "seek" after the truth, to work hard to convey what the biblical text actually meant.

Lloyd not only studied diligently, he also applied his conclusions to his own life. Often he would come to staff meetings brimming with excitement over some biblical passage he had been studying. Before preaching on the text in worship he would apply it to our life as a leadership team. If a Scripture spoke of the need for prayer, he would challenge us to spend more time in prayer. If some verse challenged him to step out in faith, he would urge us to do the same. For Lloyd, study led to obedience—both personal and institutional.

Finally, like Ezra, Lloyd devotes his life to teaching the "statutes and ordinances" of God. Every sermon is based firmly upon the Scriptures. And Lloyd does not back away from the difficult verses and passages that do not tickle modern ears. He communicates the whole counsel of God.

I readily admit that Lloyd Ogilvie models what I want to be as a communicator of God's Word. Admittedly my voice will never approach the richness of his, nor will I speak with his poetic articulation. But these qualities do not explain why God uses Lloyd so powerfully. After all, there are plenty of technically-masterful preachers who fail to move the souls of men and women. Rather, I strive to emulate the commitment of Lloyd's heart to study, to do, and to teach God's truth. This, Ezra 7 reveals, is the key—the *kî*—to God's blessing.

Following the Example of Ezra

Do you want God to bless you? Do you want God to bless your ministry? I am writing this commentary for contemporary communicators of the Bible. Thus, I assume that you have answered "yes" to these questions. If so, then your next step is to follow the example of Ezra. Allow me to lead you through a personal inventory that might help you get in line for God's blessing.

Have you set your heart upon God's truth? Have you committed your life and ministry to seeking, doing, and teaching God's word? Before you answer affirmatively and move on, reflect for a few moments. Do you yearn to know the Scriptures, or do you study simply to prepare your next lesson or sermon? Would you study even if you didn't have to teach? Those of us in Christian leadership set our hearts upon many things, some good, others not so good. We may set our hearts upon church growth, or upon being liked by our congregations, or upon having successful ministries. But genuine church growth requires a solid biblical commitment, even if preaching the Bible means we are disliked by our congregations at times. How have you set your heart?

Have you committed yourself to study God's truth? Diligent study requires time and effort. It is hard work, and there are no short cuts. Those of us who teach and preach must commit ourselves to genuine, laborious study. John MacArthur, pastor of Grace Community Church in Panorama City, California, spends thirty hours each week studying the Bible. Is it any wonder that God has blessed his ministry? Though my pastoral duties do not allow for such a lengthy time of study, I do set aside at least one day per week for this purpose, as well as several weeks each year that are wholly devoted to study. I know lay teachers in the church who spend a minimum of six hours each week in preparation for their adult Sunday school classes. Does your commitment to studying the Bible show up in your calendar?

Have you committed yourself to do God's truth? Study, no matter how important, is not sufficient alone; it must lead to obedience, even and especially when we are preparing to teach or to preach. Jesus made it clear: "My mother and My brothers are these who hear the word of God *and do it*" (Luke 8:21, emphasis added). John Wimber, pastor of Vineyard Christian Fellowship in Anaheim, California, talks about people who come to him for more sophisticated Bible studies when they have not even begun to live basic biblical truths. "I want more meat," they say. To these people he responds: "The meat is in the street." In other words, if you want real meat, begin by putting what you know into practice. Time and again the church in America has been rocked by preachers who fail to do what they proclaim. While we might point fingers at the most visible of sinners, indeed all of us fail in our obedience. But we may take solace in the fact that God did not bless Ezra because he perfectly followed the Law. No, God blessed him because he set his heart to obey. God does not require a perfect track record but a contrite and obedient heart, a heart seeking to obey God's truth.

Have you committed yourself to teach God's truth? It seems increasingly common for preachers to focus on something other than biblical teaching. We are told that God's truth simply will not sell. I read recently of a leader who attributed his denomination's lack of growth to the fact that the preachers were adhering too closely to the Bible. What nonsense! If anything, churches have lost their power today precisely because so many communicators teach various "winds of doctrine" rather than the whole truth of God. Not so with Ezra. He set his heart to teach the "stat-utes and ordinances," or the complete Law of God. Do we imitate his example, or do we shy away from difficult or controversial subjects?

I have wrestled with this question recently in my preparation of a series on "God's Guide to Good Sex." I will unabashedly preach God's revealed standards for our sexuality. I know already that some who hear me will be offended. Yet I have set my heart to teach the whole counsel of God, especially when it touches the deep needs of our life. God's Word brings life and peace, but it also brings "reproof and correction" (2 Tim. 3:16). The church today desperately needs communicators who will stand upon the Word of God, who will teach God's ways even though they are unpopular.

Psalm 119 beautifully describes the commitment of someone like Ezra, a commitment that leads to God's blessing of ministry. I would encourage you to read the entire psalm, but I will close this chapter with just a few key verses:

> Blessed are the undefiled in the way,
> Who walk in the law of the LORD
> Blessed are those who keep His testimonies,
> Who seek Him with the whole heart!
>
> *Psalm 119:1–2*

How can a young man cleanse his way?
By taking heed according to Your word.
With my whole heart I have sought you;
Oh let me not wander from Your commandments!
Your word I have hidden in my heart,
That I might not sin against You.
Blessed are You, O LORD!
Teach me Your statutes.
With my lips I have declared
All the judgments of Your mouth.
I have rejoiced in the way of Your testimonies,
As much as in all riches.
I will meditate on Your precepts,
And contemplate Your ways.
I will delight myself in Your statutes;
I will not forget Your word.

Psalm 119:9–15

Your word is a lamp to my feet
And a light to my path.
I have sworn and confirmed
That I will keep Your righteous judgments.

Psalm 119:105–106

Your testimonies are wonderful;
Therefore my soul keeps them.
The entrance of Your words gives light;
It gives understanding to the simple.

Psalm 119:129–130

My lips shall utter praise,
For You teach me Your statutes.
My tongue shall speak of Your word,
For all Your commandments are righteousness.
Let Your hand become my help,
For I have chosen Your precepts.
I long for Your salvation, O LORD,
And Your law is my delight.

Psalm 119:171–174

NOTES

1. As mentioned in the "Introduction to Ezra-Nehemiah," not all scholars place the work of Ezra during the reign of Artaxerxes I, preferring instead to place Ezra within the reign of Artaxerxes II (for example, Brockington, *Ezra, Nehemiah, and Esther,* New Century Bible [Greenwood, SC: The Attic Press, 1969], p. 20). His seventh year was 398 B.C. I opt for the traditional dating that places Ezra before Nehemiah, in the reign of Artaxerxes I. See the "Introduction" for discussion.

2. Kidner, *Ezra & Nehemiah,* p. 62.

3. Williamson, *Ezra, Nehemiah,* p. 100. For a more critical view, see R. North, "Ezra," *ABD* (New York: Doubleday, 1992).

4. Brown, Driver, and Briggs, *Lexicon,* s.v. *"kî,"* 3.

5. Fensham, *Ezra and Nehemiah,* p. 101.

6. Brown, Driver, and Briggs, *Lexicon,* s.v. *"dāraš,"* 6.

7. Suggested by Rabbi Jose in *Babylonian Talmud, Sanhedrin* 21b–22a.

8. J. M. Myers, *Ezra • Nehemiah,* The Anchor Bible (Garden City, NY: Doubleday, 1965), p. lxxiii.

9. For a discussion of Ezra's role in Jewish history, see H. G. M. Williamson, *Ezra and Nehemiah,* Old Testament Guides (Sheffield: Sheffield Academic Press [JSOT Press], 1987), pp. 69–76.

CHAPTER EIGHT

Ezra Returns to Jerusalem

Ezra 8:1–36

A QUESTION OF CONSISTENCY

Each autumn, we at Irvine Presbyterian face the challenge of financial stewardship. Within the broader context of helping people to use faithfully all of the resources entrusted to them by God, we address the specific issue of giving money to the church, which operates on a yearly pledge system. We ask members to determine in advance what they expect to give in the next year. On this basis, we formulate our budget. Of course, vital ministries and missions depend upon generous pledging. That is why stewardship sermons play such a key role during the weeks of financial planning—they provide essential education and motivation for church members.

When it comes to raising money for the church, I often wrestle with questions of consistency. Although Irvine Presbyterian utilizes a pledge model, other churches operate strictly "on faith". They simply pray, determine a budget according to their sense of God's leading, and trust that God will provide the necessary funds. Some Christian missions even boast of the fact that they never ask for money—they simply trust God. This makes me wonder: Does my stewardship approach contradict my own faith in God? Do I limit God's work by budgeting according to human promises rather than according to God's vision alone?

Other questions come to mind as I prepare the stewardship sermons, because I believe that true obedience, especially in giving, comes from the movement of the Holy Spirit in people's hearts. I also believe that Christian obedience comes as a response to God's grace and love. But do I maintain these commitments when I preach about giving to the church? Can I trust God to motivate people to give if I emphasize grace, not guilt; shalom, not shame? I must confess that a part of me wants to slip into tried and true means of getting people to give money: oughts, shoulds, guilt, fear, etc. After all, if adequate pledges are not received then valuable ministries will have to be curtailed, or even eliminated. Should my commitment to consistency place all of these at risk?

In chapter 8, Ezra confronts similar challenges as a leader: the risk of consistency, the temptation to compromise, and the danger of dealing with money. His response models for us the type of leadership needed today in the Church and in the world.

THOSE WHO ACCOMPANY EZRA (8:1–14)

8:1 These are the heads of their fathers' houses, and this is the genealogy of those who went up with me from Babylon, in the reign of King Artaxerxes:

2 of the sons of Phinehas, Gershom; of the sons of Ithamar, Daniel; of the sons of David, Hattush;

3 of the sons of Shecaniah, of the sons of Parosh, Zechariah; and registered with him were one hundred and fifty males;

4 of the sons of Pahath-Moab, Eliehoenai the son of Zerahiah, and with him two hundred males;

5 of the sons of Shechaniah, Ben-Jahaziel, and with him three hundred males;

6 of the sons of Adin, Ebed the son of Jonathan, and with him fifty males;

7 of the sons of Elam, Jeshaiah the son of Athaliah, and with him seventy males;

8 of the sons of Shephatiah, Zebadiah the son of Michael, and with him eighty males;

9 of the sons of Joab, Obadiah the son of Jehiel, and with him two hundred and eighteen males;

10 of the sons of Shelomith, Ben-Josiphiah, and with him one hundred and sixty males;

11 of the sons of Bebai, Zechariah the son of Bebai, and with him twenty-eight males;

12 of the sons of Azgad, Johanan the son of Hakkatan, and with him one hundred and ten males;

13 of the last sons of Adonikam, whose names are these—Eliphelet, Jeiel, and Shemaiah—and with them sixty males;

14 also of the sons of Bigvai, Uthai and Zabbud,
and with them seventy males.

Ezra 8:1–14

Chapter 8 begins with Ezra's list of those who *"went up with me from Babylon, in the reign of King Artaxerxes"* (v. 1). He does not list each person by name, but instead categorizes people according to their families. As would have been typical in Ezra's culture, he mentions only the males who journeyed to Jerusalem. The list identifies about 1500 men, so the entire caravan must have numbered around 5000.[1]

EZRA RECRUITS LEVITES AND TEMPLE SERVANTS (8:15–20)

15 Now I gathered them by the river that flows to
Ahava, and we camped there three days. And I
looked among the people and the priests, and found
none of the sons of Levi there.
16 Then I sent for Eliezer, Ariel, Shemaiah,
Elnathan, Jarib, Elnathan, Nathan, Zechariah, and
Meshullam, leaders; also for Joiarib and Elnathan,
men of understanding.
17 And I gave them a command for Iddo the chief
man at the place Casiphia, and I told them what they
should say to Iddo and his brethren the Nethinim at
the place Casiphia—that they should bring us
servants for the house of our God.
18 Then, by the good hand of our God upon us,
they brought us a man of understanding, of the sons
of Mahli the son of Levi, the son of Israel, namely
Sherebiah, with his sons and brothers, eighteen men;
19 and Hashabiah, and with him Jeshaiah of the
sons of Merari, his brothers and their sons, twenty
men;
20 also of the Nethinim, whom David and the
leaders had appointed for the service of the Levites,
two hundred and twenty Nethinim. All of them were
designated by name.

Ezra 8:15–20

Ezra and his companions gathered *"by the river that flows to Ahava"* (v. 15). We do not know the precise location of Ahava, but it must have been in the vicinity of Babylon.[2] While they camped in this spot for three days, Ezra surveyed those who had responded to Artaxerxes' invitation. To his chagrin, he found *"none of the sons of Levi there"* (v. 15). To remedy this situation, Ezra recruited an impressive delegation of *"leaders,"* including two men noted for their intellect and learning (v. 16). This delegation of leaders traveled from Ahava to *"Casiphia,"* another place near Babylon that we cannot identify today,[3] where they told *"Iddo the chief man at the place Casiphia"* of Ezra's need for temple servants—including Levites who could serve as assistants to the priests (v. 17). Once again God blessed the efforts of Ezra, and the delegation returned to Ahava with an impressive array of Levites and temple servants. Among the new recruits were *"Sherebiah"* and *"Hashabiah,"* who must have been leaders among the Levites (vv. 18–19). All in all, thirty-eight Levites joined Ezra, along with *"two hundred and twenty Nethinim,"* temple servants who helped the Levites (v. 20).[4]

The passage does not explain why Ezra required Levites as a part of his caravan. Presumably the temple in Jerusalem already had an ample number of Levites and temple servants. So there must be another reason for Ezra's special recruitment drive. Verse 24 suggests an answer. There, Sherebiah and Hashabiah are named explicitly among those who carried sacred temple offerings and implements from Babylon to Jerusalem. This, then, was the reason they were needed in the caravan. Ezra, an expert in God's Law, knew that only Levites were to carry the holy things for the tabernacle (Num. 1:50; 3:1–4:33). Based on this principle, he determined that only Levites should carry the gifts from Artaxerxes back to the temple in Jerusalem. Though his conviction required additional effort, Ezra endeavored to be consistent with the intent of God's Law, even when the letter of the Law did not directly address this particular situation.

SEEKING GOD'S PROTECTION (8:21–23)

21 Then I proclaimed a fast there at the river of Ahava, that we might humble ourselves before our God, to seek from Him the right way for us and our little ones and all our possessions.
22 For I was ashamed to request of the king an escort of soldiers and horsemen to help us against the

enemy on the road, because we had spoken to the
king, saying, "The hand of our God is upon all those
for good who seek Him, but His power and His wrath
are against all those who forsake Him."

23 So we fasted and entreated our God for this,
and He answered our prayer.

Ezra 8:21–23

Once the full team was assembled, Ezra *"proclaimed a fast"* so that *"we might humble ourselves before our God, to seek from Him the right way for us and our little ones . . ."* (v. 21). He did not want to begin the journey without seeking God's protection and guidance. The caravan, which was traveling from Babylon to Jerusalem during the summer months, had to take a cooler, northern route, a journey of more than 800 miles.[5] And it would be a dangerous journey, especially considering the presence of children who accompanied the adults and the vast amounts of precious metals that were being transported. Bandits could have a heyday at the expense of the returning exiles, who had risked both their possessions and their very lives by leaving Babylon.

Verse 22 implies that Ezra could have asked for a military escort to protect his party (Nehemiah had received such an escort in Neh. 2:9), but he was *"ashamed"* to do so because he had said to the king, *"The hand of our God is upon all those for good who seek Him, but His power and His wrath are against all those who forsake Him"* (v. 22). No doubt Ezra felt that to ask for royal protection would be to contradict his confession of God's protection. Therefore, he called the people to fast and to pray. Verse 23 assures us that God *"answered [their] prayer."*

When we consider the dangers the returning exiles were facing on this journey, Ezra's simple trust in God's protection is a bit unsettling. He and his companions would be sitting ducks, easy prey for marauding bandits. Hundreds if not thousands of children could be slaughtered. Yet Ezra's commitment to live consistent with what he confessed commends a daring course—a course that God honored.

HOLY GIFTS FOR THE TEMPLE (8:24–30)

24 And I separated twelve of the leaders of the
priests—Sherebiah, Hashabiah, and ten of their
brethren with them—

25 and weighed out to them the silver, the gold,
and the articles, the offering for the house of our God
which the king and his counselors and his princes,
and all Israel who were present, had offered.
26 I weighed into their hand six hundred and fifty
talents of silver, silver articles weighing one hundred
talents, one hundred talents of gold,
27 twenty gold basins worth a thousand
drachmas, and two vessels of fine polished bronze,
precious as gold.
28 And I said to them, "You are holy to the LORD;
the articles are holy also; and the silver and the gold
are a freewill offering to the LORD God of your fathers.
29 Watch and keep them until you weigh them
before the leaders of the priests and the Levites and
heads of the fathers' houses of Israel in Jerusalem, in
the chambers of the house of the LORD."
30 So the priests and the Levites received the
silver and the gold and the articles by weight, to bring
them to Jerusalem to the house of our God.

Ezra 8:24–30

The commission from Artaxerxes to Ezra included a charge to carry silver and gold from the king and other residents of Babylon to the temple in Jerusalem (7:15–19). In 8:24–30, Ezra establishes structures of responsibility and accountability for the transportation of this treasure. First of all, he set apart twelve leading priests and twelve leading Levites, including *"Sherebiah and Hashabiah"* (v. 24). To these leaders Ezra carefully *"weighed out"* all of the offerings for the temple (v. 25). This insured that all items would arrive intact, since another weighing in Jerusalem would confirm the safe passage of all the offerings.

The measures in verse 26 represent an unbelievably large quantity of silver and gold when we consider the fact that a "talent" weighed approximately seventy-five pounds.[6] This means that the silver bars and articles weighed over twenty-five tons—quite a load for twelve priests and twelve Levites! While they may have transported such a heavy amount of metal with ox carts, it is also possible that verse 26 represents some confusion of weights and measures.[7]

After weighing out the gold and silver items, Ezra declared to those who would carry them: *"You are holy to the LORD; the articles are*

132

holy also; and the silver and the gold are a freewill offering to the LORD God of your fathers" (v. 28). In others words, he said to them, "You have been set apart for this special task. The articles and offerings have also been set apart for God. They belong to him. So take special care to see that everything arrives intact." Then, just in case the transporters might be tempted to take a few silver bars, Ezra reminded them that everything would be weighed again upon their arrival in Jerusalem (v. 29).

ARRIVAL IN JERUSALEM (8:31–36)

31 Then we departed from the river of Ahava on the twelfth day of the first month, to go to Jerusalem. And the hand of our God was upon us, and He delivered us from the hand of the enemy and from ambush along the road.

32 So we came to Jerusalem, and stayed there three days.

33 Now on the fourth day the silver and the gold and the articles were weighed in the house of our God by the hand of Meremoth the son of Uriah the priest, and with him was Eleazar the son of Phinehas; with them were the Levites, Jozabad the son of Jeshua and Noadiah the son of Binnui,

34 with the number and weight of everything. All the weight was written down at that time.

35 The children of those who had been carried away captive, who had come from the captivity, offered burnt offerings to the God of Israel: twelve bulls for all Israel, ninety-six rams, seventy-seven lambs, and twelve male goats as a sin offering. All this was a burnt offering to the LORD.

36 And they delivered the king's orders to the king's satraps and the governors in the region beyond the River. So they gave support to the people and the house of God.

Ezra 8:31–36

The caravan departed from Ahava on *"the twelfth day of the first month,"* around the first of April (v. 31). They arrived in Jerusalem on "the first day of the fifth month" (8:9), about four months later. Ezra does not relate the adventures of the journey, except to note that God *"delivered us from the hand of the enemy and from ambush along the road"* (v. 31). Certainly this confirms that *"the hand of God was upon us"* (v. 31).

After three days of rest (v. 32), *"the silver and the gold and the articles"* were weighed in the temple in the presence of several religious officials (v. 33). Ezra notes that *"all the weight was written down at that time,"* implying that official records verified the successful transportation of all items from Babylon to Jerusalem (v. 34).

Upon returning to Jerusalem, the people, whose ancestors *"had been carried away captive,"* offered various sacrifices to God (v. 35). *"Twelve bulls"* and *"ninety-six rams"* (twelve times eight) represented *"all Israel,"* the full twelve tribes (v. 35). These sacrifices represented offerings of thanks to God for a safe journey, while *"twelve male goats as a sin offering"* represented sacrifices for cleansing from pagan contamination.[8]

Finally, the local officials, both *"satraps"* (provincial rulers) and *"governors,"* received the orders from the king to support Ezra (7:21–23), which, according to Ezra's witness, they followed (v. 36).

REFLECTIONS ON EZRA 8:1–36

Consistent Christian Living

I began this chapter by raising the question of consistency. What does it mean for us as Christians to live consistently according to our trust in God? The story of Ezra in chapter 8 shows one man's effort to live consonant with his faith. Although it required extra effort, Ezra recruited Levites to carry the sacred items for the temple, and although the welfare of the caravan seemed more vulnerable without it, Ezra rejected a military escort in favor of trusting God's supernatural protection.

However, Ezra's trust in God did not blind him to the realities of human nature for he established elaborate safeguards for the transportation of implements and money for the temple. Ironically, he was able to trust God for protection from bandits, but not for protection from pilfering Levites! This highlights the challenge of consistent living. Naturally, interpretations of consistency will differ according to personal experience and perspective. Later in Ezra-Nehemiah,

134

Nehemiah chooses to accept a military escort, seemingly without concern for any inconsistency between this action and his confession of God's sovereign care (Neh. 2:9).

Christians today also differ over what consistent trust in God means in practice. While in college I attended a debate between two Christian leaders. One argued that we should not buy insurance, but, rather, should trust God and the Christian community. The millions of dollars spent on insurance, he argued, could be put to far better use in God's kingdom. His opponent in the debate disagreed, arguing for a "realistic" stewardship in today's world. Who was right? Who lived more consistently with a confession of God's care and providence?

On several occasions in the past few years, I have been approached by men who needed a ride to a location several miles away. Sometimes I have offered them a ride and at other times I have declined, but each time I have wondered about the wisdom of my choice. What if this man intends me harm? If I extend love in God's name, will God always protect me? How would I feel if my wife trusted God in this way?

Pope John Paul II has traveled the world more than any of his predecessors. He rides through the streets, waving to throngs of well-wishers. However after someone attempted to assassinate him several years ago he now rides in a bullet-proof vehicle, affectionately known as "The Popemobile." Does this speak of his failure to trust God, or his wise care for his own life? What does a consistent faith in God require?

There are no simple answers to these questions. The case of Ezra shows how we may trust God alone in one case and utilize human structures in another case. Of course we can take the issue of consistency to absurd extremes, and the words of Ralph Waldo Emerson warn us against just such folly: "A foolish consistency is the hobgoblin of little minds, adored by little statesmen and philosophers and divines."[9]

Nevertheless, all Christians should ask the hard question: "Am I living consistent with my confession of faith?" For all of us, the answer must be: "No, not completely." I find it easier to trust God for my own protection than for the protection of my wife and son. Strangely, I can trust God with giant financial matters, like building a sanctuary, but sometimes I struggle to trust him for small change— like $400 for car repairs. The example of Ezra does not answer our questions definitively; rather, it encourages us to consider our lifestyles and our activities honestly and to seek the Lord for wisdom.

We should note also that when Ezra trusted God for something major, like the protection of his caravan, he did not presume upon God's care. No, he called everyone to fast and to pray for God's protection. A lackadaisical "Oh, God will take care of us" does not reflect Ezra's attitude. Only prayerful discernment reveals when and how to trust God; only prayerful obedience reflects a fully biblical trust in God's care.

Integrity in Leadership

The attempt to live with consistency between confession and action is a touchstone of Ezra's leadership. Not only did he demand integrity of himself, but he demanded it of his subordinates. (Chapters 9 and 10 will demonstrate this in further detail.) "Integrity" is based upon the Latin word "integer" meaning "whole" or "complete." Integrity exists when a person lives in a state of wholeness, in which ideas and actions cohere, and every part of life fits together in a consistent whole.

We find a distressing absence of integrity in our culture today. We suffer from what Ted Engstrom calls "Acquired Integrity Deficiency Syndrome."[10] We hope that our leaders will model integrity for us, but sadly this is not the case. On all levels of government we see officials with fractured lives full of dishonesty and self-interest. Most recently, nominees for U.S. Attorney General have been rejected because they cut corners and broke the law by hiring illegal aliens as baby-sitters. One of the "chronic problems" of organizations, according to Stephen R. Covey, is: "No integrity: values do not equal habits; there is no correlation between what I believe and what I do."[11]

Sadly, the church offers little relief from this disintegration of leadership. Pastors, elders, and evangelists seem to be falling like flies because of adultery or financial impropriety. Today, as never before, the church and the country yearn for leaders who personify integrity. In his excellent book, *Leadership is an Art*, business executive Max DePree lists qualities of future leaders. At the top of the list he calls for a leader who has "consistent and dependable integrity."[12]

Ezra exemplifies integrity in his leadership, and we would do well to imitate his example. First of all, *Ezra inspires us to do the right thing, even if this requires additional time and effort*. He recruited Levites to carry the sacred articles even though this slowed down his trip to Jerusalem. He could well have said, "Oh well, the Law doesn't actually require Levites for this particular assignment. Let's make the easy choice and go on without them." But instead he took time to do things right.

As a pastor, I face this type of challenge, too. Recently we wanted to add a small closet to one of our education buildings. Now although the city of Irvine requires a permit for even minimal building alterations, it was possible that the Building Department would never know about our one little closet. Furthermore, to obtain official approval would take extra time and money, and would inevitably complicate matters. The man responsible for the project asked me bluntly, "Should we get a permit?" As much as I hate having to jump through official hoops, my answer required little reflection, "Yes. We must do what is right." If we in church leadership do not act with honesty, how can we call others to lead lives of integrity? Even though it means we have to slow down our progress, we must consistently choose to do things in the right way.

Second, *Ezra challenges us to act consistently with our convictions*. He acted consistently with his confession of God's care. While Nehemiah later found no conflict between his faith and the acceptance of a military escort, Ezra's conscience would not support such a seemingly prudent decision. While we might debate Ezra's logic, it is not the important issue here. What does matter is that he acted with integrity, according to his personal convictions.

Without doubt, preachers differ in their convictions about how people are motivated to obedience. In the introduction to this chapter, I mentioned my own belief that right behavior follows from God's grace and love. Even the Law comes in the context of grace! While I am not reticent to proclaim God's standards for behavior, I avoid the use of manipulative emotions such as guilt or fear, no matter how successful these might be. For me, it would be wrong to preach a stewardship sermon that motivated my congregation with guilt.

I will never forget my nervousness as I entered my first stewardship season at Irvine Presbyterian. What if my convictions led to poor results? What if I decimated the church budget? Although these questions troubled me, I knew that I had to preach with integrity, with a wholeness that embraced my beliefs and my words. So I spoke of God's grace and called people to respond in freedom, and by "the good hand of God upon me," my first stewardship campaign was a financial success!

Third, *Ezra models for us a commitment to institutional integrity.* He demanded integrity from his subordinates—the priests and Levites who transported the holy materials were to be holy themselves. Further, they were not to profit personally by "borrowing" some of God's gold and silver. Ironically, Ezra's realism about human greed led him to institute a system of accountability that virtually compelled financial integrity. He did not blithely trust God, but acted to insure faithfulness to God's standards.

We who lead would do well to imitate Ezra's example. Recently, Orange County, California has been shaken by repeated episodes of greed-induced stealing by government officials and directors of nonprofit agencies. Yet churches and other Christian organizations are not immune from the plague of greed. Financial accountability must be demanded and institutionally guaranteed. In our church, we employ a network of checks and balances that makes embezzlement virtually impossible. Sometimes this is cumbersome and even humorous, nevertheless it is an important safeguard to fiscal integrity. Recently our Business Administrator needed to sign a twenty dollar check for himself. He came into my office and said, "OK, boss, I want you to watch this. I'm signing my own check for a few expenses." All for twenty dollars! When it comes to financial matters, we want to follow in Ezra's footsteps.

As I have noted above, the precise dimensions of consistency and integrity will vary from person to person, but Ezra challenges all of us not to take integrity lightly. God requires—and our world needs—leaders who will live and lead with costly, thoughtful integrity.

NOTES

1. Williamson, *Ezra, Nehemiah*, p. 110.

2. Williamson, *Ezra, Nehemiah*, p. 116; M. J. Fretz, "Ahava," *ABD* (New York: Doubleday, 1992).

3. G. A. Herion, "Casiphia," *ABD* (New York: Doubleday, 1992).

4. For discussion of the Nethinim, see commentary on Ezra 2:43-58 above.

5. Blenkinsopp, *Ezra-Nehemiah*, p. 138.

6. Williamson, *Ezra, Nehemiah*, p. 119.

7. Williamson, *Ezra, Nehemiah*, p. 119.

8. Williamson, *Ezra, Nehemiah*, p. 122.

9. R. W. Emerson, "Self Reliance," in *The American Tradition in Literature*, 3rd edition, ed., S. Bradley, R. Beatty, and E. H. Long, vol. 1 (New York: Grosset & Dunlap, 1967), p. 1135.

10. T. W. Engstrom with R. C. Larson, *Integrity* (Waco, TX: Word Books, 1987), p. 7.

11. S. R. Covey, *Principle-Centered Leadership* (New York: Simon & Schuster, 1992), p. 171.

12. M. DePree, *Leadership is an Art* (New York: Dell Publishing, 1989), p. 131.

CHAPTER NINE

Ezra Confronts Jewish Intermarriage

Ezra 9:1–10:44

THE PAINFUL SIDE OF RESTORATION

Several years ago, my wife and I decided to restore a dilapidated patio behind our home to turn it into a usable room. Short on money, but long on naïveté, we chose to do the work ourselves. For weeks we spent our free moments tearing apart the old structure. The more we worked, the more we discovered rotting timbers and a poor structural design. We spent hours in dusty, joyless demolition until we finally arrived at a base from which we could begin rebuilding. To this day, I am surprised that we made it through that first stage of restoration. When we were finally able to build and to paint, it seemed like a party compared with the preliminary work of tearing down.

But that's the way it is with restoration. Everybody loves renewal or restoration, in theory, but true restoration and rebuilding almost always require a painful process of taking apart what has gone before. And, unfortunately, it can be quite messy.

We see this side of restoration in Ezra 9 and 10. After receiving the king's commission, Ezra led a party of Jews to return to Jerusalem (Ezra 7–8). God blessed their trip with safety for the travelers and bounty for the temple. Good news abounded and national restoration appeared to be just on the horizon. But the mood changes drastically in chapter 9 as Ezra confronts widespread sin.

EZRA'S RESPONSE TO AN APPALLING REPORT (9:1–4)

9:1 When these things were done, the leaders came
to me, saying, "The people of Israel and the priests

and the Levites have not separated themselves from
the peoples of the lands, with respect to the
abominations of the Canaanites, the Hittites, the
Perizzites, the Jebusites, the Ammonites, the
Moabites, the Egyptians, and the Amorites.

2 For they have taken some of their daughters as
wives for themselves and their sons, so that the holy
seed is mixed with the peoples of those lands. Indeed,
the hand of the leaders and rulers has been foremost
in this trespass."

3 So when I heard this thing, I tore my garment
and my robe, and plucked out some of the hair of my
head and beard, and sat down astonished.

4 Then everyone who trembled at the words of
the God of Israel assembled to me, because of the
transgression of those who had been carried away
captive, and I sat astonished until the evening
sacrifice.

Ezra 9:1–4

Verse 1 begins with the phrase *"when these things were done,"*
which, in context, refers to the delivery of the goods for the temple in
chapter 8. Yet, four months have passed since Ezra arrived in Jerusalem (7:9, 10:9). So what did he do during this span of time? Could it
be that "these things" included teaching the Law to the people, which
Artaxerxes had commanded Ezra to do and which would elicit the
report of verse 1? Unfortunately, Ezra-Nehemiah does not supply
this information. For some reason, however, the leaders of Israel
came to Ezra with a report of widespread sin.

According to the report, the *"people of Israel,"* including *"the
priests and the Levites,"* had not *"Separated themselves from the
peoples of the lands"* (v. 1). Instead, they had intermarried with these
peoples and had taken *"some of their daughters as wives for themselves and their sons"* (v. 2). As a result, *"the holy seed [was] mixed with
the peoples of those lands"* (v. 2). The unusual phrase "holy seed"
blends two biblical concepts: the people of God and the seed of
Abraham.[1] It emphasizes Israel's uniqueness as a nation set apart for
God alone.

The list of foreign peoples in verse 1 represents the kind of people
found in the lands surrounding Judah. Of course we know that forming

141

relationships with these groups of people had been strictly forbidden by God in the Law. The book of Deuteronomy states bluntly:

> When the Lord your God brings you into the land which you go to possess, and has cast out many nations before you, the Hittites and the Girgashites and the Amorites and the Canaanites and the Perizzites and the Hivites and the Jebusites, seven nations greater and mightier than you, and when the LORD your God delivers them over to you, you shall conquer them and utterly destroy them. You shall make no covenant with them nor show mercy to them. *Nor shall you make marriages with them. You shall not give your daughter to their son, nor take their daughter for your son.* For they will turn your sons away from following Me, to serve other gods; so the anger of the Lord will be aroused against you and destroy you suddenly.
>
> *Deuteronomy 7:1–4 (emphasis added)*

Intermarriage with the nations was wrong because of the religious impact of mixed marriages. God forbade such marriages because foreign daughters would turn their sons away from following God (Deut. 7:4). Similarly, God instructed Israel not to enter into a covenant with someone from the surrounding nations, lest "you take of his daughters for your sons, and his daughters play the harlot with their gods and make your sons play the harlot with their gods" (Exod. 34:16). The later history of Israel shows that, in fact, intermarriage did lead to the loss of a pure relationship between the nation and God.

An especially distressing detail is added in verse 2: "*Indeed, the hand of the leaders and rulers has been foremost in this trespass.*" Whereas priests and Levites had already been numbered among the trespassers in 9:1, now we discover that other leaders had also led the decline into transgression.

Ezra did not respond nonchalantly to this distressing report. Immediately he tore his clothing, plucked hair from his head, and sat down "*astonished*" (v. 3). The Hebrew word translated as "astonished" also means "appalled, horrified."[2] Ezra's three actions, which usually accompany mourning for the dead,[3] demonstrate his shock and horror at this turn of events.

Ezra's gestures of grief not only expressed his own feelings but also drew others around him (v. 4). Verse 4 clarifies who had sinned by intermarriage: "*those who had been carried away captive.*" The problem did not involve those who had remained in the land after the Babylonian invasion, but, rather, those who were sent back to restore Judah. With fellow mourners gathered around him, Ezra sat *"astonished until the evening sacrifice,"* probably about 3:00 p.m.[4]

EZRA'S PRAYER OF CONFESSION (9:5–15)

5 At the evening sacrifice I arose from my fasting; and having torn my garment and my robe, I fell on my knees and spread out my hands to the LORD my God.

6 And I said: "O my God, I am too ashamed and humiliated to lift up my face to You, my God; for our iniquities have risen higher than our heads, and our guilt has grown up to the heavens.

7 Since the days of our fathers to this day we have been very guilty, and for our iniquities we, our kings, and our priests have been delivered into the hand of the kings of the lands, to the sword, to captivity, to plunder, and to humiliation, as it is this day.

8 And now for a little while grace has been shown from the LORD our God, to leave us a remnant to escape, and to give us a peg in His holy place, that our God may enlighten our eyes and give us a measure of revival in our bondage.

9 For we were slaves. Yet our God did not forsake us in our bondage; but He extended mercy to us in the sight of the kings of Persia, to revive us, to repair the house of our God, to rebuild its ruins, and to give us a wall in Judah and Jerusalem.

10 And now, O our God, what shall we say after this? For we have forsaken Your commandments,

11 which You commanded by Your servants the prophets, saying,' The land which you are entering to possess is an unclean land, with the uncleanness of the peoples of the lands, with their abominations which have filled it from one end to another with their impurity.

12 'Now therefore, do not give your daughters as wives for their sons, nor take their daughters to your

sons; and never seek their peace or prosperity, that
you may be strong and eat the good of the land, and
leave it as an inheritance to your children forever.'

13 And after all that has come upon us for our evil
deeds and for our great guilt, since You our God have
punished us less than our iniquities deserve, and have
given us such deliverance as this,

14 should we again break Your commandments,
and join in marriage with the people committing
these abominations? Would You not be angry with us
until You had consumed us, so that there would be no
remnant or survivor?

15 O LORD God of Israel, You are righteous, for we
are left as a remnant, as it is this day. Here we are
before You, in our guilt, though no one can stand
before You because of this!"

Ezra 9:5–15

Ezra sat appalled for several hours, perhaps *"fasting"* (v. 5). The
Hebrew word translated as "fasting" conveys more of an attitude of
humiliation than of self-denial.[5] At the time of the evening sacrifice,
Ezra offered a prayer of confession. He began by falling on his knees
in a gesture of submission to God. (Spreading one's hands was a
common posture for intercession, see 2 Chr. 6:13, for example).

Ezra's prayer began in the first-person singular, *"I am too
ashamed,"* then moved to the first-person plural as Ezra confessed
corporate sin, *"for our iniquities . . ."* (v. 6). He conveyed the gravity
of national sin by describing it as rising up to the heavens. Not only
had the Jewish iniquities *"risen higher than [their] heads"* (v. 6), but
their guilt had *"grown up to the heavens"* (v. 6). In other words, sins
had piled upon sins until the people had created a colossal dung-
heap of evil.

Verse 7 provides a brief summary of Israel's guilt, which explains
why the leaders of the nation had been punished by foreign kings.
This also explains why Judah, even at this time, was subject to foreign rule. But verses 8 and 9 testify to God's gracious treatment of his
sinful people. God had shown his favor by allowing a *"remnant"* of
the people to escape from bondage and to establish a *"peg in His holy
place"* (v. 8). The word translated as "peg" means, quite literally, a
"tent stake."[6] The peg secured the tent to keep it from blowing away

in a strong wind. The use of this term here signifies the hope that what God had established in restoration would not be blown away by Israel's sin.

Reading further we see that God not only allowed the nation to have a firm foothold in Jerusalem but also to experience *"a measure of revival in [their] bondage"*—literally, "a little relief in their bondage" (v. 8). Even when the people of God were living as *"slaves"* in a foreign land, God *"extended mercy"* to bring revival and restoration of the temple (v. 9). As elsewhere in Ezra-Nehemiah, "mercy" or *hesed* here, signifies God's faithfulness to his covenant promises. Thus, even when the people were taken away by the Babylonians, God did not forget them.

The final phrase of verse 9 seems odd: *"and to give us a wall in Judah and Jerusalem."* First of all, the wall around Jerusalem would not be rebuilt until later (Neh. 6). Second, at no time did a wall surround the entire region of Judah. Thus, the use of "wall" here no doubt signifies a metaphorical wall of protection that God provided for the people, not an actual physical barrier.[7]

Yet in spite of God's grace, the people had forsaken his commandments (v. 10). Verses 11–12 recount the commandments broken by the intermarrying Jews. The content of these verses reflects language found in many places throughout the Hebrew Scriptures (Deut. 7:1–4; 23:7; 2 Kgs. 21:16; Isa. 1:19; Mal. 2:10–11). Ezra emphasized God's commandment not to intermarry with the peoples from the land, who were *"unclean"* (v. 11), that is, morally and ritually opposed to God's holiness. Only faithful obedience would allow the Jews to leave the land *"as an inheritance to [their] children forever"* (v. 12).

Verse 13 once again emphasizes God's grace, in that he punished the people *"less than [their] iniquities deserve."* In fact he had *"given [them] such deliverance as this"*: namely, the restoration under the Persian rulers. Then Ezra asked a rhetorical question. In light of God's extra measure of grace, *"should we again break Your commandments, and join in marriage with the people of these abominations?"* (v. 13). The answer, of course, was no! The remnant in Judah should never have broken God's commandment with regard to mixed marriages. Ezra followed with another question for God, *"Would You not be angry with us until You had consumed us, so that there would be no remnant or survivor?"* (v. 14). Ezra wondered how long God would continue to extend mercy to a people who regularly rebelled against him, even in the face of extraordinary grace.

Verse 15 concludes the prayer of confession with a marked contrast between God, who is *"righteous,"* and the people who are mired in *"guilt."* Ezra admitted that *"no one can stand"* in God's presence because of the vileness of Israel's sin. Significantly, his prayer ends in despair, without even a cry for deliverance. Ezra seemed to believe that the people were beyond hope, beyond salvation.

Please note that my concluding "Reflections" in this chapter will not address Ezra's prayer of confession since Nehemiah 9:1–37 later records another confession upon which I will reflect at length.

A PROPOSAL TO SOLVE THE PROBLEM (10:1–8)

10:1 Now while Ezra was praying, and while he was confessing, weeping, and bowing down before the house of God, a very large assembly of men, women, and children gathered to him from Israel; for the people wept very bitterly.

2 And Shechaniah the son of Jehiel, one of the sons of Elam, spoke up and said to Ezra, "We have trespassed against our God, and have taken pagan wives from the peoples of the land; yet now there is hope in Israel in spite of this.

3 Now therefore, let us make a covenant with our God to put away all these wives and those who have been born to them, according to the advice of my master and of those who tremble at the commandment of our God; and let it be done according to the law.

4 Arise, for this matter is your responsibility. We also are with you. Be of good courage, and do it."

5 Then Ezra arose, and made the leaders of the priests, the Levites, and all Israel swear an oath that they would do according to this word. So they swore an oath.

6 Then Ezra rose up from before the house of God, and went into the chamber of Jehohanan the son of Eliashib; and when he came there, he ate no bread and drank no water, for he mourned because of the guilt of those from the captivity.

> 7 And they issued a proclamation throughout
> Judah and Jerusalem to all the descendants of the
> captivity, that they must gather at Jerusalem,
>   8 and that whoever would not come within three
> days, according to the instructions of the leaders and
> elders, all his property would be confiscated, and he
> himself would be separated from the assembly of
> those from the captivity.
>
> *Ezra 10:1–8*

Chapter 10 begins right on the heels of 9:15: *"Now while Ezra was praying and while he was confessing"* (v. 1). During his time of prayer *"a very large assembly of men, women, and children"* gathered around him, weeping *"very bitterly"* (v. 1). The text accentuates the size of the gathering ("very large") as well as its inclusiveness ("men, women, and children"). Ezra's public confession had drawn the masses into an attitude of profound grief and repentance for their sins.

Without explanation, chapter 10 shifts from a first-person to a third-person account of Ezra's actions. The editor of Ezra-Nehemiah may have reworded the account from Ezra's memoirs, or he may have utilized another source for this part of the story.

Although Ezra concluded his prayer without hope, a man named *"Shechaniah,"* who admitted the gravity of Israel's sin, nevertheless proposed a solution to the problem (v. 2). He recognized that the people had *"trespassed against our God,"* or literally, *"been unfaithful to our God."*[8] Yet he held out *"hope for Israel in spite of this"* (v. 2). Shechaniah suggested that the sinning men *"put away all these wives and those who have been born to them"* (v. 3). The verb translated as "to put away" is not the standard Hebrew verb for divorce, though this is certainly its sense in verse 3.[9] Continuing on, Shechaniah suggested that this should only be done, *"according to the advice of my master"* (Ezra), and *"according to the law"* (v. 3). No Hebrew law demanded or explained how one should divorce foreign wives and children. Either Shechaniah saw the divorce of pagan wives as an implication of the law prohibiting mixed marriages, or he meant that the divorces should occur according to the regulations for divorce in Deuteronomy 24:1–4.

Having offered his suggestions for action, Shechaniah placed the responsibility to carry them out with Ezra: *"Arise, for this matter is*

147

your responsibility" (v. 4). Indeed he spoke the truth, for Ezra alone had received authority from King Artaxerxes to teach and to enforce God's Law (7:25–26). Sensing Ezra's hesitation, Shechaniah added a word of encouragement, *"We also are with you. Be of good courage, and do it"* (v. 4). Sometimes even great leaders like Ezra need a nudge and a word of support in order to exercise leadership.

Ezra responded to Shechaniah's proposal in two ways. First, he made all the people, including the leaders, *"swear an oath that they would do according to this word"* (v. 5). The people swore by the oath and Ezra retired to a room belonging to *"Jehohanan,"* probably located in the temple.[10] There he continued to fast and to mourn because of the *"guilt"* of Israel (v. 6). Although he appeared to accept Shechaniah's "hope" for Israel, it would seem that Ezra scarcely felt hopeful. His private mourning emphasizes the utter authenticity of his earlier display of grief. He had not grieved publicly merely to put on a show for the people, but, rather, that they might be drawn into a spirit of repentance also.

The leaders of Judah, not just Ezra, *"issued a proclamation"* that called all the people to gather in Jerusalem immediately (v. 7). Whoever failed to appear within *"three days"* would forfeit all of his property and would be excommunicated from the nation (v. 8) Such a proclamation would certainly have received the attention and compliance of the people. It underscored how seriously the leaders viewed this situation. The time had come for national repentance and action!

NATIONAL CONSENSUS AND ACTION (10:9–17)

9 So all the men of Judah and Benjamin gathered at Jerusalem within three days. It was the ninth month, on the twentieth of the month; and all the people sat in the open square of the house of God, trembling because of this matter and because of heavy rain.

10 Then Ezra the priest stood up and said to them, "You have transgressed and have taken pagan wives, adding to the guilt of Israel.

11 Now therefore, make confession to the LORD God of your fathers, and do His will; separate yourselves from the peoples of the land, and from the pagan wives."

12 Then all the assembly answered and said with a loud voice, "Yes! As you have said, so we must do.

13 But there are many people; it is the season for heavy rain, and we are not able to stand outside. Nor is this the work of one or two days, for there are many of us who have transgressed in this matter.

14 Please, let the leaders of our entire assembly stand; and let all those in our cities who have taken pagan wives come at appointed times, together with the elders and judges of their cities, until the fierce wrath of our God is turned away from us in this matter."

15 Only Jonathan the son of Asahel and Jahaziah the son of Tikvah opposed this, and Meshullam and Shabbethai the Levite gave them support.

16 Then the descendants of the captivity did so. And Ezra the priest, with certain heads of the fathers' households, were set apart by the fathers' households, each of them by name; and they sat down on the first day of the tenth month to examine the matter.

17 By the first day of the first month they finished questioning all the men who had taken pagan wives.

Ezra 10:9–17

"All the men of Judah and Benjamin" gathered quickly in Jerusalem (v. 9) (which comes as no surprise considering the penalty for non-compliance, v. 8). They arrived on *"the twentieth"* of *"the ninth month,"* early in December. The timing explains *"the heavy rain"* that contributed to the *"trembling"* of the people (v. 9).

Ezra addressed the assembly, beginning with a brief statement of their sin. As in 10:2, the NKJV wording *"You have transgressed"* actually misses the literal and relational nuance of the Hebrew, which reads "You have been unfaithful [to God]" (v. 10). Ezra called the people to *"make confession to the LORD God"* and to *"do His will"* (v. 11). He believed that God's will for the intermarried Jews was to *"separate"* from the *"peoples of the land,"* specifically from their *"pagan wives"* (v. 11).

The gathered assembly responded with a strong affirmation of Ezra's command, qualifying their positive response with a pragmatic request (vv. 12–13). The large number of transgressing men and the terrible weather made instantaneous obedience to Ezra's command impractical, so the people asked for the implementation of the command to be delegated to leaders in the various cities, to *"the elders and judges"* (v. 14). Apparently Ezra concurred and only a handful of people opposed *"this"* suggestion (v. 15). However, the pronoun reference in verse 15 is unclear, so we do not know definitely whether they opposed Ezra's initial command or the pragmatic amendment in verse 14.

We do know that the people acted upon the plan. In the next three and a half months Ezra and other leaders questioned all who had *"taken pagan wives,"* to make sure that they had put away their wives and children (vv. 16–17).

THOSE WHO PUT AWAY PAGAN WIVES (10:18–44)

18 And among the sons of the priests who had taken pagan wives the following were found of the sons of Jeshua the son of Jozadak, and his brothers: Maaseiah, Eliezer, Jarib, and Gedaliah.

19 And they gave their promise that they would put away their wives; and being guilty, they presented a ram of the flock as their trespass offering.

20 Also of the sons of Immer: Hanani and Zebadiah;

21 of the sons of Harim: Maaseiah, Elijah, Shemaiah, Jehiel, and Uzziah;

22 of the sons of Pashhur: Elioenai, Maaseiah, Ishmael, Nethanel, Jozabad, and Elasah.

23 Also of the Levites: Jozabad, Shimei, Kelaiah (the same is Kelita), Pethahiah, Judah, and Eliezer.

24 Also of the singers: Eliashib; and of the gatekeepers: Shallum, Telem, and Uri.

25 And others of Israel: of the sons of Parosh: Ramiah, Jeziah, Malchiah, Mijamin, Eleazar, Malchijah, and Benaiah;

26 of the sons of Elam: Mattaniah, Zechariah, Jehiel, Abdi, Jeremoth, and Eliah;

27 of the sons of Zattu: Elioenai, Eliashib, Mattaniah, Jeremoth, Zabad, and Aziza;

28 of the sons of Bebai: Jehohanan, Hananiah, Zabbai, and Athlai;

29 of the sons of Bani: Meshullam, Malluch, Adaiah, Jashub, Sheal, and Ramoth;

30 of the sons of Pahath-Moab: Adna, Chelal, Benaiah, Maaseiah, Mattaniah, Bezalel, Binnui, and Manasseh;

31 of the sons of Harim: Eliezer, Ishijah, Malchijah, Shemaiah, Shimeon,

32 Benjamin, Malluch, and Shemariah;

33 of the sons of Hashum: Mattenai, Mattattah, Zabad, Eliphelet, Jeremai, Manasseh, and Shimei;

34 of the sons of Bani: Maadai, Amram, Uel,

35 Benaiah, Bedeiah, Cheluh,

36 Vaniah, Meremoth, Eliashib,

37 Mattaniah, Mattenai, Jaasai,

38 Bani, Binnui, Shimei,

39 Shelemiah, Nathan, Adaiah,

40 Machnadebai, Shashai, Sharai,

41 Azarel, Shelemiah, Shemariah,

42 Shallum, Amariah, and Joseph;

43 of the sons of Nebo: Jeiel, Mattithiah, Zabad, Zebina, Jaddai, Joel, and Benaiah.

44 All these had taken pagan wives, and some of them had wives by whom they had children.

Ezra 10:18–44

Verses 18–44 list by name those in Israel who had married and then divorced their foreign wives. Those listed first, in verses 18–22, are priests (compare 2:36–39), then verse 23 mentions the Levites. The ordering of the list reiterates the point of 9:1–2: leaders of Israel had led the nation into sin, so it was right that they should lead in painful repentance.

The chapter ends poignantly, by noting that some of the transgressors *"had wives by whom they had children"* (v. 44). Such a simple phrase undoubtedly covers a magnitude of mourning, as men sent away their beloved, albeit foreign wives and children. Indeed, restoration can be painful!

REFLECTIONS ON EZRA 9:1–10:44

Our Response to this Passage

Ezra 9–10 is a notoriously difficult Bible passage that upsets our emotional instincts. Admittedly intermarriage between Jews and pagans was wrong, but was it really necessary for families to be broken up? Did fathers have to send away their children forever? Did restoration really need to be this painful?

Then, too, the events of Ezra 10 seem to contradict our biblical and theological commitment to the sanctity of marriage. Through the prophet Malachi, who prophesied around the time of Ezra, God said: "For I hate divorce, . . . and covering one's garment with violence. . . . So take heed to yourselves and do not be faithless" (Mal. 2:16, NRSV). Even though the people had broken God's law by marrying foreign wives, was it right for them to divorce these wives? Did two wrongs make a right?

Our response to this passage depends upon a crucial distinction between *descriptive* and *prescriptive* passages of the Bible. Descriptive passages tell us what happened while prescriptive passages tell us how we should live. For example, 2 Samuel 11 describes David's adultery with Bathsheba. The fact that a great biblical character committed adultery does not mean that we should do likewise. In contrast, Exodus 20 provides a prescriptive commandment regarding adultery: "You shall not commit adultery" (Exod. 20:14). This prescribes behavior—it tells us how we should live. In fact, the command in Exodus helps us to know that David's example should not be emulated.

Like the example of David, Ezra 10 is descriptive. It tells us what God's people did in their struggle for renewal and righteousness. It informs us what Ezra believed to be God's will: divorcing pagan wives (v. 11). Yet a commitment to biblical authority does not compel us to agree with Ezra. Nowhere does God actually speak in Ezra 10, telling us through a prophet whether Ezra and the people correctly understood God's will or not.

It is important to understand this point because some people defend divorce on the basis of this very passage in Ezra 10. Their argument runs: "The men of Israel divorced their wives because they never should have been married in the first place. So, whenever a marriage should not have happened, divorce is acceptable." This argument confuses the descriptive and prescriptive aspects of the Scriptures. (It also wrenches an event out of its historical context.) At most Ezra 10 shows us that in an extreme instance God's people believed that divorce was correct. In no way does the passage indicate that God blesses divorce.

Was Ezra correct? Did God in fact approve of divorce for the inter-married men of Judah and Benjamin? Here we are caught on the horns of a dilemma. We know that the men married contrary to God's revealed will, and we know that their actions placed the holiness of Israel at risk. We also know that they should never have married pagan wives, but, on the other hand, we know that God hates divorce. Centuries later Jesus confirmed that God never commanded men to divorce their wives. He only regulated divorce because of the hardness of the human heart (Mark 10:1–12).

Was Ezra correct? Honestly, I do not know. Did God hate the continuation of pagan marriages even more than breaking them up? I am not sure. This situation reminds me of a pastoral crisis I faced recently in my ministry. A woman who came to me for counseling was the victim of extreme verbal and physical abuse. Her husband would get drunk and then beat her, often quite severely. He was completely unrepentant and uninterested in any sort of counseling. This woman asked me simply: "As a Christian, what should I do? Am I ever permitted to divorce my husband?" I had absolutely no hesitation in encouraging the woman to get away from her husband immediately, to move into a "safe-house" for battered women. But I was still plagued with the question: If restoration of the marriage never happens, and if her husband never changes, will God sanction her divorce? Questions such as these are difficult and perplexing, especially when the Scriptures do not address the case of spouse abuse directly.

Facing Tough Issues Together

The Bible realistically portrays people struggling for answers, sometimes finding and sometimes failing to find God's will. I can relate to this process. Can you? Ezra 10 provides a helpful example for those of us who confront difficult ethical issues. I am not referring to it's conclusion, but, rather, to the process revealed in the chapter.

Notice that although Ezra alone was authorized by the King to enforce the Law of God, the scribe-priest chose a different course of action in chapter 10. He did not unilaterally consider the problem, decide how to solve it, and compel the people to obey. Although he could have chosen this course of action, he opted instead for a far more participatory process.

First of all, he drew other people into his mourning over national sin. His example of mourning encouraged widespread confession and bitter tears of repentance. Second, he allowed others to participate in the decision-making process. Shechaniah actually proposed the solution (vv. 2–4), not Ezra. This prompted group ownership of the proposal (v. 5). Then, when the plan stumbled over practical difficulties, Ezra allowed the people to suggest a strategy for implementation of its details (vv. 13–14). Thus, although Ezra had the authority to work independently, he chose to draw others into all facets of the problem-solving process. He and his fellow Jews faced the tough issue of intermarriage together.

As Christians, we are the Body of Christ together. Certain members of the Body are placed in positions of special authority within the Church. But I believe that too often these members find themselves making tough decisions alone. People look to me, as their pastor, for answers that I cannot always provide. Nor should I even try to do so by myself in many cases. Although I do not shirk my authority to teach God's truth, I believe that corporate decision-making almost always leads to better decisions, particularly when the issues at hand are complex.

I developed this commitment during my years on the staff at Hollywood Presbyterian Church. Although the pastor, Lloyd Ogilive, guided the process of discernment, the staff and the elders together labored over difficult issues. For example, in the late 1980's we faced the tough issue of AIDS. Many of those in our city were HIV positive and desperately in need of care, support, and God's love. Crucial questions had to be answered. How should we reach out to them? How would our ministry to persons with AIDS mesh with our commitment to biblical morality?

For many months the pastors and elders wrestled with these issues. We studied factual data and biblical passages. We prayed. We debated. In the end, we unanimously affirmed a statement that emphasized our commitment to biblical truth and biblical love. And in the years since then, literally hundreds of men and women have received God's love and grace through the HIV-positive support group. I firmly believe that our process of corporate discernment led to a position that was far stronger than it would have been if any one of us had worked alone.

Individual Christians and Christian communities alike will face excruciatingly difficult moral choices. In so many of these situations, we who lead are responsible for the process of discernment. I believe that Ezra models a participatory process that we can all imitate to great benefit.

Desire for Righteousness

Another facet of Ezra 10 that deserves our careful consideration is the people's hunger for righteousness. Whether or not we agree with their solution, we see in Ezra, Shechaniah, and the others a heartfelt desire to do what is right and to make what is wrong, right. We also see how costly and difficult restitution can be.

Confession and forgiveness may happen in a moment. This is certainly true in our relationship with God, and is often true in human relationships as well. But complete healing and restoration may take considerable time and effort. An example is my relationship with my younger sister, Julie. One of my best friends, she and I share a deep love and mutual respect. But things have not always been good between us, for as an early adolescent I teased Julie mercilessly. Some of my sarcastic barbs made deep puncture wounds in her self-esteem. Years later, I recognized the wrongness of my former ways, and I apologized to Julie. She forgave me, but it required several years for our relationship to be completely restored. I am thankful, however, that God gave both of us the desire to bring restitution to this relationship.

How easily we give up on righteousness! With things in our world so chaotic, with brokenness and evil everywhere around us, it is easy to surrender any hope of seeing God's justice or healing. That seemed to be Ezra's conclusion at the end of chapter 9, but Shechaniah's hopefulness and zeal for righteousness made a difference, not only in Ezra, but in the nation. Oh that we would all become like Shechaniah in our willingness to stick our necks out for what is right!

Hope That Will Not Disappoint Us

Sometimes, however, in our zeal for righteousness we miscontrue God's leading no matter how honorable our intentions may be. Shechaniah illustrates this sort of well-intentioned mistake. Notice that after having recognized Israel's sin, he said, "Yet now there is hope in Israel in spite of this. Now therefore, let *us* make a covenant with our God to put away all these wives . . ." (vv. 2–3, emphasis added). Shechaniah placed his hope, not in God's mercy or covenant love, but in Israel's ability to make a covenant with God. He seemed to imply that the people could make a deal with God so he would not wipe them out.

I can empathize with Shechaniah's desire to strike a bargain with God, as I expect you can. For no matter how much we claim to believe in God's grace, most of us ultimately believe that our behavior can make God love us more. We place our hope in our ability to make things right. Then, when our hopes fail, we wonder what went wrong.

How much better it would have been for Shechaniah and for Israel if they had remembered the Psalms:

> Why are you cast down, O my soul?
> And why are you disquieted within me?
> *Hope in God,* for I shall yet praise Him
> For the help of His countenance.
>
>

Psalm 42:5 (emphasis added)

> By awesome deeds you answer us with deliverance,
> O God of our salvation;
> *you are the hope of all the ends of the earth*
> and of the farthest seas.
>
>

Psalm 65:5 NRSV (emphasis added)

> Happy is he who has the God of Jacob for his help,
> Whose hope is in the LORD his God.
>
>

Psalm 146:5

As Christians, we continue to affirm that true hope lies not in our ability to do anything but in God's power at work in us. So we read:

> Now may the *God of hope* fill you with all joy and peace in believing, that you may *abound in hope by the power of the Holy Spirit.*
>
>

Romans 15:1 (emphasis added)

> Now *hope does not disappoint, because the love of God has been poured out in our hearts by the Holy Spirit* who was given to us. For when

we were still without strength, in due time Christ died for the un-
godly.

Romans 5:5–6 (emphasis added)

Because we hope in God, not ourselves, and because the Holy
Spirit gives us true hope, we confront difficult issues from a perspective not shared by Shechaniah or Ezra. For example, the apostle
Paul faced a situation in Corinth where some Christians were divorcing their non-Christian spouses. (Perhaps they had read Ezra
10 too prescriptively!) He could have counseled these Christians to
separate from their pagan mates in order to preserve their personal
holiness, but Paul's Christian hope led him in another direction altogether:

> But to the rest I, not the Lord, say: If any brother has a wife who
> does not believe, and she is willing to live with him, let him not
> divorce her. And a woman who has a husband who does not be-
> lieve, if he is willing to live with her, let her not divorce him. For
> *the unbelieving husband is sanctified by the wife, and the unbelieving
> wife is sanctified by the husband;* otherwise your children would be
> unclean, but now they are holy. But if the unbeliever departs, let
> him depart; a brother or a sister is not under bondage in such
> cases. But God has called us to peace. *For how do you know, O wife,
> whether you will save your husband? Or how do you know, O husband,
> whether you will save your wife?*
>
> *1 Corinthians 7:12–15 (emphasis added)*

Whereas the Jews in Ezra's time feared that the pagan spouse would
ruin the holiness of the godly spouse, Paul saw things the other way
around. The inclusiveness of Christ had given him a new perspective.
Like Paul, we too hope for the salvation of the unbelieving spouse;
we do not encourage divorce of that spouse.

Such a hope, however, must rest in God alone. When I counsel
with men and women whose spouses do not know Christ, I hear of
their frustration, their desperation, and their years of quiet prayers.
They no longer hope in their own powers of persuasion or manipulation, yet they do continue to hope for their spouses' conversions. This
hope comes from the Holy Spirit and is dependent upon God alone.
This, indeed, is the only hope that will never let us down:

Blessed be the God and Father of our Lord Jesus Christ, who according to His abundant mercy has begotten us again to a living hope through the resurrection of Jesus Christ from the dead.

1 Peter 1:3

NOTES

1. Williamson, *Ezra, Nehemiah,* p. 132.
2. Brown, Driver, and Briggs, *Lexicon,* s.v. "*šāmēm.*"
3. Williamson, *Ezra, Nehemiah,* p. 132–33.
4. Williamson, *Ezra, Nehemiah,* p. 133.
5. Brown, Driver, and Briggs, *Lexicon,* s.v. "*taᶜănît.*"
6. Brown, Driver, and Briggs, *Lexicon,* s.v. "*yātēd.*"
7. Williamson, *Ezra, Nehemiah,* pp. 136–37.
8. Brown, Driver, and Briggs, *Lexicon,* s.v. "*māᶜal.*"
9. Brockington, *Ezra, Nehemiah, and Esther,* p. 92. Williamson suggests that the unusual verb might imply a discounting of the marriages as less than genuine (p. 150).
10. Williamson, *Ezra, Nehemiah,* pp. 151–54.

Restoration of the Wall Through Nehemiah

Nehemiah 1:1–7:73

The book of Ezra-Nehemiah continues now with a new focus upon the work of Nehemiah. Ezra came to Jerusalem in the seventh year of King Artaxerxes (Ezra 7:7), so, if as we suppose, this refers to Artaxerxes I, then Ezra began his work in 458 B.C. Nehemiah 2:1 dates the beginning of Nehemiah's effort in Jerusalem to the twentieth year of Artaxerxes I, or 445 B.C.—thirteen years after Ezra.

The overall structure of Ezra-Nehemiah moves from physical restoration (of the Temple), to covenantal restoration (through Ezra), back to physical restoration (of the wall), and finally to covenantal restoration (through Ezra and Nehemiah). The first seven chapters of Nehemiah focus on the second phase of physical restoration: rebuilding the wall of Jerusalem. Most of this section reproduces an autobiographical account written by Nehemiah in his memoirs. The editor of Ezra-Nehemiah appears to have utilized this source with particular fidelity.

We have seen an example of restoration leadership in Ezra. Now we observe a new leader with a unique approach to leadership. Whereas Ezra was primarily a priest and a scholar, Nehemiah is a man of the king's court—a leader with political sophistication who has lived at the right hand of power.

CHAPTER TEN

Introduction to Nehemiah

Nehemiah 1:1–11

A Proper Introduction

Often when I am introduced before giving a message, the group will hear a gracious summary of my accomplishments and responsibilities. I tend to feel not only embarrassed but also aware that such an introduction misses who I really am as a person. While working at Hollywood Presbyterian Church, however, I was often introduced by people who knew me all too well. Once, before speaking at a Christmas luncheon, a woman named Eugenia introduced me to the gathering with the usual resume. Then she added an unexpected line: "But let me tell you what really matters. When Mark was a boy, I caught him skipping church and hiding in the church storeroom. So don't be fooled by all this other stuff. Now, here's our speaker for today, Mark Roberts." Knowing the love and good humor with which Eugenia told the truth about me, I felt properly introduced—for once.

If you are like me you probably find it particularly awkward to introduce youself. People say, "Oh, just tell us a little bit about yourself." But what should you say? How can you communicate who you are? Usually I just give a few facts, in the hope that my true identity will emerge as a relationship unfolds.

Speaking of introductions, Nehemiah 1 introduces us to the person, Nehemiah. In fact, it reproduces Nehemiah's self-introduction, which is the beginning (perhaps) of what scholars call the "Nehemiah Memoir."[1] The book of Nehemiah contains extensive portions of this memoir, an autobiographical account of Nehemiah's life. Chapter 1 not only gives us facts about the man, but more importantly, it reveals his fundamental values and character as a leader.

DIRE REPORT AND DEEP RESPONSE (1:1–4)

1:1 The words of Nehemiah the son of Hachaliah. It came to pass in the month of Chislev, in the twentieth year, as I was in Shushan the citadel,

2 that Hanani one of my brethren came with men from Judah; and I asked them concerning the Jews who had escaped, who had survived the captivity, and concerning Jerusalem.

3 And they said to me, "The survivors who are left from the captivity in the province are there in great distress and reproach. The wall of Jerusalem is also broken down, and its gates are burned with fire."

4 So it was, when I heard these words, that I sat down and wept, and mourned for many days; I was fasting and praying before the God of heaven.

Nehemiah 1:1–4

Verse 1 clarifies the source of the writing. We are about to read *"The words of Nehemiah the son of Hachaliah."* The name "Nehemiah" means "the LORD comforts." The verse locates Nehemiah in both time and place, though with some ambiguity. *"Sushan the citadel,"* better known as Susa, was the winter lodging for Persian kings (it is located in modern Iran, not far from the Iraqi border). But exactly when was *"the twentieth year"*? This becomes clearer in 2:1, where the text refers to "the twentieth year of King Artaxerxes." But ancient Persia had three kings named Artaxerxes (Artaxerxes I, II, and III). So which one reigned during the life of Nehemiah? The answer comes by way of an ancient letter that identifies parties mentioned later by Nehemiah. Based on this letter, scholars conclude that he lived during the reign of Artaxerxes I.[2] Since this king ruled from 465 to 423 B.C., we conclude that Nehemiah's work began in 445 B.C. *"Chislev"* is a postexilic name for a month equivalent to our late November and early December.[3]

While Nehemiah was in Shushan, one of his *"brethren"* (a literal brother or another relative) named *"Hanani"* arrived with others from Judah (v. 2). Nehemiah inquired of them about the Jews living in Judah[4] *"and concerning Jerusalem."* In response, he was given a dire report that had two parts. First, *"the survivors . . . are there in great distress and reproach."* From chapter 5 we know that Judah faced desperate economic times because of famine in the land (5:2–5). As a result, many people had been forced to sell themselves or their children into slavery. It appeared that the nation was ripping apart at the seams. Moreover, those leaders who later would be so ready to challenge Nehemiah (2:19; 4:2–3) held pathetic little Judah in reproach. The second aspect of the dire report concerned the *"wall of Jerusalem,"* which *"is also broken down, and its gates are burned with fire"* (v. 3).

Nehemiah responded to the report by sitting down and weeping, mourning *"for many days"* (v. 4). Commentators wonder about this strong reaction to the situation in Judah. Did Nehemiah actually not know about the broken walls and the distressed society? After all, Babylon had destroyed the walls in 587 B.C., 142 years before Hanani's report. Why did Nehemiah react so profoundly? Kidner proposes that a subsequent destruction of the walls is the basis of this report (see Ezra 4:7–23).[5] Still another possibility suggests itself as well. Perhaps Nehemiah heard old news from his Judean relatives, yet, for some reason, this time his heart was deeply moved by what he had known for years. Was God preparing Nehemiah for service by opening his heart in a new way?

I see a similar experience in many Christians today who know about the pain in the world, but who live in a state of numbness. Then, one day, old news pierces their hearts. They mourn over starving children in Somalia, or millions of abortions in America. Perhaps Nehemiah heard something new from Hanani and the others, but it may also have been that God prepared him to hear the "old" news in a new way.

Not only did Nehemiah mourn and weep, he also fasted and prayed to God. Verse 4 serves as a preface to the prayer that completes the remainder of Nehemiah 1.

NEHEMIAH'S PRAYER (1:5–11)

5 And I said: "I pray, LORD God of heaven, O great and awesome God, You who keep Your covenant and mercy with those who love You and observe Your commandments,

6 please let Your ear be attentive and Your eyes open, that You may hear the prayer of Your servant

which I pray before You now, day and night, for the
children of Israel Your servants, and confess the sins
of the children of Israel which we have sinned against
You. Both my father's house and I have sinned.

7 We have acted very corruptly against You, and
have not kept the commandments, the statutes, nor
the ordinances which You commanded Your servant
Moses.

8 Remember, I pray, the word that You
commanded Your servant Moses, saying, 'If you are
unfaithful, I will scatter you among the nations;

9 but if you return to Me, and keep My
commandments and do them, though some of you
were cast out to the farthest part of the heavens, yet I
will gather them from there, and bring them to the
place which I have chosen as a dwelling for My
name.'

10 Now these are Your servants and Your people,
whom You have redeemed by Your great power, and
by Your strong hand.

11 O Lord, I pray, please let Your ear be attentive
to the prayer of Your servant, and to the prayer of
Your servants who desire to fear Your name; and let
Your servant prosper this day, I pray, and grant him
mercy in the sight of this man." For I was the king's
cupbearer.

Nehemiah 1:5–11

Since Nehemiah prayed for an extended period of time, what we
read in these verses is actually a summary of his lengthy intercession.
The prayer begins with an acknowledgement of God's nature as a
"great and awesome God" (v. 5). Nehemiah professed and submitted to
God's sovereignty, in light of which he was only a *"servant"* (vv. 6, 11).

Next, Nehemiah referred to God as *"You who keep Your covenant
and mercy with those who love You and observe Your commandments"* (v.
5). "Mercy" is a translation of the Hebrew term *hesed*. It connotes
God's faithfulness within the covenant, as the setting here makes
clear.[6] Nehemiah depended upon God's covenant faithfulness in his
supplication of verse 11.

As God's *"servant,"* who submitted to God's sovereign rule,
Nehemiah interceded for the people and confessed their sins (v. 6).

He did so, however, not as an innocent critic, but as one who also had dirty hands. He freely admitted: *"Both my father's house and I have sinned."* As a leader, Nehemiah did not exalt himself above the people, nor did he deny his own wrongdoings. The fact is, he confessed with blunt honesty: *"We have acted very corruptly against You."* He placed no "positive spin" upon the facts, one that would minimize Israel's failure. Already we perceive that Nehemiah understood that God's restoration would come to the people, not because they deserved it, but because of God's faithfulness.

In verses 8 and 9 he asks God to remember the covenant promise of national restoration by utilizing a pastiche of biblical texts that come primarily from Leviticus and Deuteronomy (Lev. 26:33; Deut. 12:5; 30:1–5). Given the conditional nature of God's promise in 1:8–9, one would expect the following verse to claim that the people had returned to God and had kept his commandments. But Nehemiah had already confessed to the contrary. Verse 10 emphasizes *God's* relationship with Israel and *God's* former acts of redemption. Again, the request in verse 11 depends not upon the people's faithfulness but upon God's. Whereas they had broken the covenant; God's *ḥesed* exceeded all human failure.

The final verse of the prayer emphasizes Nehemiah's status as God's *"servant."* This not only reiterates God's sovereignty, but also suggests that although Nehemiah served a human king, in reality, God was his one true Master. The prayer ends with a surprising supplication: *"and let Your servant prosper this day, I pray, and grant him mercy in the sight of this man"* (v. 11). The Hebrew word translated as "mercy" here is not *ḥesed*, but a different word meaning "compassion, motherly feeling."[7] Nehemiah asked for a nurturing compassion on the basis of God's covenant faithfulness as he came before "this man." But who is "this man"? The following sentence explains: *"For I was the king's cupbearer." "In the sight of this man"* adds dramatic movement to the narrative, giving the impression that Nehemiah is about to enter the courtroom of the king. The phrase propels us into the next chapter to find out what happens in the royal throne room.

As *"cupbearer to the king,"* Nehemiah held a position of honor and power. His proximity to the king gave him insight into the king's ways as well as into the affairs of the empire. The cupbearer was not merely the one who tested the king's drink to insure its safety, he also served as the king's adviser and chief supporter. Thus, as cupbearer to the king, Nehemiah enjoyed a position of luxury and authority. And given the events of chapter 2, we may conclude that Artaxerxes had a special interest in and appreciation for this young assistant.[8]

REFLECTIONS ON NEHEMIAH 1:1–11

In this chapter Nehemiah introduces himself, though he does so in a surprising manner. His position as cupbearer to the king, an honor that would earn immediate respect, does not appear until the last verse. Nehemiah did not begin by relating facts that would impress his readers, rather, he told a story that shows more deeply who he was; it reveals the fundamental character of the man and the bedrock of his leadership.

The Vulnerable Heart of a Leader

Once we understand Nehemiah's exalted status within the Persian empire, and learn, in Pfeiffer's expression, that he "was a successful man of action,"[9] we marvel at his self-introduction. In our first glimpse of Nehemiah we find him sitting down and crying for many days (v. 4)—hardly the picture of a dynamic leader! All of his actions, however, come out of his heart: a vulnerable heart, a heart able to feel pain.

As we consider other biblical leaders, Nehemiah's openness to grief does not seem surprising. Both David and Jesus wept openly (1 Sam. 30:4; 2 Sam. 15:30; Luke 19:41; John 11:35; Heb. 5:7), and Paul forthrightly shared his despair and brokenness (2 Cor. 1:8–11). Scripture shows that godly leaders feel pain. Like the Suffering Servant foretold in Isaiah, they are men and women of sorrow who are acquainted with grief (Isa. 53:3). We who lead in God's kingdom might do well to repeat the prayer of Bob Pierce, founder of World Vision: "May my heart be broken by the things that break the heart of God." If we are open to feeling God's heart for the world and its hurting people, then we will be leaders who grieve.

For many of us, the notion of leadership that includes sadness runs counter to our cultural and family values. I was raised to believe that if my sister was sad it was my job to "cheer her up." Implicitly, I learned that sadness was bad, a sorry state of heart to be avoided. At one point in my life, the thought of weeping like Nehemiah would have sent a shudder of fear down my spine. Rather, I would have felt it my duty to cheer him up!

Admittedly, I still tend to look upon the bright side. But I have discovered how God can use sadness to direct and inspire my ministry. In the Winter of 1990, I was in the midst of considering a possible move from Hollywood to Irvine. Over a period of months I sought the Lord for guidance. Should I become Pastor of Irvine Presbyterian Church if the position was offered to me? During this time, my wife and I vacationed on the California coast, and on Sunday morning we visited a small Presbyterian church. Prior to entering the service, we specifically asked the Lord to speak to our hearts about a possible move to Irvine.

Well, our prayers seemed to fall upon deaf ears. The service was dreary, the worship insipid, and the preaching weak. Not only did God fail to speak to us in an inspiring way, but we left feeling discouraged—and very sad. The feelings of sadness continued for several hours, and, bewildered, I began to pray: "Lord, why am I so sad?" Gradually I began to realize how much it grieved my heart that Christians had gathered for worship but ended up wasting their time. I sensed how much I valued responsible preaching of God's truth, and how distressed I was by a pastor whom, I felt, had cheated his congregation. As the locus of my sadness became clearer, I realized behind the feelings some growing convictions about my pastoral call. I sensed more than ever God's call to me to facilitate genuine worship, to preach the gospel, and to make sure that Sunday morning is worth every minute invested in it. I realized that God was shifting my focus of vision—from the educational ministry of one church to the ministry of preaching and worship in another. He was preparing me for a new church! And all of these discoveries came through inexplicable feelings of sadness.

However, let me clarify that in commending a vulnerability that allows for sadness, I do not intend to sanctify unhappiness. Many Christians walk around with dour faces, not because they feel the broken heart of God, but because they are mired in self-pity. The fact that someone cries for days at a time does not guarantee his or her fitness for ministry! My intent is rather to challenge popular Christianity, which emphasizes joy to such an extent that a genuine, Spirit-filled sadness has no place in the Christian life. For all Christians, and especially for leaders open to the heart of God, there is indeed "a time to weep, and a time to laugh; a time to mourn, and a time to dance" (Eccl. 3:4).

Leadership Built on a Foundation of Prayer

Notice in this passage what Nehemiah did with his grief. He did not try to forget it, nor did he simply pine away; rather, he fasted and prayed. He took his grief before God. Prayer is the place to process God's work in our hearts; it is where we discover and clarify God's call upon our lives. Prayer provides the only sure foundation for our lives and our leadership.

The Psalms teach us to grieve through prayer. Consider for example Psalm 61:1–2:

> Hear my cry, O God;
> Attend to my prayer.
> From the ends of the earth I will cry to You,
> When my heart is overwhelmed;
> Lead me to the rock that is higher than I.

But, of course, we should pray in all situations, not only in times of grief.

The purpose statement of Irvine Presbyterian Church includes a key phrase that mirrors Nehemiah's leadership. Our church is "built on a foundation of prayer." My predecessor as pastor, Ben Patterson, helped prayer to permeate every area of the church, especially its leadership structures. The Board of Elders spends extended times in prayer twice a month before official meetings; I meet each Friday morning for prayer with the elders; and all leadership groups within the church are expected to devote considerable time to prayer.

Every now and then, I read statistics about how infrequently Christian leaders in America pray. Admittedly, I can certainly relate to the difficulty of finding quality time to spend with the Lord. As a leader, my life is inundated with meetings, planning sessions, staff supervision, sermon preparations, and so on; but I must make time for prayer! The Scriptures call us again and again to leadership that is built upon a foundation of prayer. If the example of Nehemiah is not compelling enough, we need only to remember Jesus. The sinless Son of God often spent whole nights in prayer. Did that have something to do with his ability to do exactly what the Father required of him? Could that explain the power and authority with which he ministered?

Following the example of Nehemiah, we who lead should emphasize three practices in our personal prayers. First, *we should remember and confess who is in charge.* Nehemiah acknowledged God's greatness and sovereignty in contrast to himself—a mere servant. Godly leaders entrusted with authority must continually submit their agendas and egos to God, lest their own leadership become an idol. A certain sign of an impoverished prayer life is a Christian leader with an overblown ego.

Second, *the example of Nehemiah reminds us to ask God to bless our ministries.* This seems too obvious to mention, but that is precisely the point. Sometimes, in the hustle and bustle to get things done, we forget to ask for God's blessing and power. How much more God would do for us and through us if only we would ask!

Third, *the case of Nehemiah encourages us to seek God's guidance in prayer.* Although not stated specifically, we can presume that between Hanani's report to Nehemiah and his audience before the king, Nehemiah received direction from God about his ministry. When he first heard about Jerusalem, Nehemiah simply mourned and prayed; but as he prayed, he sensed God's call. We will see in chapter 2 that he also worked out the details of a plan to restore Jerusalem. Prayer provided the workshop in which God honed Nehemiah's call and and helped him to develop a strategy for "ministry."

As a pastor I have my prayer list—the matters of intercession that I bring to the Lord's attention. But I find my prayer life increasingly taken up with listening and asking questions rather than presumptuously telling God what I would like for him to do. "What should I preach about, Lord? What do you want to say through this passage? How can I help a certain staff member to work more effectively? Should we move ahead in our building plans now, or should we wait?" Now I may not hear God's voice audibly, but as I seek the Lord, as I ask my questions, God speaks within my heart and moves my heart and mind. Then I begin to feel a bit of his heart.

Since prayer lays a sure foundation under Christian leadership, we who lead in God's church and who communicate God's truth must pray. Undoubtedly you know people who seem to pray constantly. These "prayer warriors" love to pray and do so faithfully. But if you are like me and you struggle to build a strong base of prayer, let me make a two practical suggestions.

First, *find and utilize your best time and place for prayer*. I used to think that truly godly people prayed only at the crack of dawn while kneeling beside their beds. I had visions of rolling out of bed while it was still dark and falling on my knees for an extended session with God. Unfortunately, I have never been a morning person, and my bedroom is full of distractions and temptations, particularly an inviting bed! For years my prayer life suffered under the burden of my personal tendencies. Finally, some years ago, I decided to stop fighting with myself. I began to pray at the time and in the place that worked best for me. As it turned out, I prayed with greatest effectiveness when I was walking in a quiet place. So I started to plan such times into my personal calendar. As a result, the quantity and quality of my prayer times improved dramatically!

Second, *pray with other people*. To be sure, we all need private sessions of prayer, but in seasons of spiritual dryness or unusual busyness we tend to dilute our time with the Lord. For me, having regular prayer times with other people guarantees a consistency of prayer time. Then from these experiences of corporate prayer I receive energy to reestablish my own communication with God.

NOTES

1. For a recent discussion of this memoir, see H.G. M. Williamson, *Ezra and Nehemiah*, Old Testament Guides (Sheffield, England: JSOT Press, 1987), pp. 15–19.

2. Jews in Elephantine, a city in upper Egypt, wrote a letter to Bagaos, governor of Judah, in 407 B.C. In this letter they mention "Delaiah and Shelemiah, the sons of Sanballat the governor of Samaria." Sanballat figures prominently in the story of Nehemiah (for example, 2:19). Therefore, Sanballat himself ruled earlier than 407 B.C. during the reign of Artaxerxes I. For the letter, see J. B. Pritchard, ed., *The Ancient Near East: An Anthology of Texts and Pictures*, 2 vols., (Princeton: Princeton University Press, 1958), 1:279–81.

3. A helpful chart of ancient months may be found in *The Illustrated Bible Dictionary*, 3 vols. (Leicester, England: InterVarsity, 1980), 1:223.

4. The meaning of the phrase, "the Jews who had escaped, who had survived the captivity," is hard to pin down, but, as 1:3 shows, Nehemiah is asking about Jews living in Judah.

5. Kidner, *Ezra and Nehemiah*, p. 78.

6. See also R. L. Harris, *"hesed,"* *TWOT* (Chicago: Moody, 1980); and Sakenfeld, "Love," *ABD* (New York: Doubleday, 1992).

7. The term *raḥămîm* is based upon the word *reḥem*, which means "womb." Brown, Driver, and Briggs, *Lexicon*, s.v. *"reḥem, raḥămîm."*

8. For additional information on Nehemiah as cupbearer, see R. North, "Nehemiah," *ABD* (New York: Doubleday, 1992). On the mistaken notion that a cupbearer must have been a eunuch, see E. M. Yamauchi, "Was Nehemiah the Cupbearer a Eunuch?" *Zeitschrift für die alttestamentliche Wissenschaft* 92 (1980): 132–142.

9. R. H. Pfieffer, "Nehemiah," *IDB* (Nashville: Abingdon, 1962).

CHAPTER ELEVEN

Nehemiah Prepares to Rebuild

Nehemiah 2:1–20

SPIRITUAL OR PRAGMATIC LEADERSHIP

I have occasionally observed a familiar conflict between Christian leaders. It often happens in conversations about church budgets. On the one side are the "visionaries," who urge us to trust God for big things and not to be so cautious; on the other side are the "pragmatists," who argue for the wisdom of fiscal prudence. "Faith budgets," for these bottom-line thinkers, represent an ill-advised testing of God—not faithful stewardship. But visionaries challenge us "to step out of the boat in faith," and not to limit what God can do.

Although this kind of disagreement can happen in an attitude of love and mutual respect, it represents a divergence in leadership values and practices. Some leaders major in spiritual disciplines of prayer and Bible study, while others exercise practical wisdom and down-to-earth basics. Only a few, in my experience, balance the two sides of leadership: the spiritual and the pragmatic.

Nehemiah first introduces himself as a spiritual leader whose vulnerable heart breaks over the dire state of God's people. Through many tears he shares his heart with God in extended periods of intense prayer. If we only read Nehemiah 1, we might be tempted to classify Nehemiah among the visionaries whose minds are fixed on the things above, not on the practicalities of daily living. But the second chapter shows a different side of Nehemiah. Here he plays out a careful strategy in preparation for rebuilding the wall of Jerusalem. Nehemiah's example in this chapter helps to resolve the debate between those who advocate visionary leadership and those who prefer pragmatism.

NEHEMIAH SECURES THE KING'S BLESSING (2:1–8)

2:1 And it came to pass in the month of Nisan, in the twentieth year of King Artaxerxes, when wine was before him, that I took the wine and gave it to the king. Now I had never been sad in his presence before.

2 Therefore the king said to me, "Why is your face sad, since you are not sick? This is nothing but sorrow of heart." So I became dreadfully afraid,

3 and said to the king, "May the king live forever! Why should my face not be sad, when the city, the place of my fathers' tombs, lies waste, and its gates are burned with fire?"

4 Then the king said to me, "What do you request?" So I prayed to the God of heaven.

5 And I said to the king, "If it pleases the king, and if your servant has found favor in your sight, I ask that you send me to Judah, to the city of my fathers' tombs, that I may rebuild it."

6 Then the king said to me (the queen also sitting beside him), "How long will your journey be? And when will you return?" So it pleased the king to send me; and I set him a time.

7 Furthermore I said to the king, "If it pleases the king, let letters be given to me for the governors of the region beyond the River, that they must permit me to pass through till I come to Judah,

8 and a letter to Asaph the keeper of the king's forest, that he must give me timber to make beams for the gates of the citadel which pertains to the temple, for the city wall, and for the house that I will occupy." And the king granted them to me according to the good hand of my God upon me.

Nehemiah 2:1–8

Nehemiah first heard about the appalling condition of Jerusalem in the month of Chislev (1:1), but verse 1 refers to the month of Nisan, four months later.[1] The scene opens with Nehemiah functioning in his official role as cupbearer to King Artaxerxes, but something is different now—Nehemiah reveals his sadness to the king for the first time. Although he had been mourning for the past four months, only now does Nehemiah let his feelings show upon his face. Why? Though we cannot know for sure, I suspect that this open expression of sadness was the first step in Nehemiah's strategy to gain the king's support. That is, while a servant would never initiate the personal discussion that was about to occur, by appearing unhappy, Nehemiah was able to influence the king to ask what was wrong, thus gaining for himself a point of entry to make a special request of the king.

Without doubt, this strategy entailed risk. When the king asked his cup bearer why he was sad, Nehemiah became *"dreadfully afraid"* (v. 2). Knowing that he was about to ask for an unusual favor, he felt understandably nervous. This reminds me of a friend of mine who wanted to go on a short-term mission trip, but was worried that her boss would not give her the time off. Before asking for this favor, she felt exceedingly nervous, if not quite "dreadfully afraid." But I am sure that Nehemiah found himself in a much more delicate position than my friend, for if he displeased the king he could lose more than his job—his very life was on the line!

With so much at stake, Nehemiah wisely began with the ancient equivalent of "Long live the King!" (v. 3). He then explained his sadness in a most clever way: *"Why should my face not be sad, when the city, the place of my fathers' tombs, lies waste, and its gates are burned with fire?"* (v. 3). Notice that he did not mention Jerusalem or Judah at this point, nor anything having to do with the religion of Israel; rather, he framed the problem in terms a Persian king would understand. Artaxerxes could certainly relate to grieving over the desecration of ancestral burying grounds.[2] His response, *"What do you request?"* (v. 4), shows the success of Nehemiah's careful rhetoric.

Before answering, Nehemiah offered a quick prayer. Although he had spent many days and nights praying for God's guidance and blessing, he added another, presumably short and silent, request. Most of us have sent up "quickie" prayers to God: as students facing a difficult exam, as drivers spotting police lights in our rear-view mirrors, or as employees about to ask for a special favor from the boss.

Then Nehemiah framed his question in a direct manner that still honored the king by saying: *"If it pleases the king, and if your servant has found favor in your sight"* (v. 5). Following this he added a bit more information: his fathers were buried in *"Judah,"* and he wanted permission to rebuild the city in that place.

173

Any competent leader would have considered the cost of this request. Artaxerxes, who happened to have his wife near him at the time, asked: *"How long will your journey be? And when will you return?"* (v. 6). He valued Nehemiah's service and wanted to know how long he expected to be gone. Apparently, Nehemiah had thought out the details of this request in advance, because he offered a satisfactory answer to the king, who decided to allow his cupbearer to go to Judah. Although he probably gave the king a much shorter timetable, as it turns out, Nehemiah spent twelve years in Judah. Although not stated in chapter 1, we can see now that Nehemiah utilized his extended season of mourning and prayer as a time to formulate specific plans.

After securing the king's basic support, Nehemiah moved ahead in his strategy to get everything he needed from Artaxerxes. First, he asked for letters from the king to *"the governors of the region beyond the River, that they must permit me to pass through till I come to Judah"* (v. 7). The Persians regarded everything west of the Euphrates to the Mediterranean Sea as a large region "beyond the River."[3] Nehemiah anticipated that the governors in that area might be less than enthusiastic about his project and might attempt to stop him. A letter from the king would insure his safe passage.

Furthermore, Nehemiah asked for lumber from the king's own forest (v. 8). The precise location of this forest, which must have been relatively close to Jerusalem, is unknown. In ancient times Israel was much more widely forested than it is today.[4] In his request for lumber Nehemiah mentioned for the first time his desire to rebuild *"the city wall,"* which could have been the most controversial aspect of his program, since a people who wished to rebel would need a walled city. In his expanding requests for help, Nehemiah reminds me of a junior-high girl who asks her father for a new skirt. She begins with the obvious: "Dad, I need a new skirt." After he grants permission, she ups the ante: "Dad, if I get the skirt, then I'll need a new blouse as well." Pretty soon Dad is paying for a whole new outfit — all because he said "yes" to a new skirt.

The king granted Nehemiah everything he requested. Although he had been exceptionally clever in his presentation to the king, Nehemiah gave credit not to himself, but *"to the good hand of my God upon me"* (v. 8). Even though he had utilized his personal resources, he nevertheless recognized the sovereign blessing of God.

FIRST ENCOUNTER WITH THE REGIONAL LEADERS (2:9–10)

9 Then I went to the governors in the region
beyond the River, and gave them the king's letters.
Now the king had sent captains of the army and
horsemen with me.
10 When Sanballat the Horonite and Tobiah the
Ammonite official heard of it, they were deeply
disturbed that a man had come to seek the well-being
of the children of Israel.

Nehemiah 2:9–10

In order to secure safe passage through the region beyond the River, Nehemiah gave the king's letters to the governors there. Now we learn that the king also sent a small military escort, including *"captains of the army and horsemen"* (v. 9). We do not know whether Nehemiah asked for this escort, or whether the king came up with the idea himself, but, at any rate, we do know that Nehemiah accepted the military support. This stands in striking contrast to the decision of Ezra not to seek an escort because he believed it would contradict his trust in God's protection (Ezra 8:22). Although Ezra and Nehemiah both led Israel into renewal, they led with different styles, if not with different theological convictions.

Verse 10 introduces us to two men who will appear frequently throughout the book of Nehemiah: *"Sanballat the Horonite and Tobiah the Ammonite official."* The term "Horonite" identifies Sanballat's place of origin, although scholars disagree on the precise location.[5] An ancient letter identifies him as the "governor of Samaria,"[6] who would have been authorized by the Persian king. The name "Tobiah" means "God is good" in Hebrew. This fact, as well as Tobiah's close connections within Jerusalem (6:18; 13:7), have led some commentators to identify him as a Jewish man who ruled over Ammon, the region immediately east of Judah.[7] Nehemiah's identification of Tobiah as "the Ammonite" probably denotes his ethnicity. He was an Ammonite, not a Jew. The NKJV uses the translation "official" for the Hebrew word ⁾*ebed*, which actually means "slave, servant."[8] According to Williamson, Nehemiah pictures Tobiah as a "junior colleague of Sanballat," using the word ⁾*ebed* ironically.[9]

Sanballat and Tobiah were *"deeply disturbed that a man had come to seek the well-being of the children of Israel"* (v. 10). Although this may have been true, we must remember that Nehemiah offered the perspective of a bitter opponent. Perhaps Sanballat and Tobiah were not so disturbed by help for Israel as by the threat Nehemiah posed to their own self-aggrandizement. And as we will see shortly, they were right to worry about Nehemiah's influence in Jerusalem.

Nehemiah's Secret Survey of the Wall (2:11–16)

11 So I came to Jerusalem and was there three days.

12 Then I arose in the night, I and a few men with me; I told no one what my God had put in my heart to do at Jerusalem; nor was there any animal with me, except the one on which I rode.

13 And I went out by night through the Valley Gate to the Serpent Well and the Refuse Gate, and viewed the walls of Jerusalem which were broken down and its gates which were burned with fire.

14 Then I went on to the Fountain Gate and to the King's Pool, but there was no room for the animal under me to pass.

15 So I went up in the night by the valley, and viewed the wall; then I turned back and entered by the Valley Gate, and so returned.

16 And the officials did not know where I had gone or what I had done; I had not yet told the Jews, the priests, the nobles, the officials, or the others who did the work.

Nehemiah 2:11–16

Shortly after Nehemiah arrived in Jerusalem, he set out on a secret mission to survey the broken wall. He took only *"a few men"* (v. 12), presumably those who could be trusted to keep quiet, but he did not even tell these men what he was planning to do. In order to maintain utmost secrecy, he took only one animal. Verses 13 through 15 describe Nehemiah's clandestine journey around a portion of the wall. He did not circle the entire city, but only the southern portion,[10] perhaps because he did not feel a need to see the whole wall in order to assess the job awaiting him. Notice how verse 16 reiterates the secrecy of the mission.

This short passage again reveals Nehemiah as a careful strategist with a shrewd sense of timing. He wanted to evaluate the scope of the job that awaited him, yet without drawing attention to himself or giving away his plans too early. Nothing in the passage suggests that Nehemiah would have abandoned the project if it had seemed too daunting. Rather, he waited for just the right time to announce his plans to the people of Judah. Moreover, he may have realized that by making a careful survey of the wall before gaining popular support, he would be ready to capitalize upon the people's initial enthusiasm.

This section of chapter 2 reminds me of the time my wife and I stealthily attended Irvine Presbyterian Church in the months before I was called to be pastor there. We wanted to experience worship and survey the facility as ordinary congregants without being identified as pastoral candidates. We managed to avoid being greeted or having to misrepresent our intentions. Indeed, we both felt very devious, like kids playing Mission Impossible. At that point in our consideration of the church, secrecy was necessary. The time was not yet right to reveal our true interests, but we, like Nehemiah, needed to survey the task at hand.

NEHEMIAH RALLIES THE TROOPS (2:17–18)

17 Then I said to them, "You see the distress that we are in, how Jerusalem lies waste, and its gates are burned with fire. Come and let us build the wall of Jerusalem, that we may no longer be a reproach."
18 And I told them of the hand of my God which had been good upon me, and also of the king's words that he had spoken to me. So they said, "Let us rise up and build." Then they set their hands to this good work.

Nehemiah 2:17–18

After appraising the condition of the wall, Nehemiah spoke to *"them,"* the Jews of Jerusalem and the surrounding region (v. 17). He stated the problem at hand and called upon the people to participate in the solution. Then he added two incentives for motivation. First, he suggested that by building the wall he and the Jews would *"no longer be a reproach"* (v. 17). People from the surrounding lands had laughed at the sorry state of Jerusalem and had taken advantage of the people there. A rebuilt wall would end their reproach. Second,

Nehemiah told the people *"of the hand of my God which had been good upon me, and also of the king's words"* (v. 18). Nehemiah assured the people that both God and the king were on their side. They could build with confidence because they had received support from the higher authorities. So the people agreed to build and began work on the project at once (v. 18). At this point, Nehemiah's secret survey of the work bore practical fruit.

This short passage shows Nehemiah as a successful motivator of people: he identified a problem and formulated a solution, he called the people to be involved in the solution, and he motivated them to act by addressing their concerns and interests.

FIRST CLASH WITH THE OPPONENTS (2:19–20)

> 19 But when Sanballat the Horonite, Tobiah the Ammonite official, and Geshem the Arab heard of it, they laughed at us and despised us, and said, "What is this thing that you are doing? Will you rebel against the king?"
> 20 So I answered them, and said to them, "The God of heaven Himself will prosper us; therefore we His servants will arise and build, but you have no heritage or right or memorial in Jerusalem."
>
> *Nehemiah 2:19–20*

Verse 19 introduces yet another adversary, *"Geshem the Arab."* "The Arab" identifies not only his ethnic background but also his position of leadership over certain Arab peoples.[11] At first Sanballat, Tobiah, and Geshem responded by laughing at the Jews. On the one hand, their laughter was meant to discourage the builders. On the other hand, it demonstrated how lightly they took Nehemiah's efforts at restoration. Things had been so bad in Judah and the wall had been so completely destroyed that anyone who attempted to bring restoration seemed like a fool. Furthermore, the question *"Will you rebel against the king?"* should be heard as sarcasm. It was unthinkable that the people of insignificant Judah would dare to plot rebellion against the massive Persian empire, or that they would dream of rebuilding the wall of Jerusalem.

Yet the laughter and derision did not quench Nehemiah's spirit. By declaring *"the God of Heaven Himself will prosper us,"* he was admitting that, indeed, the task was too large for mere human effort (v. 20); that was precisely why Nehemiah did not place his confidence in his leadership skills, but, rather, in God. He made it clear that the opponents were to have no part in the project, nor were they welcome in Jerusalem.

This passage, while summarizing Nehemiah's first clash with his opponents, also foreshadows the problems and difficulties to come. Unfortunately, Sanballat, Tobiah, and Geshem soon returned.

REFLECTIONS ON NEHEMIAH 2:1–20

As chapter 1 reveals the spiritual side of Nehemiah's leadership, so chapter 2 reveals his practical, clever side. Now the man of tears and prayer appears as a careful strategist: one who formulates just the right way to approach the king; who carefully appraises the demolished condition of the wall without telling anyone; who makes sure he is prepared to confront his regional opponents; and who finds the best way to persuade the people to support his project.

A Leader's Sense of Timing

Nehemiah was a master of timing. Recall how he waited until the appropriate moment to show his sadness to the king, how he did not mention the walls until well into his conversation with the king, and how he kept his plans secret until he was ready to promote popular support.

We who lead today, whether in church or in the world, must also consider the matter of timing. Just because God wants something done, does not mean that we should start it right now. Often God asks us to wait for his right time. It seems I have to learn this lesson the hard way, especially when my eagerness for renewal pushes me ahead of God's schedule. The headaches that result are teaching me to wait— to consider God's timing rather than my own feelings of impatience.

A Leader's Use of Rhetoric

Nehemiah also demonstrated a mastery of rhetoric. He spoke to the king not only with due respect but with an awareness of the king's own values. By a careful choice of words he gradually moved the king along in his support. When it was time to persuade the Jews to build, again Nehemiah evidenced an ability to motivate people by appealing to their concerns and desires.

I have written this commentary for *communicators* of God's truth. I assume that readers want to teach clearly and persuade effectively. Although the word "rhetoric" sometimes has a negative connotation in English, it deserves far better. Rhetoric is the ancient and honorable art of communication. Classical rhetoricians, such as Aristotle or Cicero, taught students to understand their audience and to speak in light of the audience's concerns. Today in the Christian world we find two extremes with regard to this rhetorical axiom. On the one hand, some preachers so wish to speak to secular people that they compromise the integrity of the gospel; on the other hand, some preachers disdain any effort to communicate effectively within our cultural idiom—they "simply teach God's word."

It seems to me that as Christian leaders, teachers, and preachers, we can no longer assume that our hearers will understand us nor that they will be inclined to listen to us. We must face the fact of our secularized culture: most Americans do not know the Bible—even if they are Christians—and most American do not seek to glorify God, even if they believe in his existence. If our attempt at communication assumes biblical literacy or a desire to glorify God, then we will fail in our efforts. While I do not advocate "chopping the gospel down to size," I do take seriously the need to speak in ways that encourage a secular audience to listen.

Let me give two brief examples. First, when I begin preaching, I start from the assumption that I must earn the right to be heard. While the vast majority of my listeners are faithful members of my church, I want visitors—especially non-Christians—to listen to what I will say. So I start my sermons with stories and illustrations, with tidbits from everyday life. I want people who do not know me to think: "Hey, he lives in my world. I can relate to him. I think I'll listen." Second, I find that humor works extremely well in this task. A funny story, especially one in which I play the fool, warms up even reticent listeners.

A Leader Gathers Necessary Information

Nehemiah also demonstrates that effective leadership requires adequate information. Although we are not privy to the actual process, by the time Nehemiah approached the king he had figured out how long it would take him to complete the project. He also knew the name of the person who oversaw the king's forest near Jerusalem. Then later, before he rallied the troops to build, Nehemiah surveyed the wall to determine exactly what needed to be done. He had gathered enough information about the job that when the people were ready he was prepared to move the project ahead without wasting time.

The church I pastor in Irvine just celebrated its seventeenth birthday. As a relatively young congregation, we have only begun to build the facilities that we need for a full-orbed ministry. For the past few years we have been on the verge of building a sanctuary since we worship now in our fellowship hall. Discerning God's timing has been a major concern of our Board of Elders. Recently we realized that, in addition to seeking the Lord in prayer, we needed to seek more practical information. We embarked upon an extensive study of our community to discover what numerical growth we could expect over the next ten years. To follow up on that, we asked numerical experts to create financial models that would show us whether we could afford to build or not. We also surveyed the congregation and the staff to gather a consensus of our ministry needs. In other words, we intentionally gathered the information we needed to make a wise and informed decision as leaders. Although we did not have to sneak around the wall like Nehemiah, we did need to prepare for our project by gathering pertinent facts and information.

Finding the Balance of Spiritual and Pragmatic Leadership

I began this chapter with an observation of the common tensions between two kinds of leaders: the visionaries and the pragmatists. I suggested the possibility of finding a balance between their different approaches to leadership. We see that balance in Nehemiah. In chapter 1 we saw the spiritual or visionary nature of his leadership, then in chapter 2 we learned of his practical approach to leadership. Nehemiah definitely models a balance that we can develop in our own leadership.

But while his approach is balanced, I would suggest also that Nehemiah does not weigh spiritual and pragmatic leadership as equal. His memoirs in chapter 1 testify to a *precedence* of the spiritual over the practical. Recall that before he strategized and persuaded, Nehemiah prayed. For all godly leaders, prayer must come first.

Nehemiah also illustrates a *permeation* of the spiritual within the practical. Notice that although chapter 1 focuses on prayer, Nehemiah's spiritual awareness does not end with that chapter. In 2:4 he offers another short prayer before addressing the king; in 2:8 he attributes his success to "the good hand of God"; in 2:18 he tells the people about God's good hand; and in 2:20 he counters the derision of his adversaries by confessing his faith in God's blessing. Furthermore, as we see Nehemiah's plan unfold in chapter 2, we realize that he developed this plan during the season of prayer summarized in chapter 1. The spiritual dimension of leadership not only took precedence for Nehemiah, it also permeated his pragmatic actions.

Although I do not find it easy to keep the spiritual and the pragmatic aligned in balance, I am encouraged by men and women who have learned to integrate their faith with every aspect of their lives. One man in my congregation is the vice-president of a highly successful automobile company. He oversees a multi-billion dollar division, with phenomenal results. I recently asked this man what was the basis of his leadership. His immediate response was: "I pray about everything. I couldn't do anything without prayer." My surprise at this wonderful answer may have revealed my own tendency to drive a wedge between the spiritual and the practical. But I was encouraged by his example, as I am by the example of Nehemiah, to keep growing toward balanced leadership.

I believe that few of us will consistently achieve the balance of my friend, or of Nehemiah. *That is one reason why God has placed us in leadership together.* Whereas the Old Testament elevates singular leaders, kings, and prophets who served their community, the New Testament teaches that leadership is to be shared by the Body of Christ. Yes, certain people will serve as elders, pastors, and overseers, but even their leadership should be shared with the Body being served. Admittedly, corporate leadership of this kind is not always efficient; my life would be much simpler if I had the authority to make all the decisions in my church. But if I did, my church would suffer from the limitations of my character and leadership style. It may take longer to process key decisions through the Board, but in that context the visionaries and the pragmatists can sharpen each other as iron sharpens iron. Cooperative leadership reflects the proper biblical balance seen in Nehemiah.

NOTES

1. The Jewish calendar usually places Nisan as the first month of the year (late March, early April). Yet Nehemiah regards Nisan as still within the twentieth year of Artaxerxes (2:1), even though he had previously referred to Chislev of the twentieth year. Apparently he used a calendar in which Nisan was not the first month (Williamson, *Ezra, Nehemiah,* pp. 169–70).

2. Peoples of the ancient Near East gave great attention to the proper burial of the dead, as can be seen in the elaborate and well-preserved tombs that have been uncovered by modern archaeologists. See W. L. Reed, "Burial," *IDB* (Nashville: Abingdon, 1962).

3. See the discussion of Ezra 4:11.

4. Williamson, *Ezra, Nehemiah,* p. 181.

5. H.G.M. Williamson, "Sanballat," *ABD* (New York: Doubleday, 1992).

6. See the letter in Pritchard, ed., *The Ancient Near East,* 1:281.

7. For example, Blenkinsopp, *Ezra-Nehemiah,* p. 219.

8. Brown, Driver, and Briggs, *Lexicon,* s.v. "ʿebed."

9. Williamson, *Ezra, Nehemiah,* p. 183. See also T. C. Eskenazi, "Tobiah," *ABD* (New York: Doubleday, 1992).

10. A helpful map of Nehemiah's journey appears in Kidner, *Ezra & Nehemiah,* p. 85.

11. N. A. Williams, "Geshem," *ABD* (New York: Doubleday, 1992).

CHAPTER TWELVE

Teamwork in Rebuilding the Wall

Nehemiah 3:1–32

READING BETWEEN THE LINES OF A LIST

The tedious list of names in Nehemiah 3 reminds me of commencement—of listening patiently to an endless series of names, waiting for that moment when my name, or the name of my child, or friend, or grandchild is called. Inevitably, people cheer when that special moment comes. The spokesperson at the podium pleads with the audience to "refrain from applause until the end," to no avail. This is undoubtedly one of the most frequently unheeded requests in modern civilization. Families and friends simply must cheer when that special name is finally called.

I wonder if Nehemiah 3 received such a response when it was read in Israel. Did descendants of Zaccur cheer when his name was read (v. 2)? Did relatives of Malchijah wait expectantly for his name to be called (v. 31)?

Unfortunately, this chapter offers no such excitement for us. In fact, we are probably tempted to skip it altogether. It seems simply to provide a detailed list of who rebuilt which section of the wall. Hardly compelling reading! But careful scrutiny of the list uncovers insights for the modern reader. Actually, the chapter addresses pivotal theological questions about how God works in the world and how we can participate in this work.

LIST OF BUILDERS AND THEIR ASSIGNMENTS (3:1–32)

> 3:1 Then Eliashib the high priest rose up with his brethren the priests and built the Sheep Gate; they consecrated it and hung its doors. They built as far as the Tower of the Hundred, and consecrated it, then as far as the Tower of Hananel.

2 Next to Eliashib the men of Jericho built. And next to them Zaccur the son of Imri built.

3 Also the sons of Hassenaah built the Fish Gate; they laid its beams and hung its doors with its bolts and bars.

4 And next to them Meremoth the son of Urijah, the son of Koz, made repairs. Next to them Meshullam the son of Berechiah, the son of Meshezabel, made repairs. Next to them Zadok the son of Baana made repairs.

5 Next to them the Tekoites made repairs; but their nobles did not put their shoulders to the work of their Lord.

6 Moreover Jehoiada the son of Paseah and Meshullam the son of Besodeiah repaired the Old Gate; they laid its beams and hung its doors, with its bolts and bars.

7 And next to them Melatiah the Gibeonite, Jadon the Meronothite, the men of Gibeon and Mizpah, repaired the residence of the governor of the region beyond the River.

8 Next to him Uzziel the son of Harhaiah, one of the goldsmiths, made repairs. Also next to him Hananiah, one of the perfumers, made repairs; and they fortified Jerusalem as far as the Broad Wall.

9 And next to them Rephaiah the son of Hur, leader of half the district of Jerusalem, made repairs.

10 Next to them Jedaiah the son of Harumaph made repairs in front of his house. And next to him Hattush the son of Hashabniah made repairs.

11 Malchijah the son of Harim and Hashub the son of Pahath-moab repaired another section, as well as the Tower of the Ovens.

12 And next to him was Shallum the son of Hallohesh, leader of half the district of Jerusalem; he and his daughters made repairs.

13 Hanun and the inhabitants of Zanoah repaired the Valley Gate. They built it, hung its doors with its bolts and bars, and repaired a thousand cubits of the wall as far as the Refuse Gate.

14 Malchijah the son of Rechab, leader of the district of Beth Haccerem, repaired the Refuse Gate; he built it and hung its doors with its bolts and bars.

15 Shallun the son of Col-Hozeh, leader of the district of Mizpah, repaired the Fountain Gate; he built it, covered it, hung its doors with its bolts and bars, and repaired the wall of the Pool of Shelah by the King's Garden, as far as the stairs that go down from the City of David.

16 After him Nehemiah the son of Azbuk, leader of half the district of Beth Zur, made repairs as far as the place in front of the tombs of David, to the man-made pool, and as far as the House of the Mighty.

17 After him the Levites, under Rehum the son of Bani, made repairs. Next to him Hashabiah, leader of half the district of Keilah, made repairs for his district.

18 After him their brethren, under Bavai the son of Henadad, leader of the other half of the district of Keilah, made repairs.

19 And next to him Ezer the son of Jeshua, the leader of Mizpah, repaired another section in front of the Ascent to the Armory at the buttress.

20 After him Baruch the son of Zabbai carefully repaired the other section, from the buttress to the door of the house of Eliashib the high priest.

21 After him Meremoth the son of Urijah, the son of Koz, repaired another section, from the door of the house of Eliashib to the end of the house of Eliashib.

22 And after him the priests, the men of the plain, made repairs.

23 After him Benjamin and Hasshub made repairs opposite their house. After them Azariah the son of Maaseiah, the son of Ananiah, made repairs by his house.

24 After him Binnui the son of Henadad repaired another section, from the house of Azariah to the buttress, even as far as the corner.

25 Palal the son of Uzai made repairs opposite the buttress, and on the tower which projects from the king's upper house that was by the court of the prison. After him Pedaiah the son of Parosh made repairs.

26 Moreover the Nethinim who dwelt in Ophel made repairs as far as the place in front of the Water Gate toward the east, and on the projecting tower.

186

27 After them the Tekoites repaired another
section, next to the great projecting tower, and as far
as the wall of Ophel.

28 Beyond the Horse Gate the priests made
repairs, each in front of his own house.

29 After them Zadok the son of Immer made repairs
in front of his own house. After him Shemaiah the son of
Shechaniah, the keeper of the East Gate, made repairs.

30 After him Hananiah the son of Shelemiah, and
Hanun, the sixth son of Zalaph, repaired another
section. After him Meshullam the son of Berechiah
made repairs in front of his dwelling.

31 After him Malchijah, one of the goldsmiths,
made repairs as far as the house of the Nethinim and
of the merchants, in front of the Miphkad Gate, and as
far as the upper room at the corner.

32 And between the upper room at the corner, as
far as the Sheep Gate, the goldsmiths and the
merchants made repairs.

Nehemiah 3:1–32

At the close of chapter 2, Nehemiah had successfully persuaded
the people of Judah to join him in rebuilding the wall. They intended
to begin work, in spite of ridicule from their neighboring opponents.
Not only did Nehemiah motivate the people, he also organized them
effectively as demonstrated by the list of builders and their assignments. While the list is not exhaustive, it does offer an overall picture
of the work in progress.[1]

Notice that the list is strikingly inclusive. The builders came from
diverse regions of Judah (for example, the *Tekoites* in v. 5, and the *inhabitants of Zanoah* in v. 13) and from diverse professions (*the goldsmiths*
and *the perfumers*, v. 8). Both sexes worked on the wall (*Shallum* and
his daughters in v. 12), and even leaders from Judah got their hands
dirty: including *the high priest* and *his brethren the priests* (v. 1), the
Levites (v. 17), and many district *leaders* (vv. 9, 12, etc.). In fact
Malchijah, the *"leader of the district of Beth Haccerem, repaired the Refuse
Gate"* (v. 14).[2] This was probably not prime territory to work in—
downwind from the city dump—but someone of authority, who
might have used his influence to gain a better assignment, was willing to complete this necessary but disagreeable task.

Yet, not everyone participated in Nehemiah's rebuilding project. Note in verse 5 that the *nobles* from Tekoa *"did not put their shoulders to the work of their Lord."* The Hebrew of this text reads literally: "but their nobles did not put their neck to the service of their lords." In other words, the leading citizens from Tekoa were not willing to submit to the leadership of Nehemiah (and his associates). As a result, the common folk from the region of Tekoa repaired two sections of the wall without any assistance from their nobles (vv. 5, 27).

Actually, it comes as no surprise that some persons of power and status in Judah failed to support Nehemiah. In our offices, our schools, and often in our churches, we too encounter "nobles" who will not submit to leadership. These individuals invariably cause problems for leaders. As an example, I think of a good friend of mine who entered a new pastorate about two years ago. The Pastor Nominating Committee from the church had found him to be a person with broad vision and proven leadership, so the congregation called him enthusiastically to be their pastor. The first few months of his tenure seemed to prove the rightness of the decision. New ministries were initiated and many new members joined the church.

But not everyone liked the changes. A few of the most influential and wealthy members of the church gathered to confront their new pastor. In a nutshell they said: "You are changing our church and we don't like it. We don't want all of those new people here." After months of patient and diligent struggle, my friend realized that his leadership never would be accepted in that church. Prayerfully and painfully he resigned—just two years after accepting the position.

REFLECTIONS ON NEHEMIAH 3:1–32

God Works Through People

As a native Californian, I am intrigued by the lush forests of New England. And I marvel that throughout the densely-overgrown region, one finds hundreds of small farms hewn out of the woods. Local folklore includes the story of a pastor in New Hampshire. While out on his visitation rounds one day he came upon a farmer laboring in the fields. Eager to compliment his parishioner, the pastor stated, "Say, you and God have certainly done a wonderful job out here." With typical New England wit, the farmer responded, "Yeah, but you should have seen what God did alone."[3] The wise farmer knew whose hands had done the work!

Likewise, rebuilding the wall in Jerusalem was God's work. God stirred up Nehemiah in chapter 1 and enabled him to be sent to Jerusalem in chapter 2. To his opponents, Nehemiah stated boldly, "The God of heaven Himself will prosper us; therefore we His servants will arise and build . . ." (2:20). Later when the wall was completed, Nehemiah commented that "this work was done by our God" (6:16).

But God worked through people: through Nehemiah and the hard-working men and women of Judah. Nehemiah 3 is a reminder to us that the work of God happens when the people of God labor. Of course God can do whatever he wishes, but usually he chooses to work through those who belong to him, who respond to his direction. This was true in the days of Nehemiah—and it was true in the New Testament. It is still true today.

Now "God works through people" may sound like an overworked truism, but reminders of God's methods help us to understand his truths and to act responsibly. Too often we use the assurance that "God wants to do this work" as an excuse not to act ourselves. Yes, God wants to bring the lost to faith. Yes, he desires justice for the oppressed—but this does not free us from all responsibility. In fact, it places the responsibility squarely with us, because as Christians we are called to do the work of God in this world.

And knowing that God works through us should encourage us, especially when we labor faithfully without necessarily *feeling* God's assistance. It should also motivate us to get busy with *God's business.* Certainly God wants to love our neighbors and colleagues—*through us!* He wants to bring peace to Los Angeles, to the Balkan states, to all areas of the earth—through his people who "do justly, love mercy, and walk humbly with their God" (Micah 6:8).

Leadership On All Levels

In Chapter 3 Nehemiah demonstrated balanced and strategic leadership. Based on a spiritual foundation of prayer (1:4–11), he organized effectively and delegated thoroughly. He succeeded at one of the essential yet complex tasks of leadership: to translate broad vision into measurable, bite-sized projects.

Those who are called to lead often try to do it all themselves. Why? Because delegating responsibility requires time and effort. Working with people can be cumbersome. "I will just do it myself" too frequently is the simple escape-approach that is preferred. But the example of Nehemiah reminds us that leaders of God's people are charged with the responsibility of mobilizing and empowering the people to do God's work. In fact, if in my pastoral leadership I can do it all myself, then my "all" is too small! As a pastor-teacher in the Church of Christ, I accept the challenge of "equipping the saints for the work of ministry, for the edifying of the Body of Christ" (Eph. 4:12). The "saints" at Irvine Presbyterian Church are to do the work of God as I equip them and support their efforts.

This does not mean, however, that I should not get my hands dirty with tangible acts of service. Nehemiah 3 portrays leaders, even the high priest, who got involved in building the wall. When we who lead consider ourselves above the fray, we act more like the Tekoite nobles than like the majority of the Judean leaders who were willing to get their hands dirty to accomplish God's work.

One of my favorite examples of "hands-on" leadership occurred when I was Pastor of Educational Ministries at Hollywood Presbyterian Church. Linda, a high-level executive for a major entertainment company, dressed impeccably and carried herself regally. She exercised leadership not only in the workplace but also in the church as an elder of vision and spiritual maturity. One day as I was making my rounds through the Sunday school, I noticed Linda in our classroom of three-year olds. Flawlessly dressed, as always, she was sitting on the floor, playing with an unruly mob of children. Noticing my gaze, she seemed embarrassed to be seen so far out of character. Yet, I thought it was wonderful. Here was a leader who was not above getting down on the floor to love children for the sake of Christ! Mature leaders know when to organize and delegate—and when to get their hands dirty in humble service.

God's Work Necessitates Total Participation

As Nehemiah 3 reminds us, the work of God happens most effectively when everyone participates. Judeans of both genders, from various occupations, diverse locations, and social classes—all joined in the great restoration project. The wall was completed in record time (6:15) because everybody worked hard.

Growing up in Los Angeles during the 1960s, I rooted for the L.A. Lakers. The team fared extremely well, due largely to two outstanding players: Jerry West and Elgin Baylor. They were—and still are— two of the most remarkable athletes ever to play basketball. Six times in the 60's the Lakers played in the championship series. Yet, agonizingly, six times they were defeated by the Boston Celtics. With diligent loyalty, I soon began to despise the Celtics. I wondered why they were better than the Lakers—frustratingly and consistently better. Although the Celtic team was talented (including the likes of Bill Russell and John Havlicek), it could not match the raw talent of the Lakers, who sometimes had two first-team NBA players when the Celtics had none. No, the Celtics were not superior because of all-star talent—but because they were coached to use 100 percent of their personnel. Red Auerbach, the Celtic coach, insisted that every member of the team contribute his strengths. The Celtics prevailed because every player offered all that he had to give.

Most churches, even notably successful ones, function more like the Lakers than the Celtics. In my own congregation, a highly talented and committed group of all-stars carries the team. Key players serve on committees, teach Sunday school, and give sacrificially of their time, strength, and finances. And although their dedication is noble, sometimes in their effort to serve they unintentionally preclude others from becoming involved. They tend to carry the rest of the team.

Nehemiah 3 is a reminder that the work of God happens most effectively when everyone participates. If it is the responsibility of people to do God's work, then it is the responsibility of leaders to help them accomplish that work. As a pastor, I regularly remind my congregation of their need to do God's bidding. But I'm increasingly aware that I also need to guide and direct them in this process. Many are willing, but they simply don't know where to serve—they can't find their place in the wall.

Here, my duty as pastor differs from that of Nehemiah, however, for although I may have an accurate idea of ministry needs, Christians serve according to the direction and empowerment of the sovereign Spirit. It would be easy to simply assign jobs, but my singular delegation would be theologically suspect and practically unwise. Recognizing the sovereignty of God's Spirit and the responsibility we share, my colleagues in leadership and I encourage each member of our church to do the following:

- **Pray for God's guidance.** If you pray, "Lord, I'm willing; show me where to serve," he will respond. After all, it is his work!

- **Look around.** Often God calls us into ministries right where we are. Your section of the wall may be right in front of you.

- **Consult with Christian friends.** Discernment of our place in ministry should happen in the context of prayerful community.

- **Receive guidance from church leaders.** Although they are not charged with Nehemiah's authority, church leaders often have a clear sense of God's direction and an awareness of ministry needs.

- **Follow your heart.** Feelings of passion, compassion, and even joy can guide you to your section of the wall.

- **Utilize the church's "Answering the Call" guidebook.** The leadership of Irvine Presbyterian has developed a concise guide to the various ministries in the church. The guide outlines precise needs and opportunities, which enables interested members to pray for God's guidance in an informed way.

Finding Meaning in Our Piece of the Wall

God intends to work in this world through us. And surely the Church of Christ needs the participation of each member, just as each member needs to experience the joy and fulfillment of contributing to God's work. We spend so much of our lives on projects destroyed "by moth and rust" (Matthew 6:19). What a fulfilling contrast to see our efforts contribute to God's great work on earth!

I was speaking recently with one of the outstanding leaders from my congregation about his contribution to God's work at Irvine Presbyterian. This man has given sacrificially and generously throughout the short history of the church as an elder, church treasurer, chairman of committees, Sunday school teacher, and the list goes on. In our conversation, however, he did not mention all of these contributions; rather, he spoke with special fondness about painting the first building on the church property. His tangible action, though humble and thankless, made a difference and he felt a proper godly pride.

We all need to experience the joyful sense of contributing to God's work. Our lives find ultimate meaning in knowing that we have labored—as parents, as church workers, as doers of justice, as communicators of God's gracious truth and love—for what will last.

NOTES

1. Myers, *Ezra • Nehemiah*, pp. 112–13.

2. Others translations speak of the "Dung Gate." But "Refuse Gate" is probably more accurate given the Hebrew term used.

3. Story found in B.A. Botkin, ed., *A Treasury of New England Folklore*, rev. ed. (New York: American Legacy Press, 1989), p. 82. Ref. to "Lancaster" by O. G. Veazie; Manuscripts of the Federal Writers' Project of the Works Progress Administration for the State of New Hampshire.

CHAPTER THIRTEEN

Confronting and Overcoming Opposition

Nehemiah 4:1–6:19

JUST WHEN YOU THOUGHT IT WAS SAFE

In 1975, Steven Spielberg shocked America with his classic film, *Jaws*. Following the story line of Peter Benchley's novel, a mammoth great white shark terrorized Amity, a fictional New England coastal village. Newspapers in 1975 reported an actual decline in beach tourism during the popular run of this movie. To this day, the bass tones of John Williams' score from the movie strike terror in the hearts of America's moviegoers. But 1975 passed, and we returned to the beaches. Then 1978 brought the return of the shark to poor Amity— "just when you thought it was safe to go back into the water . . . ," or so the ad for *Jaws 2* warned.

Something about the *Jaws* series rings true. I am not thinking of great white sharks attacking humans—which happens very rarely— but of the "just when you thought it was safe" motif. So often it seems that just when our lives seem to be going well, disaster strikes. Take last Wednesday for instance. I experienced God working in amazing ways. A member of my small study group shared with new openness; my afternoon counseling appointments reminded me of God's ability to heal broken hearts; and to top things off, my evening committee meeting progressed smoothly with cooperative excitement. In short, I ended the day rejoicing! But, "just when I thought it was safe . . . ," Thursday rolled around. It began with an emergency phone call from my mother because my grandfather had to be rushed to the hospital. And so the day went. A colleague updated me on a project with a note that summed up my day perfectly: "Sort of bleak. See me."

And these ups and downs are not limited to the personal level. We also experience them on a worldwide scale. Communism declines, the Berlin Wall crumbles, and South African apartheid is on the ropes. But, "just when we think it is safe . . . ," Saddam Hussein invades Kuwait and we are quickly plunged into war.

Nehemiah knew the "just when you thought it was safe" syndrome all too well. Remember how everything was running along smoothly for him (chapters 2 and 3)? The king had blessed his venture and had provided supplies. The people had rallied around him and had begun to work energetically. Then Nehemiah experienced his version of *Jaws* 2. Suddenly in chapters 4–6 he is confronted with opposition, not only from his enemies but even from his own people. Here we can learn from Nehemiah's example how to overcome adversity in our lives and in our ministries.

NEHEMIAH CONFRONTS MOCKERY (4:1–6)

4:1 But it so happened, when Sanballat heard that we were rebuilding the wall, that he was furious and very indignant, and mocked the Jews.

2 And he spoke before his brethren and the army of Samaria, and said, "What are these feeble Jews doing? Will they fortify themselves? Will they offer sacrifices? Will they complete it in a day? Will they revive the stones from the heaps of rubbish—stones that are burned?"

3 Now Tobiah the Ammonite was beside him, and he said, "Whatever they build, if even a fox goes up on it, he will break down their stone wall."

4 Hear, O our God, for we are despised; turn their reproach on their own heads, and give them as plunder to a land of captivity!

5 Do not cover their iniquity, and do not let their sin be blotted out from before You; for they have provoked You to anger before the builders.

6 So we built the wall, and the entire wall was joined together up to half its height, for the people had a mind to work.

Nehemiah 4:1–6

Nehemiah's opponents, *Sanballat* and *Tobiah the Ammonite*, appear once again with their familiar tone of derision (see the discussion of 2:19 above). Sanballat mocked the Jews in a voice that must have been full of animosity and spite. Were he living today, he might have said: "Who do these Jews think they're kidding? Be serious! They're going to rebuild the wall from all of that junk? They're crazy!" (v. 2). Tobiah the Ammonite added his denigration: "A little fox would break down whatever they build!" (v. 3). The passage implies that Sanballat and Tobiah mocked the Jews not only for personal pleasure, but also to discourage the builders.

Nehemiah responded with a fervent prayer: "O God, get revenge on them! Let them be overthrown! Don't forgive their sins!" (vv. 4–5). Now that's quite a prayer—one, in fact, that has caused considerable consternation for preachers and commentators. Like individuals in some of the Psalms (for example Ps. 21), Nehemiah prayed in an aggressively hostile manner. He was neither polite nor kind. So how are we to understand this prayer? And what are we to learn from it?

Once again, we must remember that this passage shows us how Nehemiah prayed, not necessarily how we should pray. It illustrates; it does not instruct. As Christians who know of Christ's call to love our enemies and of his death for them, we would hardly choose to imitate Nehemiah's example. Nevertheless, two aspects of Nehemiah's prayer deserve our attention—and even emulation.

First, notice that Nehemiah *prioritized prayer*. When mocked, he did not shout back; he turned to God. Now I have to confess that in times of conflict and criticism, prayer does not always top my list of responses. How tempting it is to respond by plotting a counterattack, or to forget planning altogether and to launch instead into a defensive tirade. Nehemiah may have spoken in an unneighborly fashion, but at least he did so in conversation with God, not with Sanballat and Tobiah.

Second, Nehemiah *prayed honestly*. He told God exactly what he wanted, with startling candor. What a contrast to our carefully-edited prayers that say nothing offensive or embarrassing. But our pretense of civility does not fool God, for he looks upon our hearts. Moreover, by screening everything we say in prayer, we miss the vitality and transforming power of honest conversation with God.

As a pastor, I talk almost daily with people who feel deep disappointment with God—who wonder, Why has God let me down?

Why hasn't God helped me to get a job? Why didn't God save my marriage? Why is he letting my father suffer? They vent their anger in tears and desperate voices, yet in prayer they mask their discouragement and anger, saying stoically, "Let your will be done." But that is not what they really want! Nor does it communicate their true feelings about God. Only when people learn to tell the truth in prayer, no matter how unattractive the truth might be, will they enter into genuine, intimate relationship with God. Don't we see this forthright, perilous honesty throughout the Psalms? And even on the lips of Jesus in the Garden of Gethsemane? Like Nehemiah, let us learn that God is big enough to hear prayers that authentically reveal our thoughts and emotions.

After all was said and done, it certainly seems that Nehemiah's prayerful response achieved its purpose because the workers continued to labor until the wall reached *"half its height"* (v. 6). In spite of insults from opposing leaders, *"the people had a mind to work."*[1]

NEHEMIAH CONFRONTS THE THREAT OF ATTACK (4:7–23)

7 Now it happened, when Sanballat, Tobiah, the Arabs, the Ammonites, and the Ashdodites heard that the walls of Jerusalem were being restored and the gaps were beginning to be closed, that they became very angry,

8 and all of them conspired together to come and attack Jerusalem and create confusion.

9 Nevertheless we made our prayer to our God, and because of them we set a watch against them day and night.

10 Then Judah said, "The strength of the laborers is failing, and there is so much rubbish that we are not able to build the wall."

11 And our adversaries said, "They will neither know nor see anything, till we come into their midst and kill them and cause the work to cease."

12 So it was, when the Jews who dwelt near them came, that they told us ten times, "From whatever place you turn, they will be upon us."

13 Therefore I positioned men behind the lower parts of the wall, at the openings; and I set the people according to their families, with their swords, their spears, and their bows.

14 And I looked, and arose and said to the nobles, to the leaders, and to the rest of the people, "Do not be afraid of them. Remember the Lord, great and awesome, and fight for your brethren, your sons, your daughters, your wives, and your houses."

15 And it happened, when our enemies heard that it was known to us, and that God had brought their plot to nothing, that all of us returned to the wall, everyone to his work.

16 So it was, from that time on, that half of my servants worked at construction, while the other half held the spears, the shields, the bows, and wore armor; and the leaders were behind all the house of Judah.

17 Those who built on the wall, and those who carried burdens, loaded themselves so that with one hand they worked at construction, and with the other held a weapon.

18 Every one of the builders had his sword girded at his side as he built. And the one who sounded the trumpet was beside me.

19 Then I said to the nobles, the rulers, and the rest of the people, "The work is great and extensive, and we are separated far from one another on the wall.

20 Wherever you hear the sound of the trumpet, rally to us there. Our God will fight for us."

21 So we labored in the work, and half of the men held the spears from daybreak until the stars appeared.

22 At the same time I also said to the people, "Let each man and his servant stay at night in Jerusalem, that they may be our guard by night and a working party by day."

23 So neither I, my brethren, my servants, nor the men of the guard who followed me took off our clothes, except that everyone took them off for washing.

Nehemiah 4:7–23

When mockery failed to stop the rebuilding, the enemies of Judah threatened to attack (vv. 8, 11). They did not intend to actually take control of the city, but merely to *"create confusion"* (v. 8) and to *"cause the work to cease"* (v. 11). Sanballat and Tobiah had rallied a considerable alliance (including *"the Arabs, the Ammonites, and the Ashdodites"*) against tiny Judah (v. 7). Nehemiah and his band were surrounded, with Sanballat and the Samaritans to the north, Tobiah and the Ammonites on the east, the Arabs (with Geshem [2:19]?) to the south, and the Ashdodites on the west.

Once again, Nehemiah responded by praying (v. 9). In addition, the Jews *"set a watch against them day and night"* (v. 9) and prepared for an attack.

Now, apparently, the threat of attack from surrounding nations weakened the spirits of the Jews. *"Then Judah said"* here refers to circulating, common gossip. So the word on the street was: "Everybody is getting tired. And all of the rubbish is getting in our way" (v. 10). Thus while mockery had no effect, military intimidation did. And the enemies kept issuing threats, promising to attack secretly in order to bring the rebuilding efforts to a halt (v. 11). As a result, frightened Jews from outlying areas, who felt particularly vulnerable, repeatedly complained of their fears to Nehemiah. *"Ten times"* probably means "again and again."[2]

Confronted with a discouraged populace, menacing neighbors, and innumerable complaints, Nehemiah gathered the people together, fully armed and ready for battle. By positioning this congregation *"behind the lower parts of the wall, at the openings"* (v. 13), Nehemiah guaranteed that their enemies would see the strength and readiness of the Jews.[3] Once they were in place, Nehemiah delivered a rousing pep talk, calling on the people to keep their focus on God, who is *"great and awesome"* (v. 14). With their mind-set properly focused, the people of Judah were ready to fight for their families.

Once again, Nehemiah's defensive strategy was successful (v. 15). The danger of immediate attack subsided and the builders returned to their labors. But from that time onward, Nehemiah and his crew remained prepared for a surprise attack at all times.

Verses 16–23 outline some of their preparations:

- Half of Nehemiah's servants stood guard while the others worked (4:16).

- The builders bore arms while laboring on the wall (4:17–18).

- A long-distance communication system was deployed (4:18–20).

- The workers camped in Jerusalem in order to protect the city (4:21–22).

Verse 23 indicates that even Nehemiah and his fellow leaders stayed with the workers who camped out in Jerusalem.[4] Undoubtedly, Nehemiah's willingness to join in the hardships, spurred the people on in their commitment (v. 23).

How did the Jews respond to threats against their welfare? After praying, they prepared for battle. As verse 6 states, the people had a *mind to work*—a commitment that is illustrated vividly throughout the rest of the chapter. The laborers certainly would not have found it pleasant to work all day encumbered with weapons at their side, nor would camping in Jerusalem have been a privilege. Yet in spite of difficulties and dire threats, the wall continued to rise.

REFLECTIONS ON NEHEMIAH 4:1–23

Prayer and Preparation: Strange Bedfellows?

In chapter 4, Nehemiah responds to his opponents with a combination of prayer and preparation for battle. Again we see the familiar balance in his leadership between the spiritual and the pragmatic. But is there a tension, perhaps even a contradiction in this balance? If Nehemiah sincerely trusted God, why did he prepare the people for battle? Is it possible that he did not believe what he said to the people: "*Our God will fight for us*" (v. 20)? And if did believe it, why did he prepare the builders to fight? Does he trust God, or doesn't he?

Of course deliberations of this sort are carried out most easily within the comfortable confines of our homes, studies, and churches, safely out of the actual line of fire. But there are Christians throughout the world who live daily under the shadow of death threats. Some of my close friends minister in a gang-infested neighborhood of Hollywood, California where drive-by shootings are a common experience. You can be sure we have discussed at length the difficult tension between trusting God and taking steps to provide personal security.

This also brings to mind an occasion during my tenure at Hollywood Presbyterian Church when I faced a situation similar to that of Nehemiah. The pastors and congregants consistently endeavored to care for the clutches of homeless people who lived near the church, most of whom received our efforts with gratitude and appreciation. One time, however, my colleague Ralph Osborne and I attempted to

200

help one homeless man, Richard, to no avail. He was not satisfied with our offerings of food, shelter, counseling, and prayer. He seemed to be consumed with a smoldering anger. He mocked our ministry yelling: "You are a bunch of hypocrites! You don't really love people at all!" Soon he started to picket the church and threatened to contact the news media. When these efforts to manipulate were not successful, he added the ultimate threat: "Next Sunday I will come to church and shoot you and Rev. Osborne." Two days later I received an emergency phone call from Richard's wife. "I've left him," she cried. "And I'm afraid because he thinks he's Charles Manson—and he has a gun!"

You can imagine that we did plenty of praying that week. Coincidentally, Ralph and I were sharing the pulpit in worship leadership the following Sunday morning. We and many others prayed fervently for safety, and for Richard to be touched by God. But, I freely admit, we also hired special security guards to protect the church that morning. As it turned out, Richard did come to church, but without his gun. And although the security guards did have to ask him to leave, he cooperated without making a fuss.

When Ralph and I had to confront this threat to our lives, we found that prayer and tangible preparation complemented each other perfectly. We saw God work through our prayers and through our preparation. These two elements need not be contradictory. I can assure you, under the right circumstances they go nicely hand in hand!

But, having said this, I must recognize my own tendency to prepare exhaustively while praying minimally. When I face conflict, prayer sometimes fails to take top priority on my "to do" list. Yet, as we will see below, this is a costly mistake for Christians to make.

Preparing for Opposition

For Christians, the "just when you thought it was safe . . ." syndrome is no mere coincidence. The New Testament teaches clearly that God's people should expect opposition, because we are at war. Paul puts it this way:

> Finally, my brethren, be strong in the Lord and in the power of His might. Put on the whole armor of God, that you may be able to stand against the wiles of the devil. For we do not wrestle against flesh and blood, but against principalities, against powers,

against the rules of the darkness of this age, against spiritual hosts of wickedness in the heavenly places.

Ephesians 6:10–12

Christians are in a battle against spiritual forces. The universe contains not only God and natural beings, but a spiritual adversary and a host of supernatural forces. While to some contemporary thinkers this perspective may seem antiquated and irrelevant, the reality of spiritual warfare fills the pages of the New Testament. And as western Christians become increasingly aware of Christian experience throughout the world, which invariably includes visible activities of evil spiritual forces, we are realizing the value of embracing the biblical understanding of spiritual warfare—even if this conflicts with our prescribed, secularistic culture. Without going overboard and attributing the loss of a parking space to traffic demons, we Christians must squarely face the opposition.

But how can we be prepared to oppose these evil spiritual forces? Paul provides the answer in Ephesians 6:13–14:

Therefore, take up the whole armor of God, that you may be able to withstand in the evil day, and having done all, to stand. Stand therefore, having girded your waist with truth, having put on the breastplate of righteousness, and having shod your feet with the preparation of the gospel of peace; above all, taking the shield of faith with which you will be able to quench all the fiery darts of the wicked one. And take the helmet of salvation, and the sword of the Spirit, which is the word of God.

We prepare for spiritual battle by putting on the whole armor of God: truth, righteousness, peace, faith, salvation, and the Word of God. In order to fight against our spiritual opponents, we must "put on" these attributes. Essentially Paul is saying: "Major in the majors! Focus on the essentials of Christian faith! Don't get hung up in the fine print!" In other words, we prepare for spiritual warfare, not by focusing on the Devil and his forces, but by stressing the core aspects of Christian faith.

Fighting God's Fight

Once we have prepared ourselves with the armor, how do we fight these spiritual battles? Curiously, many who teach this passage from

Ephesians do not go beyond verse 17. They focus on the armor without explaining what we are to do once it is on! Yet verse 18, which is grammatically dependent upon verse 17, continues with further instructions. It shows us how to actually fight the battle:

> Praying always with all prayer and supplication in the Spirit, being watchful to this end with all perseverance and supplication for all the saints—and for me. . . .
>
> *Ephesians 6:18–19*

Paul's instructions are very clear: we fight by praying. To be sure, spiritual warfare entails other activities, including preaching, witnessing, praying for the sick, casting out demons, and so on, but at the center stands prayer. That is why our tendency to minimize prayer is so dangerous. To disregard prayer is to discard our primary weapon. To fight effectively, we must recognize that prayer is more effective than multiple other activities, including: planning, persuasion, theological apologetics, preaching, etc.

I am continually amazed by the power of God released in prayer. Problems that seem beyond a solution, people who seem beyond redemption—these God touches miraculously, when I stop to pray. For example, some time ago I faced a personnel problem that seemed insoluble. A staff member under my charge seemed completely incompetent to fulfill her job description. I was distressed over the likelihood of firing her, not only because of the inevitable hurt feelings, but also because of the danger of strife within the church for this woman was a highly respected church member.

Repeatedly I brought my concern before the Lord in prayer, but, frankly, with almost no expectation that my prayer would be answered. "But God who is rich in mercy" surprised me once again (Eph. 2:4). Through the intervention of his Spirit—no other explanation makes sense—he transformed this woman into someone who quickly exceeded the requirements of her position. To this day she continues in her job, serving with excellence and effectiveness.

Yet, as I regularly remind my congregation—and myself—we cannot be content with past spiritual victories. We cannot afford to forget our primary commitment to prayer—prayer that demands our time and our energy. For we no longer live in a society where Christian values and perspectives can be assumed. The myth of "Christian America" has been shattered. And though some saints feel called to fight against secularism in the political arena, in the schools, in the churches, and in the marketplace, our best efforts will bear sour fruit if their roots do not grow deep in the soil of prayer.

Are we praying for our cities? For our leaders? For our schools? Do we pray faithfully for pastors and other Christian leaders, or do we simply shake our heads when they fall? Parents, do you pray for your children? Do you pray with them, so they can learn how to pray? Do we pray individually? And corporately? In the privacy of our prayer closets, do we pray with a Nehemiah-like honesty? Do we tell God the truth?

Nehemiah faced opposition, and so will we. Just when we think it is safe, a spiritual battle will come our way, like the great white shark in the water of Amity. But we can *"remember the Lord, great and awesome"* (v. 14). We can rejoice in the fact that *"our God will fight for us"* (v. 20). So, with expectation of victory, let us put on the armor and fight!

NEHEMIAH CONFRONTS INTERNAL CONFLICT (5:1–19)

Just when Judah was finally able to withstand threats from outside, what should happen but internal squabbles erupted. Just when it seemed safe to build again, the citizens of Judah cried out to Nehemiah with ominous complaints. Thus, in contrast to the previous chapter where Nehemiah had to deal with threats from outside of Judah, here in chapter 5 we will see him confront and overcome conflict within Judah.

THE PEOPLE COMPLAIN (5:1–5)

5:1 And there was a great outcry of the people and their wives against their Jewish brethren.

2 For there were those who said, "We, our sons, and our daughters are many; therefore let us get grain, that we may eat and live."

3 There were also some who said, "We have mortgaged our lands and vineyards and houses, that we might buy grain because of the famine."

4 There were also those who said, "We have borrowed money for the king's tax on our lands and vineyards.

> 5 Yet now our flesh is as the flesh of our
> brethren, our children as their children; and indeed
> we are forcing our sons and our daughters to be
> slaves, and some of our daughters have been brought
> into slavery. It is not in our power to redeem them,
> for other men have our lands and vineyards."
>
> *Nehemiah 5:1–5*

The people cried out *"against their Jewish brethren,"* who had been profiting from the misfortune of the masses (v. 1). Even *"their wives"* cried out (v. 1)—probably because they had been left alone by husbands who were working on the wall in Jerusalem.

The text distinguishes three groups of protesters. The first group complained: "We need food for our large families" (v. 2). The second group complained: "We have mortgaged our property for food" (v. 3). Group three added: "We have borrowed money to pay our taxes" (v. 4). (Specifically, they had to pay the *"king's tax,"* a property tax based on the productivity of the land.)[5] Verse 5 may summarize a terrible complaint experienced by all three parties: due to financial hardships they had been forced to sell their children into slavery. This practice, abhorrent both to modern readers and to those who complained to Nehemiah, allowed people in debt to keep their means of livelihood while working to redeem their children back from the slave master.

While such slavery was not prohibited in the Law, it was strictly regulated (Ex. 21:2–11). For example, the Jews were commanded to regard their fellow Jews as hired laborers, not as slaves (Lev. 25:39–43). However, in Nehemiah's situation, the phrase *"some of our daughters have been brought into slavery"* (v. 5) implies in the original language either that their daughters had been forced to marry their owners or that they had been sexually molested.[6] Naturally this intensifies the offense.

How did this sorry state of affairs come about? Verse 3 mentions a famine in the land, which may or may not have been related to Nehemiah's building project. For certain, Nehemiah himself bears at least some responsibility for Judah's economic woes, for at his call farmers and other laborers left their homes and businesses to work in Jerusalem. As a result, their families were abandoned to face extreme financial and physical vulnerability. Moreover, as depicted in chapter 4,

Nehemiah's project so distressed Judah's neighbors that trade between Jews and other regions probably stopped altogether. At best it was reduced significantly. Then when these economic hardships overwhelmed the land, those with financial resources jumped at the chance to profit from the misfortune of their fellow Jews. While the majority of citizens faced economic hardships, a few wealthy nobles and rulers (v. 7) took advantage of the situation. They loaned money to their fellow Jews and took property as security. From some they even purchased their children as slaves.

NEHEMIAH'S RESPONSE (5:6–13)

6 And I became very angry when I heard their outcry and these words.

7 After serious thought, I rebuked the nobles and rulers, and said to them, "Each of you is exacting usury from his brother." So I called a great assembly against them.

8 And I said to them, "According to our ability we have redeemed our Jewish brethren who were sold to the nations. Now indeed, will you even sell your brethren? Or should they be sold to us?" Then they were silenced and found nothing to say.

9 Then I said, "What you are doing is not good. Should you not walk in the fear of our God because of the reproach of the nations, our enemies?"

10 I also, with my brethren and my servants, am lending them money and grain. Please, let us stop this usury!

11 Restore now to them, even this day, their lands, their vineyards, their olive groves, and their houses, also a hundredth of the money and the grain, the new wine and the oil, that you have charged them."

12 So they said, "We will restore it, and will require nothing from them; we will do as you say." Then I called the priests, and required an oath from them that they would do according to this promise.

13 Then I shook out the fold of my garment and said, "So may God shake out each man from his house, and from his property, who does not perform this promise. Even thus may he be shaken out and emptied."

> And all the assembly said, "Amen!" and praised the
> LORD. Then the people did according to this promise.
>
> *Nehemiah 5:6–13*

When Nehemiah heard the people's cries, he *"became very angry"* (v. 6). The same passion he expressed in chapter 1 reappears here, this time as anger over the injustice done to God's people. But Nehemiah did not act in the adrenaline rush of anger. Rather he took time to devote *"serious thought"* to what his response should be (v. 7). Not only was the rebuilding project at risk, but the very future and unity of God's people in Judah was at risk.

It is significant to me that Nehemiah responded first by confronting *"the nobles and rulers"*: *"Each of you is exacting usury from his brother"* (v. 7). "Exacting usury," or charging exorbitant interest, is one possible translation of the Hebrew, though verse 7 does not employ the usual terms for charging interest. A better paraphrase would be: Each of you is acting like a "pawnbroker" with his own brother![7] Charging unfair interest was only one aspect of the offense. It also included accepting property as security for loans and receiving children as slaves.

After confronting the offenders directly, Nehemiah summoned *"a great assembly,"* including the accused, the victims, and others to serve as witnesses (v. 7). There he confronted the nobles and rulers with the folly of their actions. First, he referred to the redemption of Jewish slaves by their fellow Jews, including perhaps the nobles and rulers (v. 8). These same nobles and rulers had been instrumental in buying back Jews who had previously been sold into slavery in foreign lands. Now they were owning Jewish slaves themselves! How contradictory! By highlighting this contradiction, Nehemiah underlined the fundamental kinship between the Jews, which had been epitomized in the redemption process and denied by intra-Jewish slavery. The offenders listened to the charges against them in a silence that betrayed their guilt.

Second, Nehemiah appealed to national pride. What the nobles and rulers were doing was not only shattering Judean unity, it was also making the nation a laughingstock among other nations. Those from whom Jewish slaves had been redeemed would certainly snicker at the absurdity of Jews now buying their own kin as slaves.

As the narrative continues, we find a shockingly candid admission by Nehemiah: *"I also, with my brethren and my servants, am lending them money and grain. Please, let us stop this usury!"*(v. 10). As in the case of verse 7, "usury" is probably not a correct translation. The final phrase should read: "Please, let us stop acting as pawnbrokers!" Because Nehemiah uses similar language in verses 7 and 10, and because he uses the second person in "let us stop," he obviously includes himself among the offending creditors. Bluntly and publicly, Nehemiah admitted that he and his associates had been loaning money; they had been acting as pawnbrokers with their own people!

In light of the offense in which he shared, Nehemiah called the lenders to *"restore"* all personal property held as security for loans (v. 11). They were also to give back the *"hundred"* that had been charged (v. 11). This term may indicate the percentage of interest, one-hundredth per month, or twelve percent per annum. It may also mean simply "percentage" in general.[8] In either case, the lenders were to give back all profit made on the loans. Although the text does not state that slaves should be returned, this is certainly implied from the context. Nor does it state explicitly that all loans were to be forgiven, though this may also be implied, especially from *"we . . . will require nothing from them"* (v. 12).[9]

The lenders, thoroughly chastened, hastened to agree to Nehemiah's demands. Nehemiah summoned the *priests*, probably to serve as witnesses who would guarantee fulfillment of what had been promised (v. 12). Then he performed a symbolic gesture to motivate the creditors even more. He shook out *"the fold of [his] garment,"* and said, *"So may God shake out each man from his house, and from his property, who does not perform this promise"* (v. 12). The fold of a garment was the ancient equivalent of a pocket. By emptying his fold while uttering these words, Nehemiah was stating dramatically: "If you don't do as you have promised, may God take away all of your possessions."

The combination of strategies was successful, and the passage ends on a positive note: *"Then the people did according to this promise"* (v. 13).

NEHEMIAH'S SACRIFICE (5:14–19)

14 Moreover, from the time that I was appointed
to be their governor in the land of Judah, from the
twentieth year until the thirty-second year of King
Artaxerxes, twelve years, neither I nor my brothers
ate the governor's provisions.

15 But the former governors who were before me laid burdens on the people, and took from them bread and wine, besides forty shekels of silver. Yes, even their servants bore rule over the people, but I did not do so, because of the fear of God.

16 Indeed, I also continued the work on this wall, and we did not buy any land. All my servants were gathered there for the work.

17 And at my table were one hundred and fifty Jews and rulers, besides those who came to us from the nations around us.

18 Now that which was prepared daily was one ox and six choice sheep. Also fowl were prepared for me, and once every ten days an abundance of all kinds of wine. Yet in spite of this I did not demand the governor's provisions, because the bondage was heavy on this people.

19 Remember me, my God, for good, according to all that I have done for this people.

Nehemiah 5:14–19

This passage provides several tidbits of historically-significant material. For example, here we learn for the first time that Nehemiah was *"governor"* of Judah, and that he served in this position for a term of *"twelve years."* However, we do not know the precise identity of the *"former governors"* (v. 15), nor whether they ruled over Judah alone, or over a broader region of the Persian empire.

In 5:14–19 the sacrificial aspect of Nehemiah's leadership is emphasized. He did not profit financially from his office, nor *"buy any land"* (v. 16). Neither did he collect *"the governor's provisions,"* which included food, drink, and money (vv. 14–15). Even though as governor Nehemiah had to feed many local officials as well as visiting dignitaries, he paid the bill out of his personal resources. And what a bill it must have been—for a daily supply of *"one ox and six choice sheep,"* not to mention *"fowl"* and *"all kinds of wine"* (v. 18)! Yet Nehemiah's sensitivity to the "heavy bondage" already placed upon the people led him to drain his personal resources rather than add to the people's bondage (v. 18). In typical style, Nehemiah ends this section with a prayer, asking God to *"remember"* him for all that he has done for Judah (v. 19).

Looking back over these verses (14–19), which interrupt the chronology of chapters 4–6 with historical data from an extended period of Nehemiah's service, we might wonder why they are included here. It may be that they are placed here to offset the scandal of Nehemiah's admission of guilt in 5:10. The verses also demonstrate how Nehemiah learned from his mistakes, moving from opportunistic to sacrificial leadership. Thus, since these verses contrast Governor Nehemiah's sacrificial leadership with the self-serving actions of the lenders in verses 1–13 (including himself), they do fit thematically in chapter 5 even though they seem to interrupt the chronological flow of chapters 4–6.

REFLECTIONS ON NEHEMIAH 5:1–19

How to Respond to Conflict and Complaint

Without doubt, Christian leaders will face opposition and conflict, not only from outside agitators, but from internal agitators as well. What Nehemiah experienced in chapter 5 is all too common, even (perhaps especially) among God's covenant people. I am thinking in particular of a friend of mine who has been pastoring a church for about two years. Recently he spoke about his ministry in grateful terms: "Never have I seen God so much at work in my ministry. He is changing lives, bringing newness and growth. It is wonderful to behold." Then my friend continued, "But never have I experienced so much criticism in my life. It has been especially hard on my family."

How are we who lead to respond to criticism and conflict? How should parents react when their teen-agers accuse them of being "unfair"? How should we deal with conflict in church, in our businesses, in schools, and within friendships? Nehemiah's actions in chapter 5 illustrate several basic principles of how to respond to conflict and complaint, but four in particular seem to stand out.

1. Listen

Nehemiah writes, *"And I became very angry when I heard their outcry and these words"* (v. 6). The story indicates that he heard not only physiologically but empathetically as well. Nehemiah truly heard the

210

cries of those who were being financially devastated—even though their cries implicated him!

Listening is one of the most important and most frequently ignored facets of leadership. To listen takes time and effort. It requires openness to new and even uncomfortable information. It may even conflict with our sense that leaders must be "out in front of the pack" telling everyone else what to do. Nevertheless, effective leaders listen.

In their best-selling book, *In Search of Excellence*, Peters and Waterman conclude concisely, "The excellent companies are better listeners."[10] Top-notch organizations and individuals listen with special care when people express their misgivings and frustrations. In the second volume of the "Excellence" series, Peters and Austin observe that successful companies regard complaints, not as something to be avoided, but as "a luscious, golden opportunity."[11] Such attitudes seem paradoxical, but it seems to me they confirm Nehemiah's example.

And that is why, as a pastor, I expect all leaders at Irvine Presbyterian (including myself) to be intentional listeners. Effective listening happens formally (in letters, office visits, and meetings), as well as informally (in casual conversations and phone calls). I encourage members of my congregation to share their concerns honestly with me, even when these are criticisms. In fact, just recently I asked parishioners to write me a letter about their experiences in our church because people generally are more willing to share openly and honestly in a written format. So far I have been pleased with the response. Criticisms have been intermixed with encouragements, but all have reflected a loving concern for me and the church. And I know that even though we will never be able to please everyone in our responses, I also know that people will usually feel satisfied and supported if they have been heard. Listening goes a long way, even in times of disagreement.

2. Think It Over

Nehemiah's reaction upon hearing of the people's suffering was to get angry. Although many of us have been conditioned to avoid anger, leaders throughout the Bible both felt and acted in anger. Now anger can be a valuable force, motivating us to affirmative action, but it can also be like a loose garden hose with the water turned on full-throttle, flailing about aimlessly—doing much more harm than good.

In the early days of my ministry I learned the truth of this the hard way. A few weeks after I began serving as College Director at Hollywood Presbyterian, I spoke at our college winter retreat. When I finished teaching late one evening, a collegian began to challenge what I had said—in a most uncharitable manner. In anger, I started to defend myself. Then he responded in anger, and so we continued, disputing in anger, for seven hours! Although completely exhausted at the end of our ordeal, we were no closer to mutual understanding than when we began.

Yes, Nehemiah felt angry, but he waited to act until he had given *"serious thought"* to his response (v. 6). Contemplating a response is like reaching out with a strong hand to grab that thrashing hose, to direct it carefully and productively in watering the garden. When we face conflict or complaint, and especially when this provokes us to anger, we need to take time to think and to pray. In these quiet moments we are able to reflect calmly, to get to the root of the problems we face. Thankfully, I have learned when people criticize my preaching not to confront them immediately. No more seven-hour arguments for me! Instead, I suggest a time when we can sit down together to talk about their concerns. And in these meetings I make a conscious effort to think before I answer. Admittedly, my success rate varies, but the positive effects encourage me to keep trying!

But while we are talking about criticism, I should add that potential critics would also do well to imitate Nehemiah's example. Too often complaints are delivered in anger, without time for objective reflection and evaluation. Yet, on the other hand, some people never communicate their frustrations even when they should. I have forewarned my congregation that there will be times when I will disappoint and frustrate them. But when this happens, I have asked that they think the matter over carefully. Then, I counsel, "If the issue turns out to be inconsequential—drop it. But if it really matters to you, come talk to me. Whatever you do, don't store up your anger!"

3. Confront Directly

Nehemiah went first to the nobles and officials who had been lending money. He stated without hesitation, *"Each of you is [acting as a creditor with] his brother"* (v. 7). Notice that he did not begin by calling a great assembly. That took place only after direct personal confrontation with the offenders.

212

In contrast to Nehemiah, we often find it easier and more psychologically satisfying to avoid direct confrontation. We tell everyone else what is wrong instead. Yet this clearly contradicts the forthright teaching of Jesus in Matthew 18:15: "If another member of the church sins against you, go and point out the fault when the two of your are alone. If the member listens to you, you have regained that one" (NRSV). During my years of ministry in Hollywood, I frequently heard Lloyd Ogilvie say to our staff, "Never say about someone something you are unwilling to say to that person within 24 hours." If staff discussions required that I say something negative about someone in the congregation, then it was my duty to talk directly with that person. Lloyd would also say, "Keep short accounts." And true to his own advice, if I ever did anything to offend him or if there seemed to be some discomfort between us, I would inevitably receive a telephone call from him, not for the purpose of putting me in my place, but to build understanding and a close working relationship.

Because I observed the value of these principles firsthand, I have followed Lloyd's example in my own ministry at Irvine. Periodically someone will come to me with a complaint about a staff member whom I supervise. In almost every case I will ask, "Have you talked with Mike about this?" or "Have you spoken to Larry yet?" And my staff does the same for me when complaints focused in my direction come first to their ears. We are learning together that direct confrontation is never comfortable, but it is always necessary in cases of complaint or criticism.

4. Openly Admit Your Mistakes

Nehemiah's admission of guilt startles us with its candor. Perhaps because we have grown accustomed to the endless denials and evasions of our political leaders. They do not necessarily speak falsely, they simply "misspeak." Rather than admit their mistakes, they blame just about everyone else—the other political party, or the media, or the Japanese, or their predecessors. Rarely do we observe our leaders freely admitting their failures. It seems that "I was wrong" doesn't play well on the six o'clock news.

But Nehemiah's openness about his failures should not be relegated to the museum of ancient leadership. Peters and Waterman, in *In Search of Excellence*, testify to the importance of tolerating failure: "A special attribute of the success-oriented, positive, and innovating environment, is a substantial tolerance for failure." They quote one business leader who claims, "You need the ability to fail. You cannot innovate unless you are willing to accept mistakes." Not surprisingly, the freedom to fail must be exemplified by leaders. "Tolerance for failure is a specific part of the excellent company culture—and that lesson comes directly from the top. Champions have to make lots of tries and consequently suffer some failures or the organization won't learn."[12]

My friend, Tom, told me about his experience with admitting failure. As a manager in a large organization, one of his responsibilities is to talk with subordinates about company lay-offs. In a recent communication he conveyed information that, unknown to him, was strictly confidential. During the next executive staff-meeting the company president expressed chagrin that privileged information had been leaked. Tom, knowing he had been the source of that leak, faced a tough choice: to feign ignorance at the risk of his integrity, or to admit his mistake at the risk of his reputation. He chose to confess, and in the presence of his fellow executives received a patronizing lecture from the company president. But in a later conversation the president told Tom privately how impressed he had been by Tom's gutsy honesty.

Corporate America needs leaders who can say, "I was wrong." So does government—and so does the church. But many of us live in an environment that provides no room for error. I live and minister in Irvine, California—a city well-known as America's most thoroughly planned community. All development follows a master plan designed by "the experts." Irvine strives for perfection, and in arrogant moments pretends to have attained it. But such a claim places a heavy burden upon the citizenry. We do not make room for failure in Irvine—it simply doesn't fit the plan. Yet in the midst of this desert of pretentious perfectionism, the churches in Irvine (including Irvine Presbyterian) can offer an oasis of grace. For we Christians already know that we are failures, and we can freely admit it because we also know that God forgives us by grace and loves us without limits.

NEHEMIAH CONFRONTS PERSONAL ATTACKS (6:1–19)

Swatting Spiritual Mosquitoes

One summer my wife, Linda, and I backpacked in the High Sierra west of Bishop, California. After cresting the Sierra at Piute Pass, we settled in Hutchinson Meadow: a remote, idyllic spot at the convergence of two rivers. After setting up camp, I set out to fish for golden trout—a Sierra fisherman's prize. Within minutes I had snagged my first "golden," followed by many others during the next hours.

It seemed as if Linda and I had found true paradise on earth, except for one thing—mosquitoes . . . millions of mosquitoes. There in beautiful Hutchinson Meadow we had stumbled into the World's Fair of mosquitoes. And they were more than happy to greet us enthusiastically. We soaked our skin with pungent insect repellent that kept the bugs from landing, but they continued to swarm inches away. And some of the more daring ones tried biting through our clothing—a tactic that worked, unfortunately. The cloud of mosquitoes created such a distraction that normal chores were impossible. Even fishing for golden trout proved to be tiresome. Finally, after two hectic nights of fighting those mini-vampires, we came to our senses and moved our camp to a higher elevation.

Those mosquitoes remind me of Nehemiah's predicament in chapter 6. The rebuilding project had been moving ahead in spite of frustrating opposition: challenges from the outside as neighboring opponents threatened Judah and challenges from within as internal strife threatened to destroy Judean unity. But in chapter 6, the threats are no longer against the nation. Instead, they are directed against Nehemiah. We see him facing a swarm of pesky spiritual "mosquitoes" that threaten to distract him from his task in Jerusalem. This is a good opportunity for us to observe how he successfully swatted these "mosquitoes" and to learn how we should respond when we are attacked personally, or are tempted to divert our attention from God's call upon our lives.

AN ATTEMPT TO DISTRACT AND ENDANGER NEHEMIAH (6:1–4)

6:1 Now it happened when Sanballat, Tobiah, Geshem the Arab, and the rest of our enemies heard that I had rebuilt the wall, and that there were no breaks left in it (though at that time I had not hung the doors in the gates),

2 that Sanballat and Geshem sent to me, saying, "Come, let us meet together among the villages in the plain of Ono." But they thought to do me harm.

3 So I sent messengers to them, saying, "I am doing a great work, so that I cannot come down. Why

should the work cease while I leave it and go down to
you?"

4 But they sent me this message four times, and I
answered them in the same manner.

Nehemiah 6:1–4

The workers had almost finished the wall. All that remained was
to hang the doors. Then *Sanballat, Tobiah,* and *Geshem the Arab* (v. 1),
who had opposed Nehemiah from the beginning (2:10, 19), tried once
again in desperation to derail the project. This time, however, they
used a different tactic—they threatened Nehemiah personally.

At first glance their invitation to a conference does not appear fore-
boding: "*Come, let us meet together among the villages in the plain of Ono*" (v.
2). So why did Nehemiah suspect ill will: "*But they thought to do me
harm*" (v. 2)? Certainly, past experience with Sanballat and his co-
horts would have raised his suspicion, but the key to the sinister
purpose of the meeting is its location. Note that Sanballat and Tobiah
did not offer to come to Jerusalem; rather, they invited Nehemiah to a
distant region. The word translated *among the villages* may, rather, be
the name of a village or region near Ono: Kephirim or Hakkephirim.[13]
"The plain of Ono" was located more than twenty-five miles northwest of Jerusalem, either on the edge of Judah or outside of the
border in an area between Samaria and Ashdod. In either case, Ono
would not be a safe place for Nehemiah to meet these men, for they
could easily capture or kill him there. Furthermore, a trip to Ono
would be at least a two-day journey, if not more, which would distract Nehemiah from finishing the work on the wall.

Wisely, Nehemiah declined the offer of a meeting: "*I am doing a great
work, so that I cannot come down*" (v. 3). If it sounds boastful to say "I am
doing a great work," perhaps we should understand Nehemiah to
mean, "I have a big job right here. I cannot leave with all of my responsibilities." "*Four times*" Sanballat and Tobiah attempted to lure
Nehemiah away from Jerusalem, and four times he declined (v. 4).
The persistence of his enemies did not overcome Nehemiah's resolve.

Keeping Focused

Although Nehemiah declined to meet with his enemies not simply
because he was choosing priorities but because he suspected that his

well-being was at risk, his answer to his potential detractors can still remind us how we should respond when we face potentially distracting opportunities. For example, Nehemiah said "no" to his enemies by stating his priorities and commitments: "I have a big job right here, and I won't take on anything else right now." He remained focused on the task at hand. I imagine that Nehemiah would have responded similarly even to friends wishing to throw a party in his honor.

How difficult it is to stay focused on what really matters! While most of us do not encounter threatening invitations, we do face a tempting buffet of options and opportunities. And, like most people at a buffet, we fill our plates far too full! Parents who value time with their children end up chauffeuring more than parenting as they transport their youngsters to endless activities. Lay ministers who serve effectively in one area of the church soon find themselves facing other tempting invitations: "Since you're such a fine Sunday School teacher, we'd like you to serve on our committee, or lead a Bible study, or serve as a deacon."

Nor are pastors free from these temptations. In fact, we may be more prone to them! For instance, though my top priority in ministry is to pastor my congregation, I find myself easily tempted by invitations to preach elsewhere, to serve on boards, or to take on writing assignments (like this commentary!). Of course it is not always wrong for me to minister in other settings as God sovereignly directs, but I have to recognize my own tendency to lose focus, and thereby to diminish my effectiveness as a pastor—not to mention my effectiveness as a husband and a father. Like Nehemiah, we must learn to evaluate new opportunities in light of God's higher call upon our lives. We need to remember that staying focused means sometimes saying no.

I was reminded of the importance of focus when I had lunch at McDonald's the other day. While waiting for my order, I noticed a phrase affixed to several surfaces behind the counter: Quality, Service, Cleanliness, and Value. In fact, this phrase determines the focus of McDonald's worldwide enterprise. These basic priorities shape the operation and growth of the company on all levels. Managers are promoted and restaurants are applauded—all in light of their faithfulness to "Quality, Service, Cleanliness, and Value." Surely the phenomenal success of McDonald's can be attributed, at least in part, to the company's unwavering focus upon its priorities. Like McDonald's motto, Nehemiah's response challenges us to keep focused on our priorities, on what really matters. Why? To swat the mosquitoes of distraction!

ATTEMPT TO LIBEL NEHEMIAH (6:5–9)

5 Then Sanballat sent his servant to me as before, the fifth time, with an open letter in his hand.

6 In it was written: It is reported among the nations, and Geshem says, that you and the Jews plan to rebel; therefore, according to these rumors, you are rebuilding the wall, that you may be their king.

7 And you have also appointed prophets to proclaim concerning you at Jerusalem, saying, "There is a king in Judah!" Now these matters will be reported to the king. So come, therefore, and let us consult together.

8 Then I sent to him, saying, "No such things as you say are being done, but you invent them in your own heart."

9 For they all were trying to make us afraid, saying, "Their hands will be weakened in the work, and it will not be done."

Now therefore, O God, strengthen my hands.

Nehemiah 6:5–9

Since Nehemiah refused to be distracted, Sanballat tried another approach to disrupt the work. He dispatched his servant with *"an open letter"* (v. 5). The Hebrew emphasizes that the correspondence was unsealed. Clearly Sanballat was less interested in communicating with Nehemiah than in spreading rumors through a libelous, unsealed letter. No doubt the servant made sure that many "eyes" saw the letter en route from Samaria to Jerusalem.

Sanballat's letter contained two libelous accusations: (1) The *"Jews plan to rebel"* against the Persians; and (2) Nehemiah intends to become *"king"* (v. 6). Allegedly, Nehemiah had *"appointed prophets"* in Jerusalem to hail him as king, an action that, if true, would support the second accusation. Also included in the letter was a promise from Sanballat to notify the Persian king of Nehemiah's grandiose plans— a threat that is reminiscent of the letter found in Ezra 4–5. But, as usual, Sanballat's primary purpose was not to inform on Nehemiah;

rather, it was to incite division and disunity within Judah. Which is precisely why he sent an "open letter." No doubt he reasoned that if common Judeans began to "see" Nehemiah as a self-centered opportunist, they would stop supporting him and his building project.

Nehemiah responded tersely to these accusations: *"No such things as you say are being done, but you invent them in your own heart"* (v. 8). Sanballat may have contrived these accusations, or they may have been circulating *"among the nations and Geshem"* (v. 6). Nevertheless, the accusations served Sanballat's purpose of denigrating Nehemiah. Projecting onto Nehemiah the selfish motives Sanballat would relate to himself, this power-hungry opponent could not have comprehended Nehemiah's desire to serve Judah and to build the wall simply for Judah's good and for God's glory. No, he would have assumed the motivation to be a quest for power and glory.

True to his character, Nehemiah simply dismissed the charges and prayed for strength (v. 9). There is no evidence that he composed a letter of defense for the Persian king, nor that he engaged in an "open-letter war" with Sanballat. He simply stated the truth as he knew it, prayed, and moved on.

Trusting in the Truth

How tempting it must have been for Nehemiah to respond with a detailed defense! I can imagine that he worried about those who had seen the open letter. Surely, he must have had a twinge of concern about how the King of Persia would respond to the charges. But, apparently, Nehemiah did little more than offer a concise denial and a short prayer for strength.

How was Nehemiah able to carry on without engaging his opponent in epistolary battle? To be sure, Nehemiah trusted God for strength and protection, but he also trusted in the truth. Knowing the utter falsehood of the libelous claims against him, Nehemiah seemed to believe that the truth would prevail without the investment of costly time and energy in defending his honor.

Current politicians would do well to imitate Nehemiah—and voters would be relieved. As I write, we are in the middle of a cantankerous and increasingly mean election for president. President George Bush, Governor Bill Clinton, and independent candidate Ross Perot are pummeling each other with rumors and innuendoes. Each campaign employs an "opposition research" staff to find individuals like Geshem who are willing to discredit the opposing candidates. As a political outsider I don't know how much truth lies behind the carefully crafted innuendoes, but I do wonder why candidates don't trust in the truth as their chief defense. Whining, excuses, elaborate denials, counter-attacks—all of these incline me to believe that "something is rotten in the state of these politicians' lives," even if I don't know exactly what it is!

By God's grace, I have not been the victim of vicious personal attacks on my ministry, but on one occasion I did find Nehemiah's example of trusting in the truth to be helpful. While serving as a Pastor of Educational Ministries, I worked hard to increase the educational staff, especially in the youth ministry and children's ministry. Opportunities for changing lives were plentiful, but we desperately needed additional staff members to serve as coaches for a growing team of lay ministers. I received strong support from the Board of Elders, staff, and congregation—with one exception. A particularly influential elder opposed me every step of the way. To a mutual friend he explained: "Mark just wants to build his own kingdom, to add to his own power." Now, I will admit to times of self-interested motives in ministry, and in this instance there may have been a part of me that enjoyed the signs of success and growth, but this was certainly not the whole story, as I consider my own heart.

I felt sad that this elder simply could not understand my desire to reach more young people through an expanded education ministry. And since he never came to me directly with these charges, I never felt inclined to defend myself against them. I believed that truth would prevail without undue effort on my part, and, in fact, it did. We proceeded with the program I had suggested and ultimately this elder even became a friend.

Though it does not always happen this way, truth often swats the mosquitoes of false charges without requiring that we wave our arms in defense until we are exhausted. Like Nehemiah, we can trust in the truth because God upholds the truth. In the words of the psalmist:

> By [God] I can crush a troop,
> and by my God I can leap over a wall.
> This God—his way is perfect;

the promise of the LORD proves true;
he is a shield for all who take refuge in him.

Psalm 18:29–30 NRSV

AN ATTEMPT TO DISGRACE NEHEMIAH (6:10-14)

10 Afterward I came to the house of Shemaiah the
son of Delaiah, the son of Mehetabel, who was a
secret informer; and he said, "Let us meet together in
the house of God, within the temple, and let us close
the doors of the temple, for they are coming to kill
you; indeed, at night they will come to kill you."
11 And I said, "Should such a man as I flee? And
who is there such as I who would go into the temple
to save his life? I will not go in!"
12 Then I perceived that God had not sent him at
all, but that he pronounced this prophecy against me
because Tobiah and Sanballat had hired him.
13 For this reason he was hired, that I should be
afraid and act that way and sin, so that they might
have cause for an evil report, that they might
reproach me.
14 My God, remember Tobiah and Sanballat,
according to these their works, and the prophetess
Noadiah and the rest of the prophets who would have
made me afraid.

Nehemiah 6:10–14

The next attempt to distract Nehemiah originated from an obscure
Jewish prophet named *Shemaiah* (v. 10). According to the NKJV, he was
"*a secret informer*," though the translation of the Hebrew here is uncertain (v. 10).[14] It is certain, however, that he was hired by *Tobiah* and
Sanballat to discredit Nehemiah publicly (vv. 12–13). The fact that
Nehemiah went to Shemaiah's house suggests that the prophet must
have been a person of some influence. Indeed, a few verses later we
learn that Tobiah, in particular, had strong ties with leaders in Judah.
Shemaiah "prophesied" to Nehemiah: your enemies "*are coming to
kill you*," even this very night (v. 10). But the prophet had a plan to
save Nehemiah's life: "*Let us meet together in the house of God, within
the temple*." He proposed that the leader of Judah hide, not only

221

within the larger temple structure (*"the house of God"*), but specifically within the *"temple"* itself— in the holy place just outside of the Holy of Holies.[15] But Nehemiah was not a priest and, as such, had no right to enter the holy place. If carried out, Shemaiah's proposal would disgrace Nehemiah in two ways. First, it would cause him to commit a ritual transgression by going where priests alone were allowed. (Numbers 18:7 not only limits entrance to priests, but sentences a trespasser to death.) Second, by hiding to save his own life, Nehemiah would be seen as a coward, a poor leader for Judah.

Nehemiah's response addresses both aspects of the attempt to disgrace him. First he says, *"Should such a man as I flee?"* (v. 11). In other words, "I'm a leader, a man of boldness and responsibility. How can I run away in times of danger? That would be inconsistent with my personality and my responsibility." Second, he says, *"And who is there such as I who would go into the temple to save his life?"* (v. 11). A paraphrase of his response might be, "I am a commoner, a lay person; I am not a priest. I cannot go into the temple to save my life. In fact, I might lose it by trespassing in the holy place!"

Curiously, only after he rejected the false prophecy did Nehemiah *"perceive that God had not sent him at all, but that he pronounced this prophecy against me because Tobiah and Sanballat had hired him"* (v. 12). The text does not explain how Nehemiah identified Tobiah and Sanballat as the instigators of this plot. Undoubtedly they had hoped that fear would motivate Nehemiah to *"sin"* by entering the temple (v. 13), thus disgracing himself publicly. But their plot was foiled by Nehemiah's firm rejection. The passage closes with a prayer that mentions, without elaboration, other *"prophets"* who were collaborating with Tobiah and Sanballat (v. 14).

Know Who You Are

The attempt to trick Nehemiah through false prophecy failed, but not because he immediately saw through the deception. Rather, Nehemiah rejected the suggestion on the basis of his own identity: on the basis of who he was and who he was not. Nehemiah knew his inner character, and this self-image determined his behavior. Only later did he recognize the devious nature of the plot and its origin.

To the suggestion that he hide from danger, Nehemiah responded by pointing to his character and to his role as a leader. Timidity did not fit with Nehemiah's identity, nor did an overriding self-interest. No, Nehemiah knew himself as a courageous, responsible leader, and his actions reflected that abiding self-concept and self-esteem.

Yet Nehemiah did not have an overblown sense of his own self-importance. He was not like a prominent baseball star who recently completed five days of suspension from the team. Upon his return, a reporter asked the star what he had been thinking about during his suspension. "The magnitude of me," was his answer.[16] No, Nehemiah knew the limits of his personal magnitude. He was not a priest, and therefore could not enter the temple, even to save his own life.

We will be able to swat spiritual mosquitoes best when we know who we are. When I listen to parishioners mired in guilt over sins confessed and forgiven years ago, I often respond by reminding them of who they are in Christ: forgiven ones, not perfect ones; those for whom Christ died; those who have been raised with Christ. Others sense God's call into ministry, but fear they will fail. These folks need to hear once again who they are in Christ: a temple of the Holy Spirit; members of Christ's Body who are gifted for ministry; soldiers in God's army.

At the same time, like Nehemiah we must not become too sure of ourselves. Sadly, I watch fellow pastors become embroiled in difficulties because they do not know their own limitations. Sometimes they enter into therapeutic relationships that demand psychological training beyond their capabilities. Sometimes those who have the privilege of preaching get carried away with their own authority. They stray far afield, speaking as experts about topics in which they are mere novices.

Admittedly, at times I will touch upon matters in preaching that go beyond my realm of expertise: parenting skills, financial management, political concerns. But I speak with greater caution than when I preach the gospel of Christ. I know without reservation that Christ died for our sins, but who am I to walk boldly into the realms of adolescent parenting and offer detailed rules for discipline, when I don't have teen-aged children or special training in adolescent psychology. By knowing and admitting precisely who I am as a pastor, I can lead with a careful balance of boldness and humility. By knowing who we are in Christ, we will be ready to swat the mosquitoes of compromise and personal aggrandizement.

COMPLETION OF THE WALL (6:15–16)

15 So the wall was finished on the twenty-fifth
day of Elul, in fifty-two days.
16 And it happened, when all our enemies heard
of it, and all the nations around us saw these things,
that they were very disheartened in their own eyes; for
they perceived that this work was done by our God.

Nehemiah 6:15–16

The *"wall was finished on the twenty-fifth day of Elul,"* or in late September. Amazingly, the entire project took only *"fifty-two days."* It was a testimony to Nehemiah's exceptional leadership, and it caused the *"enemies"* of Nehemiah to be *"very disheartened"* (v. 16). Their attempts to interrupt the project had failed dismally. So miraculous was the timing of completion that the opponents *"perceived that this work was done by our God"* (v. 16).

I wonder. Would those outside of the church say this about our activities? Are we attempting anything for God that requires a desperate dependence upon him? Or do we always take the safe road, allowing our observers merely to say: "My, how well organized and hard working are the people in that church."

One might expect that the completion of the wall would have received more fanfare in the text. As it stands, this great achievement is hidden rather obscurely between accounts of conspiracies to topple Nehemiah. Later, in chapter 12, the wall will be dedicated in a splendid celebration, but for now its completion appears as a mere parenthetical comment. Given what follows in chapters 8–12, however, the book of Ezra-Nehemiah clarifies that the wall itself is not the point. Regardless of how important it was, the wall only provided a secure environment for what really mattered: the covenant people of God living righteously as God's people.

OPPOSITION CONTINUES (6:17–19)

17 Also in those days the nobles of Judah sent
many letters to Tobiah, and the letters of Tobiah came
to them.
18 For many in Judah were pledged to him,
because he was the son–in–law of Shechaniah the son

of Arah, and his son Jehohanan had married the
daughter of Meshullam the son of Berechiah.
   19 Also they reported his good deeds before me,
and reported my words to him. Tobiah sent letters to
frighten me.

Nehemiah 6:17–19

Having mentioned the completion of the wall, Nehemiah quickly
turns aside to recount the conspiratorial actions of his opponents, especially Tobiah. This clever antagonist had influential connections
within Judah, in part because he and his son had married into distinguished Jewish families. Curiously, Tobiah's *"son Jehohnan had
married the daughter of Meshullam the son of Berechiah"* (v. 18)—the
same Meshullam mentioned in 3:4 as a worker on the wall. Possibly
Tobiah's brother-in-law also labored on the wall (3:29). These men
supported Nehemiah, yet worked for reconciliation between their
leader and their relative, Tobiah. Not only did Nehemiah reject this
opportunity for diplomacy, but Tobiah also seemed to have little interest in building a relationship with Nehemiah, since he sent letters
to frighten him (v. 19). Thus, constantly opposing each other, Tobiah
and Nehemiah seem to agree on only one thing: the irreconcilability
of their conflict.

NOTES

1. For commentary on the people and work, see the discussion of
Nehemiah 3, above.
2. What the people from the outlying areas actually said is not
clear in the original. They may have requested special attention from
Nehemiah himself. See the discussion in Williamson, *Ezra, Nehemiah,*
pp. 221–22, 226–27.
3. Williamson, *Ezra, Nehemiah,* pp. 226–27.
4. The last phrase of the verse provides a peculiar and amusing
puzzle. The NKJV (following the KJV) of 4:23 reads: *"So neither I, my
brethren, my servants, nor the men of the guard who followed me took off
our clothes, except that everyone took them off for washing."* Other translations of the final phrase read differently. The NIV, for example, ends

this way: "Each had his weapon, even when he went for water." The NRSV offers another nuance: "each kept his weapon in his right hand." The MT literally reads "a man his weapon the waters," and the phrase does not appear in the LXX. For a technical discussion, see Williamson, pp. 223–24. The original meaning of the text cannot be ascertained with certainty. But I find the NKJV's concern for cleanliness to be somewhat amusing. The translators were obviously concerned with the disagreeable implications of the fact that Nehemiah and his men had spent many days working and sleeping in the same clothes.

5. Williamson, *Ezra, Nehemiah*, p. 238.

6. Where the NKJV translates the Niphal feminine participle of *kābaš* as "*have been brought into slavery*," the NRSV uses "have been ravished." See Brown, Driver, and Briggs, *Lexicon*, p. 461; and Fensham, *Ezra and Nehemiah*, p. 192.

7. Kidner, *Ezra & Nehemiah*, p. 96.

8. Williamson, *Ezra, Nehemiah*, p. 233.

9. On the absolution of loans, see Fensham, *Ezra and Nehemiah*, p. 195, and Kidner, *Ezra & Nehemiah*, p. 96.

10. T. J. Peters and R. H. Waterman, Jr., *In Search of Excellence: Lessons from America's Best-Run Companies* (New York: Warner Books, 1984), p. 193.

11. T. Peters and N. Austin, *A Passion for Excellence: The Leadership Difference* (New York: Warner Books, 1986), p. 97.

12. Peters and Waterman, *In Search of Excellence*, p. 223.

13. Because this village is unknown, scribes and translators of the Hebrew have read "among the villages," which in Hebrew resembles the name "*Hakkephirim*."

14. Translations vary widely, for example: "*who was a secret informer*" (NKJV); "who was confined to his house" (NRSV); "who was looking extremely worried" (Williamson, *Ezra, Nehemiah*, p. 249). The precise meaning of the Hebrew term *ʿaṣûr* is uncertain. A literal translation would be "shut up, restrained" (Brown, Driver, and Briggs, *Lexicon*, p. 783).

15. Brown, Driver, and Briggs, *Lexicon*, p. 228.

16. From "Morning Briefing," by S. Howard-Cooper, LA Times, June 29, 1992, C:2. Excerpted from D. Schaap, *Joy in Mudville*.

CHAPTER FOURTEEN

Jerusalem After the Wall

Nehemiah 7:1–73

This chapter concludes Nehemiah's effort to rebuild the wall. It begins with his assignment of guards for Jerusalem, then moves into an extended genealogical list.

GUARDING JERUSALEM (7:1–3)

7:1 Then it was, when the wall was built and I had hung the doors, when the gatekeepers, the singers, and the Levites had been appointed,

2 that I gave the charge of Jerusalem to my brother Hanani, and Hananiah the leader of the citadel, for he was a faithful man and feared God more than many.

3 And I said to them, "Do not let the gates of Jerusalem be opened until the sun is hot; and while they stand guard, let them shut and bar the doors; and appoint guards from among the inhabitants of Jerusalem, one at his watch station and another in front of his own house."

Nehemiah 7:1–3

With the wall complete and the doors finally in place, the residents of Jerusalem might become lax and trust their security to the wall alone. But Nehemiah preempts such laxity by assigning leaders to guard the city and its new wall. *Hanani*, Nehemiah's brother, appeared first in chapter 1 when he brought to Nehemiah the dire report about Jerusalem that initiated the rebuilding process. *"Hananiah the leader of the citadel"* is not only a military leader, but a person of model integrity (v. 2). Nehemiah entrusted the care of the city only to those deserving of his trust.

The Hebrew in verse 3 is difficult to translate. The NKJV rendering, "*Do not let the gates of Jerusalem be opened until the sun is hot,*" probably misses the original intention. Rather, it should read: "the gates should not remain open when the sun is hot, and guards might be drowsy." In other words, during siesta time, the gates should be closed.[1]

Registration of Residents (7:4–73)

4 Now the city was large and spacious, but the people in it were few, and the houses were not rebuilt.

5 Then my God put it into my heart to gather the nobles, the rulers, and the people, that they might be registered by genealogy. And I found a register of the genealogy of those who had come up in the first return, and found written in it:

6 These are the people of the province who came back from the captivity, of those who had been carried away, whom Nebuchadnezzar the king of Babylon had carried away, and who returned to Jerusalem and Judah, everyone to his city.

7 Those who came with Zerubbabel were Jeshua, Nehemiah, Azariah, Raamiah, Nahamani, Mordecai, Bilshan, Mispereth, Bigvai, Nehum and Baanah.

The number of the men of the people of Israel:

8 the sons of Parosh, two thousand one hundred and seventy-two;

9 the sons of Shephatiah, three hundred and seventy-two;

10 the sons of Arah, six hundred and fifty-two;

11 the sons of Pahath-Moab, of the sons of Jeshua and Joab, two thousand eight hundred and eighteen;

12 the sons of Elam, one thousand two hundred and fifty-four;

13 the sons of Zattu, eight hundred and forty-five;

14 the sons of Zaccai, seven hundred and sixty;

15 the sons of Binnui, six hundred and forty-eight;

16 the sons of Bebai, six hundred and twenty-eight;

17 the sons of Azgad, two thousand three hundred and twenty-two;

18 the sons of Adonikam, six hundred and sixty-seven;

19 the sons of Bigvai, two thousand and sixty-seven;

20 the sons of Adin, six hundred and fifty-five;

21 the sons of Ater of Hezekiah, ninety-eight;

22 the sons of Hashum, three hundred and twenty-eight;

23 the sons of Bezai, three hundred and twenty-four;

24 the sons of Hariph, one hundred and twelve;

25 the sons of Gibeon, ninety-five;

26 the men of Bethlehem and Netophah, one hundred and eighty-eight;

27 the men of Anathoth, one hundred and twenty-eight;

28 the men of Beth Azmaveth, forty-two;

29 the men of Kirjath Jearim, Chephirah, and Beeroth, seven hundred and forty-three;

30 the men of Ramah and Geba, six hundred and twenty-one;

31 the men of Michmas, one hundred and twenty-two;

32 the men of Bethel and Ai, one hundred and twenty-three;

33 the men of the other Nebo, fifty-two;

34 the sons of the other Elam, one thousand two hundred and fifty-four;

35 the sons of Harim, three hundred and twenty;

36 the sons of Jericho, three hundred and forty-five;

37 the sons of Lod, Hadid, and Ono, seven hundred and twenty-one;

38 the sons of Senaah, three thousand nine hundred and thirty.

39 The priests: the sons of Jedaiah, of the house of Jeshua, nine hundred and seventy-three;

40 the sons of Immer, one thousand and fifty-two;

41 the sons of Pashhur, one thousand two hundred and forty-seven;

42 the sons of Harim, one thousand and seventeen.

43 The Levites: the sons of Jeshua, of Kadmiel, and of the sons of Hodevah, seventy-four.

44 The singers: the sons of Asaph, one hundred and forty-eight.

45 The gatekeepers: the sons of Shallum, the sons of Ater, the sons of Talmon, the sons of Akkub, the sons of Hatita, the sons of Shobai, one hundred and thirty-eight.

46 The Nethinim: the sons of Ziha, the sons of Hasupha, the sons of Tabbaoth,

47 the sons of Keros, the sons of Sia, the sons of Padon,

48 the sons of Lebana, the sons of Hagaba, the sons of Salmai,

49 the sons of Hanan, the sons of Giddel, the sons of Gahar,

50 the sons of Reaiah, the sons of Rezin, the sons of Nekoda,

51 the sons of Gazzam, the sons of Uzza, the sons of Paseah,

52 the sons of Besai, the sons of Meunim, the sons of Nephishesim,

53 the sons of Bakbuk, the sons of Hakupha, the sons of Harhur,

54 the sons of Bazlith, the sons of Mehida, the sons of Harsha,

55 the sons of Barkos, the sons of Sisera, the sons of Tamah,

56 the sons of Neziah, and the sons of Hatipha.

57 The sons of Solomon's servants: the sons of Sotai, the sons of Sophereth, the sons of Perida,

58 the sons of Jaala, the sons of Darkon, the sons of Giddel,

59 the sons of Shephatiah, the sons of Hattil, the sons of Pochereth of Zebaim, and the sons of Amon.

60 All the Nethinim, and the sons of Solomon's servants, were three hundred and ninety-two.

61 And these were the ones who came up from Tel Melah, Tel Harsha, Cherub, Addon, and Immer, but they could not identify their father's house nor their lineage, whether they were of Israel:

62 the sons of Delaiah, the sons of Tobiah, the sons of Nekoda, six hundred and forty-two;

63 and of the priests: the sons of Habaiah, the sons of Koz, the sons of Barzillai, who took a wife of the daughters of Barzillai the Gileadite, and was called by their name.

64 These sought their listing among those who were registered by genealogy, but it was not found; therefore they were excluded from the priesthood as defiled.

65 And the governor said to them that they should not eat of the most holy things till a priest could consult with the Urim and Thummim.

66 Altogether the whole assembly was forty-two thousand three hundred and sixty,

67 besides their male and female servants, of whom there were seven thousand three hundred and thirty-seven; and they had two hundred and forty-five men and women singers.

68 Their horses were seven hundred and thirty-six, their mules two hundred and forty-five,

69 their camels four hundred and thirty-five, and donkeys six thousand seven hundred and twenty.

70 And some of the heads of the fathers' houses gave to the work. The governor gave to the treasury one thousand gold drachmas, fifty basins, and five hundred and thirty priestly garments.

71 Some of the heads of the fathers' houses gave to the treasury of the work twenty thousand gold drachmas, and two thousand two hundred silver minas.

72 And that which the rest of the people gave was twenty thousand gold drachmas, two thousand silver minas, and sixty-seven priestly garments.

73 So the priests, the Levites, the gatekeepers, the singers, some of the people, the Nethinim, and all Israel dwelt in their cities.
When the seventh month came, the children of Israel were in their cities.

Nehemiah 7:4–73

God urged Nehemiah to take a census of all residents of Jerusalem according to their genealogy (v. 5). For this registration he used a registry of persons who had returned to Judah in the day of Cyrus, more than ninety years earlier. The list that is given in verses 6–72 essentially repeats the list found in Ezra 2:2–73. The few minor discrepancies between the two lists undoubtedly reflect the difficulty of textual transmission. For commentary on the list, see the discussion of Ezra 2 in Chapter 2, above. Note, too, that verse 73 is transitional. Its final sentence (73b) probably should have been the beginning of chapter 8.

NOTES

1. Williamson, *Ezra, Nehemiah,* p. 270.

Restoration of Covenant Life, Phase Two: Ezra and Nehemiah Together

Nehemiah 8:1–13:30

Several features of the text indicate a change in perspective and sources between chapters 7 and 8. The first person singular of Nehemiah's memoirs is replaced by a third person description ("I did . . . Nehemiah did . . ."). Surprisingly, Ezra returns on the scene after an unexplained absence of thirteen years (and seven chapters). Interestingly, in chapters 8–10 he plays a more dominant role than Nehemiah, who virtually disappears until the latter part of chapter 12. The rebuilt wall, finished in chapter 6, receives no further mention until chapter 12. Rather, the focus turns to the Law and to its ordering of covenant life among God's people.

Chapters 8–10 are particularly challenging to scholars. The question of the sources used by the editor of Ezra–Nehemiah elicits a variety of responses,[1] but the tougher question has to do with the relationship between Ezra and Nehemiah. Chapters 8–10 describe these two leaders as contemporaries, sharing together in the restoration of Judah, but their togetherness seems awkward. We find no genuine partnership, but only an occasional juxtaposition of names (for example, 8:9). Throughout chapters 8 and 9 Nehemiah seems virtually absent, as did Ezra during Nehemiah's endeavors to build the wall. The uneasy joining of Ezra and Nehemiah in these chapters has led some scholars to conclude that they did not, in fact, work together. Rather, these commentators propose, the editor of Ezra-Nehemiah joined the two leaders for his theological purposes.[2]

In the Introduction to Ezra-Nehemiah, I discussed briefly the historical relationship between Ezra and Nehemiah, concluding that there is no compelling reason to reject the historicity of the present account.[3] Incongruities may be explained without moving Ezra's service after Nehemiah's. But scholars who argue for the historical accuracy of Ezra-Nehemiah often miss the theological significance of the editor's telling of events. It is not enough to say that he told the story as it happened. Rather, he carefully shaped his story and the underlying sources to make a potent theological statement. This statement stands, whether or not the events described happened in precisely the order depicted. So, while we may accept the overlapping ministries of Ezra and Nehemiah, we must also consider the textual puzzles involved. Why, indeed, does Nehemiah play such an inconspicuous role in the climax of the book named for him?

The overall structure of Ezra-Nehemiah provides a clue to this mystery. The book of Ezra commences with the rebuilding of the temple and culminates with the work of Ezra, who brings the Law to Judah. Similarly, Nehemiah begins with the rebuilding of the wall and ends with the ordering of community life according to the Law. In each book, building lays the foundation for the Law. The material and the spiritual go hand-in-hand. While the material happens first, ultimately the spiritual takes precedence.

Nehemiah chapters 8–10 form the literary and theological apex of Ezra-Nehemiah.[4] There, within the newly-rebuilt walls and centered around the rebuilt temple, the Law reorders the life of God's people—the covenant is renewed. Although Nehemiah and Ezra both contribute to this restoration process, ultimately Ezra takes precedence as the one who reads and teaches the Law.

Chapters 11–13 contain some items of interest, including the dedication of the wall, but they pale in comparison to chapters 8–10. In fact, Ezra-Nehemiah ends more with a whimper than a bang, as we shall see in chapter 13.

NOTES

1. See, for example, the discussions in Williamson, *Ezra, Nehemiah,* pp. 275–76, 279–86, 305–10.

2. Childs, *Introduction,* pp. 634–37.

3. In addition to the "Introduction" above, see also: Williamson, *Ezra, Nehemiah,* pp. xxxix–xliv; Kidner, *Ezra & Nehemiah,* pp. 146–58.

4. Childs, *Introduction,* pp. 635–37.

CHAPTER FIFTEEN

Renewal Through Understanding and Celebrating the Law

Nehemiah 8:1–18

A NEW VIEW OF THE LAW

My friend John loves to study the Bible. Although he has never attended seminary, he knows the Scriptures more thoroughly than many pastors. Over forty years ago, John committed his leisure time to meticulous Bible study. Today I enjoy talking with him about the meaning of specific passages because inevitably he helps me to see God's truth in new ways. John studies the Bible, not out of a sense of duty or guilt, but out of sheer love. He has a zeal for God's truth and celebrates when he discovers new facets of that truth.

I wish we were all more like John. Many of us who believe in Christ have fallen into a familiar, tragic pattern. When we first accepted the Lord, we eagerly studied the Scriptures. We used study guides, we took notes, and we enthusiastically marked up our brand new Bibles. But as the years passed, we grew increasingly nonchalant about God's truth. Now we find Bible study to be more of a chore than a delight. We may even think of God's Law as something that ruins our fun rather than as something that calls forth celebration.

Nehemiah 8 challenges our complacent approach to the Bible and our tendency to associate God's Law with grudging obedience. The completion of the wall in chapter 6 sets the stage for chapter 8. God's people finally have adequate physical protection, so it is time for spiritual rebuilding. And here, after a mysterious thirteen year absence, Ezra reappears to lead the people into renewal as God's covenant people whose lives are ordered by the Law. Meanwhile,

235

Nehemiah steps into the background during this season of spiritual restoration.

READING AND UNDERSTANDING THE LAW (8:1–8)

8:1 Now all the people gathered together as one man in the open square that was in front of the Water Gate; and they told Ezra the scribe to bring the Book of the Law of Moses, which the LORD had commanded Israel.

2 So Ezra the priest brought the Law before the assembly, of men and women and all who could hear with understanding, on the first day of the seventh month.

3 Then he read from it in the open square that was in front of the Water Gate from morning until midday, before the men and women and those who could understand; and the ears of all the people were attentive to the Book of the Law.

4 So Ezra the scribe stood on a platform of wood which they had made for the purpose; and beside him, at his right hand, stood Mattithiah, Shema, Anaiah, Urijah, Hilkiah, and Maaseiah; and at his left hand Pedaiah, Mishael, Malchijah, Hashum, Hashbadana, Zechariah, and Meshullam.

5 And Ezra opened the book in the sight of all the people, for he was standing above all the people; and when he opened it, all the people stood up.

6 And Ezra blessed the LORD, the great God. Then all the people answered, "Amen, Amen!" while lifting up their hands. And they bowed their heads and worshiped the LORD with their faces to the ground.

7 Also Jeshua, Bani, Sherebiah, Jamin, Akkub, Shabbethai, Hodijah, Maaseiah, Kelita, Azariah, Jozabad, Hanan, Pelaiah, and the Levites, helped the people to understand the Law; and the people stood in their place.

8 So they read distinctly from the book, in the Law of God; and they gave the sense, and helped them to understand the reading.

Nehemiah 8:1–8

In the seventh month (7:73), or late September, the people gathered (*"as one man"*) in an open area near the *"Water Gate"* (v. 1). We are surprised to find here that, Ezra now returns to the scene of events. Having brought *"the Book of the Law of Moses"* (v.1), he began to read from it. We cannot be sure exactly how much of the Torah (Genesis, Exodus, Leviticus, Numbers, Deuteronomy) Ezra brought, but we do know that he read for six hours, so apparently it was a substantial portion. (v. 3).

The gathered assembly included a variety of persons: not only *"men,"* but also *"women and all who could hear with understanding"* (v. 2). Those children who were old enough to understand the Law joined the assembly. The Bible, especially the book of Deuteronomy, regularly includes children in religious education, highlighting their importance as persons of faith (Deut. 4:10; 11:19; 31:12–13; Ps. 34:11; 78:5).

Typical of Ezra-Nehemiah, verses 3–8 do not provide a sequential ordering of events, but, rather, a summary of the entire proceedings. So we find that in order to be seen and heard in the reading, Ezra stood *"on a platform of wood which they had made for the purpose"* (v. 4), and which was large enough for other leaders to stand alongside him. This description reminds me of the President's State of the Union address, an occasion when he stands at the podium with an impressive array of leaders in the background.

When Ezra opened the book of the Law, or more accurately, when he unrolled the scroll, all the people stood as a gesture of respect (v. 5). When Ezra blessed the Lord, the people rejoined *"'Amen, Amen!' while lifting up their hands"* (v. 6). Then they bowed down and worshiped God *"with their faces to the ground"* (v. 6). For those of us accustomed to worshiping "decently and in order" (usually in a seated position), all of this sounds suspiciously Catholic or Charismatic, except for the "Amen" part, which seems a bit Baptist. I can imagine many Presbyterian preachers skipping this verse altogether in their exposition. Yet while they are not the focus of chapter 8, verses 5–6 do paint a noteworthy picture of fully participatory worship. Oh, that we all, regardless of our particular Christian tradition, would learn to worship God with all of our heart, all of our mind, and all of our strength. The people of Israel challenge us to become active participants in the worship of God.

Ezra read from the Law *"from morning until midday,"* or for about six hours. Throughout this extended period of time, *"the ears of all the*

people were attentive to the Book of the Law" (v. 3). What a startling observation! I cannot imagine any congregation of Western Christians
standing for six hours while the preacher reads the Scriptures. In fact,
a couple of weeks ago I read an article strongly urging preachers to
limit their expositions to the attention span of most people: seventeen
minutes! Why were the people able to listen for half a day? First, their
oral culture (before television and printing presses) nourished well-
developed listening skills. Second, they obviously hungered to know
the Law of God, which had been ignored for so long. During the
physical rebuilding of Jerusalem the people grew in their desire for
spiritual rebuilding based upon the Law.

As we continue reading, verses 7–8 amplify the picture a bit further. Not only did Ezra read from the Law, but many Levites,
including those named in 8:7, *"helped the people to understand the Law."*[1]
The Levites *"read distinctly from the book"* (v. 8), perhaps "paragraph
by paragraph,"[2] and then *"gave the sense."* They interpreted the passage and helped those gathered *"to understand the reading."* Diverse
forms of the verb "to understand" appear throughout this chapter
(vss. 2, 3, 7, 8, 9, 12, 13).[3] This repetition of the verb highlights the focus on understanding the Law—not simply hearing it or blindly
obeying it. (See below.) We do not know whether the Levites taught
during the six hours mentioned in v. 3, or at another time. The passage seems to imply that subsequent to the reading they divided the
large assembly into smaller groups for explanation and discussion:
an ancient version of "Sunday school."

THE PEOPLE RESPOND (8:9–12)

9 And Nehemiah, who was the governor, Ezra
the priest and scribe, and the Levites who taught the
people said to all the people, "This day is holy to the
LORD your God; do not mourn nor weep." For all the
people wept, when they heard the words of the Law.
10 Then he said to them, "Go your way, eat the
fat, drink the sweet, and send portions to those for
whom nothing is prepared; for this day is holy to our
LORD. Do not sorrow, for the joy of the LORD is your
strength."
11 So the Levites quieted all the people, saying,
"Be still, for the day is holy; do not be grieved."

12 And all the people went their way to eat and
drink, to send portions and rejoice greatly, because
they understood the words that were declared to them.

Nehemiah 8:9–12

When the people heard and understood the Law, they began to weep (v. 9). We can only imagine why. Perhaps they were convicted of sin, or perhaps they realized that their suffering could have been prevented if only they and their ancestors had obeyed God's precepts. Whatever their reason, although it seems an appropriate response to the Law, the leaders (including Nehemiah, Ezra, and the Levites) rebuked the people for their tears: *"This day is holy to the* LORD *your God; do not mourn nor weep"* (v. 9). Instead, they encouraged the people to celebrate and to throw a great party, *"for the joy of the* LORD *is your strength"* (v. 10). The phrase *"eat the fat"* here means, in our parlance, "eat the best cuts of meat"; or, in other words, "Go have prime rib and filet mignon!" And those who did not have food appropriate for a party were to be invited anyway. Everyone was to celebrate and rejoice. (Weeping in response to the Law will be encouraged later, in chapter 9, but rejoicing comes first.)

The leaders prevailed upon the people, who *"went their way to eat and drink, to send portions [to those who didn't have any] and rejoice greatly, because they understood the words that were declared to them"* (v. 12). Verses 1–12 not only emphasize an understanding of the Law, but identify this understanding as the cause for the joyful celebration. Just imagine! The people threw a giant party, to which all were invited, because they comprehended the Law!

THE FEAST OF BOOTHS (8:14–18)

13 Now on the second day the heads of the
fathers' houses of all the people, with the priests and
Levites, were gathered to Ezra the scribe, in order to
understand the words of the Law.

14 And they found written in the Law, which the
LORD had commanded by Moses, that the children of
Israel should dwell in booths during the feast of the
seventh month,

15 and that they should announce and proclaim
in all their cities and in Jerusalem, saying, "Go out to
the mountain, and bring olive branches, branches of
oil trees, myrtle branches, palm branches, and
branches of leafy trees, to make booths, as it is
written."
16 Then the people went out and brought them
and made themselves booths, each one on the roof of
his house, or in their courtyards or the courts of the
house of God, and in the open square of the Water
Gate and in the open square of the Gate of Ephraim.
17 So the whole assembly of those who had
returned from the captivity made booths and sat
under the booths; for since the days of Joshua the son
of Nun until that day the children of Israel had not
done so. And there was very great gladness.
18 Also day by day, from the first day until the
last day, he read from the Book of the Law of God.
And they kept the feast seven days; and on the eighth
day there was a sacred assembly, according to the
prescribed manner.

Nehemiah 8:13–18

Once again, in their desire *"to understand"* the Law, the leaders of
Judah gathered to hear from Ezra. This time they learned about the
Feast of Booths as prescribed in Leviticus 23:34–43. The Feast of
Booths, which is sometimes called The Feast of Tabernacles or simply
Sukkoth (the Hebrew word meaning "booths"), begins on the fifteenth day of the seventh month (in early fall, Lev. 23:34). It includes
days of rest, special offerings, feasting on newly harvested fruits, and
living in booths for seven days (Lev. 23:42). By living in temporary
structures of brush and sticks, the Israelites remembered the sojourn-
ing of their ancestors in the wilderness (Lev. 23:43). It sounds to me
like the ancient Israelite version of Church Family Camp!

Needless to say, when the leaders heard about the Feast of the
Booths, they called all of Judah to participate in the festival (v. 15).
For the first time in a long time, everyone was involved and the feel-
ing of joy predominated: *"And there was very great gladness"* (v. 17).
The people obeyed the Law, not with sullen severity, but with exu-
berant celebration!

240

The Importance of Understanding

Throughout this chapter, the understanding of God's Law is high-lighted. For example, those gathered included *"all who could hear with understanding"* (v. 2); the Levites *"helped the people to understand the Law"* (v. 8); and once they did understand, they threw a great party to celebrate that *"they understood the words that were declared to them"* (v. 12). Ezra and the other leaders were not satisfied simply to read the Law and leave the people to make of it what the would. No, they labored not only to declare God's truth but to make sure people understood it.

What an example for those of us who communicate God's truth today! We who teach and preach would profit from taking this example to heart. In the abstract, most of us would like our listeners (worship participants, Bible-study members, Sunday school students, etc.) to understand what we communicate. But how seriously do we take this goal? Do we ever verify that the listeners have understood what we have taught or preached? Can we assume that if we present truth in an interesting and compelling manner, understanding will naturally follow? Undoubtedly, such an assumption would regularly prove to be false.

Although I occasionally teach Bible studies and small groups, my principal venue for teaching is the Sunday worship service. I work hard to prepare my sermons for this service by studying the text, by searching for appropriate illustrations, and by prayerfully considering applications. I am committed to helping my congregation understand God's truth, and that is a prodigious challenge. For each Sunday I preach to a diverse gathering of people, from fourth-grade children, through junior-high youth, to folks who come from Regents Point, a nearby retirement community. My congregation includes people who are still in elementary school, as well as many who have earned doctorates in various fields. How can I communicate with fourth graders while keeping college professors interested?

There are three rules of thumb that help me with this formidable assignment:

- While preparing my sermons, *I mentally picture my congregation:* I see the junior highers in the first two rows; I envision my friends from Regents Point, Ida and Stewart; I remember those who are mature in Christ; and I remember those who are not yet Christians. As I visualize these parishioners, I ask the Lord, "What would *you* like to say to these people? How can I help them understand *your* truth this week?"

- *I try to include in my sermon something for everyone.* That is not to say I try to please everyone all the time. Rather, in each sermon I try to include at least something for most of those gathered. Admittedly, this is not easy since I do not think like either a fourth-grader or a grandmother. But the extra effort put into trying to think like them, to identify with their needs and interests, pays off in increased understanding among the congregants. For example, my sermon on Nehemiah 8 began with an illustration from "The Simpsons," those laughable cartoon characters. While not everyone in the congregation could identify with that illustration, the kids loved it. In fact, I received a prized memento from a junior-high student who drew a picture of Bart Simpson, with this caption: "From a Junior Higher who loved your sermon about Bart."

- *I listen intentionally to all congregants,* especially when they tell me what works (or does not work!) in my sermons. I have found it particularly effective to listen to individuals whose life experience I do not share: ethnic minorities, senior adults, children, singles, parents of teenagers, etc. The truth of the matter is, I question how anyone can be an effective communicator without being an attentive listener.

Nehemiah 8 further demonstrates that the goal of understanding must be shared both by those who teach and by those who learn. Thus, no matter how carefully I have prepared and delivered my sermon, understanding requires effort on the part of my listeners. They must pay attention, and in this process must engage both mind and heart. Unfortunately, many people who have gone to church for a lifetime have developed a habit of turning off their minds in church. But this is certainly not the case of Ezra and the people in Nehemiah 8. With this example in mind, I frequently remind my congregation of their responsibility on Sunday mornings: to worship God actively, to think energetically, and to participate completely.

This passage also demonstrates the inadequacy of an exclusively lecture-style education model in the church. To be sure, we must proclaim God's truth. Indeed, I am a dyed-in-the-wool expository preacher and I value a lecture format in Sunday school. But this is not sufficient for a thorough learning process. Ezra knew this, and that is why a team of Levites taught the people in smaller groups. Complete education requires a setting that allows for interaction between teacher and student, for questions and answers, discussion, and personal engagement.

Most of us agree with this instructional format when we are talking about children and youth, but we may find it more difficult to agree that the same principles hold true for adults as well. But that is precisely why I encourage all members of Irvine Presbyterian Church, young and old alike, to participate regularly in a smaller group, either a Sunday school class or a support group, or both.

I also feel that we who teach and preach should place ourselves in situations where we can learn from others, where we are not responsible for providing the lesson. A pattern of regular proclamation without renewed understanding and learning from others is a prelude to spiritual burnout. That is why each week I meet with a group of men for Bible study. In this context, I gather not only a new understanding of the text but new challenges for my daily life as well.

The Results of Understanding

Nehemiah 8 not only teaches the value of understanding, it also reminds us that understanding is not the culmination of hearing God's truth. Notice that when the people grasped the sense of the Law they responded, both emotionally and behaviorally. The wept and they rejoiced; they went out and celebrated, and then participated in the prescribed Feast of Booths. Comprehensive communication of God's truth fosters a mental change that leads to transformation of the heart and lifestyle. When have I succeeded as a preacher? When my congregation understands, when their hearts are changed, and when they alter their lives in obedience to God's truth. It is tragic to observe Christians who have spent a lifetime in church and in Christian education classes, yet whose lives remain unchanged. Their minds have been informed, but their hearts have not been touched. We must not approach teaching God's Word as an educational elective, but, rather, as a life-transforming requirement.

As communicators of God's Word we must accept the challenge of changing lives. We must preach and teach so that men and women, boys and girls, young and old will know Christ and will have their lives recreated by his power. And, I might add, *his power* is the key! No sooner do I recognize my calling to change lives than I have to confess my inability to do the job. I will labor with all my strength to bring about transformation in people's lives, but I cannot do it without God! When I embrace my full calling as a preacher, at the same time I admit my utter dependence upon the Holy Spirit. I recognize my need, not only to prepare and preach with fervor, but to pray with faithfulness. Life-transforming understanding occurs not only when the communicator and the learners have endeavored to teach and to learn, but when the Holy Spirit, by his power, convicts, cleanses, heals, and transforms.

The Law Enriches Our Lives

God's Law leads not only to sorrow but to vibrant joy. When we fully understand the Law, it is time to throw a party, because God gives the Law, not to preclude our pleasure, but to maximize it. This could probably be said of all good laws—like the laws at summer camp. I knew that one of the foundational camp rules was: Do not throw rocks. But to a young boy the rocks cried out: "Throw me! Throw me!" Unfortunately, I learned the hard way why rock-throwing was discouraged when a flying rock struck my face just an inch from my eye—a painful and potentially disastrous experience! Now you would think that this would have convinced me not to throw rocks. But sometime later as a group of us were hiking along a stream, I spied a still pool of water, and, at my feet, one of those "talking" rocks. In a flash of impishness, I hurled the rock towards the inviting pool . . . only to hit another boy right on top of his head! His enjoyment of the outing was greatly diminished—as was mine when the leaders found out who had thrown the rock!

In retrospect, God's Law tells us what to do and what not to do. It is given, not to ruin our lives, but to enrich them. When we understand God's truth, when it affects our hearts and impacts our lives, then we will know fullness of joy. Then we will *"eat the fat"* and *"drink the sweet"* of God's kingdom in anticipatory celebration of the world to come.

244

NOTES

1. The NKJV of 8:7 reads, ". . . *Hanan, Pelaiah, and the Levites.*" While this correctly translates the Hebrew (*ḥānān pělā'yâ wěhalěwiyyim*), the "*and*" is either a scribal mistake (Williamson, *Ezra, Nehemiah* p. 278), or an explanative *waw*. The persons listed by name are Levites.

2. Williamson, *Ezra, Nehemiah*, pp. 277–78.

3. The text uses primarily Hiphil forms of the root *bîn*, which means "to understand, to comprehend" (*TWOT*, p. 103; Brown, Driver, and Briggs, *Lexicon,* pp. 106–7).

CHAPTER SIXTEEN

Renewal Through Confession

Nehemiah 9:1–37

To Tell the Truth

As a child, each week I looked forward to the television show, "To Tell the Truth." It began with three contestants who claimed to be the show's featured guest. Each contestant would claim: "My name is Mike Barris." "My name is Mike Barris." "My name is Mike Barris." Then the announcer would explain what made Mike Barris so unusual—typically a unique experience, profession, or hobby—and a panel of celebrity judges would accept the challenge of identifying the genuine Mike Barris by asking questions of each contestant, two of whom would fabricate clever answers. After the panel of judges had made its best guess, the announcer would ask: "Will the real Mike Barris please stand up?" After teasing the audience for a few moments, Mike Barris would stand.

That show is a bit like Nehemiah 9, which could be titled "To Tell the Truth." Although most commentaries and Bibles call it something like "National Confession" or "The People Confess Their Sins," the chapter actually illustrates the nature of confession as telling the truth. In Nehemiah 8 Ezra read the Law to the people, who responded emotionally—first with weeping, then with joyful celebration. They continued in "very great gladness" by keeping the Feast of Booths (8:17). Now the scene shifts and the mood becomes more serious as the people engage in an extended confession.

Description of the Assembly (9:1–5)

9:1 Now on the twenty-fourth day of this month the children of Israel were assembled with fasting, in sackcloth, and with dust on their heads.

> 2 Then those of Israelite lineage separated
> themselves from all foreigners; and they stood and
> confessed their sins and the iniquities of their fathers.
>   3 And they stood up in their place and read from
> the Book of the Law of the LORD their God for one-
> fourth of the day; and for another fourth they
> confessed and worshiped the LORD their God.
>   4 Then Jeshua, Bani, Kadmiel, Shebaniah, Bunni,
> Sherebiah, Bani, and Chenani stood on the stairs of
> the Levites and cried out with a loud voice to the
> LORD their God.
>   5 And the Levites, Jeshua, Kadmiel, Bani,
> Hashabniah, Sherebiah, Hodijah, Shebaniah, and
> Pethahiah, said: "Stand up and bless the LORD your
> God Forever and ever! "Blessed be Your glorious
> name, Which is exalted above all blessing and praise!
>
> *Nehemiah 9:1–5*

The Feast of the Booths in chapter 8 ended on the twenty-first day, with an additional day for a sacred assembly (8:18). After an interval of another day, the people gathered again, *"on the twenty-fourth day of this month"* (v. 1). Three behaviors commonly associated with grief accentuate the solemnity of this occasion: the people fasted, they wore sackcloth, and they put dust on their heads (v. 1). In a gesture reminiscent of Ezra 6:21, *"those of Israelite lineage separated themselves from all foreigners."* Their separation is understandable in light of the confession of national and ancestral sins that follow, in which foreigners would have no part.

As in other parts of this book, verses 2–5 provide an overview of events, not a sequential ordering. For *"one-fourth of the day"* an unspecified *"they"* (possibly the Levites) read from *"the Book of the Law."* Then, *"for another fourth"* an unspecified *"they"* (perhaps the leaders and the people) *"confessed and worshiped the LORD their God"* (v. 3). Sometime during this process, teams of Levites *"stood on the stairs of the Levites"* (a type of platform) to cry out to God and to lead in worship (vv. 4–5).

The verb "to confess" appears in verses 2 and 3: *"they stood and confessed their sins," "for another fourth they confessed."* Although this verb means "to acknowledge one's sins," it has a broader sense as well. It is used in the Hebrew Bible for recognition or acknowledgement of what

247

is true about a person or about God.[1] Confession, therefore, may include a recital of God's nature or his works as well as a statement of human sins. In Hebrew, as in New Testament Greek (or in Latin, from which the English word derives), confession includes the characteristic of telling the truth—the truth about God and the truth about one's own self.

Verse 5 includes the Levites' call to the people to *"stand up and bless the* LORD *your God."* A blessing of God follows and flows into the confession beginning in verse 6. At one point these items may have been distinct, but the editor of Ezra-Nehemiah blended them into a single unit.[2]

THE CONFESSION (9:6–37)

6 You alone are the LORD;
   You have made heaven,
   The heaven of heavens, with all their host,
   The earth and everything on it,
   The seas and all that is in them,
   And You preserve them all.
   The host of heaven worships You.
7 You are the LORD God,
   Who chose Abram,
   And brought him out of Ur of the Chaldeans,
   And gave him the name Abraham;
8 You found his heart faithful before You,
   And made a covenant with him
   To give the land of the Canaanites,
   The Hittites, the Amorites,
   The Perizzites, the Jebusites,
   And the Girgashites—
   To give it to his descendants.
   You have performed Your words,
   For You are righteous.
9 "You saw the affliction of our fathers in Egypt,
   And heard their cry by the Red Sea.
10 You showed signs and wonders against
      Pharaoh,
   Against all his servants,
   And against all the people of his land.
   For You knew that they acted proudly against
      them.

248

So You made a name for Yourself, as it is this
  day.
11 And You divided the sea before them,
  So that they went through the midst of the sea
    on the dry land;
  And their persecutors You threw into the deep,
    As a stone into the mighty waters.
12 Moreover You led them by day with a cloudy
    pillar,
  And by night with a pillar of fire,
  To give them light on the road
  Which they should travel.
13 You came down also on Mount Sinai,
  And spoke with them from heaven,
  And gave them just ordinances and true laws,
  Good statutes and commandments.
14 You made known to them Your holy Sabbath,
  And commanded them precepts, statutes and
    laws,
  By the hand of Moses Your servant.
15 You gave them bread from heaven for their
    hunger,
  And brought them water out of the rock for
    their thirst,
  And told them to go in to possess the land
  Which You had sworn to give them.
16 "But they and our fathers acted proudly,
  Hardened their necks,
  And did not heed Your commandments.
17 They refused to obey,
  And they were not mindful of Your wonders
  That You did among them.
  But they hardened their necks,
  And in their rebellion
  They appointed a leader
  To return to their bondage.
  But You are God,
  Ready to pardon,
  Gracious and merciful,
  Slow to anger,
  Abundant in kindness,
  And did not forsake them.

249

18 Even when they made a molded calf for themselves,
   And said, 'This is your god
   That brought you up out of Egypt,'
   And worked great provocations,
19 Yet in Your manifold mercies
   You did not forsake them in the wilderness.
   The pillar of the cloud did not depart from
       them by day,
   To lead them on the road;
   Nor the pillar of fire by night,
   To show them light,
   And the way they should go.
20 You also gave Your good Spirit to instruct them,
   And did not withhold Your manna from their
       mouth,
   And gave them water for their thirst.
21 Forty years You sustained them in the
       wilderness,
   They lacked nothing;
   Their clothes did not wear out
   And their feet did not swell.
22 Moreover You gave them kingdoms and nations,
   And divided them into districts.
   So they took possession of the land of Sihon,
   The land of the king of Heshbon,
   And the land of Og king of Bashan.
23 You also multiplied their children as the stars
       of heaven,
   And brought them into the land
   Which You had told their fathers
   To go in and possess.
24 So the people went in
   And possessed the land;
   You subdued before them the inhabitants of
       the land,
   The Canaanites,
   And gave them into their hands,
   With their kings
   And the people of the land,
   That they might do with them as they wished.
25 And they took strong cities and a rich land,
   And possessed houses full of all goods,

250

Cisterns already dug, vineyards, olive groves,
And fruit trees in abundance.
So they ate and were filled and grew fat,
And delighted themselves in Your great
goodness.
26 "Nevertheless they were disobedient
And rebelled against You,
Cast Your law behind their backs
And killed Your prophets, who testified
against them
To turn them to Yourself;
And they worked great provocations.
27 Therefore You delivered them into the hand of
their enemies,
Who oppressed them;
And in the time of their trouble,
When they cried to You,
You heard from heaven;
And according to Your abundant mercies
You gave them deliverers who saved them
From the hand of their enemies.
28 But after they had rest,
They again did evil before You.
Therefore You left them in the hand of their
enemies,
So that they had dominion over them;
Yet when they returned and cried out to You,
You heard from heaven;
And many times You delivered them
according to Your mercies,
29 And testified against them,
That You might bring them back to Your law.
Yet they acted proudly,
And did not heed Your commandments,
But sinned against Your judgments,
'Which if a man does, he shall live by them.'
And they shrugged their shoulders,
Stiffened their necks,
And would not hear.
30 Yet for many years You had patience with them,
And testified against them by Your Spirit in
Your prophets.

Yet they would not listen;
Therefore You gave them into the hand of the
   peoples of the lands.
31 Nevertheless in Your great mercy
You did not utterly consume them nor forsake
   them;
For You are God, gracious and merciful.
32 "Now therefore, our God,
The great, the mighty, and awesome God,
Who keeps covenant and mercy:
Do not let all the trouble seem small before
   You
That has come upon us,
Our kings and our princes,
Our priests and our prophets,
Our fathers and on all Your people,
From the days of the kings of Assyria until this
   day.
33 However You are just in all that has befallen us;
For You have dealt faithfully,
But we have done wickedly.
34 Neither our kings nor our princes,
Our priests nor our fathers,
Have kept Your law,
Nor heeded Your commandments and Your
   testimonies,
With which You testified against them.
35 For they have not served You in their kingdom,
Or in the many good things that You gave
   them,
Or in the large and rich land which You set
   before them;
Nor did they turn from their wicked works.
36 Here we are, servants today!
And the land that You gave to our fathers,
To eat its fruit and its bounty,
Here we are, servants in it!
37 And it yields much increase to the kings
You have set over us,
Because of our sins;
Also they have dominion over our bodies and
   our cattle

> At their pleasure;
> And we are in great distress.
>
> *Nehemiah 9:6–37*

The confession contains a rich recounting of biblical history from creation through the time of Nehemiah. It begins with the recognition of the one Creator God (v. 6), moves through the covenant with Abraham (vv. 7–8), on to the deliverance of the Exodus (vv. 9–12), and finally narrates the Mosaic covenant and the establishment of the Law (vv. 13–15). The remainder of the confession moves back and forth between the sin of the people and God's gracious but increasingly corrective response. Notice particularly the familiar hymnic elements that highlight God's faithful and forgiving nature: *"But You are God, / ready to pardon, / gracious and merciful, / slow to anger, / abundant in kindness"* (v. 17; see Exod. 34:6; Ps. 86:15; 103:8; Lam. 3:22). Other elements of the confession echo well-known biblical themes and phrases:

- *"Their clothes did not wear out / And their feet did not swell"* (v. 21); see Deut. 8:4.

- *"So they took possession of the land of Sihon, / The land of the king of Heshbon, / And the land of Og king of Bashan"* (v. 22); see Deut. 1:4; Josh. 2:10; Ps. 135:11.

- *"When they cried to You, / You heard from heaven; / And according to Your abundant mercies / You gave them deliverers who saved them"* (v. 27); see Judg. 2:18.

Indeed, each line of this confession could have been footnoted with references to many biblical passages.[3]

Verse 33 sums up the essence of the confession succinctly: *"However You are just in all that has befallen us; / For You have dealt faithfully, / but we have done wickedly."* Although God had been patient, merciful, forgiving, and always faithful, the people of God had been rebellious, forgetful, sinful, and consistently faithless in their covenant relationship with him. This explains the discomforting condition of Judah in the day of Nehemiah:

> *Here we are, servants today! / And the land that You gave to our fathers . . . yields much increase to the kings / You have set over us,*

/ Because of our sins; / Also they have dominion over our bodies and
our cattle / At their pleasure; / And we are in great distress (vv. 36–37).

The people of God were reaping what they had sown. They deserved
their sentence of servitude to foreign kings. The confession of chapter
9 offers no excuses—only an admission of the people's perpetual
guilt in contrast to God's perpetual grace. The covenant renewal of
chapter 10 stands, not upon any confidence that the people have in
themselves but upon God's continued and undying faithfulness.

REFLECTIONS ON NEHEMIAH 9:1–37

Confession—Telling the Whole Truth

In Nehemiah 9, we read that the people gathered together, clothed
in signs of mourning, to confess their common sins. Those foreigners
who did not share a sinful ancestry stood apart so that all of the
confessors could acknowledge where they and their predecessors
had erred. John Calvin considers this a prime example of "general,
public confession," when "the people are guilty of some transgression in common."[4]

But, notice that *confession of sin is not the main theme* of 9:6–37. Yes,
the people confessed their sins and dressed in penitential garb. But
more verses of this national confession describe God and his faithfulness than the rebellious acts of the people. Human sin plays a
supporting role to the dominance of God's starring role. Nehemiah 9
is, primarily, a confession of faith and only secondarily a confession
of sin.

As noted above, the Hebrew verb "to confess" means more than
"to admit one's sin." More accurately, it means "to acknowledge, to
affirm, to recognize," or, as I have suggested, "to tell the truth." The
people gathered for confession, not merely of their faults, but of their
faults and of God's super-abundant grace. They told the truth about
themselves, and, more importantly, they told the truth about God.

In English we use the word "to confess" with similar diversity. At
times in church we "confess our sins;" at other times we "confess our
faith." Simply stated, we say what we know to be true. Witnesses in
the courtroom are asked: "Will you tell the truth, the whole truth, and
nothing but the truth?" Although we usually associate confession

with criminals, in fact the witness is asked to make a full confession of information that is pertinent to the situation. Likewise, when the people of Israel confessed their corporate sin, they made a complete confession: they told the whole truth, not only about themselves, but also about their God.

Look again at the structure of vv. 6–37:

- *God's greatness in creation, covenant, redemption* (6–15)
- The people's hardening of their necks (16–17a)
- *God's grace* (17b)
- The people's idolatry (18)
- *God's mercies* (19–25)
- The people's disobedience (26)
- *God's discipline and salvation* (27)
- The people's evil (28a)
- *God's deliverance* (28b)
- The people's stiff necks (29)
- *God's patience, judgment, and mercy* (30–31)

Notice how confession alternates between admission of sin and acknowledgement of God's gracious character and actions.

Usually, when we confess our sin we fail to tell the whole truth. I don't mean that we overlook certain sins, although this can certainly be the case, but, rather, that in our worship services and private devotions we tend to separate "confession of faith" from "confession of sin." Why do we do this? Wouldn't we be much better off to imitate the people in Nehemiah 9, to tell the whole truth about God and ourselves when we acknowledge our misdeeds before the Lord? There are two reasons why I believe this would be better for us.

1. Telling the Whole Truth Highlights the Nature of Sin

It is distressing but true—our society minimizes sin. In our valiant efforts to explain human behavior, we recoil from blunt recognition of sin as evil. Although the words "sin," "wicked," and "evil" appear over 1800 times in the Bible, they rarely find their way into public or even religious discourse today. The efforts to understand our actions, to look for causes, and to identify compulsions are not necessarily wrong. The disciplines of psychology and sociology have their rightful place. But materialism is more than a sociological phenomenon—it is sin. Angry outbursts may indeed stem from childhood conditioning, but they are still sinful. We Christians have developed a particular skill in minimizing our sin by comparing ourselves with others. "Yes, I may be a bit materialistic, but at least I'm not as bad as my neighbor." "Indeed, I may say mean things in anger, but you should have seen my father when he was mad!"

Yet all of our efforts to dilute sin dissipate in the presence of our holy, righteous God. As long as we compare ourselves with others we can play this self-justification game. But when we place our sins alongside the attributes and actions of God, feeble excuses to discount our wickedness fail miserably. Juxtaposed to God, each of us stands out as what we truly are: sinners and rebels against God, who are lost completely apart from his mercy. It is a matter of being compared to the incomparable.

Something similar happened to one of our friends who decided to run a marathon. Although Nancy jogged regularly, she had never run in a marathon, nor had she actively participated in organized athletics. My wife and I volunteered to run with Nancy to keep her company while she prepared for the upcoming race. Over the months we ran longer and longer distances, sometimes covering fifteen miles in a single workout. Compared with us, Nancy seemed to be a fine athlete. But she sensed a need for more strenuous training, so she joined a local track club. Instead of being enthusiastic about this advanced step, Nancy returned from her first official workout greatly discouraged. "I'm no good at all!" she lamented. "Next to those runners I just waddle along. It's pitiful." I tried to encourage Nancy. "Don't worry. You'll improve. Pretty soon you'll be running right with the others." But my words had little impact, and Nancy continued to be despondent over her training at the club.

Finally, I decided to visit the club to see if things were really as bad as she claimed. As we had agreed, I met Nancy at Santa Monica City College, home of the Santa Monica Track Club. And it didn't take me long to realize what Nancy's problem was. She had joined the world's most prestigious track club! As the workout began, I watched, incredulous. There was Nancy running right alongside the best runners in the world! As Nancy did her laps, she was passed by several Olympic champions and world-record holders—including Evelyn Ashford and Carl Lewis. Yes, in comparison with these marvelous athletes, Nancy did appear to waddle. And so would I, if I could ever work up the courage even to walk on the same track with them!

Compared with my wife and me, Nancy ran well. But next to the fastest runners in history, her performance appeared weak. Something similar happens when we begin to compare our sins. When we set them up next to the failures of others, it is possible to excuse our puny peccadillos; but when we see our sin in the light of God's greatness and glory, we know ourselves as we truly are. And we are compelled to acknowledge the vileness of our sin.

Though this may be uncomfortable, it is essential for genuine spiritual renewal. As Andrew Murray noted, "Any deep spiritual revival must needs be preceded and accompanied by a deeper sense of sin."[5] Only when we see ourselves as we truly are—sinners, lost without God—will our hearts be genuinely open for healing, forgiveness, and profound cleansing. By confessing both who we are and who God is, we lay the groundwork for spiritual restoration.

2. Telling the Whole Truth Encourages Us to Confess Our Sin

The second rationale for confessing our sin and God's nature together confronts a paradox. Since this juxtaposed confession highlights the truly vile nature of our sin, one might suppose that telling the whole truth would discourage open admission of sin. But, in fact, the opposite is true. By confessing the faithfulness of God, while confessing our sin, we discover greater freedom to tell the truth about ourselves.

Notice again what the people of Israel confessed about God:

> But you are God,
> Ready to pardon,
> Gracious and merciful,
> Slow to anger,
> Abundant in kindness,
> And did not forsake [Your people].
> Even when they made a molded calf for themselves,
> And said, "This is your god

That brought you up out of Egypt,"
And worked great provocations,
Yet in Your manifold mercies
You did not forsake them in the wilderness. (9:17–19)

But after they had rest,
They again did evil before You.
Therefore You left them in the hand of their enemies,
So that they had dominion over them;
Yet when they returned and cried out to You,
You heard from heaven;
And many times You delivered them according to
Your mercies. (9:28)

Without question, God is holy. He cannot tolerate sin; nor can sin tolerate God. While God's holiness underscores the foulness of our sin, the mercy of God invites us to confess our sin. The very nature of God beckons us to tell him the truth. In the words of John Calvin:

> Since it is the Lord who forgives, forgets, and wipes out sins, let us confess our sins to him in order to obtain pardon. He is the physician; therefore, let us lay bare our wounds to him. It is he who is hurt and offended; from him let us seek peace. He is the discerner of hearts, the one cognizant of all thoughts; let us hasten to pour out our hearts before him. He it is, finally, who calls sinners: let us not delay to come to God himself.[6]

Calvin's phrasing, "He is the physician," reminds me of the ritual of preparation for major surgery. Most people approach surgery with at least a twinge of fear, which they counteract by talking about the talents and expertise of their doctors. As I visit "pre-op" patients in the hospital, I hear the same lines over and over: "My doctor is excellent. She has a great reputation. She has done this surgery hundreds of times. I trust my doctor." It is a litany of reassurance, for those seeking to find the courage to go through with surgery, and yet it makes me wonder if we shouldn't approach confession of sin in the same manner. If we shouldn't confess: "My God is excellent. He has a great reputation. He has dealt with sinners like me millions of times. I know I can trust my God." Because based upon such a confession, we can then conclude with Calvin, "Let us not delay to come to God himself."

Telling the Whole Truth and the Cross

We cannot speak truly and fully of the grace of God without mentioning the Cross of Christ. Because God is *"ready to pardon, Gracious and merciful, Slow to anger, and abundant in kindness"* (v. 17), he sent his only Son to die for us. As Oswald Chambers noted:

> The love of God means Calvary, and nothing less; the love of God is spelt on the Cross and nowhere else. The only ground on which God can forgive me is through the Cross of my Lord.
>
> We trample the blood of the Son of God under foot if we think we are forgiven because we are sorry for our sins. The only explanation of the forgiveness of God and of the unfathomable depth of His forgetting is the Death of Jesus Christ. Our repentance is merely the outcome of our personal realization of the Atonement which He has worked out for us.[7]

The Apostle Paul put it this way in writing to the Romans: "God demonstrates His own love toward us, in that while we were still sinners, Christ died for us" (Rom. 5:8). This stands at the center of the whole truth about God.

The celebration of Communion provides a vital context in which we can tell the truth about God and ourselves. In the sacrament of the Lord's Supper we confess the marvelous, sacrificial grace of God. We also receive tangible reminders of this sacrifice: the bread and the wine of the sacrament. In receiving these elements, we also confess our sinfulness, our utter need for God's forgiveness. We remember Paul's admonition to the Corinthians: "Examine yourselves, and only then eat of the bread and drink of the cup" (1 Cor. 11:28, NRSV). But in light of Nehemiah 9, perhaps our confession of sin before communion should be intermingled with confession of the greatness and faithfulness of God.

Recently, prior to receiving the Lord's Supper, I led the congregation in an extended prayer of full confession. This prayer imitated the structure of Nehemiah 9, alternating between confession of God's nature and confession of our sin. We remembered God's faithfulness; and we remembered our unfaithfulness. We thanked God for his patience; and we admitted our impatience, especially with him. Then we came together at the Table of Christ to confess, through our action, the whole truth and nothing but the truth: "Christ Jesus came into the world to save sinners—of whom I am chief" (1 Tim. 1:15).

Will the real sinner please stand up—to receive the grace of God in Christ Jesus, who died for us that we might live!

NOTES

1. 9:2 and 3 use the Hithpael of *yādâ*. See *TWOT*, s.v.; and Brown, Driver, and Briggs, *Lexicon*.

2. The RSV and NRSV make a break between verses 5 and 6, adding the phrase "And Ezra said." This appears in the LXX (2 Esdras 19:6), but not in the MT or other versions. It was probably added to the LXX by a scribe who wanted to highlight the role of Ezra. The NKJV reading, which omits "and Ezra said," is preferable (Williamson, pp. 303–4).

3. For a helpful and exhaustive list of biblical passages behind this confession, see Myers, *Ezra • Nehemiah*, pp. 167–69.

4. J. Calvin, *Institutes of the Christian Religion*, 3.4.11. Trans. by F. L. Battles, in The Library of Christian Classics edition (Philadelphia: Westminster, 1960).

5. A. Murray, *Revival* (Minneapolis: Bethany House, 1990), p. 92

6. J. Calvin, *Institutes*, 3.4.9.

7. O. Chambers, *My Utmost for His Highest* (New York: Dodd, Mead & Company, 1935), pp. 324, 343.

CHAPTER SEVENTEEN

Renewal of the Covenant with God

Nehemiah 9:38–10:39

"I Do" All Over Again

Every now and then, I am privileged to perform a ceremony for couples wishing to renew their wedding vows. Two years ago, Jaime and Maria approached me with a request for such a ceremony. They had been married for almost twenty years and wanted to reaffirm their vows of love and commitment in a public ceremony. As preparations for the service proceeded, their nervous anticipation increased. Finally the special night of ceremony arrived. In front of two hundred friends and family members, they renewed their vows of marriage, saying "I do" all over again. It was a poignant moment, not only for these two, but for many of us who sensed a similar need for renewal in our marriages.

This ceremony reminds me of the people of Israel and their relationship with God shortly after they finished building the wall of Jerusalem (v. 6). You will recall that Ezra's reading of the Law had given birth to a joyful celebration (v. 7). This in turn led to a time of national confession, after which the people felt the need to say "I do" to God all over again.

Sealing the Firm Agreement (9:38–10:29)

38 "And because of all this, We make a sure covenant, and write it; Our leaders, our Levites, and our priests seal it."
10:1 Now those who placed their seal on the document were: Nehemiah the governor, the son of Hacaliah, and Zedekiah,

2 Seraiah, Azariah, Jeremiah,

3 Pashhur, Amariah, Malchijah,

4 Hattush, Shebaniah, Malluch,

5 Harim, Meremoth, Obadiah,

6 Daniel, Ginnethon, Baruch,

7 Meshullam, Abijah, Mijamin,

8 Maaziah, Bilgai, and Shemaiah. These were the priests.

9 The Levites: Jeshua the son of Azaniah, Binnui of the sons of Henadad, and Kadmiel.

10 Their brethren: Shebaniah, Hodijah, Kelita, Pelaiah, Hanan,

11 Micha, Rehob, Hashabiah,

12 Zaccur, Sherebiah, Shebaniah,

13 Hodijah, Bani, and Beninu.

14 The leaders of the people: Parosh, Pahath-Moab, Elam, Zattu, Bani,

15 Bunni, Azgad, Bebai,

16 Adonijah, Bigvai, Adin,

17 Ater, Hezekiah, Azzur,

18 Hodijah, Hashum, Bezai,

19 Hariph, Anathoth, Nebai,

20 Magpiash, Meshullam, Hezir,

21 Meshezabel, Zadok, Jaddua,

22 Pelatiah, Hanan, Anaiah,

23 Hoshea, Hananiah, Hasshub,

24 Hallohesh, Pilha, Shobek,

25 Rehum, Hashabnah, Maaseiah,

26 Ahijah, Hanan, Anan,

27 Malluch, Harim, and Baanah.

28 Now the rest of the people—the priests, the Levites, the gatekeepers, the singers, the Nethinim, and all those who had separated themselves from the peoples of the lands to the Law of God, their wives, their sons, and their daughters, everyone who had knowledge and understanding—

29 these joined with their brethren, their nobles, and entered into a curse and an oath to walk in God's Law, which was given by Moses the servant of God, and to observe and do all the commandments of the LORD our Lord, and His ordinances and His statutes:

Nehemiah 9:38–10:29

In the Hebrew text of Nehemiah, verse 38 of chapter 9 is actually the first verse of chapter 10. Although it provides a transition between the two chapters, it actually serves as a better introduction to chapter 10 than as a conclusion to chapter 9. For this reason I have included it in the commentary on chapter 10.

Verse 38 begins, *"And because of all this,"* indicating that the covenantal renewal of chapter 10 was based upon the confession of chapter 9: a confession that emphasized not so much the repeated failure of Israel as the repeated mercy of God. The leaders of Israel did not make *"a sure covenant"* with God because of their sin, nor in order to earn God's approval. Rather, they made the convenant on the basis of God's grace—in response to his mercy.

In reality, the people did not make a *"covenant"* at all. The NKJV supplies this word, though it is lacking in the Hebrew original, which reads: "we are cutting a firm agreement and writing it." Although Hebrew speakers generally "cut" a covenant, here the word "covenant" is replaced by "firm agreement."[1] "Firm agreement" might be a synonym of "covenant,"[2] but I suspect that it reflects a deeper theological principle.[3] The Bible regularly describes God as the one who makes covenants with people; only rarely are people said to make a covenant with God.[4] So, in chapter 10, the Israelites do not make a covenant with God, rather, they make a firm agreement to live according to the former covenant that God had established through Moses. As 10:29 states, the people *"joined with their brethren, their nobles, and entered into a curse and an oath to walk in God's Law, which was given by Moses the servant of God. . . ."* Thus, the original terms used in 9:38 suggest a theologically profound truth: God is the covenant maker; his people are the covenant renewers.

By sealing the covenant, the leaders of Judah, including *Nehemiah*, demonstrated their support of the firm agreement. One aspect of this list that is a bit surprising is the fact that there is no mention of Ezra. Scholars have suggested various theories for this omission, but the most persuasive theory recognizes that the list calls out leaders according to their families, and Ezra is a son of *"Seraiah"* (v. 2).[5]

The priests, Levites, and secular leaders who sealed the covenant took a stand for God, much as the signers of the Declaration of Independence took a stand for political freedom in the United States over two hundred years ago. They led by costly example, not by coercion. The text of 10:28 clarifies that those who "signed on" with the leaders did so on the basis of their *"knowledge and understanding."* This extended not only to heads of families but to *"their wives, their sons, and their daughters"* (v. 28) as well.

Even in this solidly patriarchal society, each person had to make his or her own choice to support the firm commitment of the leaders. And we who lead today would do well to consider how faithfully we imitate this example. Do we lead our people by living exemplary lives and taking stands according to our convictions? Or do we coerce and compel those who follow us to do what we want them to do? Are we helping our people to grow as mature decision makers, or do we keep them in moral infancy by treating them as immature children?

The *"rest of the people"* (v. 28) joined with *"the nobles"* by entering into *"a curse and an oath to walk in God's Law"* (v. 29). The language of curses and oaths sounds strange to modern ears, but notice that they not only swore to walk obediently, they also swore to be punished if they failed to walk obediently. This is what to enter into a curse means. Often covenants, including those between God and people, had curses associated with them. For example, on Mt. Ebal when Moses told the people the consequences of disobeying God's Law, he said, "The LORD will strike you with consumption, with fever, with inflammation, with severe burning fever, with the sword, with scorching, and with mildew" (Deut. 28:22). Now that's enough to encourage covenantal faithfulness!

Even with unspecified curses, however, the people chose to join with their leaders in making a new commitment to God. They agreed *"to walk in God's Law . . . and to observe and do all the commandments of the LORD our Lord, and His ordinances and His statutes"* (v. 29). They consented to do all that the Law required. In fact, as we will see below, the people actually agreed to do more than the Law required. They aspired to a thoroughgoing obedience, above and beyond the letter of the Law.

SPECIFIC TENETS OF THE FIRM AGREEMENT (10:30–39)

30 We would not give our daughters as wives to the peoples of the land, nor take their daughters for our sons;

31 if the peoples of the land brought wares or any grain to sell on the Sabbath day, we would not buy it

from them on the Sabbath, or on a holy day; and we would forego the seventh year's produce and the exacting of every debt.

32 Also we made ordinances for ourselves, to exact from ourselves yearly one-third of a shekel for the service of the house of our God:

33 for the showbread, for the regular grain offering, for the regular burnt offering of the Sabbaths, the New Moons, and the set feasts; for the holy things, for the sin offerings to make atonement for Israel, and all the work of the house of our God.

34 We cast lots among the priests, the Levites, and the people, for bringing the wood offering into the house of our God, according to our fathers' houses, at the appointed times year by year, to burn on the altar of the LORD our God as it is written in the Law.

35 And we made ordinances to bring the firstfruits of our ground and the firstfruits of all fruit of all trees, year by year, to the house of the LORD;

36 to bring the firstborn of our sons and our cattle, as it is written in the Law, and the firstborn of our herds and our flocks, to the house of our God, to the priests who minister in the house of our God;

37 to bring the firstfruits of our dough, our offerings, the fruit from all kinds of trees, the new wine and oil, to the priests, to the storerooms of the house of our God; and to bring the tithes of our land to the Levites, for the Levites should receive the tithes in all our farming communities.

38 And the priest, the descendant of Aaron, shall be with the Levites when the Levites receive tithes; and the Levites shall bring up a tenth of the tithes to the house of our God, to the rooms of the storehouse.

39 For the children of Israel and the children of Levi shall bring the offering of the grain, of the new wine and the oil, to the storerooms where the articles of the sanctuary are, where the priests who minister and the gatekeepers and the singers are; and we will not neglect the house of our God.

Nehemiah 10:30–39

The people promised to obey all of God's Law (v. 29) and, in addition, made specific promises concerning: intermarriage (v. 30), the sabbath (v. 31), and support for the temple and its personnel (vv. 32–39). Some of the specific tenets of these promises simply restate biblical laws (for example, bringing *"the firstfruits of the ground"* to the temple [10:35; see Lev. 23:10]), but most extend or reinterpret biblical precedents (for example, bringing *"the firstfruits of all fruit of all trees"* went beyond the requirements of the Law). Therefore, as we look in this agreement for tenets of the agreement in the Mosaic Law, we find something resembling but not exactly the same as the Mosaic agreement.

The Law needed to be extended because the life-setting of God's people had changed since the time God originally gave the Law. Verse 31 provides an apt illustration. The Ten Commandments stated clearly that one should not work on the sabbath (Exod. 20:8–10), therefore, the Israelites refrained from selling anything on the sabbath. But between the giving of that law and the time of Nehemiah, the situation of God's people had changed. Foreigners had come to live within Judah who had no reservations about selling and buying goods on the sabbath (see 13:16). So the question arose: In light of the sabbatical law, could Jews buy on the sabbath? Verse 31 answers the question negatively: neither selling nor buying on the sabbath was acceptable. So the people instituted an ancient version of "Blue Laws" that prohibited commerce on the sabbath. They reinterpreted the Law to fit their new situation.

Thus, the specific promises contained in this agreement reflect the issues and crises of Nehemiah's day. These included the problem of intermarriage with *"the peoples of the land"* (this had already been an issue in Ezra 9); indebtedness (previously dealt with in 5:1–13); and inadequate support for the temple and its ministry (a crisis later in Nehemiah's tenure of leadership, 13:10–13). Given the likelihood that Malachi prophesied around the time of Nehemiah,[6] we have another witness to the people's utter failure to provide acceptable tithes and offerings to God (Mal. 1:7–8; 12–14; 3:8–10).

Other commentaries provide detailed explanations of verses 30–39.[7] The meaning of most of the tenets is clear,[8] even if their rationale is not always as obvious. Verse 39 sums up the majority of the tenets simply: *"We will not neglect the house of our God."*

Applying God's Standards to New Situations

The people of Israel applied the Law to their current situation, and we are certainly in the same position today. Biblical standards continue to be authoritative, but many do not speak immediately to our life-settings. As we seek to obey God, we are challenged to reinterpret his standards in our new situations.

This was the case recently for a group of businessmen I meet with each week. In our Bible study, we have been working our way through the Sermon on the Mount, and last week we pondered the Golden Rule: "In everything do to others as you would have them do to you; for this is the law and the prophets" (Matt. 7:12; NRSV). We began to discuss how this might impact our professional lives. Since each of us serves as supervisor for a number of employees, we asked what it would mean to supervise in the way that we would like to be supervised. A lively discussion ensued; one that stuck with me for several days. Later, in a meeting of the Personnel Commission of my church, I shared some thoughts about how we might change some of our personnel policies for the benefit of our employees. As a result, we have now instituted several of these changes, all on the basis of making Matthew 7:12 relevant to life today.

All of us—not just pastors, but lawyers, editors, salespeople, teachers, students, and others—have the responsibility of applying God's timeless standards to the worlds in which we live. Indeed, this is true for Christian institutions as well as for individuals. For example, God has called Irvine Presbyterian Church to be one of his churches in Irvine. Without question, Irvine Presbyterian congregants are called to worship God, to communicate his truth, and to extend his love; we are called to live as the Body of Christ. Now while God's fundamental call to us does not change, the way we respond to this call will and must change. In other words, the exact shape of our obedience will depend upon the changing world around us.

To illustrate, our local paper, *The Orange County Register*, recently ran a cover story with this headline: "More People, Jobs in OC's Future. New Report Gives Detailed Forecast of Area's Growth."[9] The story charted the future growth in our county, indicating that while fifteen years ago the population of Orange County was more than 75 percent white, fifteen years from now whites will be a minority. This means that Irvine Presbyterian Church, now predominantly white in membership, must seriously consider the changing faces of its neighbors, especially with regard to the Great Commission. The call to make disciples has not changed, but how the congregants of Irvine Presbyterian make disciples in Irvine, California will be changing in the years to come.

We live in a world that changes more rapidly every day. Not only do we confront more changes, but the pace of change itself accelerates dramatically. It is hard to keep up with what is happening in our communities, not to mention our counties, states, countries, and the entire world. Yet we must find ways to meet this challenge. In his excellent new book on a Christian's place in tomorrow's world, *Wild Hope,* Tom Sine urges Christians to take change seriously:

> [I]f we don't begin in our lives, professions, and churches to anticipate both the new challenges and the new opportunities the twenty-first century brings us, we will quite literally be buried alive in the onrushing avalanche of change. No longer can we drive headlong into the future with our eyes fixed on our rearview mirrors.[10]

Like the people of Israel in Nehemiah 10, we must apply God's permanent standards to a world in constant transformation.

Renewing Our Commitment to God's Covenant

We Christians, like the Jews, are people of God's covenant. Through the prophet Jeremiah, God first promised a new covenant:

> Behold, the days are coming," says the LORD, "when I will make a new covenant with the house of Israel and with the house of Judah—not according to the covenant that I made with their fathers in the day that I took them by the hand to lead them out of the land of Egypt, My covenant which they broke, though I was a husband to them," says the LORD. "But this is the covenant that I will make with the house of Israel: After those days, says the LORD: I will put My law in their minds, and write it on their hearts; and I will be their God, and they shall be My people. No more shall every man teach his neighbor, and every man his brother, saying, 'Know the LORD,' for they all shall know Me,

from the least of them to the greatest of them," says the LORD. "For I will forgive their iniquity, and their sin I will remember no more."

Jeremiah 31:31–34

In this light, we hear the words of Jesus at the Last Supper: "This cup is the new covenant in My blood. This do, as often as you drink it, in remembrance of Me" (1 Cor. 11:25). Jesus becomes the "mediator of a new covenant" through his death (Heb. 9:15; 12:24), and we who believe in him have become the new covenant people of God.

God promised that in the new covenant we would know him intimately. As Christians we often talk about "having a personal relationship with Christ," but do we—really? Do we know God intimately? Do we enjoy spending time with him? Do we live in true fellowship with Christ? Are we experiencing the new covenant offered through the blood of Jesus?

I find myself in need of several types of covenant renewal. On the one hand, I require a *daily recommitment* of my life to Christ. At some point each day, preferably at the beginning, I must say to the Lord: "Lord, I belong to you. You are my God. Use me this day for your purposes and for your glory." Additionally, I need the *weekly renewal* that comes in worship. I look forward to singing God's praise and to joining with my sisters and brothers as we reaffirm our faith in song, in confession, and in prayer. Beyond that, I find our *monthly communion services* at Irvine Presbyterian to be especially helpful in my relationship with Christ. Here I literally remember and recommit myself to the "new covenant" in Christ's blood. But, in addition to these regular times of spiritual renewal, my faith journey is marked by *certain watershed events* in which I renew my covenantal relationship with God in a profound way.

The most recent of these events occurred when I received the call to be pastor of Irvine Presbyterian Church. Through that event, God took me to a deeper level of commitment to him and participation in his covenant than I had experienced previously. And I fully expect that before too long I will once again be confronted with the opportunity to surrender even more of myself to God, to live anew within his covenant of grace.

Renewing Our Commitment in Reliance Upon God's Amazing Grace

Yet a word of caution must be added here, because whenever we consider renewing our covenant with God we run the risk of trying to earn his grace. We may be tempted to say: "If I can only get my life together, then I'll be acceptable to God. If I can only be good enough, then God will love me." But as Nehemiah and the people knew, such arrogance only turns out to be folly. In their confession of sin (v. 9), the people remembered with excruciating detail how they had broken their covenant with God. They remembered how, again and again, God had been more than faithful in his endless mercy. The covenant renewal of Nehemiah 10 is not an attempt to earn back God's favor, it is a response, in gratitude, to his favor already given. Remember, the people did not make a covenant with God—they renewed their commitment to the covenant God had already made with them, on the basis of his overwhelming grace.

And so should we. Whenever we renew our covenantal relationship with God, we do so because God's Spirit has drawn us, for our very desire for renewal comes from the Holy Spirit. Indeed, the more I grow as a Christian, the more I realize my own imperfections and failures. Renewing my relationship with Christ no longer grows out of a youthful idealism; I no longer believe I can be a "pretty great Christian for God." Now, when I renew my faith in Christ, I know all too well my past failures, and my penchant to fail again. I know that renewal comes from God's grace in my life, and I look ahead with certainty to the times when I will, once again, need to depend on more of God's grace.

> O to grace how great a debtor,
> Daily I'm constrained to be!
> Let Thy goodness, like a fetter,
> Bind my wandering heart to Thee:
> Prone to wander, Lord, I feel it;
> Prone to leave the God I love;
> Here's my heart, O take and seal it;
> Seal it for Thy courts above.[11]

There is something particularly touching about renewing vows after experiences of pain and failure. Three years ago, my wife and I attended a marriage retreat. As a final exercise in the retreat, we were encouraged to write new wedding vows. I took some time to reflect upon where we had been as a couple and then I wrote new vows. Linda and I joined with another couple, and, one by one, we read our new vows to our spouses. Not one of us finished the reading without

270

shedding some tears—a decided change from our wedding at which neither of us cried.

What was different this time? In my new vows I repeated many of the same lines we had spoken to each other years earlier, "for better or for worse; in sickness and in health; in joy and in sorrow;" but this time I said the same words differently. When I said, "For better or for worse," now I knew some of what "for worse" included. I knew all too well my foibles as a husband—and Linda's gracious forgiveness. When in our original wedding I had said, "In sickness and in health, in joy and in sorrow," little did I know that within five years my father and Linda's mother would both die from cancer. Sickness and sorrow we knew all too well. So in renewing my vows to Linda, the words came with deeper sorrow and deeper joy. I remembered the days when I would return home after a day of nursing my Dad and would have nothing left for Linda, yet she stood by me "in sickness and in health." Later I was able to return the gift when her mother suffered and died. So as I uttered my new vows, my heart overflowed with an appreciation of grace: the grace of my forgiving wife and the grace of God who stayed with us in the valley of the shadow of death.

The grace of God enables us to renew our covenant with him—the Covenant Maker. Not only do we respond to him with first-time commitment, but also with frequent times of renewal. In the words of "Amazing Grace,"

> Through many dangers, toils and snares,
> I have already come;
> 'Tis grace hath brought me safe thus far,
> And grace will lead me home.[12]

God's grace, revealed and confirmed to us through the death of Christ, beckons us home. In covenant renewal we come home to God and say to him "I do"—all over again.

NOTES

1. In an odd mixing of terms, 9:38 (10:1, MT) says that the people are "cutting a firm agreement." Although the NKJV translates ʾămānâ

as "sure covenant," it literally means "faith, support" (Brown, Driver, and Briggs, *Lexicon*, p. 53) or "a settled provision" (*TWOT*, p. 52). The NRSV prefers "a firm agreement." The word "covenant" (*běrît*) does not appear. But the verb translated as "to make" is, literally, "to cut" (*kārat*). This reminds the Hebrew reader of the usual expression for making a covenant, "to cut a covenant." So the language suggests a covenantal tone, though without saying directly that the people make a covenant with God.

2. Myers, *Ezra • Nehemiah*, p. 173.

3. Blenkinsopp, *Ezra-Nehemiah*, p. 312.

4. See 2 Chronicles 29:10 and Ezra 10:3 for the exceptions.

5. See Ezra 7:1. This suggestion comes from Kidner, *Ezra & Nehemiah*, p. 114.

6. Kaiser, p. 433.

7. See, for example, Williamson, *Ezra, Nehemiah*, pp. 333–39; and Fensham, *Ezra and Nehemiah*, pp. 239–41.

8. The meaning of 10:36 is not clear at first. According to Numbers, the people were *"to bring the firstborn of our sons and our cattle"* to the priest, and to pay a fee to redeem these firstborn (Num. 18:15–18; but compare Deut. 15:19–23).

9. Cathy Taylor, "More people, jobs in OC's future," *Orange County Register*, 8/9/92, A1.

10. T. Sine, *Wild Hope* (Dallas: Word Publishing, 1991), p. 4.

11. Third verse of "Come, Thou Fount of Every Blessing," by Robert Robinson.

12. Third verse of "Amazing Grace," by John Newton.

CHAPTER EIGHTEEN

Ordering a Renewed People

Nehemiah 11:1–12:26

Once again in our study of Ezra-Nehemiah we encounter several tedious lists (see Ezra 2; 8:1–14; 10:20–44; Neh. 3; 7:6–73; 10:1–27). Although many teachers and preachers would justifiably skip the lists in chapters 11–12, these texts do show us something substantial about the life of God's covenant people. For the purposes of this commentary, I will treat each list briefly and will conclude with some reflections that may guide the communicator who intends to teach or preach on these lists. I would refer those desiring a fuller treatment of the lists to other commentaries.[1]

SETTLERS IN JERUSALEM (11:1–24)

11:1 Now the leaders of the people dwelt at Jerusalem; the rest of the people cast lots to bring one out of ten to dwell in Jerusalem, the holy city, and nine-tenths were to dwell in other cities.

2 And the people blessed all the men who willingly offered themselves to dwell at Jerusalem.

3 These are the heads of the province who dwelt in Jerusalem. (But in the cities of Judah everyone dwelt in his own possession in their cities—Israelites, priests, Levites, Nethinim, and descendants of Solomon's servants.)

4 Also in Jerusalem dwelt some of the children of Judah and of the children of Benjamin. The children of Judah: Athaiah the son of Uzziah, the son of Zechariah, the son of Amariah, the son of Shephatiah, the son of Mahalalel, of the children of Perez;

5 and Maaseiah the son of Baruch, the son of Col-Hozeh, the son of Hazaiah, the son of Adaiah, the son of Joiarib, the son of Zechariah, the son of Shiloni.

6 All the sons of Perez who dwelt at Jerusalem were four hundred and sixty-eight valiant men.

7 And these are the sons of Benjamin: Sallu the son of Meshullam, the son of Joed, the son of Pedaiah, the son of Kolaiah, the son of Maaseiah, the son of Ithiel, the son of Jeshaiah;

8 and after him Gabbai and Sallai, nine hundred and twenty-eight.

9 Joel the son of Zichri was their overseer, and Judah the son of Senuah was second over the city.

10 Of the priests: Jedaiah the son of Joiarib, and Jachin;

11 Seraiah the son of Hilkiah, the son of Meshullam, the son of Zadok, the son of Meraioth, the son of Ahitub, was the leader of the house of God.

12 Their brethren who did the work of the house were eight hundred and twenty-two; and Adaiah the son of Jeroham, the son of Pelaliah, the son of Amzi, the son of Zechariah, the son of Pashhur, the son of Malchijah,

13 and his brethren, heads of the fathers' houses, were two hundred and forty-two; and Amashai the son of Azarel, the son of Ahzai, the son of Meshillemoth, the son of Immer,

14 and their brethren, mighty men of valor, were one hundred and twenty-eight. Their overseer was Zabdiel the son of one of the great men.

15 Also of the Levites: Shemaiah the son of Hasshub, the son of Azrikam, the son of Hashabiah, the son of Bunni;

16 Shabbethai and Jozabad, of the heads of the Levites, had the oversight of the business outside of the house of God;

17 Mattaniah the son of Micha, the son of Zabdi, the son of Asaph, the leader who began the thanksgiving with prayer; Bakbukiah, the second among his brethren; and Abda the son of Shammua, the son of Galal, the son of Jeduthun.

18 All the Levites in the holy city were two hundred and eighty-four.

19 Moreover the gatekeepers, Akkub, Talmon,
and their brethren who kept the gates, were one
hundred and seventy-two.

20 And the rest of Israel, of the priests and
Levites, were in all the cities of Judah, everyone in his
inheritance.

21 But the Nethinim dwelt in Ophel. And Ziha
and Gishpa were over the Nethinim.

22 Also the overseer of the Levites at Jerusalem
was Uzzi the son of Bani, the son of Hashabiah, the
son of Mattaniah, the son of Micha, of the sons of
Asaph, the singers in charge of the service of the
house of God.

23 For it was the king's command concerning
them that a certain portion should be for the singers, a
quota day by day.

24 Pethahiah the son of Meshezabel, of the
children of Zerah the son of Judah, was the king's
deputy in all matters concerning the people.

Nehemiah 11:1–24

Prior to the completion of the wall, Jerusalem had been under-populated for obvious reasons, but now that security could be guaranteed, it was time to resettle the capital city. By casting lots, one-tenth of the Israelites were chosen to move to Jerusalem. Verse 2 emphasizes that those who moved did so *"willingly."* Literally, they volunteered.[2] Those elected to remain in their own villages *"blessed"* the ones who offered to move, presumably because it entailed considerable sacrifice.

Verses 3–24 provide a categorical listing of those who settled in Jerusalem:

- *"The children of Judah"* (vv. 4–6)
- *"The sons of Benjamin"* (vv. 7–9)
- *"The priests"* (vv. 10–14)
- *"The Levites"* (vv. 15–18)
- Others (vv. 19–24)

Every now and then the list adds an item of special interest, such as noting that some of the men were *"valiant"* (v. 6), *"mighty men of valor"* (v. 14), *"Nethinim"* (v. 21; see commentary on Ezra 2:43), or leaders with particular responsibilities (vv. 21–24).

VILLAGES WHERE PEOPLE SETTLED (11:25–36)

25 And as for the villages with their fields, some of the children of Judah dwelt in Kirjath Arba and its villages, Dibon and its villages, Jekabzeel and its villages;
26 in Jeshua, Moladah, Beth Pelet,
27 Hazar Shual, and Beersheba and its villages;
28 in Ziklag and Meconah and its villages;
29 in En Rimmon, Zorah, Jarmuth,
30 Zanoah, Adullam, and their villages; in Lachish and its fields; in Azekah and its villages. They dwelt from Beersheba to the Valley of Hinnom.
31 Also the children of Benjamin from Geba dwelt in Michmash, Aija, and Bethel, and their villages;
32 in Anathoth, Nob, Ananiah;
33 in Hazor, Ramah, Gittaim;
34 in Hadid, Zeboim, Neballat;
35 in Lod, Ono, and the Valley of Craftsmen.
36 Some of the Judean divisions of Levites were in Benjamin.

Nehemiah 11:25–36

Those who were not chosen by lot to live in Jerusalem settled in the surrounding villages. Rather than giving specific names of individuals, this list records the villages in which they settled.

IDENTIFYING THE PRIESTS AND LEVITES (12:1–26)

12:1 Now these are the priests and the Levites who came up with Zerubbabel the son of Shealtiel, and Jeshua: Seraiah, Jeremiah, Ezra,
2 Amariah, Malluch, Hattush,
3 Shechaniah, Rehum, Meremoth,
4 Iddo, Ginnethoi, Abijah,
5 Mijamin, Maadiah, Bilgah,
6 Shemaiah, Joiarib, Jedaiah,
7 Sallu, Amok, Hilkiah, and Jedaiah. These were

the heads of the priests and their brethren in the days of Jeshua.

8 Moreover the Levites were Jeshua, Binnui, Kadmiel, Sherebiah, Judah, and Mattaniah who led the thanksgiving psalms, he and his brethren.

9 Also Bakbukiah and Unni, their brethren, stood across from them in their duties.

10 Jeshua begot Joiakim, Joiakim begot Eliashib, Eliashib begot Joiada,

11 Joiada begot Jonathan, and Jonathan begot Jaddua.

12 Now in the days of Joiakim, the priests, the heads of the fathers' houses were: of Seraiah, Meraiah; of Jeremiah, Hananiah;

13 of Ezra, Meshullam; of Amariah, Jehohanan;

14 of Melichu, Jonathan; of Shebaniah, Joseph;

15 of Harim, Adna; of Meraioth, Helkai;

16 of Iddo, Zechariah; of Ginnethon, Meshullam;

17 of Abijah, Zichri; the son of Minjamin; of Moadiah, Piltai;

18 of Bilgah, Shammua; of Shemaiah, Jehonathan;

19 of Joiarib, Mattenai; of Jedaiah, Uzzi;

20 of Sallai, Kallai; of Amok, Eber;

21 of Hilkiah, Hashabiah; and of Jedaiah, Nethanel.

22 During the reign of Darius the Persian, a record was also kept of the Levites and priests who had been heads of their fathers' houses in the days of Eliashib, Joiada, Johanan, and Jaddua.

23 The sons of Levi, the heads of the fathers' houses until the days of Johanan the son of Eliashib, were written in the book of the chronicles.

24 And the heads of the Levites were Hashabiah, Sherebiah, and Jeshua the son of Kadmiel, with their brothers across from them, to praise and give thanks, group alternating with group, according to the command of David the man of God.

25 Mattaniah, Bakbukiah, Obadiah, Meshullam, Talmon, and Akkub were gatekeepers keeping the watch at the storerooms of the gates.

26 These lived in the days of Joiakim the son of Jeshua, the son of Jozadak, and in the days of

> Nehemiah the governor, and of Ezra the priest, the
> scribe.
>
> *Nehemiah 12:1–26*

At first glance these verses appear to be a confusing conglomeration of odd names, but the collection does follow a basic outline:

- *"The priests and the Levites who came up with Zerubbabel"* (vv. 1–9)
- High priests from the time of Zerubbabel to the time of Nehemiah and beyond (vv. 10–11)
- Priests *"in the days of Joiakim"* (the high priest between Zerubbabel and Nehemiah; vv. 12–21)
- Levites during many generations (vv. 22–26)

The various categories in the list indicates the continuity in priestly and Levitical leadership between the first return of Jews under Cyrus and the days of Ezra and Nehemiah (and beyond). Since the right to serve in the temple passed from father to son, the list verified who had the authority to serve in the renewed community. The inclusion of the list here in Nehemiah confirms that the "proper authorities" were serving in the temple.

REFLECTIONS ON 11:1–12:16

Renewal and the Ordered Community

The covenant renewal of chapter 10 precedes the lists of chapters 11 and 12. According to Ezra-Nehemiah, renewal does not conflict with order, but, rather, it leads to order. Presumably, a proper ordering of the settlers in Jerusalem and the organization of the temple ministry would prolong the renewal that began with the rebuilding of the temple and culminated in the signing of a firm agreement (chapter 10).

Of course order can squelch genuine renewal. Sometimes in our churches we embrace so much order that the Holy Spirit, who moves where he wills (John 3:8), has no room to move! That is not to say that spiritual freedom and order are enemies. On the contrary, in 1 Corinthians 12–14, Paul encourages the free exercise of spiritual gifts while at the same time he provides rules by which these gifts can operate "decently and in order" (1 Cor. 14:40).

Presbyterians relish the orderliness of tradition. We quote with passion Paul's line that "all things should be done decently and in order," though we usually forget that "all things," in context, refers to "spiritual gifts." We become nervous about the exercise of these gifts for fear that the order we relish will be shaken. If anything, we err too far in the direction of order. Speaking for myself and the church I pastor, we definitely need the fresh wind of the Spirit to blow through our midst, to dishevel our formal, constrained order. Our Presbyterian motto is, after all, *ecclesia reformata semper reformanda:* The reformed church, always being reformed. But, surely, too much attachment to an established order will prevent the Holy Spirit from continuing to "re-form" us.

Yet order itself is not necessarily an obstruction to renewal, although some new churches would say so. I watch with interest (and occasional envy) as Christians break off to form new churches. They insist that their church will be different, with an ongoing experience of renewal that will not be hampered by excessive order. However, as these churches grow, they face the inevitable demands of institutionalization. As long as a charismatic founder leads the church, all may be well; but who will assist and someday replace that leader? Eventually, structures of authority begin to appear. Then someone who thinks he speaks with God's authority begins to teach heresy. Responsible leaders step in to discipline this individual and create creedal statements to prevent other outbursts. Soon, the renewed community that shucked off its shackles of order has developed its own order[3]—an order that is necessary in the process of maturation.

We who yearn for renewal in our churches, and those of us who are blessed to experience it, must live in the creative tension between order and renewal, between form and reformation. In our openness to receive God's new wine, at times we will discard old wineskins, but we will need new wineskins to replace them.

Knowing Your Leaders

Nehemiah is careful to identify the spiritual leaders of Israel; those who serve as priests and Levites appear by name along with their ancestry, which establishes their authority to minister. Those who live in a renewed community need to know the qualifications and validity of the leaders they are called to follow.

Some contemporary Christians seem squeamish about identifying leaders. Newly established churches sometimes affirm "the priesthood of all believers" to the extent that few members accept any leadership labels. Still, leaders in other settings recoil from the suggestion that they be recognized publicly as leaders; they prefer to serve behind the scenes. Yet, in 1 Thessalonians 5:12 Paul writes, "And we ask you, brothers and sisters, to know those who labor among you, who lead you in the Lord, and who admonish you" (author's translation). When leaders are known, they can lead through the example of their lives in addition to the impact of their teaching, preaching, and guidance. Furthermore, when leaders are known, they can also be held accountable for their personal behavior and their leadership.

At Irvine Presbyterian Church, we realized that with a growing number of new members and visitors in our congregation, many did not know the elders and deacons. Had they wanted to turn to one of these leaders for counsel or guidance they would not have known to whom they could turn. To solve this problem, one of our members, a professional photographer, took photos of the leaders, and we posted these in a central location. The point of this project was not to boast about leadership authority, but to allow the leadership to be known as leaders. It may be an unusual idea but one I think Nehemiah would have approved of!

NOTES

1. See Williamson, *Ezra, Nehemiah,* pp. 341–66; Fensham, *Ezra and Nehemiah,* pp. 242–54.

2. The Hebrew uses a Hithpael form of *nādab,* with the meaning "to volunteer" (Brown, Driver, and Briggs, *Lexicon*).

3. The process of institutionalization is explored in P. L. Berger and T. Luckmann, *The Social Construction of Reality: A Treatise in the Sociology of Knowledge* (Garden City, NJ: Doubleday, 1967).

CHAPTER NINETEEN

Dedication of the Wall

Nehemiah 12:27–43

I LOVE A PARADE

Growing up in Southern California, my family regularly attended the Rose Parade on New Year's Day. My mind swirls with memories of those magic mornings: waking before dawn, bundling up with mittens and ski caps, walking in crowds of hurrying parade enthusiasts, anticipating a stunning pageant of floats and bands.

I loved a parade then—and I still do—but the closest I have come to participating in a parade was my graduation processional at Harvard. Several weeks after submitting my doctoral dissertation, I flew back to Cambridge, Massachusetts for the ceremony. The other doctoral students and I, fully decked out in academic regalia of bright crimson robes, marched through Harvard yard amid crowds, banners, music, and buoyant jubilation. Pageantry abounded everywhere— lot's of pomp and plenty of circumstance. I felt the exuberant joy of having finished a long project—something I had missed in the Federal Express office when I actually completed twelve years of graduate school by mailing off an approved dissertation. Not until the moment of parade and pageantry did I feel like I had truly graduated.

Now when the wall was finished (6:15), we were not told of any celebration or dedication. The flow of the narrative continued for several chapters as an indication that the wall was not an end in itself, but only a means to the end of a renewed covenant people. Chapters 8–10 form the emotional apex of Ezra-Nehemiah as both leaders work together to usher in a new era of covenantal commitment. Finally, in chapter 13, we read of the joyous celebration. The people of Judah dedicated the wall with great pageantry. In fact, their ceremony would compete for dramatic impact with any Harvard graduation, presidential inauguration, or holiday parade.

PREPARATION FOR CELEBRATION (12:27–30)

> 27 Now at the dedication of the wall of Jerusalem they sought out the Levites in all their places, to bring them to Jerusalem to celebrate the dedication with gladness, both with thanksgivings and singing, with cymbals and stringed instruments and harps.
> 28 And the sons of the singers gathered together from the countryside around Jerusalem, from the villages of the Netophathites,
> 29 from the house of Gilgal, and from the fields of Geba and Azmaveth; for the singers had built themselves villages all around Jerusalem.
> 30 Then the priests and Levites purified themselves, and purified the people, the gates, and the wall.
>
> *Nehemiah 12:27–30*

Although we do not hear the voice of Nehemiah clearly until verse 31, in verse 27 his narration of events continues (resuming from 7:5). In preparation for the dedication, *"the Levites"* were gathered from their places of residence. Not only did they assist the priests, but the Levites also provided the music in the temple. Special *"singers,"* who may or may not have been Levites, also gathered in Jerusalem from the surrounding villages (vv. 28–29).

Once the appropriate personnel had arrived, *"the priests and Levites purified themselves, and purified the people, the gates, and the wall"* (v. 30). Religious purification in the Old Testament took various forms, including washings, ritual sprinklings, sacrifices, fasting, and sexual abstinence.[1] The priests and Levites participated in one or more of these means of ritual preparation. Even the gates and the wall were purified, though the text does not explain how.

Preparation for the dedication involved gathering the participants and directing them to prepare themselves through rites of purification. Although the text does not say so explicitly, Nehemiah also prepared for the dedication by planning a large-scale pageant of parades, choirs, and sacrifices. The descriptions given in verses 31–43 reflect careful design and implementation.

DEDICATION OF THE WALL (12:31–43)

31 So I brought the leaders of Judah up on the wall, and appointed two large thanksgiving choirs. One went to the right hand on the wall toward the Refuse Gate.

32 After them went Hoshaiah and half of the leaders of Judah,

33 and Azariah, Ezra, Meshullam,

34 Judah, Benjamin, Shemaiah, Jeremiah,

35 and some of the priests' sons with trumpets— Zechariah the son of Jonathan, the son of Shemaiah, the son of Mattaniah, the son of Michaiah, the son of Zaccur, the son of Asaph,

36 and his brethren, Shemaiah, Azarel, Milalai, Gilalai, Maai, Nethanel, Judah, and Hanani, with the musical instruments of David the man of God. Ezra the scribe went before them.

37 By the Fountain Gate, in front of them, they went up the stairs of the City of David, on the stairway of the wall, beyond the house of David, as far as the Water Gate eastward.

38 The other thanksgiving choir went the opposite way, and I was behind them with half of the people on the wall, going past the Tower of the Ovens as far as the Broad Wall,

39 and above the Gate of Ephraim, above the Old Gate, above the Fish Gate, the Tower of Hananel, the Tower of the Hundred, as far as the Sheep Gate; and they stopped by the Gate of the Prison.

40 So the two thanksgiving choirs stood in the house of God, likewise I and the half of the rulers with me;

41 and the priests, Eliakim, Maaseiah, Minjamin, Michaiah, Elioenai, Zechariah, and Hananiah, with trumpets;

42 also Maaseiah, Shemaiah, Eleazar, Uzzi, Jehohanan, Malchijah, Elam, and Ezer. The singers sang loudly with Jezrahiah the director.

43 Also that day they offered great sacrifices, and rejoiced, for God had made them rejoice with great joy; the women and the children also rejoiced, so that the joy of Jerusalem was heard afar off.

Nehemiah 12:31–43

To begin the dedication, Nehemiah divided the people into two groups. Each group contained:

- *a large thanksgiving choir* (12:31, literally a "thanksgiving"[2])
- a significant lay leader (*Hoshaiah*, 12:32; Nehemiah, 12:38)
- other leaders (12:32–34, 40)
- priests with trumpets (12:35–36, 41)
- other musicians, including the Levites (12:36,42)

From the point where they had gathered, Nehemiah sent one group counterclockwise along the top of the wall, and he directed another group in a clockwise direction. After walking around on most of the wall, both groups converged at the temple (v. 40). There, while *"the singers sang loudly with Jezrahiah as their director"* (v. 42), the priests *"offered great sacrifices"* (v. 43). All the people *"rejoice[d] with great joy,"* including *"the women and the children"* (v. 43). Their rejoicing was so loud that it *"was heard afar off"* (v. 43). This description reminds us of Ezra 3:13, where the combination of weeping and rejoicing "was heard afar off." But now weeping had passed; only deafening rejoicing remained.

REFLECTIONS ON 12:27–43

The people of God dedicated the wall in Jerusalem with an elaborate worship service. To me, this passage suggests how we also might worship God more fully. As the Israelites celebrated God's provision of a wall, so we gather as Christians to celebrate God's grace offered through Christ. As they dedicated the wall, so we dedicate ourselves in worship. Nehemiah 12:27–43 offers four aspects of effective worship: pausing, preparation, participation, and physical expression.

Pausing to Celebrate

The people of Judah paused to dedicate the wall. Levites from a wide area took time away from their appointed duties to celebrate this event. All the people—including religious and secular leaders—stepped back from their daily tasks in order to celebrate. The text does not indicate exactly how long the dedication lasted, but it must have lasted at least a day, and for many the preparations probably required much more time.

When we gather for worship, we also pause, stepping back from our typically busy lives to focus on God. Sadly, the notion of pausing for anything has become increasingly foreign to our culture. We fill our lives with endless activities, rushing through them at a frenetic pace. It is not surprising that worship often gets lost in the shuffle.

But God created us to pause. He created us to live in a steady rhythm in which we rest from our labors one day each week. The sabbath was created for us so that we might pause for refreshment, for rest, and for worship. You and I must build into our lives time to pause, to enjoy God—and to enjoy life.

It is not easy for me to pause. And, frankly, I chaff at having to take time to celebrate. As soon as I have finished one project, my pragmatism presses me forward onto the next one. Consequently, too often I miss the joy along the way. Believe it or not, I would have missed my graduation ceremonies from Harvard had it not been for the insistence of my adviser, my wife, and a few friends. But how much poorer my life would be if I had always let my work-ethic take command of my life! Likewise, as we consider our relationship with God, we need to take time to pause, to reflect, to pray, and to celebrate with other believers.

Preparation for Worship

The priests and Levites prepared for their service by purifying themselves. Whatever physical action this entailed, it provided these religious leaders with a chance to prepare their hearts for serving God. If they washed their clothes, for example, focusing on physical cleanliness gave them the opportunity to consider their spiritual readiness for worship.

Unfortunately, I do not know many Christians who prepare for worship. To be sure, those of us who lead worship prepare our sermons or rehearse our anthems. But do we set aside time to prepare our hearts to bow in the presence of God? If not, could this be why we find worship so boring?

Perhaps we need to consider how we can prepare for worship. Some of us might begin on Saturday evening, setting aside a time for reflection and prayer. Before going to church on Sunday morning, my wife spends an hour listening to Christian music, writing in her journal, and praying—preparing her heart and her mind for worship. But as I watch the members of my church arriving in a rush, often trailing two or three young children after them, I realize that times of quiet are few and far between for many of them. So we have added a new feature to Sunday morning worship. Five minutes before our service officially begins, the pastors and choir members take their seats. David, our church pianist, plays a meditative song to focus our attention. For these five minutes we prepare to worship God by quieting our spirits, reflecting on God, and allowing the Holy Spirit to move in our hearts. It is my hope that this experience will enrich our corporate worship each Sunday and will encourage us to take even more time on our own to prepare to worship God.

Participation in Worship

The people of Israel did not dedicate the wall by sitting and listening; they participated by processing (v. 38) and by rejoicing (v. 43). Undoubtedly, they were led in song by the Levites and other music directors. As a result of their active participation the singing was heard from far away.

It seems that in the past two decades Western Christians have rediscovered the participatory nature of true worship. Some of us have made this discovery through exposure to "charismatic" worship; others through participating in more liturgical traditions; and still others by visiting foreign countries, especially those in the Southern Hemisphere. We have come to realize what has always been true, that worship is not something we observe, it is something we do. My predecessor at Irvine Presbyterian, Ben Patterson, did a marvelous job of teaching the congregation that worship is a performance—indeed, a performance in which God is the audience and the congregants are the performers.[3] Those who lead worship are only prompters, they are not performers to be observed by the congregation.

But many Christians seem to have missed the recent renaissance in worship. They still attend worship each Sunday in order to watch the show, to get something out of the sermon, to be inspired, and to go home. These reasons may be worthy, but they are not worship. True worship occurs when we communicate with God, when we offer our praise, our love, and our very lives to him.

As a pastor, I am concerned with how easily we fall into an observational mode in church. But it may be that the arrangements of our church services encourage this mode. For example, the pastors, along with the choir, sit in front of the congregation like actors on a stage. They are dressed in formal worship attire, while the average church member wears common clothing. With the exception of one or two hymns, the worshipers simply watch and listen to the action on the platform. Is it any wonder that so little genuine, participatory worship occurs on Sunday mornings?

Although I preach a sermon each Sunday, and our choir provides wonderful music, our Director of Worship and I work hard to ensure that those who lead, whether in speech or in song, are the prompters of the worshipers, not the entertainers. We maximize congregational participation through songs and prayers. We have chosen not to wear clerical robes and we plan the physical arrangement of the service to communicate clearly to our congregants: "You are the performers, God is the audience, and we are simply the prompters."

Physical Expression in Worship

In their service of dedication, the Israelites marched around the city walls. They sang and rejoiced with such gusto that neighbors from miles around heard the noise. They were involved physically as well as mentally and spiritually.

Indeed, the Old Testament abounds with physical expressions of worship. People sing, shout, stand, kneel, bow, clap their hands, raise their hands, and dance. In fact, rarely do we read that they simply sit. Indeed, in the biblical view, God sits enthroned while worshipers kneel or stand before him as a gesture of submission and servitude.

I come from a Christian tradition that minimizes and even discourages physical expressions of worship. When we sing, we sing quietly; when we confess our faith, we do so with reverent reservation. We emphasize the intellectual component of true worship, with some slight allowance for the emotional with great restraint. Certainly, true worship involves the mind, for we think about God and communicate cognitively with him in worship, but perhaps we need to learn more about loving God with all of our heart, and all of our soul, and all of our strength (Deut. 6:5).

Singing, one of the physical expressions of worship, is central to biblical worship. The dedication in Nehemiah 12 illustrates this principle distinctly. Ten of the seventeen verses in 12:27–43 mention something musical. Levites came from miles around to play their instruments and sing in the choir. The people participated by singing with great joy—and with great volume. If we turn to the Psalms we find that they reiterate the fundamental role of singing in worship (for example, Psalms 91, 95, 96, 98, 100). All of this brings to mind the words of Martin Luther, who was effusive in his praise of music:

> I wish to see all arts, principally music, in the service of Him who gave and created them. Music is a fair and glorious gift of God. I would not for the world forego my humble share of music. Singers are never sorrowful, but are merry, and smile through their troubles in song. Music makes people kinder, gentler, more staid and reasonable. I am strongly persuaded that after theology there is no art that can be placed on a level with music; for besides theology, music is the only art capable of affording peace and joy of the heart . . . the devil flees before the sound of music almost as much as before the Word of God.[4]

Perhaps more than in any other medium of worship, singing unites our hearts, souls, minds, and bodies.

Of course mere physical expression of worship that does not emanate from the heart does not honor God. On the other hand, our bodies can influence our hearts to genuinely experience worship. When I kneel in prayer, for example, I often find my heart unexpectedly humbled before God. And I can imagine that, as the people of Israel walked upon the wall they had finished by God's grace, heartfelt thanksgivings began to well up inside of them. As they sang loud praises, surely their hearts filled with even more joy. Wouldn't our worship be enriched if we began to follow Psalm 95 literally?

> Oh come, let us sing to the LORD!
> Let us shout joyfully to the Rock of our salvation.
> Let us come before His presence with thanksgiving;
> Let us shout joyfully to Him with psalms.
> For the LORD is the great God,
> And the great King above all gods.
> In His hand are the deep places of the earth;
> The heights of the hills are His also.
> The sea is His, for He made it;

And His hands formed the dry land.
O come, let us worship and bow down;
Let us kneel before the LORD, our Maker.
For He is our god,
And we are the people of His pasture,
And the sheep of His hand.

Psalm 95:1–7

NOTES

1. See Exod. 19:10, 14–15; Lev. 16:28; Num. 8:5–8; 19; and Williamson, *Ezra, Nehemiah,* p. 373.

2. "Thanksgiving choir" translates *tôdâ,* which means "thanksgiving" (Brown, Driver, and Briggs, *Lexicon*).

3. B. Patterson attributes this idea to Søren Kierkegaard, in his excellent book, *The Grand Essentials* (Waco, TX: Word Books, 1987) p. 91.

4. Martin Luther, quoted in F. Bock, ed., *Hymns for the Family of God* (Nashville: Paragon, 1976), opposite hymn #1.

CHAPTER TWENTY

A Day of Obedience

Nehemiah 12:44–13:3

This short passage serves as a transition between the climactic dedication in 12:27–43 and the later work of Nehemiah in 13:4-31. It summarizes the covenant life of Israel after the wall had been built, while it presents the issues to be considered in the rest of chapter 13. The passage does not appear to have come from Nehemiah's memoirs, but from the hand of the editor.

ISRAEL GIVES THE REQUIRED PORTIONS (12:44–47)

44 And at the same time some were appointed over the rooms of the storehouse for the offerings, the firstfruits, and the tithes, to gather into them from the fields of the cities the portions specified by the Law for the priests and Levites; for Judah rejoiced over the priests and Levites who ministered.
45 Both the singers and the gatekeepers kept the charge of their God and the charge of the purification, according to the command of David and Solomon his son.
46 For in the days of David and Asaph of old there were chiefs of the singers, and songs of praise and thanksgiving to God.
47 In the days of Zerubbabel and in the days of Nehemiah all Israel gave the portions for the singers and the gatekeepers, a portion for each day. They also consecrated holy things for the Levites, and the Levites consecrated them for the children of Aaron.

Nehemiah 12:44–47

Verse 44 begins with the phrase: *"and at the same time."* In fact, the Hebrew reads literally, "on that day," repeating a phrase used in 12:43 and again in 13:1. Although this gives an impression of activities that occurred on the same day in which the wall had been dedicated, verse 47 shows the editor's broader intention: *"In the days of Zerubbabel and in the days of Nehemiah."* This passage describes a time that begins with the dedication but continues for an unspecified period of time.[1]

In ancient times, persons were appointed to supervise the storehouse of tithes for those who served in the temple (v. 44). They also gathered these tithes *"from the fields of the cities"* (v. 44). Here it appears that the people were more than willing to offer the required portions, since *"Judah rejoiced over the priests and Levites who ministered"* (v. 44). Under the influence of Nehemiah, the people ordered their life according to God's covenant and even took joy in the sacred institutions.

Verses 45–46 outline the activities of *"the singers and the gatekeepers."* When David established the order for Priests and Levites (1 Chronicles 23–24), he also formed divisions of musicians and gatekeepers (1 Chronicles 25–26). *"Asaph,"* one of the most noted music leaders, authored many psalms (for example, Psalm 82). By mentioning the singers and the gatekeepers, the author paints a picture of a temple that was completely operational, one in which all ministries occurred as in the former days.

Verse 47 further indicates that, not only was the temple fully staffed, but *"all Israel"* supported the ministry by giving the required tithes and other portions. Under Nehemiah's leadership, the temple and the nation functioned according to covenantal stipulations.

SEPARATION FROM FOREIGNERS (13:1–3)

13:1 On that day they read from the Book of Moses
in the hearing of the people, and in it was found
written that no Ammonite or Moabite should ever
come into the assembly of God,
    2 because they had not met the children of Israel
with bread and water, but hired Balaam against them
to curse them. However, our God turned the curse
into a blessing.
    3 So it was, when they had heard the Law, that
they separated all the mixed multitude from Israel.

Nehemiah 13:1–3

Once again the book of Ezra-Nehemiah addresses the issue of separation from foreigners (see Ezra 6:21; 9–10). As mentioned above, the phrase *"on that day"* means, "during that period of time," not "on the very day in which the wall was dedicated." (Verse 4 supports this interpretation by showing that a considerable period of time had passed before "that day" of verse 1).

The leaders read a passage from Deuteronomy, *"the Book of Moses,"* that is summarized in 13:1–2. The legal text was:

> An Ammonite or Moabite shall not enter the congregation of the LORD; even to the tenth generation none of his descendants shall enter the assembly of the LORD forever, because they did not meet you with bread and water on the road when you came out of Egypt, and because they hired against you Balaam the son of Beor from Pethor of Mesopotamia, to curse you. Nevertheless the LORD your God would not listen to Balaam, but the LORD your God turned the curse into a blessing for you, because the LORD your God loves you.
>
> *Deuteronomy 23:3–6*

Upon hearing this passage, the Israelites *"separated all the mixed multitude from Israel"* (v. 3). We do not know exactly what they did , but Williamson suggests that they excluded persons of foreign descent from religious gatherings.[2] The emphasis here is not on the precise nature of the actions, but on the fact that the people obeyed the Law. We might picture the writer of the book looking back with nostalgia upon a time when all Israel endeavored to obey the Torah. Sadly, as we will soon see, this period did not last for long. Unfortunately, the sun quickly set upon Israel's day of obedience.

NOTES

1. The Hebrew phrase usually identifies a particular point or period in time. See Brown, Driver, and Briggs, *Lexicon,* s.v. *"yôm,"* 7g. Here it is used more indefinitely.

2. Williamson, *Ezra, Nehemiah,* p. 386.

CHAPTER TWENTY-ONE

Shoring Up Restoration Life: Nehemiah's Second Term

Nehemiah 13:4–31

Not Quite "Happily Ever After"

A friend of mine who works in the movie industry told a fascinating story that illustrates how we value happy endings. Studio executives were getting ready to release one of the most lucrative movies of the past few years. Before doing so, however, they showed the film to a number of focus groups: carefully selected viewers who would represent the movie-going population. The focus groups strongly disliked the movie, which, of course, was bad news for the studio. The viewers objected strongly to the movie's realistic but sad ending. It was a "downer," they said. So the producers went back to the drawing board, reshot a happy ending, and showed it to focus groups once more. This time the film received enthusiastic, positive comments, especially about its "upbeat" ending. So the film was released in its new form, to the delight of millions of moviegoers, not to mention the delight the studio executives who had turned a financial disaster into a highly lucrative venture.

We can bemoan the materialism of Hollywood or the superficiality of our culture, but the fact remains: we love a happy ending. We want the good guys to win. So in light of this sentiment, I seriously doubt that Hollywood will ever make a movie about Nehemiah, at least not an accurate one. Focus groups would certainly say that, in the end, Ezra-Nehemiah is a "downer." The editor of the book had every chance to finish on a high note—the dedication of the wall in chapter 12 ends with a joyful celebration (12:43), and the transition in 12:44–13:3 shows the covenantal faithfulness of Judah—but things fall apart in the rest of chapter 13. In Williamson's apt phrase, the book "seems to peter out in a series of reforms."[1] We are compelled to complete our reading of Ezra-Nehemiah with a gloomy dose of realism. Yet our task must be to determine the significance of this melancholy ending, to ask what we can learn from a story that would never be a success at the box office.

In 13:4–31, Nehemiah returns as narrator to tell about his final term as governor of Judah. The passage can be divided into three sections, each beginning with a temporal reference ("Now before this," "In those days") and ending with a prayer for remembrance ("Remember me"). Each section describes one way in which the people had forsaken their covenantal vows, as well as Nehemiah's decisive response to their unfaithfulness. The theme of the chapter is holiness.

RESTORING THE HOLINESS OF THE TEMPLE (13:4–14)

4 Now before this, Eliashib the priest, having authority over the storerooms of the house of our God, was allied with Tobiah.

5 And he had prepared for him a large room, where previously they had stored the grain offerings, the frankincense, the articles, the tithes of grain, the new wine and oil, which were commanded to be given to the Levites and singers and gatekeepers, and the offerings for the priests.

6 But during all this I was not in Jerusalem, for in the thirty-second year of Artaxerxes king of Babylon I had returned to the king. Then after certain days I obtained leave from the king,

7 and I came to Jerusalem and discovered the evil that Eliashib had done for Tobiah, in preparing a room for him in the courts of the house of God.

8 And it grieved me bitterly; therefore I threw all the household goods of Tobiah out of the room.

9 Then I commanded them to cleanse the rooms; and I brought back into them the articles of the house of God, with the grain offering and the frankincense.

10 I also realized that the portions for the Levites had not been given them; for each of the Levites and the singers who did the work had gone back to his field.

11 So I contended with the rulers, and said, "Why is the house of God forsaken?" And I gathered them together and set them in their place.

12 Then all Judah brought the tithe of the grain and the new wine and the oil to the storehouse.

13 And I appointed as treasurers over the storehouse Shelemiah the priest and Zadok the scribe, and of the Levites, Pedaiah; and next to them was Hanan the son of Zaccur, the son of Mattaniah; for they were considered faithful, and their task was to distribute to their brethren.

14 Remember me, O my God, concerning this, and do not wipe out my good deeds that I have done for the house of my God, and for its services!

Nehemiah 13:4–14

The opening phrase, *"Now before this,"* refers to 13:1–3. Before the Israelites separated from the mixed multitude, a priest named *"Eliashib"* (probably not the High Priest by this name)[2] had been given responsibility for the *"storerooms"* of the Temple. It is not clear whether he was an ally, or perhaps even a relative of Tobiah,[3] the arch rival of Nehemiah (see 2:19; 4:3, 7; 6:1, 14, 17–19), but it is clear that he allowed Tobiah to use a large storeroom of the Temple, presumably to extend his business and political contacts in Jerusalem. This reveals two discouraging factors. For one, it indicates that the required offerings were not being given for the support of the Temple ministry, hence the empty storeroom. For another, Tobiah was a gentile, an Ammonite (2:19), who should not have been allowed in the sacred areas of the Temple. Tobiah's presence in the storeroom designated for holy implements caused the room to be desecrated. And it is perplexing that this compromise of the Temple's holiness and integrity did not appear to matter to Eliashib or to his fellow priests.

Meanwhile, Nehemiah had left Jerusalem and returned to King *"Artaxerxes"* (v. 6). His initial twelve-year stay ended in the *"thirty-second year"* of the king's reign (see 5:14). Nehemiah does not say how many years passed before, once again, he obtained *"leave from the king"* in order to return to Jerusalem. He also does not mention being sent as governor, but his authoritative actions in chapter 13 make this a likely possibility. All we know is that *"after certain days"* Nehemiah

295

arrived in Jerusalem, there to find *"the evil that Eliashib had done for Tobiah, in preparing a room for him in the courts of the house of God"* (v. 7).

Nehemiah reacted with strong emotion: he was *"bitterly"* grieved (v. 8). He not only felt strongly, but he acted decisively. He threw *"all the household goods of Tobiah out of the room,"* and commanded that the *"rooms"* be cleansed.⁴ (Christian readers cannot help but see a fore-shadowing of Jesus' own cleansing of the Temple.) Finally, Nehemiah restocked the storeroom with the *"articles"* and *"offerings"* originally intended to be stored there.

At this time Nehemiah discovered that the *"portions for the Levites had not been given them; for each of the Levites and the singers who did the work had gone back to his field"* (v. 10). Although not stated, the text seems to imply that the Levites and singers had left their ministry to provide for themselves because their support from the temple had ceased. When the Temple was functioning properly, these ministers were supported fully by offerings given for their livelihood. But when these were withheld, the Levites and singers could not con-tinue with their sacred tasks. This appears to explain why they had returned to their fields.

Nehemiah held the *"rulers"* (the civic officials) accountable for the failed support of the Levites and singers (v. 11). He *"contended"* with the leaders, saying: *"Why is the house of God forsaken?"* Incred-ibly, the people had done precisely what they had promised not to do in the covenant of chapter 10. In 10:39 they had pledged: "And we will not neglect the house of our God." (The Hebrew word translated there as "neglect" comes from the same root as the word for "forsaken" in 13:11.)⁵ Therefore, when Nehemiah accused the leaders (and implicitly the people) of neglecting or forsaking the Temple, he was actually accusing them of breaking the covenant made in chapter 10. And as we shall see, each incident in chapter 13 follows this same pattern: the people break their covenantal vows from chapter 10.

After contending with the leaders, Nehemiah reinstated the for-saken ministers in their proper places (v. 11). (*"I gathered them together"* refers to the Levites, not to the leaders.) Under Nehemiah's command, *"all Judah"* once again brought the appropriate offerings to the storehouse and, thus, restored full support for the Temple staff. This time, however, he guaranteed that the guardians of the storehouse would be more *"faithful"* than the compromising Eliashib (v. 13);

296

Nehemiah himself appointed the storehouse *"treasurers,"* choosing people distinguished for their integrity.

This portion of 13:4–31 ends with the first of three prayers in which Nehemiah asked God to remember him. Additionally he asked: *"Do not wipe out my good deeds that I have done for the house of my God, and for its services!"* (v. 14). "Good deeds" is translated from the Hebrew word *hesed*, which means "my acts of faithfulness."[6] This original word is often used of actions done in light of the covenant. Here, whereas the Israelites had forsaken the covenant they had made to honor the Temple, Nehemiah acted faithfully and fulfilled his covenant vow to the LORD. His actions were not simply "good deeds," but deeds done in covenant faithfulness to God. Nehemiah asked God not to *"wipe out"* his actions, perhaps reflecting the fact that his earlier deeds on behalf of the Temple had been wiped out—not by God, but by an unfaithful people and especially by their unfaithful leaders.

RESTORING THE HOLINESS OF THE SABBATH (13:15–22)

15 In those days I saw in Judah some people treading wine presses on the Sabbath, and bringing in sheaves, and loading donkeys with wine, grapes, figs, and all kinds of burdens, which they brought into Jerusalem on the Sabbath day. And I warned them about the day on which they were selling provisions.

16 Men of Tyre dwelt there also, who brought in fish and all kinds of goods, and sold them on the Sabbath to the children of Judah, and in Jerusalem.

17 Then I contended with the nobles of Judah, and said to them, "What evil thing is this that you do, by which you profane the Sabbath day?

18 Did not your fathers do thus, and did not our God bring all this disaster on us and on this city? Yet you bring added wrath on Israel by profaning the Sabbath."

19 So it was, at the gates of Jerusalem, as it began to be dark before the Sabbath, that I commanded the gates to be shut, and charged that they must not be opened till after the Sabbath. Then I posted some of my servants at the gates, so that no burdens would be brought in on the Sabbath day.

20 Now the merchants and sellers of all kinds of
wares lodged outside Jerusalem once or twice.

21 Then I warned them, and said to them, "Why
do you spend the night around the wall? If you do so
again, I will lay hands on you!" From that time on
they came no more on the Sabbath.

22 And I commanded the Levites that they should
cleanse themselves, and that they should go and
guard the gates, to sanctify the Sabbath day.

Remember me, O my God, concerning this also,
and spare me according to the greatness of Your mercy!

Nehemiah 13:15–22

The second section of 13:4–31 begins with a general indicator of
time: *"In those days"* (v. 15). Sometime during his second term of office, probably soon after his return to Jerusalem, Nehemiah observed
the people dishonoring the Sabbath. Many who lived in the country-
side around Jerusalem were working on the Sabbath: making wine
and transporting produce into the city for sale (v. 15). Immediately,
Nehemiah warned the transgressors not to sell goods on the Sabbath.

Moreover, *"men of Tyre"* who lived in Jerusalem brought their goods
into the city and sold them *"to the children of Judah"* (v. 16). Residents of
ancient Tyre were well known in antiquity as merchants, and they
had sent colonies of Tyrians throughout the Mediterranean world.[7]
As Gentiles, they did not follow the Sabbath law, of course, but by
setting up shop on the Sabbath they were corrupting the Judeans.
Nehemiah did not rebuke the Tyrians, but, rather, contended with
"the nobles of Judah," who must have been buying Tyrian goods (v. 17).

Nehemiah warned the nobles not to *"profane"* the Sabbath by reminding them of their *"fathers"* or ancestors who had disobeyed the
Sabbath law and, thereby, had brought destruction upon God's
people (vv. 17–18). Perhaps he was thinking of prophetic passages
such as Jeremiah 17:19–27 and Ezekiel 20:12–24, where it was recorded that ignoring the Sabbath had brought judgment upon the
people. Nehemiah feared that by *"profaning the Sabbath"* again, the
nobles would bring *"added wrath upon Israel."*

Not satisfied with his attempt to persuade the people, Nehemiah
then commanded the gates of Jerusalem to be shut and to be guarded
during the Sabbath so that no merchants could enter (v. 19). For a
while the sellers camped outside the gates, perhaps hoping to sell

goods to individuals who left from the city during the Sabbath (v. 20), but when Nehemiah threatened these merchants with physical violence, they stopped coming to Jerusalem on the Sabbath (v. 21).

Finally, Nehemiah commanded the *"Levites"* to *"cleanse themselves"* and *"guard the gates"* (v. 22.) This was an unusual assignment for the Levites, who typically served within the Temple. The fact that the Levites were to cleanse themselves ritually for such a mundane task seems particularly odd. Yet it indicates the sacredness of the assignment in Nehemiah's view. By guarding the gates, the Levites would *"sanctify the Sabbath day."* They would make sure it was holy—set apart from other days. True holiness, according to Nehemiah, pertains not only to what happens within the Temple precincts, but, equally, to life outside in the holy city.

Once more, we should note that the people broke a covenant vow they had made earlier. In 10:31 they had promised: "If the peoples of the land bring wares or any grain to sell on the Sabbath day, we will not buy it from them on the Sabbath, or on a holy day." But, several years later they did in fact transact business on the Sabbath. Nehemiah exercised his authority to restore the sanctity of the Sabbath and to insure the ongoing faithfulness of the people. By locking the city gates and posting guards, however, he exposed his distrust of the people and their own convictions. Had he expected them to keep the Sabbath, guards would not have been necessary. Sadly, but realistically, his expectations led in the opposite direction.

The prayer of remembrance that concludes this section evinces a spirit of resignation rather than of hope. Not only did Nehemiah seek God's recollection of his effort to sanctify the Sabbath, but he asked God: *"Spare me according to the greatness of Your mercy!"* (v. 22). People don't usually ask to be spared when they are enthusiastic about their achievements! But perhaps Nehemiah foresaw the potential for Israel's destruction once again with the people's disobedience, not only of the Ten Commandments, but also of their own specific promises. He was asking to be spared, not because of his own faithfulness, but because of God's great mercy. The original language uses the same word found in 13:14: *ḥesed*. The word literally means "kindness or mercy" but often connotes actions or attitudes that are shaped by covenantal commitment.[8] Even as Nehemiah performed "acts of covenant faithfulness," he depended upon God's "covenant faithfulness" for his own salvation.

Restoring the Holiness of the People (13:23–31)

23 In those days I also saw Jews who had married women of Ashdod, Ammon, and Moab.

24 And half of their children spoke the language of Ashdod, and could not speak the language of Judah, but spoke according to the language of one or the other people.

25 So I contended with them and cursed them, struck some of them and pulled out their hair, and made them swear by God, saying, "You shall not give your daughters as wives to their sons, nor take their daughters for your sons or yourselves.

26 "Did not Solomon king of Israel sin by these things? Yet among many nations there was no king like him, who was beloved of his God; and God made him king over all Israel. Nevertheless pagan women caused even him to sin.

27 "Should we then hear of your doing all this great evil, transgressing against our God by marrying pagan women?"

28 And one of the sons of Joiada, the son of Eliashib the high priest, was a son-in-law of Sanballat the Horonite; therefore I drove him from me.

29 Remember them, O my God, because they have defiled the priesthood and the covenant of the priesthood and the Levites.

30 Thus I cleansed them of everything pagan. I also assigned duties to the priests and the Levites, each to his service,

31 and to bringing the wood offering and the firstfruits a appointed times.

Remember me, O my God, for good!

Nehemiah 13:23–31

The final section of 13:4–31 begins with a familiar temporal expression: *"In those days"* (v. 23). This time Nehemiah observes yet another instance of covenant breaking: some people of Judah *"had married women of Ashdod, Ammon, and Moab."* Now Ashdod was a city about forty miles due west of Jerusalem, while Ammon and Moab were large regions on the east of Judah. Verse 24 indicates that intermarriage with Ashdodites was the chief issue here since Nehemiah observed that children with Ashdodite mothers *"could not speak the language of Judah, but spoke according to the language of one or the other people."*

In response, Nehemiah not only confronted those who had intermarried, he hit them, pulled out their hair, and forced them to swear that they would not marry non-Jews. Specifically, he made them say: *"You shall not give your daughters as wives to their sons, nor take their daughters for your sons or yourselves"* (v. 25). This repeats almost verbatim what the people had originally promised in the covenant renewal of chapter 10 (see 10:30).

Nehemiah's exaggerated reaction may seem rash to modern readers. His actions not only of confronting, but hitting and pulling hair seem to be violent over-reactions. While I cannot defend Nehemiah's pugilistic actions, I would hasten to explain why he felt so strongly about the wrongness of mixed marriage. On one level, intermarriage threatened the religious integrity of Israel. Moreover, as verse 24 indicates, it was also a threat to the cultural survival of the Hebrew people for mixed marriages produced children who could not speak the traditional language—the chief conveyance of culture. Finally, Nehemiah recognized the sinfulness of intermarriage and the tendency of pagan wives to lead their husbands into sin and false religions. Solomon, renowned for his wisdom, exemplified for Nehemiah the risk of marrying pagan wives (12:26; see 1 Kings 11, especially verses 2–4). For Nehemiah, Israelite religion, culture, and obedience to God had all been compromised by the mixed marriages.

Yet so lightly did the people regard the issue that even a priest had married a pagan woman—a daughter of Nehemiah's principal enemy, Sanballat the Horonite (13:28; on Sanballat, see 2:19; 4:1–2, 7; 6:1–9, 14). Nehemiah asked God to remember their sin, "because they [had] defiled the priesthood and the covenant of the priesthood and the Levites" (see Malachi 2:4–8).

The whole issue of intermarriage is not unique to Nehemiah, of course. Ezra dealt with the problem in detail in Ezra 9–10. There the people not only repented of marrying pagans but divorced their pagan wives and sent them away. The fact that Nehemiah makes no reference to this event and does not require the divorcing of pagan wives has vexed commentators. How could Nehemiah act as if Ezra had never addressed or solved the problem? Does the repetition of this problem in Nehemiah 13 mean that Ezra's effort ultimately failed?

Many solutions to this problem have been suggested.[9] Given the account in 13:23–31, it seems to me that Ezra's effort did, over the years, lose its effectiveness, at least in some regions.[10] The people had promised to abstain from mixed marriage, but they did not keep their word. Perhaps Nehemiah realized that those who had married Ashdodite women had so little regard for the Law that a reference to Ezra's actions would have had little impact. This may also explain why Nehemiah did not insist upon breaking up the mixed marriages.

Verses 30–31 summarize Nehemiah's efforts to reestablish a state of holiness within Israel and to refurbish the ministry of priests and Levites. Significantly, Nehemiah talks about what he has accomplished without mentioning the support of the people. Indeed, although he compelled the people to bring proper offerings, to honor the Sabbath, and to abstain from mixed marriages, nowhere in the chapter do we see evidence of their enthusiasm for his labors. The fact that Nehemiah had to appoint treasurers (v. 13) and guards (vv. 19–22) is surely an indication of the people's reticence to be reformed.

In his final prayer, Nehemiah asked simply: *"Remember me, O my God, for good!"* (v. 31). Nehemiah was too astute not to feel his relative impotence. As governor he could enforce obedience, but his work of restoration was slowly slipping away. Previously he had asked God not to wipe out his deeds of covenant faithfulness (13:14) and to spare him according to God's own covenant faithfulness (13:22). Here, perceiving that his good deeds might not be spared, Nehemiah asked only to be remembered for good. The NIV captures the sense well in translating: "Remember me with favor, O my God" (v. 31). Nehemiah asked God to remember, not his great and lasting successes, but simply himself.

REFLECTIONS ON NEHEMIAH 13:4–31

The Realism of Nehemiah

The story of Nehemiah ends, in the words of T. S. Eliot, "not with a bang, but a whimper."[11] The era of sweeping restoration and widespread, popular enthusiasm had ended. Each promise made by the people in chapter 10 was broken in chapter 13. Although Nehemiah still had the power to enforce obedience, he moved the people to holiness in deed only, not in heart. And chapter 13 provides no indication that they gladly followed him in his ongoing reformation.

The conclusion of Ezra-Nehemiah reflects a sad yet compelling realism. In his memoirs, Nehemiah told the truth, even when the truth hurt. The editor of Ezra-Nehemiah could have ended on the high note of 12:43, with its joyous celebration; instead, he told "the whole truth, and nothing but the truth." I wonder if he compiled the accounts of Ezra and Nehemiah in a day when the unfaithfulness of chapter 13 was even more rampant. Perhaps he told the story of restoration to foreshadow and explain the failure of restoration in his own day.

Speculation aside, we certainly see in Ezra-Nehemiah the sort of realism that fills the pages of Scripture. The biblical writers were not afraid to tell the truth, even when their own heroes played the fool: Moses disobeyed God by striking the rock rather than speaking to it (Numbers 20:7–12); David committed adultery with Bathsheba (2 Samuel 11); and the disciples regularly misunderstood Jesus, even to the point of denying him.

Biblical realism, such as found in Ezra-Nehemiah, commends the Scriptures to those who seek the unvarnished truth. We live in a day of spin doctors who repackage reality to sell it to a gullible public. In the most recent presidential election we watched several debates between the major candidates. Before each debate we were told that the contest was a "must win" for each candidate. Then, no matter how ineffective the performance, immediately after the debate we were assured by campaign spokespersons that each candidate had done splendidly, "hitting the ball out of the park," and so on. Today in the western world we almost expect our leaders to color the truth, or even to be outright shady characters. Sadly, the same could be said for religious leaders as well.

But the Bible tells it as it is. And so do biblically-committed leaders. The more we tell the truth, the more we will earn a hearing in our churches and in our world. This lesson impressed me in a recent Board meeting at my church. We were discussing some changes I had made in the structure of worship, and several elders insisted that I had moved too quickly without adequately informing them or explaining things to the congregation. As I considered their position, God granted me the grace to say, "You know, I think you're right. I did move too quickly. That was a mistake." I could hardly believe the difference my straightforward admission made in the tone of the meeting. A potentially combative encounter became open and mutually supportive. As I look back upon that moment, I can trace the beginning of a deeper trust between the elders and me. It all depends upon a willingness to see what is real and to speak honestly about it.

Conformed—Or Transformed?

What was Israel's fundamental problem? Why did the reforms of Ezra and Nehemiah fail, at least in part? In Nehemiah 13 we see God's people allowing the world to invade what should be holy, set apart for God alone. They failed to live holy lives with respect to the Temple, the Sabbath, and marriage; Eliashib invited the gentile Tobiah to operate within the Temple; foreign traders tempted the Jews to dishonor the Sabbath; and men of Judah married foreign wives, only to bear children who could not even speak Hebrew. Even though adultery with pagan nations had repeatedly brought national destruction, God's people still abandoned their holy status to join with the world.

We contemporary Christians face similar pressures to compromise our holiness. In our efforts to be accepted by the world we allow nonbiblical values to "live within the church." We want preachers to stop talking about sin because "it is offensive to modern ears." The idea of keeping the Sabbath rarely enters our minds. We fill our lives to the brim, rushing from one thing to another, filling the Lord's day with shopping, chores, and extra hours in the office. Then we wonder why we are so exhausted and "stressed out." Whereas the Bible teaches us to honor marriage and keep the bed "undefiled" (Hebrews 13:4), marital infidelity seems commonplace today, even among Christians—not to mention Christian leaders.

Time and again, Israel allowed the world and its fallen idols to invade her life. In Paul's words, she became "conformed to this world" (Rom. 12:2). Though our offenses differ, we Christians regularly come up short in the same way. Surely we need to hear once again Paul's call to holy living, and to respond in gracious obedience.

> I beseech you therefore, brethren, by the mercies of God, that you
> present your bodies a living sacrifice, holy, acceptable to God,

which is your reasonable service. And do not be conformed to
this world, but be transformed by the renewing of your mind,
that you may prove what is that good and acceptable and perfect
will of God.

Romans 12:1–2

Notice that true transformation requires more than coerced holiness;
it begins with an inner transformation that flows out into tangible
acts of faithfulness. Notice also that Paul's request is based on God's
mercies, which are revealed through the death of Christ on the cross,
in which God establishes a new covenant with his people.

Successful Leadership

In Ezra and Nehemiah we have observed outstanding leadership.
Both men moved a nation into a season of rebuilding and renewal,
and both experienced measurable success in their efforts. Ezra taught
the people to obey the Law, and Nehemiah led the people to rebuild
Jerusalem's fallen wall. Together, Ezra and Nehemiah oversaw a fundamental renewal of the covenant between God and his chosen
nation.

But our delight in the successes of our heroes stumbles over the
dreary and dismal accounts of chapter 13. A couple of decades after
Ezra's victory over intermarriage, many Jews continued to marry pagan women. For all of Nehemiah's efforts to protect Jerusalem from
the world by building a wall, pagan influences continued to invade
and to corrupt God's people. When righteous behavior occurred, it
happened not because a renewed people chose to act in covenant
faithfulness, but only because Nehemiah still had the power to coerce
their obedience. We would be inclined to say that, in the end, Ezra
and Nehemiah failed as leaders.

On one level they did, in fact, fail. If we measure success by the
pervasive and lasting transformation of Israel, then neither Ezra nor
Nehemiah ultimately succeeded. But we find within the prayers of
chapter 13 a different way to measure leadership. First, Nehemiah
asked God to remember his deeds of covenant faithfulness (*ḥesed*, v. 14).
Later, he asked the LORD to spare him according to God's great mercy
(*ḥesed*, v. 22). Finally, Nehemiah prayed for God simply to remember
him—not his works, but himself—with favor. In the end, Nehemiah's

success may be evaluated, not on the basis of walls completed or laws enforced, but in light of his *faithfulness to God* and *God's covenant*. Similarly, God weighs Nehemiah's efforts, not by how much or how little he accomplished, but in light of God's own faithful mercy. To the end, Nehemiah tried to honor God and to lead in light of the covenant. He succeeded, not by persuading the nation to follow him, but by living and leading faithfully before God. And where he fell short, God's mercy compensated. What matters most in the end is not Nehemiah's achievements, but his character and his relationship with God.

During my years in ministry, I have occasionally faced severe testing of my calling and commitment. At times I have wondered if I would keep my job. I have been forced to consider what ultimately matters to me as a Christian and as a leader. What I have discovered is this: When I stand before God one day, I want to know that I have tried to be faithful to him. That is what I want most of all. Who knows, perhaps I will lose my job some day because of foolish decisions or hurried changes. After I die, I can envision being in the presence of God, who will say: "Mark, you really blew it back then—royally. But I know you wanted the best. You tried to be faithful." That will be enough for me. Was Jesus successful? Hardly, by worldly standards. But he was faithful, even to death. Therefore God highly exalted him (Phil. 2:9), and through his death, God's ultimate purpose for the universe was accomplished.

Because we are called to faithfulness as leaders, and because our evaluation depends ultimately on God's faithfulness in Christ, we can lead with joyful freedom. I will be the first to admit that I don't always experience this, but I believe it is available. Joyful freedom comes from knowing that we are called to faithfulness, not to worldly success. My church may never grow from ten to ten thousand, people may never invite me to share the secrets of my splendid successes, but I can lead with glad abandon because, in the words of the gospel hymn: "I serve a risen savior, He's in the world today." All genuine leadership begins and ends at this point—we are servants of Jesus Christ. He is our Lord, who directs our ministries, and he is our Savior, who judges us with a faithfulness shaped by the cross and the new covenant in his blood.

NOTES

1. Williamson, *Ezra, Nehemiah,* p. 402.

2. Williamson, *Ezra, Nehemiah,* p. 386.

3. The Hebrew, which literally means "close to him," can also mean "related to him" (Brown, Driver, and Briggs, *Lexicon,* s.v. "*qārôb*"). The NRSV translates "who was related to him."

4. The plural "rooms" seems odd, but probably indicates Nehemiah's conviction that Tobiah had contaminated an area larger than the single room that he had used (Williamson, *Ezra, Nehemiah,* p. 387).

5. Both come from the Hebrew root ʿ*āzab,* "to leave, forsake."

6. The Hebrew word is *hăsāday,* literally, "my acts of *hesed.*"

7. A. S. Kapelrud, "Tyre," *IDB* (Nashville: Abingdon, 1962); H. J. Katzenstein and D. R. Edwards "Tyre," *ABD* (New York: Doubleday, 1992).

8. Brown, Driver, and Briggs, *Lexicon,* s.v. "*hesed.*" See especially R. L. Harris, "*hesed,*" *TWOT* (Chicago: Moody, 1980); and Sakenfeld, "Love."

9. For example, see Williamson, *Ezra, Nehemiah,* pp. xliii–xliv, 398–99; Kidner, *Ezra and Nehemiah,* pp. 152–53.

10. Williamson believes that Nehemiah addressed a local problem only (Williamson, *Ezra, Nehemiah,* pp. 398–99).

11. T.S. Eliot, "The Hollow Men."

SECTION TWO:

The Book of Esther

Esther 1:1–10:3

Why Study Esther?

On the surface, the Book of Esther appears to be similar to Ezra and Nehemiah, the books that precede it in English Bibles.[1] All three tell a story of Jewish life under Persian rule. They include Persian kings in starring roles, they depict Jewish prominence in the royal court, and they portray anti-Jewish efforts that were defeated through Jewish ingenuity—but here the similarities end. Divergence between Ezra-Nehemiah and Esther is seen, for example, in their widely differing perspectives on marriage between Jews and Gentiles. Twice in Ezra-Nehemiah the heroes take drastic action to break apart marriages between Jews and Gentiles. Turning the page to Esther, however, a Jewish heroine marries a Gentile king—an event that saves the Jewish people from destruction. Nowhere does the text suggest anything morally or religiously suspect about her marriage. In fact, she receives honor as Queen Esther, wife of a pagan king. Thus, although both Ezra-Nehemiah and Esther depict Jewish life in the early Persian period, each interprets this life from a widely different perspective.

This difference impacts our efforts to determine why we should study Esther. For Ezra-Nehemiah, I enthusiastically provided four reasons to study that two-volume work. For Esther, however, I have found enthusiasm more elusive. And I am not the first interpreter of Esther to wrestle over its value. As we will see below, even Jewish rabbis debated the inspiration of Esther, although they ultimately decided in its favor. The great medieval rabbi Maimonides ranked Esther second in value only to the Mosaic law.[2] Nevertheless, the modern Jewish scholar Samuel Sandmel admits that he would "not be grieved if the book of Esther were somehow dropped out of scripture."[3]

If Jews have questioned the value of Esther, Christians have been even more perplexed by its dubious character. Martin Luther minced no words when he said:

> I dislike the Book of Esther and that of II Maccabees, for they Judaize too much and contain pagan naughtiness. Yet by this

time the horrible thing has happened that the Book of Esther has a greater reputation among the Jews than Isaiah or Daniel. . . .[4]

Then writing early in this century, Lewis Paton complained: "Morally, Est. falls below the general level of the OT, and even of the Apocrypha."[5] Otto Eissfeldt wraps up his introduction to Esther with this judgment: "But Christianity, extending as it does over all peoples and races, has neither occasion nor justification for holding on to it."[6] And B. W. Anderson discourages communicators from spending too much time on Esther:

> If a Christian minister is faithful to the context, he will not take his text from Esther; and if the leader of a church-school class shows any Christian discernment, he will not waste time trying to show that the heroes of the book are models of character, integrity, and piety.[7]

On the contrary, other Christian (and most Jewish) interpreters defend the value of Esther. *The Pulpit Commentary* provides 176 full pages of homiletic jewels from Esther, showing that "a valuable moral lesson pervades the whole narrative" and "the providence of God is strikingly and memorably displayed."[8] The British Bible teacher, Ian Thomas, although speaking as a modern Christian, echoes the medieval accolades of Maimonides: "I know of no other single book in the whole of the Old Testament which more lucidly illustrates the principles governing the Christian life."[9]

Although I share the concerns aired by Luther and others, I accept the canon of Scripture as it is. I believe not only that God inspired the writers of biblical documents, but also that the Holy Spirit guided the peculiar process by which these documents were included in the canon. Thus, I conclude that God has placed Esther in our Bible for a reason. One might answer the question "Why study Esther?" with the mountaineer's favorite answer: "Because it's there!" If, however, the nature of Esther causes so many commentators to doubt it's value, we might wonder with H. A. Ironside: "Why has [God] inspired so strange a book?"[10]

My best answer to the question "Why study Esther?" will be the commentary itself. For I have found that when properly interpreted, Esther encourages us to grapple with pressing moral issues in light of God's wisdom. The ethnic rivalry pictured in Esther is frightfully modern—Jews continue to be in mortal conflict with their neighbors in the Middle East and ethnic strife covers the globe, from Bosnia, to South Africa, to the streets of Los Angeles. In short, the Book of Esther raises issues that are our issues, whether we like them or not. The story forces us to think about racism and ethnic conflict. Finally, Esther challenges us to consider how we should live in this world, where we find ourselves, like the Jews of Persia and Christians of Asia Minor, pilgrims and strangers (1 Pet. 1:1). Esther upsets our comfortable assumptions about how we should live and communicate God's truth in an alien world.

THE STORY OF ESTHER

The story of Esther begins during the reign of Ahasuerus (Xerxes), King of Persia (486-465 B.C.). He threw a lavish party for government officials with wine flowing freely (chap. 1). At some point in the party, Ahaseurus, drunk with wine, commanded his wife to show off her beauty for his guests, but Queen Vashti refused. Her refusal precipitated a national crisis: What if her insubordination encouraged all Persian wives to despise their husbands? So upon the advice of his counsel, the king demoted Vashti from her royal post.

Afterwards, an elaborate procedure began for the selection of a new queen (chap. 2). "Beautiful young virgins" from throughout the empire gathered for months of supervised beautification. When they were deemed sufficiently prepared, they appeared before the king, one by one. Esther, the orphaned cousin of Mordecai, entered the royal beauty contest, though without revealing her Jewish heritage; and Ahasuerus, smitten by her beauty, crowned Esther as his new queen. Around this time Mordecai discovered a plot against the king, and by notifying Esther, was able to save the king's life.

At this point, the villain of the story, Haman, appeared on the scene (chap. 3). Because the king had appointed him to a position of leadership, everyone in Persia bowed down before Haman—everyone, that is, except Mordecai the Jew. Haman's extreme anger with Mordecai compelled him to seek, not only revenge against Mordecai, but also the slaughter of all the Jews throughout the kingdom. Using his leverage with the king, Haman issued a decree calling for the destruction of all Jews on a certain day of the ancient month Adar—a date that was established by lot.

Mordecai and Esther responded to Haman's plot with deep distress (chap. 4). After some debate between them about strategy, Mordecai convinced Esther to risk her life by approaching the king on behalf of the Jews. Esther commanded Mordecai, in return, to make sure that all Jews in the city fasted in support of her effort.

When Esther approached the king, he received her with favor (chap. 5). Then, rather than immediately making her appeal, she invited the king and Haman to a private banquet. During this feast, Ahasuerus offered any gift to Esther, up to half of his kingdom. In response, she simply asked him and Haman to join her for another banquet. Meanwhile, Haman, exceedingly impressed with himself, built a gallows for Mordecai that towered over seventy-five feet.

That night King Ahasuerus could not sleep (chap. 6). To help him fall asleep his servants read from the royal records. Coincidentally, they related how Mordecai had saved the king's life by revealing an assassination plot. In a burst of gratitude, Ahasuerus decided to honor Mordecai. Just then Haman entered the royal chambers and Ahasuerus asked him what to do for "the man whom the king delights to honor." Haman, thinking that the king intended to honor him, proposed a lavish ceremony. To his horror, Haman's plan backfired and he was chosen to escort Mordecai throughout the city, lauding him before all the citizens. After this debacle, even Haman's wife predicted her husband's imminent doom.

When the king and Haman arrived for Esther's next banquet, she finally revealed her Jewishness and claimed that Haman's plot was actually a plot against her and her people (chap. 7). When Haman begged Esther for mercy, the king viewed his approach as a lewd assault. Consequently, Haman was hanged immediately on the very gallows that he had constructed for Mordecai.

Following Haman's death, the king honored Esther and Mordecai by giving them Haman's own house (chap. 8). Esther begged Ahasuerus to revoke his decree against the Jews, but he could not do so because an official royal decree was irrevocable in Persia. However, he did invite Mordecai to issue a contrary decree permitting the Jews to defend themselves against their attackers. After his meeting with the king, Mordecai appeared in royal clothing, to the delight of all citizens, both Jews and Persians.

When the day for Jewish slaughter finally arrived, Adar 13, the Jews were well prepared to defend themselves (chap. 9). In the capital and throughout the nation they overwhelmed their enemies. Then Esther asked the king for yet another day for the Jews to protect their lives. So, on the following day, Adar 14, the Jews in the capital fought against their enemies again, while the Jews in the provinces feasted and rejoiced. On the fifteenth day of the month the Jews in the capital celebrated. Then Mordecai sent letters to all the Jews establishing the fourteenth and fifteenth of Adar as days for celebration. These days were called Purim, because Haman had cast the lot (or *pur*, in Babylonian) to determine the date on which he planned to slaughter the Jews. Esther also exercised her royal authority to confirm the celebration and dating of Purim.

The Book of Esther ends with a testimony to the greatness of Mordecai, who was second in Persia, next to King Ahasuerus (chap. 10). Surprisingly, Queen Esther is not mentioned further.

THE PUZZLES OF ESTHER

Although it relates a simple, engaging story, the Book of Esther contains numerous puzzles that perplex interpreters. Perhaps no other book of the Bible challenges the commentator with so many basic riddles.

Esther's Secularism

One of the riddles is Esther's secularism, which strikes even the casual reader as unusual. In fact, the book lacks religious elements almost entirely. God is never mentioned, although the Persian king appears 190 times in 167 verses.[11] Although Esther and her people fast before her audience with the king (4:16), the text never mentions prayer. In fact, all of the basic characteristics of Judaism fail to appear in Esther including the temple, the priesthood, Jewish history, the Law, the prophets, the covenant, Moses, and the land of Israel. At most we find a vague reference to God's providence in Mordecai's appeal to Esther in 4:14:

> For if you remain completely silent at this time, relief and deliverance will arise for the Jews *from another place,* but you and your father's house will perish. *Yet who knows whether you have come to the kingdom for such a time as this?*

So much for the presence of God in Esther, which is otherwise without obvious religious content. Ancient scribes, concerned about the absence of God and other religious elements from Esther, added 107 verses to the original text, however, these are not found in canonical Esther, but are gathered in the Apocryphal book entitled "Additions to Esther."[12]

Esther's secularism poses a problem for those of us committed to its place within the canon of sacred Scripture. Why was this piece of literature even included within the inspired writings? What does God want to say through a book that scarcely recognizes his existence? Any interpretation of Esther must deal honestly with the puzzle of its secularism. (I propose one approach to this puzzle below in "The Purpose of Esther").

Esther as History?

Upon first reading, Esther appears to be a straightforward historical account of events within the Persian empire. Indeed, the author shows a detailed knowledge of Persian politics, culture, and language.[13] The action purportedly takes place during the third (1:3), seventh (2:16), and twelfth years of King Ahasuerus (3:7). The figure of King Ahasuerus, better known by his Greek name, Xerxes, is familiar from other sources, especially the Greek historian Herodotus. In fact, the king's personality in the Book of Esther correlates closely with what can be known about him from Herodotus and other sources.[14] Yet other characters in Esther do not appear in nonbiblical writings, although archaeologists have found evidence of a Persian official named "Mordecai."[15] Finally, the book closes with a direct reference to a historical source, "The chronicles of the Kings of Media and Persia" (10:2).

All of these factors convince many commentators that Esther contains a historical and trustworthy account of events, yet historical improbabilities and contradictions between Esther and other ancient sources have led other scholars to doubt its historicity. I will only highlight a few of these inconsistencies here; extensive analysis may be found elsewhere.[16]

In the category of historical improbabilities, we have to consider the lavish banquet of King Ahasuerus that lasted for 180 days (1:4). This is also true of the process by which Esther became queen. For instance, although she underwent twelve months of beauty treatments (2:12), no official ever asked anything about her family or her race (2:20). Surely this would be highly unusual, especially if Persian queens could come only from noble Persian families, as claimed by Herodotus.[17]

While other commentaries list several additional historical improbabilities,[18] the most serious contradiction between Esther and Herodotus concerns the identity of the Persian queen. According to the Book of Esther, Esther herself reigned from the seventh year of Ahasuerus (2:16; 3:7), but Herodotus identifies Amestris as the queen during this period of time.[19] Even if the name "Amestris" were shortened to "Esther" (which seems questionable), we can hardly equate Esther with the viciously vengeful Amestris.[20] (Additional contradictions between Esther and secular histories, too numerous to mention here, are listed elsewhere.)[21]

Whereas earlier in this century many scholars completely rejected the historicity of Esther, regarding it as completely fictional, now most commentators recognize the historical underpinnings of the story.[22] They contend that the story of Esther rests upon actual events of Persian history, but that these events have been told by an author who exercised considerable literary freedom. In this view, Esther is not mere history, but is, more accurately, a "historical novel."[23]

Some commentators bristle at the notion that Esther is anything but unadorned history. One writes,

> This story is not fiction, the creation of some author's imagination. It is history—plain and simple; names, places, dates and customs are all related on the historical level. Unless we begin with this premise, the story will have little meaning for us.[24]

(Curiously, the commentary that follows this quotation never shows how the meaning of Esther relates to its historicity). Yet we must ask why the story has meaning for us only if it is historical. Does the mere fact of its historicity validate Esther as being relevant for our lives? Hardly! Those of us who affirm the authority of Scripture too often back ourselves into a historical or literary corner without carefully considering the facts. If Esther intends merely to tell what actually happened long ago, then any exaggeration would contradict its intention and deny its infallibility. If, on the other hand, Esther intends to tell a story that is based on history but embellished for literary and educational purposes, then improbabilities and contradictions do not destroy the integrity of the book. At any rate, we cannot assume that Esther is history until we have thoroughly explored its nature and contents.

Analogously, I have heard some Christians argue that the parable of the Good Samaritan must be historically true, otherwise it has no value. They contend that Jesus would not tell a story unless it were true. But how do they know this? By an actual study of the parables? Of course not! Rather they project onto the words of Jesus their own prejudices, which include the denigration of fiction and the veneration of simple history. In the hope of supporting biblical authority, these well-intentioned Christians actually reject the Bible "as it is." Similarly, the question of whether Esther is fully historical in all of its details, or is merely a literary retelling of history, cannot be settled *a priori*. If the literary genre of the work is something other than simple history, or if elements of the text prove to be nonhistorical, then we may conclude that the author of Esther never intended to record mere facts. We must take Esther on its own terms, as we should every portion of Scripture. The higher our commitment to the Bible as God's Word the more we will base our interpretations upon the Bible itself, rather than upon our theological presuppositions about what biblical authority demands.[25]

Esther and Purim

Although most Christians are relatively unfamiliar with the story of Esther, Jews immediately recognize it as the *Megillâ* (Hebrew for "scroll, book") that is read each year during the festival of Purim.[26] Purim, though celebrated faithfully by most Jews, is not a religious holiday like the Day of Atonement. Rather, it is a joyous, even uproarious celebration of freedom and redemption. The holiday centers around the public reading of the Scroll of Esther when verses that speak of Mordecai and redemption are read with zeal, while children make raucous noise whenever Haman's name is mentioned. During Purim people send gifts of food and money to their friends and to the poor. Though they celebrate the festival exuberantly, contemporary Jews do not uniformly obey the command of one ancient rabbi, who said: "It is the duty of a man to mellow himself [with wine] on Purim until he cannot tell the difference between 'cursed be Haman' and 'blessed be Mordecai.'"[27]

The Book of Esther is overtly identified with the establishment of the feast of Purim (3:7; 9:20–28). As it stands, the obvious purpose of the book is to provide a rationale for this Jewish festival. (The name "Purim" [Hebrew, *pûrîm*] relates to the Babylonian word *"pur,"* which means "lot," according to 3:7.) Archaeologists have discovered an ancient cube-shaped die dating from the Assyrian Empire that is inscribed with the word *"pûru,"* or "lot."[28] Although Esther accurately describes the meaning of *"pur,"* the precise historical origins of the festival of Purim elude scholarly grasp.[29] The oldest reference to the festival, apart from the book of Esther, appears in the Apocryphal Jewish writing of 2 Maccabees. There, the fourteenth day of Adar is celebrated as "Mordecai's day" (2 Macc. 15:36). Curiously, this passage mentions neither Esther nor the feast of Purim.

Christians often react to the celebration of Purim with scorn. H. A. Ironside offers a representative comment: "At the present time [Purim] has degenerated into a season of godless merry-making, and is more patriotic than devotional in character."[30] Within Judaism, the popularity of Purim depends, in part, upon its undisputed patriotism and merry-making. Yet this celebration of political deliverance speaks profoundly to people who have suffered bondage, persecution, and slaughter from ancient times up to our own day.[31] But Purim is basically a secular, nationalistic holiday, and, thus, Christian readers wrestle with the meaning of the book and with its identification as canonical Scripture.

Esther as Sacred Scripture

The relationship between the book of Esther and the development of Purim seems to have been a factor in securing its place among inspired writings, although we cannot be certain of this.[32] The rabbinic Counsel of Jamnia in A.D. 90 did not appear to establish Esther as sacred Scripture,[33] and as late as the third-century A.D. the rabbis wondered about its inspiration:

> Rab Judah said in the name of Samuel; [The scroll] of Esther does not make the hands unclean. Are we to infer from this that Samuel was of opinion that Esther was not composed under the inspiration of the holy spirit?[34]

Yet other rabbis disagreed with Samuel, claiming that Esther was in fact inspired (and would, therefore, make the hands unclean). Indeed, some rabbis placed Esther virtually on a par with the Torah itself.[35] Throughout the ages, Esther has been among the most popular of biblical writings for Jews. It has inspired more Jewish art, literature, and music than any other biblical document.[36]

Christians have been less enthusiastic about Esther than Jews. Historically, the book was regarded as canonical by Christians on the Roman side of the Mediterranean world, but not by those in its northeastern portions.[37] Although it was accorded canonical status by the councils of Hippo (A.D. 393) and Carthage (A.D. 397), Esther was not the subject of a Christian commentary until A.D. 836.[38] Even though many Christians have disparaged Esther (see "Why Study Esther?" above), it nevertheless has earned a place in the Christian canon of Scripture, probably on the basis of Jewish acceptance of the book. Furthermore, C. F. Keil and F. Delitzsch attest to Esther's "religious foundation," "which has obtained and secured its position in the canon of the inspired books of the O.T."[39] This foundation, however, must not be over-emphasized by interpreters who wish to minimize the challenge of Esther's secularism.

A LITERARY INTRODUCTION TO ESTHER

Author and Audience

The text does not identify the author of Esther, and it is quite possible that more than one writer contributed to the canonical Book of Esther. But for our purposes, and for the sake of clarity, I will refer to a single author and will use the masculine pronoun.

The book itself offers little information about its author. Given the pro-Jewish tone of the story, we may assume that the author was Jewish, even if he wrote from a secular perspective. He shows interest in and knowledge of the affairs of the Persian Empire but has nothing to say about life in Judah. It would be reasonable to assume, therefore, that the author lived in the eastern Diaspora (Babylon, Persia).[40] The author's knowledge of Persian royal affairs hints that he may have served in some official role, but such knowledge could possibly have been gained from secondary sources.

320

The text also does not identify the readers for whom Esther was written. However, given the nature of the story, we may assume that the author was writing primarily for Jewish readers in the Diaspora. They faced the same basic question confronted by Esther, Mordecai, and other Jews within the story: How do we live in a Gentile world?

Sources

The Book of Esther purportedly identifies some of its sources: the writings of Mordecai and Esther (9:20, 30), and Persian royal chronicles (2:23; 6:1; 10:2), but these sources may be part of the author's literary imagination. Clearly, he knew the story of Esther from some source, either oral or written. David Clines has proposed a five-stage development of Esther, including various sources and redactions.[41] However, in this commentary we will consider the canonical text in its present form without delving into questions of previous stages of development.

Date

Esther provides only general parameters for its date (or dates, if it was written in stages). Scholars use a variety of methods for dating ancient Hebrew documents, several of which involve linguistic complexities that go beyond the scope of this commentary.[42] Simply stated, the language of Esther (late Hebrew, with some Persian words) locates it sometime in the fourth or third centuries B.C. For example, one distinctive feature of Esther is its basically positive attitude toward Gentile rule.[43] This would suggest the latest possible date for Esther as sometime prior to the Maccabean period (second century B.C.), when strong anti-Gentile sentiment was prevalent among the Jews.[44] This observation supports a date for Esther in the fourth or third centuries B.C.

Genre

The identification of the genre of a piece of writing helps the reader to interpret it correctly.[45] Along with several contemporary scholars, I classify Esther as a "historical novel,"[46] or more accurately, a "historical novella," since it is too short to be a full novel. A novella ("short novel") is a work of fiction featuring a carefully-woven plot that moves from tension to resolution.[47] As the plot unfolds, the characters develop. According to W. Lee Humphreys, in a novella "Human beings grow and disintegrate before our eyes as the plot runs its course."[48] This genre of literature has several purposes: to entertain, to reflect life, and to offer moral lessons for the reader.[49] Although a fictional novella does not relate actual events, it nevertheless reveals truth about life.[50]

This last feature of a novella helps to explain why such a work might be included in the canon of Scripture. It explains why the story of Esther can inspire and instruct without historical confirmation of every last detail. A contemporary example might help to illustrate this point. One of last year's finest movies was Robert Redford's film, *A River Runs Through It*. This touching film about faith, family, and fly-fishing is based upon the autobiographical novella by Norman Maclean, a former professor at the University of Chicago.[51] Using experiences from his childhood, Maclean tells a story that conveys the essence of his young life, yet he recasts some of the historical details in order to tell a better story. *A River Runs Through It* speaks poignantly of the delights and challenges of human life. It tells a thoroughly human and profoundly moving story, even though it does not reproduce the facts of Maclean's life chronologically. Thus, although it is not historically true at every point, it is profoundly "true" in its portrayal of life. If a historical novella written in this century can move us to laughter, to tears, and to reflection, couldn't this also be true of a similar work written centuries earlier?

Structure

The author of Esther has carefully structured his story, specifically in his use of the literary principle of reversal.[52] That is, events that flow in one direction early in the story are matched by events the flow in the opposite direction later in the story. The following chart, adapted from the work of Yehuda Radday, suggests an outline of this reversal structure in Esther:

Opening and Background	Ch. 1
The King's First Decree	Chs. 2–3
The Clash between Haman and Mordecai	Chs. 4–5

The King's Sleepless Night	(6:1)
Mordecai Defeats Haman	Chs. 6–7
The King's Second Decree	Chs. 8–9
Epilogue	Ch. 10[53]

Radday helps us to see the balance within the story, which turns upon the pivotal events of the king's sleepless night, however, his proposal minimizes the importance of Esther. Reversal comes in full force with chapter 6, but Esther's success before the king in chapter 5 certainly foreshadows the later events. Moreover, to entitle chapters 6-7 as "Mordecai defeats Haman" misses completely the fact that Esther defeated Haman through her own ingenuity, and Mordecai merely reaped the benefit of her success. Therefore I would suggest the following adaptation of Radday's structure, one that more accurately reflects the complexity of the story and the essential role of Esther:

Prelude to the Story of Esther (1:1–22)
  Mordecai and Esther in Relationship with the King (2:1–23)
    A Royal Decree to Destroy the Jews Issued by Haman (3:1–15)
      Esther Responds to Haman's Plot (4:1–5:8)
        Haman's Prideful Obsession (5:9–14)
          The King's Sleepless Night (6:1–3)
        Haman's Prideful Obsession Leads to Shame (6:4–14)
      Esther Defeats Haman (7:1–10)
    A Royal Decree to Save the Jews Issued by Mordecai (8:1–17)
  Mordecai and Esther Establish Purim (9:1–32)
Epilogue in Praise of Mordecai (10:1–3)

Literary Elements

Most commentators recognize that the Book of Esther features plot more than characterization,[54] because a novella of this length does not facilitate complex character development. It does, however, allow the author to tell a good story. He shapes his material to maximize the reader's entertainment, especially by creating suspense and by structuring the story to emphasize the reversal of fate.[55]

Another dominant literary element of Esther are motifs and themes. Sandra Berg's informative study includes banquets (and fasts) as well as the response to kingly authority among the motifs,[56] and she identifies major themes of power, loyalty, and reversal.[57] In general, Esther also provides an example of another popular Jewish motif: the success of Jews in Gentile courts (compare the stories of Joseph and Daniel).[58]

According to Carey Moore, the author of Esther emphasizes plot to the exclusion of characterization. "In the Hebrew version," Moore observes, "it is more asserted than illustrated that Mordecai was wise and good; while beautiful and courageous, Esther nonetheless seems to be almost two-dimensional, lacking in depth."[59] I would contend, however, that the text of Esther never unambiguously asserts or illustrates Mordecai's wisdom and goodness. Mordecai is more mysterious and complex than Moore recognizes. Moreover, through the narrative Esther's distinctive character emerges from any two-dimensional aspect as she develops from a beautiful girl controlled by men to a wise woman who exercises power over men. As the commentary below will show, the Book of Esther fulfills one of the strategic expectations for a novella in its development of Esther's character.[60]

THE PURPOSE OF ESTHER

On a superficial level, the author of Esther certainly intends to entertain his readers. Plot, action, suspense, and reversal all make for an enjoyable story, as does the classic conflict between good and evil. Additionally, Esther provides a basis for the celebration of Purim, which Chapter 9 clarifies beyond any question. But does this exhaust the intended purpose of the book? I believe that the connection of Esther and Purim does not fully account for the purpose of the book or for its most unusual feature—its secularism. It seems to me that a complete understanding of the purpose of this book must include an explanation of the absence of God and other religious elements from its prose.

Shemaryahu Talmon purports to solve the riddle of Esther's secularism by seeing it as a "historicized wisdom-tale" that enacts standard wisdom motifs.[61] Both in plot and in characterization, Esther reflects familiar maxims of wisdom such as those set forth in the book of Proverbs.[62] Talmon cites more than a dozen examples where the story of Esther illustrates proverbial Jewish wisdom.[63] His thesis gains credibility, not only from the correlation between Esther and Proverbs, but also from the peculiar nature of Jewish wisdom.[64]

In scholarly discussions, "wisdom" refers to a type of literature, an educational movement in the ancient world that focused on training leaders for the king's court, and a way of living that depended upon "practical knowledge of the laws of life and of the world, based upon experience."[65] Although scholars do not agree on all aspects of Jewish wisdom, most recognize its "cosmopolitan"[66] or "international"[67] character. Whereas other writings in the Hebrew Bible emphasize God's unique, historical relationship with Israel, works of wisdom literature (Proverbs, Job, Ecclesiastes) focus on experiences shared by all people and tend not to mention key elements of salvation history (the Law, the covenant, the priesthood, etc.). Moreover, as Gerhard von Rad notes, "For wisdom, questions of faith entered in only on the periphery of its field. It works with reason, in its simplest form as sound common sense."[68] The type of ancient wisdom that was used to train leaders for the royal courts especially "prefers secular vocabulary."[69] If, as Talmon proposes, Esther is a story meant to illustrate the maxims of common wisdom, then we should not be surprised by its secularism. The fact that Esther focuses on life in the king's courts gives further support to Talmon's thesis, since wisdom often derived from and addressed itself to courtly affairs—using secular language.

While his thesis has been well received by some scholars,[70] others have denied its validity. James Crenshaw faults Talmon for failing to deal with the "nonwisdom elements" of Esther, especially its fierce nationalism that diverges from wisdom's universalism.[71] Robert Gordis notes that Jewish wisdom, such as found in Proverbs, involves God regularly and explicitly.[72] To say that Esther is a wisdom tale does not, in his view, adequately explain its secularism. In my opinion, Talmon has shown that the plot and characterization of Esther reflect the maxims of wisdom to a considerable degree. In the commentary below I will point out many correlations between wisdom and Esther, adding to Talmon's own observations. It seems to me undeniable that the author of Esther has shaped his story according to popular Jewish wisdom. This fact does not, however, completely explain the purpose of Esther and its peculiar secularism. Jewish sages mentioned God, even if they did so in a cosmopolitan manner. Thus, we might certainly expect a story shaped by wisdom to mention Esther's "fear of the Lord," for example (compare Prov. 1:7). So, while many aspects of Esther do reflect proverbial Jewish wisdom, we must explain the book's secularism on a different basis than that proposed by Talmon.

Gordis proposes an alternative theory for the peculiar nature of Esther. He attempts to show that the book is a unique genre within the Bible, in which a Jewish author attempts to write a royal chronicle as if he were a Gentile scribe of the Persian court.[73] Although this theory does account for odd features of Esther, Gordis' evidence is strained.[74] Without any Persian royal chronicles for comparison, we cannot even test his theory. Moreover, the example of King Cyrus shows that Persian royal documents could liberally mention gods, including the God of Israel.[75] Finally, if indeed Gordis is correct, then the author of Esther failed dismally in his attempt to portray himself as a Persian scribe since all Jewish and Christian readers before Gordis have missed the point for over 2000 years.

Although the proposals of Talmon and Gordis have been less than persuasive, two more recent studies of Esther connect its purpose with its historical setting and literary genre. Michael Fox contends that the author of Esther is a diaspora Jew writing for other Jews in the Diaspora. The book attempts to answer questions such as: "How can Jews best survive and thrive in the diaspora?"[76] According to Fox, the story of Esther teaches Jewish people how to live in a foreign land.[77] W. Lee Humphreys concludes similarly that "the author seeks to assert to the reader that it is possible for Jews in the diaspora to live full and effective lives in a world that at times is alien and threatening, but is ultimately hospitable."[78] I have already suggested that Esther is a historical novella written in the fourth or third centuries B.C. by a Jew of the eastern Diaspora who wrote for other Jews in his situation. Since a novella often intends to edify the reader through moral instruction, we would expect Esther to offer edification and education for its readers: Jews trying to live in an alien land. Indeed, a careful reading of the story suggests exactly this: The author writes to help Jews "survive and thrive" in the Diaspora.

Why, then, is Esther so secular in its orientation? The answer to this question is to be found in the author's opinion on how Jews can live and even prosper in their Gentile world. Various approaches to this issue were employed by Jews in the Persian and Hellenistic periods. Some envisioned hope in the form of apocalyptic deliverance

(Daniel 7-12, for example); others yearned for a nationalistic revival of the state of Israel (the Maccabees, for example). The author of Esther, however, believed that Jews could live and even flourish within a Gentile empire. If, like Queen Esther, they ordered their lives by popular wisdom, then diaspora Jews could achieve greatness even while gaining victory over their enemies. The author offers a secular, pragmatic approach to living as strangers in a strange land.

The Book of Esther models this secularism in its communication about matters of faith. The commentary will show how the author commends reticence in communication through his portrayal of Esther. Even as Esther says no more than is necessary to gain her advantage, so the author of the book says no more about his faith than is necessary. His secularism in story-telling exemplifies a pragmatic, accommodating approach to diaspora life and communication. It also testifies to the ambiguity of living in this world without the benefit of prophets or other divine spokespersons.[79] Sometimes we can say with confidence, "God will save us;" at other times we can only suggest, like Mordecai, "Perhaps help will come from another place." The story of Esther teaches its Jewish readers that, even in times of ambiguity, adherence to traditional values and popular wisdom will guide them to success, as it did for Esther.

THE DISTINCTIVE APPROACH OF THIS COMMENTARY

This commentary employs a distinctive approach that reflects the unique nature of Esther and the particular focus of the Communicator's Commentary series. Each chapter begins with a popular, thematic introduction followed by a close examination of the text as it relates to issues relevant to today's preacher or teacher. Like a fine piece of literature, Esther tells its story in such a way that one does not need extensive historical or linguistic data to understand its main themes.

After basic exegesis of each section of Esther, I pinpoint salient *literary aspects* of the passage under consideration. Special attention is given to matters of plot and characterization, or to how the story illustrates Jewish wisdom. Finally, since Esther appears in the Christian canon, I reflect on the *implications of the text for Christian readers*. Within this section I often address the relevance of Esther for women. Since the story features a woman as heroine, it urges this sort of investigation. Furthermore, since Esther regularly serves as curriculum for women's Bible studies, this commentary will be particularly helpful for teachers who communicate in this setting. I hope to show, however, that the Book of Esther offers much of value for all teachers and readers, both women and men.

RESOURCES FOR STUDYING ESTHER

Several commentaries offer interpretive help for today's communicator. Unfortunately, my effort precedes the Word Biblical Commentary volume on Esther (and Ruth) by Fred Bush. From my conversations with Dr. Bush during the past months, I expect that his commentary will take first place in my library on Esther. Among existing commentaries, I recommend two. Carey Moore's effort in The Anchor Bible is learned, balanced, and useful. Unfortunately it is a bit dated, but Moore's article on the "Book of Esther" in *The Anchor Bible Dictionary* provides a valuable supplement to his commentary. Joyce Baldwin's treatment of Esther in the Tyndale Old Testament Commentary Series is also quite helpful, in addition to being evangelical in theology and brief in scope.

Readers who want extensive linguistic data will profit from Lewis Paton's contribution to the International Critical Commentary, and from the extensive treatment of Esther in Keil and Delitzsch's *Commentary on the Old Testament*. Both of these works show their age, however. One making a serious study of Esther should also read two recent publications: *The Book of Esther: Motifs, Themes and Structure,* by Sandra Beth Berg; and *Character and Ideology in the Book of Esther* by Michael V. Fox.

NOTES

1. Hebrew Bibles follow a different order in which Esther follows Lamentations and precedes Daniel. In Hebrew the book is called *mĕgillat ʾestēr*, the Book or Scroll of Esther.
2. C. A. Moore, "Esther, Book of," *ABD*, II:635.
3. S. Sandmel, *The Enjoyment of Scripture* (New York: Oxford University Press, 1972), p. 44.

4. M. Luther, *Table Talk*, 3391a. Reference and translation from H. Bornkamm, *Luther and the Old Testament*, trans. E. Gritsch and R. Gritsch (Philadelphia: Fortress, 1969), p. 189.

5. L. B. Paton, *A Critical and Exegetical Commentary on the Book of Esther*, International Critical Commentary (New York: Scribner, 1908), p. 96.

6. O. Eissfeldt, *The Old Testament: An Introduction*, trans. P. R. Ackroyd (New York: Harper and Row, 1965), pp. 511–12.

7. B. W. Anderson, "The Place of the Book of Esther in the Christian Bible," *Journal of Religion* 30 (1950): 42.

8. H. D. M. Spence and J. S. Exell, eds. *The Pulpit Commentary, vol. 7: Ezra, Nehemiah, Esther, and Job* (Grand Rapids, Michigan: Eerdmans, 1950), p. 3.

9. W. I. Thomas, *If I Perish . . . I Perish: The Christian Life as Seen in Esther* (Grand Rapids: Zondervan, 1967), p. 15. Thomas treats Esther as an allegory for the Christian life. Ahasuerus is the human soul; Esther the spirit; Haman the flesh; Mordecai the Holy Spirit.

10. H. A. Ironside, *Joshua • Ezra • Nehemiah • Esther* (Neptune, NJ: Loizeaux Brothers, 1983 [Esther orig. pub. 1905]), p. 8.

11. C. A. Moore, *Esther*, Anchor Bible (Garden City, NY: Doubleday, 1971), p. xxxii.

12. See C. A. Moore, "Additions to Esther," *ABD* (New York: Doubleday, 1992).

13. Moore, *Esther*, p. xxxv.

14. Moore, *Esther*, p. xli.

15. D. J. A. Clines, "Mordecai," *ABD* (New York: Doubleday, 1992).

16. See, for example, Keil and Delitzsch, *Commentary*, pp. 304–12; J. G. Baldwin, *Esther*, Tyndale Old Testament Commentaries (Downers Grove: InterVarsity, 1974), pp. 16–24; Paton, *Book of Esther*, pp. 64–67; Moore, *Esther*, pp. xxxiv–lxvi. Robert Gordis has made a recent defense of the essential historicity of Esther ("Religion, Wisdom and History in the Book of Esther—A New Solution to an Ancient Crux," *Journal of Biblical Literature* 100 [1981]: 382–88).

17. Herodotus, *Histories*, 3:84. See the Loeb Classical Library edition, *Herodotus*, trans A. D. Godley, 4 vols. (Cambridge: Harvard University Press, 1960–1961).

18. Paton, *Book of Esther*, pp. 73–75; Moore, *Esther*, p. xlv.

19. Herodotus, *Histories*, 7:114; 9:112.

20. Gordis repeats the familiar argument that "Esther" is a shortened form of "Amestris" (Gordis, "Religion," p. 384). Even if this

were true, which cannot be proven linguistically, the Amestris who brutally maims an innocent woman can hardly be the same as Esther. See the account in Herodotus, *Histories*, 9:107–12, esp. 112.

21. See, for example, Moore, *Esther*, pp. xlv–xlvi; Paton, *Book of Esther*, pp. 71–72.

22. Baldwin, *Esther*, pp. 23–24; Moore, *Esther*, pp. lii–liii; Gordis, "Religion," p. 388.

23. Moore, *Esther*, p. lii.

24. W. Broomall, "Esther," in *The Biblical Expositor*, ed. C. F. H. Henry, 3 vols. (Philadelphia: Holman Co., 1960), 3:396.

25. See, for example, the discussion in W. S. LaSor, D. A. Hubbard, F. W. Bush, *Old Testament Survey* (Grand Rapids: Eerdmans, 1982), pp. 626–27.

26. See the helpful article, "Purim," in *Encyclopedia Judaica*, 16 vols. (Jerusalem: Keter, 1972), 13:1390–95.

27. *Megillâ* 7b. English translation of the Talmud from *The Babylonian Talmud, Seder Mo^ced*, trans. I. Epstein, 4 vols. (London: Socino, 1938).

28. Baldwin, *Esther*, pp. 22–23.

29. Most scholars do not believe that the festival of Purim came into being in the manner suggested by the Book of Esther. See, for example, Moore, *Esther*, pp. lxvi–xlix.

30. Ironside, *Esther*, p. 115.

31. I would encourage anyone critical of Purim to read the personal testimony of the Jewish scholar, M. Fox, in *Character and Ideology in the Book of Esther* (Columbia, SC: University of South Carolina Press, 1991), pp. 11–12.

32. Moore, *Esther*, p. xxiv.

33. Moore, "Esther," *ABD* 2:635. Here Moore states, "there is not a shred of evidence that the book of Esther was canonized by the Academy of Jabneh (i.e., Council of Jamnia) ca. 90." Notice that this reverses Moore's earlier assessment (Moore, *Esther*, p. xxii).

34. *Babylonian Talmud, Megillâ* 7a.

35. *Jerusalem Talmud, Megillâ* 70d. Reference in LaSor, Hubbard, and Bush, *Old Testament Survey*, p. 627.

36. *Encyclopedia Judaica*, 16 vols. (Jerusalem: Keter, 1972), s.v. "Scroll of Esther."

37. Moore, *Esther*, p. xxv. See the map, pp. xxvi–xxvii.

38. Moore, *Esther*, p. xxxi.

39. Keil and Delitzsch, *Commentary*, p. 317.

40. R. K. Harrison, *Introduction to the Old Testament* (Grand Rapids: Eerdmans, 1969), p. 1087.

41. D. J. A. Clines, *The Esther Scroll: The Story of the Story* (Sheffield, England: JSOT, 1984), pp. 115–38. See the helpful summary of Clines' work in *ABD*, II:640–41.

42. See, for example, Paton, *Book of Esther*, pp. 62–63

43. S. B. Berg, *The Book of Esther: Motifs, Themes and Structure*, SBL Dissertation Series 44 (Missoula, MT: Scholars, 1979), p. 170.

44. *ABD*, II:641.

45. G. W. Coats, "Genres: Why Should They Be Important For Exegesis?" *Saga, Legend, Tale, Novella, Fable: Narrative Forms in Old Testament Literature*, ed. G. W. Coats, Journal for the Study of the Old Testament Supplemental Series 35 (Sheffield, England: JSOT, 1985), p.9.

46. Moore, *Esther*, p. lii.

47. See the helpful article by W. L. Humphreys: "Novella," *Saga, Legend, Tale, Novella, Fable: Narrative Forms in Old Testament Literature*, ed. George W. Coats. Journal for the Study of the Old Testament Supplemental Series 35 (Sheffield, England: JSOT Press, 1985) pp. 82–96. In this discussion of Esther as a novella I am also indebted to Fred Bush.

48. Humphreys, "Novella," p. 92.

49. Humphreys, "Novella," pp. 94–95.

50. Humphreys, "Novella," pp. 83, 86–87.

51. N. Maclean, *A River Runs Through It and Other Stories* (New York: Pocket Books, 1992 [orig. University of Chicago, 1976]).

52. See Berg, *Esther*, pp. 106–13.

53. This chart is adapted from one by Y. T. Radday, in "Chiasm in Joshua, Judges, and Others," *Linguistica Biblica*, 3 (1973):9; reproduced in Berg, *Esther*, p. 108.

54. For example, Moore, *Esther*, p. liii.

55. Moore, *Esther*, p. lxi.

56. Berg, *Esther*, pp. 31–93.

57. Berg, *Esther*, pp. 96–113.

58. Eissfeldt, *Introduction*, p. 508.

59. Moore, *Esther*, p. liv.

60. Humphreys, "Novella," p. 84. See also W. L. Humphreys, "The Story of Esther and Mordecai: An Early Jewish Novella," *Saga, Legend, Tale, Novella, Fable: Narrative Forms in Old Testament Literature*, ed. George W. Coats, Journal for the Study of the Old Testament Supplemental Series 35 (Sheffield, England: JSOT Press, 1985), pp. 97–113.

61. S. Talmon, "Wisdom in the Book of Esther," *Vetus Testamentum* 13 (1963): 419–55.

62. Talmon, "Wisdom," p. 427.

63. Talmon, "Wisdom," pp. 433–48.

64. I have found several overviews of wisdom to be particularly helpful: "Wisdom Literature," *Old Testament Survey*, pp. 533–46; G. von Rad, *Old Testament Theology*, 2 vols. (New York: Harper and Row, 1962), 1:418–53; R. E. Murphy, "Wisdom in the OT,"*ABD* (New York: Doubleday, 1992). More extensive treatments of wisdom may be found in: J. L. Crenshaw, *Old Testament Wisdom: An Introduction* (Atlanta: John Knox, 1981); and G. von Rad, *Wisdom in Israel*, trans. J. D. Martin (London: S. C. M., 1972).

65. von Rad, *Theology*, 1:418.

66. Talmon, "Wisdom," p. 430.

67. LaSor, Hubbard, and Bush, *Old Testament Survey*, p. 544.

68. von Rad, *Theology*, 1:435.

69. J. L. Crenshaw, "Wisdom in the OT," *IDB Supplementary Volume* (Nashville: Abingdon,1976), p. 952.

70. Moore, *Esther*, pp. xx, xxxiii–iv.

71. J. L. Crenshaw, "Methods for Determining Wisdom Influence upon 'Historical Literature'," *Journal of Biblical Literature* 88 (1969): 141–2. See also Fox, Character, pp. 142–43.

72. Gordis, "Religion," p. 374.

73. Gordis, "Religion," p. 375.

74. See Gordis, "Religion," pp. 375–78; Fox, *Character*, p. 144.

75. See Ezra 1:2–4 and my commentary on this section, which includes quotations from the Cyrus Cylinder, an autobiographical piece of writing by Cyrus himself.

76. Fox, *Character*, p. 4.

77. Fox, *Character*, pp. 4–5.

78. Humphreys, "Esther and Mordecai," p. 112.

79. Fred Bush, in conversation.

Outline of Esther

I. Prelude to the Story of Esther (1:1–22)

   A. Introduction to King Ahasuerus (1:1–9)
   B. Queen Vashti Dethroned (1:10–22)

II. Esther Becomes Queen (2:1–18)

   A. Plan to Select a New Queen (2:1–4)
   B. Introduction to Mordecai and Esther (2:5–7)
   C. Esther Promoted to Queen (2:8–18)

III. Mordecai Saves the King's Life (2:19–23)

IV. Haman Issues a Royal Decree to Destroy the Jews (3:1–15)

   A. Mordecai Defies Haman (3:1–4)
   B. Haman's Angry Response to Mordecai (3:5–7)
   C. Haman Persuades the King to Issue a Decree Against the Jews (3:8–15)

V. The Response of Esther and Mordecai to Haman's Plot (4:1–17)

   A. Mordecai and the Jews Mourn (4:1–3)
   B. Esther and Mordecai Debate Esther's Response (4:4–17)

VI. Esther Gains the King's Favor (5:1–8)

   A. Esther Approaches the King (5:1–5)
   B. Esther's First Banquet (5:6–8)

VII. Haman's Prideful Obsession (5:9–14)

VIII. The King Honors Mordecai Over Haman (6:1–14)

   A. The King's Sleepless Night (6:1–3)
   B. Haman Forced to Honor Mordecai (6:4–11)
   C. Haman's Downfall Predicted (6:12–14)

IX. Esther Defeats Haman (7:1–10)

X. Mordecai Issues a New Royal Decree for Jewish Self-Defense (8:1–17)

   A. Esther Appeals for Her People (8:1–8)
   B. A New Royal Decree Written by Mordecai (8:9–14)
   C. The Impact of Jewish Vindication (8:15–17)

Prelude to the Story of Esther

Esther 1:1–22

LIFESTYLES OF THE RICH AND FAMOUS

Each week millions of Americans tune in to the television program "Lifestyles of the Rich and Famous." We peer curiously into the private lives of the wealthy, marveling at their lavish homes and envying their power and privilege. Our fascination with fame and fortune is nothing new. Just as today's reporters tell us more than we need to know about Prince Charles, Elizabeth Taylor, Michael Jackson, and Hillary Rodham Clinton, so ancient authors told tales of famous kings and queens.

Certainly the Book of Esther begins like a segment of "Lifestyles of the Rich and Famous." The story commences in the courts of a king during an extravagant party. It piques our interest with tales of excessive drinking and marital disharmony. The author of Esther definitely knew how to entice his readers into the story. In the process of capturing our attention, the first chapter of Esther not only introduces one of the major characters of the book but also lays a necessary foundation for the rest of the story.

ESTHER 1:1–9. INTRODUCTION TO KING AHASUERUS

1:1 Now it came to pass in the days of Ahasuerus (this was the Ahasuerus who reigned over one hundred and twenty-seven provinces, from India to Ethiopia),

2 in those days when King Ahasuerus sat on the throne of his kingdom, which was in Shushan the citadel,

3 that in the third year of his reign he made a feast for all his officials and servants—the powers of Persia and Media, the nobles, and the princes of the provinces being before him—

4 when he showed the riches of his glorious kingdom and the splendor of his excellent majesty for many days, one hundred and eighty days in all.

5 And when these days were completed, the king made a feast lasting seven days for all the people who were present in Shushan the citadel, from great to small, in the court of the garden of the king's palace.

6 There were white and blue linen curtains fastened with cords of fine linen and purple on silver rods and marble pillars; and the couches were of gold and silver on a mosaic pavement of alabaster, turquoise, and white and black marble.

7 And they served drinks in golden vessels, each vessel being different from the other, with royal wine in abundance, according to the generosity of the king.

8 In accordance with the law, the drinking was not compulsory; for so the king had ordered all the officers of his household, that they should do according to each man's pleasure.

9 Queen Vashti also made a feast for the women in the royal palace which belonged to King Ahasuerus.

Esther 1:1–9

The story of Esther takes places during *"the days of Ahasuerus"* (v. 1). Scholars almost unanimously identify Ahasuerus with the Persian king better known by his Greek name, Xerxes. He reigned from 486 to 465 B.C., after Cyrus (Ezra 1) and Darius (Ezra 5–6), but before Artaxerxes 1 (Ezra 7–10, Neh. 1–13). The number of provinces over which Ahasuerus is said to have ruled, *"one hundred and twenty-seven,"* cannot be verified from other ancient sources. In the context of the story, this large number emphasizes the vast holdings and power of the king. Verse 2 adds that Ahasuerus ruled from *"Shushan the citadel,"* a city better known as Susa (located in modern Iran, not far from the Iraqi border).

In the *"third year of his reign,"* Ahasuerus threw an opulent party for the leaders of his kingdom (v. 3). This party, which lasted for an unbelievable period of time (180 days), gave Ahasuerus an opportunity to exhibit *"the riches of his glorious kingdom and the splendor of his excellent majesty"* (v. 4). The hyperbolic language of verse 4 underlines the outlandish pomp of the whole affair.

Even after six months of partying Ahasuerus was not finished. Immediately after ending his exclusive fete, he *"made a feast"* for all the residents of Susa, including the "little people" (v. 5). This open celebration displayed the king's luxurious interior decorations, as well as his generous provision of wine *"in golden vessels"* (vv. 6–7). Not only did Ahasuerus have a golden goblet for each party goer, but each goblet was unique in design.[1] This detail emphasizes again the unspeakable wealth of the king, who had enough golden vessels for every citizen of the capital.

The precise meaning of verse 8 is elusive, though its basic sense is clear. The king supplied generous quantities of wine, enough for each person to drink his fill. The phrase translated in the NKJV as *"In accordance with the law, the drinking was not compulsory"* may be better understood in the rendering of the NIV: "By the king's command each guest was allowed to drink in his own way." By implication, since the supply of wine was unlimited, many people from the city freely drank to the point of drunkenness.

Verse 9 introduces another character in the story, *"Queen Vashti."* Unlike Ahaseurus, her name is not known from historical sources, such as the *Histories* of Herodotus. Though the text does not explain why, it states that she *"made a feast for the women."* (Persian custom did not force men and women to celebrate separately.) Though it is brief, verse 9 not only introduces Vashti, but sets the stage for the next segment of the story when the Queen is absent from the king's banquet.

QUEEN VASHTI DETHRONED (1:10–22)

10 On the seventh day, when the heart of the king was merry with wine, he commanded Mehuman, Biztha, Harbona, Bigtha, Abagtha, Zethar, and Carcas, seven eunuchs who served in the presence of King Ahasuerus,

11 to bring Queen Vashti before the king, wearing her royal crown, in order to show her beauty to the people and the officials, for she was beautiful to behold.

12 But Queen Vashti refused to come at the king's command brought by his eunuchs; therefore the king was furious, and his anger burned within him.

13 Then the king said to the wise men who understood the times (for this was the king's manner toward all who knew law and justice,

14 those closest to him being Carshena, Shethar, Admatha, Tarshish, Meres, Marsena, and Memucan, the seven princes of Persia and Media, who had access to the king's presence, and who ranked highest in the kingdom):

15 "What shall we do to Queen Vashti, according to law, because she did not obey the command of King Ahasuerus brought to her by the eunuchs?"

16 And Memucan answered before the king and the princes: "Queen Vashti has not only wronged the king, but also all the princes, and all the people who are in all the provinces of King Ahasuerus.

17 For the queen's behavior will become known to all women, so that they will despise their husbands in their eyes, when they report, 'King Ahasuerus commanded Queen Vashti to be brought in before him, but she did not come.'

18 This very day the noble ladies of Persia and Media will say to all the king's officials that they have heard of the behavior of the queen. Thus there will be excessive contempt and wrath.

19 If it pleases the king, let a royal decree go out from him, and let it be recorded in the laws of the Persians and the Medes, so that it will not be altered, that Vashti shall come no more before King Ahasuerus; and let the king give her royal position to another who is better than she.

20 When the king's decree which he will make is proclaimed throughout all his empire (for it is great), all wives will honor their husbands, both great and small."

21 And the reply pleased the king and the princes, and the king did according to the word of Memucan.

22 Then he sent letters to all the king's provinces, to each province in its own script, and to every people in their own language, that each man should be

master in his own house, and speak in the language of
his own people.

Esther 1:10–22

According to 1:4–9, King Ahasuerus spent the 186 days prior to the day indicated by verse 10 in one extended party. On the final day of his celebration, *"the heart of the king was merry with wine"* (v. 10). Since Hebrew speakers considered the heart to be the center of thought, we might paraphrase the verse in this way: "On the seventh day, when wine had gone to the king's head. . . ." Accordingly, such a drunken state would explain his curious behavior in the following verses.

The king commanded his *"eunuchs"* to bring Queen Vashti into the celebration in order that her dazzling beauty might be displayed to all of the party goers (vv. 10–11). In the ancient world, eunuchs had charge of royal wives and concubines for the obvious reason that there was no danger they would molest these women. Ahaseurus' command to the eunuchs should not surprise us. Since he had already sponsored a six-month party to show off his wealth and power (v. 4), why wouldn't he want to show off his beautiful wife as well?

Queen Vashti's response, however, is surprising, given the authority the king had over her very life. Why did she refuse to come before the king and his party (v. 12)? Some ancient Jewish theorists have proposed that Ahasuerus intended for Vashti to appear only in *"her royal crown"* (v. 11), but the original text does not support this reading. B. W. Jones theorizes that when Persian wives attended banquets with their husbands, they departed when the heavy drinking began leaving behind only the concubines and prostitutes.[2] Therefore, Vashti's appearance at this advanced stage of the party would be an insult to her royal dignity. The text does not explain Vashti's response; rather, it emphasizes the king's response to her refusal: *"therefore the king was furious, and his anger burned within him"* (v. 12).

After Vashti refused to appear before the king, he consulted with his royal advisers, who are called *"wise men"* (v. 13). If the Hebrew text is accurate,[3] then these wise men were astrologers, people who *"understood the times,"* and experts in *"law and justice"* (v. 13). Kings in the ancient world, like political leaders today, surrounded themselves with advisers. Verse 14 accentuates the importance of those consulted by Ahasuerus. By implication, Vashti's act of insubordination was an extremely serious matter—it deserved the attention of the king's top counselors. Of course this interaction also provides a background for future developments as the story unfolds. That is, the main conflict in the book is the result of poor advice given to Ahasuerus, which is later resolved through good advice. Thus, by establishing the fact that the king depended upon his advisers, verses 13–22 intensify the significance of their advice.

When Ahasuerus asked his wise men what to do about Vashti's disobedience (v. 15), one of the advisers, *"Memucan,"* responded by pointing out the dire implications of her behavior. Not only had she *"wronged the king, but also all the princes, and all the people who are in all the provinces of King Ahasuerus"* (v. 16). She had wronged all Persians by acting in such a way that *"all women . . . will despise their husbands in their eyes"* (v. 17). He suggested that her insubordination would incite a nationwide insurgence of uppity wives against poor downtrodden husbands. Memucan pressed the king to act quickly (v. 18) since news of Vashti's refusal was already spreading among the upper class women of Persia. He proposed that soon there would be no end to *"contempt"* from wives and *"wrath"* from their despised husbands (v. 18). Given the undisputed dominance of men within the Persian empire, Memucan's estimation of Vashti's crime is a comical exaggeration. Undoubtedly, the purpose of the author here is to contrast the king's best advisers' responses of pathetic panic with the self-assured response of Queen Vashti.

In verse 19 we find Memucan's specific proposal: The king should issue a decree that *"Vashti shall come no more before King Ahasuerus."* Her *"royal position"* shall be given to another who is worthier than Vashti. By communicating this decree throughout the entire empire, the king would inspire *"all wives"* to *"honor their husbands, both great and small"* (v. 21). Yet irony abounds in Memucan's proposal. Notice that Vashti's sentence provided exactly what she had wanted: not to appear before the king. And although the wives might honor their husbands (even the small husbands!), they would not do so because their husbands deserved honor, but simply out of fear of punishment.

Verse 19 also contains a significant phrase that figures prominently in the story of Esther: *"so that it will not be altered."* A better translation would be: "Let [a royal decree] be recorded in the laws of the Persian and the Medes, *which cannot be repealed."* The impact of the conclusion of the story in chapters 8–10 depends heavily upon the fact that Persian royal decrees could not be revoked (see 8:7–8).

The final verses of chapter 1 recount Ahasuerus' response: he was pleased with Memucan's advice and acted accordingly (v. 21). So verse 22 states that he sent letters to all the provinces of his realm, using indigenous languages. However, this is one of the aspects of Esther that seems historically improbable. For while historical documents verify that Persian officials used Aramaic to communicate across their vast empire, it would have been highly unlikely for a king's decree to be translated into the vast number of regional languages and dialects that were spoken throughout the empire.[4] Yet by adding this improbable detail, the author does not intend to mislead the reader, but to highlight the ridiculous paranoia of Ahasuerus and Memucan. They were so afraid of women that they went to absurd lengths to insure that everyone in the empire would do what the culture already demanded and guaranteed would be done anyway.

Note too that the last phrase of verse 22 seems completely out of place: *"and speak in the language of his own people."* However, a slight correction in the Hebrew allows for a sensible translation: "that each man should be master in his own house, and say whatever suited him."[5]

LITERARY ASPECTS OF ESTHER 1:1–22

Chapter 1 serves as a prelude to the Book of Esther. It introduces the motif of feasting, which runs throughout the book;[6] it sets the stage for action in the Persian royal courts; and it adds details that explain certain aspects of the story. For example: why Ahasuerus needs to find a new queen (chap. 2); why Esther might fear the king's anger (chap. 4); the role and significance of royal advisers (chaps, 3, 6, 7, and 8); and why the king cannot revoke his decree (chap. 8).

Chapter 1 also introduces a major character of the story: King Ahasuerus. He is portrayed as wealthy and powerful, yet curiously threatened by the power of women, especially his wife. He loves to party and allows his drinking to hamper his better judgment. His volatile anger threatens anyone who crosses him, including the queen herself.

Although Esther 1 superficially glorifies the power of the king, in fact it portrays him as a ruler who fails to measure up to the standards of Jewish wisdom. Jewish proverbs often focused on the theme of leadership. In fact, so-called courtly wisdom instructed kings and royal

341

advisers in the art of government, but by the standards of the proverbs, Ahasuerus miserably failed "Leadership 101." His behavior in chapter 1 shows him to be the sort of ruler people dread, according to a series of sayings in Ecclesiastes:

> Woe to you, O land, when your king is a child
> And your princes feast in the morning!
> Blessed are you, O land, when your king is the son of nobles,
> And your princes feast at the proper time—
> For strength and not for drunkenness!
> Because of laziness the building decays,
> And through idleness of hands the house leaks.
>
> *Ecclesiastes 10:16–18*

What an accurate picture of Ahasuerus, who urged his princes to feast, not only in the morning, but for 180 consecutive days! Drunkenness characterized the king's party, which surely contributed to at least half a year of laziness and idleness.

Ahasuerus' love for strong drink also contradicts proverbial wisdom. A mother advises the unknown King Lemuel in this way:

> It is not for kings, O Lemuel,
> It is not for kings to drink wine,
> Nor for princes intoxicating drink;
> Lest they drink and forget the law,
> And pervert the justice of all the afflicted.
>
> *Proverbs 31:4–5*

Conversely, Ahasuerus drank wine to the point of drunkenness. In that intoxicated condition he commanded his queen to do something inappropriate, and then took away her royal position because of a ridiculous fear. How apt that Jewish proverbs warn all people— not only kings—about the power of wine to corrupt behavior and judgment:

> Wine is a mocker,
> Intoxicating drink arouses brawling
> And whoever is led astray by it is not wise.
>
> *Proverbs 20:1*

> Do not look on the wine when it is red,
> When it sparkles in the cup,
> When it swirls around smoothly;
> At the last it bites like a serpent,
> And stings like a viper.
> Your eyes will see strange things,
> And your heart will utter perverse things.
>
> *Proverbs 23:31–33*

Ahasuerus exemplifies the foolish man who drinks to excess, then is led astray and utters strange things.

Finally, the king's quick temper in response to Vashti identifies him as a fool:

> A fool's wrath is known at once,
> But a prudent man covers shame.
>
> *Proverbs 12:16*

> He who is quick-tempered acts foolishly,
> And a man of wicked intentions is hated.
>
> *Proverbs 14:17*

> He who is slow to wrath has great understanding,
> But he who is impulsive exalts folly.
>
> *Proverbs 14:29*

In fact, according to Jewish wisdom, those who control their temper are even better than those who have political or military power:

> He who is slow to anger is better than the mighty,
> And he who rules his spirit than he who takes a city.
>
> *Proverbs 16:32*

Overall, the author of Esther has painted a picture of Ahasuerus that shows him as a foolish king: he corrupts his leaders, promotes laziness, drinks excessively, acts strangely when drunk, and allows his anger to get out of control. The characterization of Ahasuerus in chapter 1 has been shaped in light of traditional proverbs so that the Jewish reader will scorn the king.

The first chapter of Esther also abounds with exaggeration: the king's feast lasts for six months, each citizen of the capital drinks wine from a unique, golden goblet, and Vashti's disobedience threatens every household in the empire! The fact is, the author of Esther exaggerates purposely to entertain the reader and to highlight the foolishness of the Persian leaders. Hyperbole amuses the reader, who sees, for example, the absurdity of Memucan's speech and the king's decree.[7] On one level, lavish descriptions of royal parties appear to laud Persian imperial wealth, but surely a six-month party goes beyond the limits of acceptable conspicuous consumption. As B. W. Jones observes, the author of Esther is not praising the Persian government, rather, he is laughing at it.[8] In other words, exaggeration helps the reader to get the joke.

Other comic elements that appear in chapter 1 include the excessive male response to Vashti's "strength", which strikes the reader as absurd. Would her single act of insubordination actually have ruined family life throughout the empire? Then, ironically, Vashti received as punishment exactly what she had wanted in the first place: freedom from coming before the king. Overall, this chapter successfully satirizes the Persian government even while appearing to praise it.[9]

ESTHER 1:1–22 FROM A CHRISTIAN PERSPECTIVE

Are We Like Ahasuerus—or Jesus?

I find it interesting that even without a knowledge of Persian customs, readers intuitively sense the offensive nature of Ahasuerus' command to Vashti. Rather than receiving the respect she deserved as wife and queen, Vashti was degraded to an object of beauty, a sign of her husband's prowess. Without any regard for her feelings, Ahasuerus wanted to parade her before his drunken friends.

Yet our culture, too, regularly places women in the position of Vashti, a position where they feel demeaned by a society that tends to value their appearance more than their character. Beauty contests, swimsuit issues of sports magazines, and even Barbie dolls tell women and girls that good looks count more that anything else. Yet most who hear this message know that they will never measure up to the media's airbrushed standards. They feel defeated as well as degraded. Many contemporary women who read the Book of Esther relate more readily to Vashti than to Esther herself. They can relate to the woman who stood up against a husband who valued her only as an object of beauty rather than as person worthy of respect and love.

Could there be a greater contrast between the attitude of Ahasuerus and that of Jesus? Even women who might have lost their right for respect found Jesus to be someone who saw them as people, not as objects. When a prostitute washed his feet with her tears, the Pharisees criticized him because he allowed himself to be touched by "a sinner" (Luke 7:39). But Jesus did not see before him a sinner or a prostitute; he saw a woman who loved, who was forgiven, and who had been saved by her faith (Luke 7:47–50). He did not see an object of lust or scorn, but a person who could give and receive love.

Unfortunately, Christians are not immune from the offense of devaluing women (and others). Sometimes we act more like Ahasuerus than Jesus—when Christian men see women only as objects of admiration, or of lust, or when Christian parents fail to respect their children, treating them as valuable only for adult pleasure. Not long ago, I was invited to the home of a family from the church I serve. After a delicious meal, the father decided that his son was going to put on a violin concert for the dinner guests. The son declined, saying that he had other things to do and that he really didn't have anything ready to play, but the father insisted, without even stopping to hear his son's hesitations. The father's devaluing message came across loud and clear: "You exist for our pleasure. Now go in there and make us happy!" But Jesus calls us to see people as valuable individuals, not as objects. His example reminds us that people do not exist for our pleasure, but, rather, to be loved, to love others, and to give delight to God.

Are We Like Memucan—or Peter?

Memucan's response to Vashti's strength reminds me of comments I have heard from some men about women in leadership: "If we let women have positions of authority in the church, pretty soon they'll be running everything. They'll chase the men out of the church." This sounds exactly like the humorous paranoia of Memucan, but it is not funny. The church often chugs along on half its cylinders because of male insecurities about women exercising power.

Unfortunately for those who identify with Memucan, the Holy Spirit falls equally upon men and women. In his Pentecost sermon Peter shows that the outpouring of the Spirit upon Christians fulfills the prophecy of Joel:

> And it shall come to pass in the last days, says God,
> That I will pour out of My Spirit on all flesh;
> Your sons and your daughters shall prophesy,
> Your young men shall see visions,
> Your old men shall dream dreams.
> And on My menservants and on My maidservants,
> I will pour out my Spirit in those days;
> And they shall prophesy.
>
> *Acts 2:17–18*

The Holy Spirit empowers both men and women for the ministry of Christ. Of course some Christians have theological reservations about women's service in leadership roles, and some of these reservations rest upon carefully executed biblical interpretation. But all too often, men use theological arguments to disguise their Memucan-like fears. Now I am not suggesting that all who oppose the ordination of women, for example, do so out of fear, but I do believe that fear often dictates such policy and even some of our theology. Like Memucan, we imagine the worst-case scenario, scrambling to solve problems that will never exist and exhausting ourselves in the attempt—simply because we are afraid.

In his excellent book, *Jesus and Addiction*, Don Williams shows how Jesus can set us free from the fears that bind us and our churches.[10] According to Williams, only through the free and fearless Jesus will we become free and fearless ourselves. No longer will we hide behind the foolish masks of Ahasuerus: conspicuous consumption, pride, arrogance, drunkenness, and anger. No longer will we glorify ourselves by treating others as objects. No longer will we guarantee our power by keeping others in chains. No longer will we fear women who are empowered by the Holy Spirit. Through Christ, we will experience a contagious freedom to be shared with others. We will see people as Jesus sees them, and by his Spirit we will receive power to empower others—both women and men.

NOTES

1. For a picture of a golden goblet like those described in these verses, see Moore, *Esther*, plate 6.

2. B. W. Jones, "Two Misconceptions About the Book of Esther," *Catholic Biblical Quarterly* 38 (1977): 171–81.

3. Moore and others make a minor change in the Hebrew, reading "laws" instead of "times" in 1:12 (Moore, p. 9).

4. Paton, *Book of Esther*, pp. 160–61.

5. Moore, *Esther*, pp. 11–12.

6. Berg, *Esther*, pp. 31–35.

7. Jones, "Two Misconceptions," p. 173.

8. Jones, "Two Misconceptions," p. 174.

9. Clines, *Esther Scroll*, p. 31.

10. D. Williams, *Jesus and Addiction: A Prescription to Transform the Dysfunctional Church and Recover Authentic Christianity* (San Diego, CA: Recovery Publications, 1993).

CHAPTER TWO

Esther Becomes Queen

Esther 2:1–23

RIDING THE TIDE OF HUMAN AFFAIRS

In the fourth act of Shakespeare's *Julius Caesar*, Brutus and Cassius debate whether to attack their enemies immediately or to wait for another time. Brutus, arguing for a hasty strike, utters these famous lines:

> There is a tide in the affairs of men
> Which, taken at the flood, leads on to fortune;
> Omitted, all the voyage of their life
> Is bound in shallows and in miseries.[1]

My friend Jon has a knack for riding the tide of human affairs to fortune. A few years ago he started a business in his garage. As opportunities for growth came his way, Jon risked everything to take advantage of them. Soon he moved out of his garage into a new facility. Quickly outgrowing that location, his company took over a large industrial building. Today, Jon has just relocated his operation into an even larger structure that provides sufficient room for his burgeoning collection of high-tech equipment and a growing staff of over sixty employees. A casual observer might say that Jon caught the tide of luck at its peak.

The second chapter of Esther paints a similar picture of Mordecai and Esther, the hero and heroine of the book. Not only did they find themselves in the right place at the right time, but they wisely took advantage of opportunities for personal advancement. Chapter 2 introduces us to these central characters and explains how they were in strategic positions to influence the fate of the Jewish people.

THE PLAN TO SELECT A NEW QUEEN (2:1–4)

2:1 After these things, when the wrath of King Ahasuerus subsided, he remembered Vashti, what she had done, and what had been decreed against her.

2 Then the king's servants who attended him said: "Let beautiful young virgins be sought for the king;

3 and let the king appoint officers in all the provinces of his kingdom, that they may gather all the beautiful young virgins to Shushan the citadel, into the women's quarters, under the custody of Hegai the king's eunuch, custodian of the women. And let beauty preparations be given them.

4 Then let the young woman who pleases the king be queen instead of Vashti." This thing pleased the king, and he did so.

Esther 2:1–4

A period of time passed between chapters 1 and 2, although the phrase *"after these things"* does not specify precisely how much time (v. 1). Apparently, it was enough time for *"the wrath of King Ahasuerus,"* which had been so intense, to subside. Now the king *"remembered Vashti, what she had done, and what had been decreed against her."* Although not expressed explicitly, this verse seems to imply that Ahasuerus regretted his rash response to Vashti's refusal to present herself at his party.[2] Josephus, a Jewish historian from the first century A.D., interprets Ahasuerus' feelings in this way:

> Now, although the king was in love with her [Vashti] and could not bear the separation, he could not, because of the law, be reconciled to her, and so he continued to grieve at not being able to obtain his desire.[3]

Because of the king's decree against Vashti (1:19–22), he could not take her once more as his queen.

The response of the king's servants also implies that he regretted his decision to banish Vashti (vv. 2–4). They suggested a way to follow through on Memucan's opinion that Vashti's "royal position" be given "to another who is better than she" (1:19). An official search would be made throughout the entire Persian empire, so that *"all the beautiful young virgins"* might come to the palace (v. 3). From among

349

these Ahasuerus would select as queen *"the young woman who pleases the king"* (literally, "who pleases the eyes of the king"; v. 4). This suggestion *"pleased the king"* (literally, "pleased the eyes of the king"; v. 4). Note here the repetition of this Hebrew phrase, which accentuates the hedonistic nature of Ahasuerus; he liked to be pleased, whether by the beauty of women or by the soundness of advice. He sought his own pleasure above everything else.

The young women would be gathered into "the women's quarters," (in Hebrew, "the house of women"; v. 3), a sequestered area of the king's palace. There they would join the king's harem, to be used for his pleasure, whether or not they became the new queen. *"Hegai the king's eunuch"* supervised the harem. (The Greek historian Herodotus identifies a man named "Hēgias" as an officer of King Xerxes.)[4] Eunuchs were commonly trusted with the care of royal wives and concubines as they did not pose a threat of sexual mistreatment for the women. In this position, Hegai would oversee the extensive *"beauty preparations"* for each of the candidates for queen (see v. 12 below).

INTRODUCTION TO MORDECAI AND ESTHER (2:5–7)

> 5 In Shushan the citadel there was a certain Jew whose name was Mordecai the son of Jair, the son of Shimei, the son of Kish, a Benjamite.
> 6 Kish had been carried away from Jerusalem with the captives who had been captured with Jeconiah king of Judah, whom Nebuchadnezzar the king of Babylon had carried away.
> 7 And Mordecai had brought up Hadassah, that is, Esther, his uncle's daughter, for she had neither father nor mother. The young woman was lovely and beautiful. When her father and mother died, Mordecai took her as his own daughter.
>
> *Esther 2:5–7*

The next passage introduces the reader to *"Mordecai"* and *"Esther,"* the two major characters of the book. The Hebrew wording, which emphasizes Mordecai's Jewishness, reads "A Jewish man was in Susa the citadel and his name was. . . ." The odd phrase clarifies beyond a shadow of a doubt the ethnic identity of Mordecai—a major factor in the plot of Esther. The name, "Mordecai," is a Hebrew translation of the Babylonian name, "*Mardukâ*," the name of a Babylonian god, Marduk.

Verse 5 identifies Mordecai in typical Hebrew fashion by naming his ancestors and tribe. Although verse 6 presents a puzzle for interpreters, the NKJV has solved this puzzle for English readers by placing the word "*Kish*" in italics, because it does not appear in the Hebrew but has been added by the translators. According to the rules of Hebrew grammar, verses 5 and 6 state that Mordecai had been deported from Judah by "*Nebuchadnezzar*." If this were true, however, then Mordecai would have been over 100 years old by the time of Ahasuerus. For this reason the translators of the NKJV agree with many scholars who regard Kish, not Mordecai, as the subject for verse 6, even though this is grammatically odd.[5] (For the deportation of "*Jeconiah*," see 2 Kings 24:8–12, where he is called "Jehoiachin.")

In verse 7 we are introduced to Esther. Like many Jews living in foreign lands,[6] she had two names, a Hebrew name, "*Hadassah*," and a Gentile name, "*Esther*." Most scholars agree that the name "*Hadassah*" meant "myrtle (tree),"[7] and the name "Esther" comes either from the Persian word meaning "star" or from the name for the Babylonian goddess "Ishtar."[8] In this verse we also learn two key details about Esther, both of which substantially support the story that follows. The first is that Esther was "*lovely* and *beautiful*." The Hebrew would actually be translated more accurately as "lovely in form and features" (NIV). Again, repetition is used to emphasize her famous good looks. Indeed, the ancient rabbis identified Esther as one of the four most beautiful women in the world.[9] The second detail is that Esther was an orphan who was raised by her cousin, Mordecai, a man whom she regarded as her own father. This fact not only explains the parent-child relationship between Mordecai and Esther, but also heightens the emotional power of her story—a beautiful young woman who rises from the low social status of an orphaned immigrant to the highest possible position as queen of the empire.

ESTHER PROMOTED TO QUEEN (2:8–18)

8 So it was, when the king's command and
decree were heard, and when many young women
were gathered at Shushan the citadel, under the

custody of Hegai, that Esther also was taken to the king's palace, into the care of Hegai the custodian of the women.

9 Now the young woman pleased him, and she obtained his favor; so he readily gave beauty preparations to her, besides her allowance. Then seven choice maidservants were provided for her from the king's palace, and he moved her and her maidservants to the best place in the house of the women.

10 Esther had not revealed her people or family, for Mordecai had charged her not to reveal it.

11 And every day Mordecai paced in front of the court of the women's quarters, to learn of Esther's welfare and what was happening to her.

12 Each young woman's turn came to go in to King Ahasuerus after she had completed twelve months' preparation, according to the regulations for the women, for thus were the days of their preparation apportioned: six months with oil of myrrh, and six months with perfumes and preparations for beautifying women.

13 Thus prepared, each young woman went to the king, and she was given whatever she desired to take with her from the women's quarters to the king's palace.

14 In the evening she went, and in the morning she returned to the second house of the women, to the custody of Shaashgaz, the king's eunuch who kept the concubines. She would not go in to the king again unless the king delighted in her and called for her by name.

15 Now when the turn came for Esther the daughter of Abihail the uncle of Mordecai, who had taken her as his daughter, to go in to the king, she requested nothing but what Hegai the king's eunuch, the custodian of the women, advised. And Esther obtained favor in the sight of all who saw her.

16 So Esther was taken to King Ahasuerus, into his royal palace, in the tenth month, which is the month of Tebeth, in the seventh year of his reign.

17 The king loved Esther more than all the other women, and she obtained grace and favor in his sight

more than all the virgins; so he set the royal crown
upon her head and made her queen instead of Vashti.
    18 Then the king made a great feast, the Feast of
Esther, for all his officials and servants; and he
proclaimed a holiday in the provinces and gave gifts
according to the generosity of a king.

Esther 2:8–18

The next section of chapter 2 describes how Esther the Jewish orphan became Esther the Queen of Persia. Along with other "beautiful
young virgins" from the empire (v. 3) Esther was gathered into the
palace at Susa, under the jurisdiction of Hegai the eunuch (v. 8).
There, for some reason, she stood out to Hegai and *"obtained his favor"*
(v. 9). The text does not explain precisely why he favored Esther, but
it does imply that she earned a preferred position on the basis of
something more than physical beauty. As a result of Hegai's esteem,
Esther received many benefits: additional beauty treatments, seven
excellent maidservants, and the best room in women's quarters (v. 9).
Her rise to a place of honor replays a familiar Hebrew scenario, in
which the lowly Jew succeeds even in the midst of adversity. (Note
the similar example of Joseph in the Egyptian prison, Gen. 39:20–21).
    Verse 10 adds the significant detail that Esther did not reveal to the
Persian authorities her Jewish background. It is likely that this factor
could have eliminated her from the royal competition, for according
to Herodotus, only daughters of noble Persian families could become
queen.[10] Although we are not told why Esther kept her lineage a secret, the intent of verse 10 is to portray her, not as scheming or
deceitful, but, rather, as obedient to her surrogate father. Esther was
not only beautiful, she was also a faithful and submissive daughter.
Moreover, her ability to be discreet about her lineage discloses her
wisdom (see below). Finally, Esther's secrecy about her ethnic background is an important detail for the development of the rest of the
story. Had Ahasuerus known that she was a Jew, either he would not
have selected her as queen or he would not have brought the Jews to
the point of extinction (chap. 3).
    Mordecai continued to be concerned about the fate of Esther (v.
11). Thus, although he was not permitted to communicate with her
directly, he walked *"in front of* [or, "near"] *the court of the women's
quarters"* in hopes of hearing something about her welfare. Mordecai

was a typical worried father who loved his adopted daughter and yearned for her well-being.

Verses 12–14 describe the process by which the virgins were prepared and then presented to the king. First of all, each woman received a year of cosmetic treatments, including six months of treatments with *"oil of myrrh"* and six months of aromatizing with a special type of incense burner (v. 12). (The phrase *"perfumes and preparations"* actually means "fumigation with other cosmetics".)[11] Following her year of preparation, each virgin would appear before the king with whatever items she chose to augment the king's pleasure (v. 13). After appearing before the king and spending the night with him (no doubt providing sexual favors), the young woman would return to the harem where she would then reside in a separate facility overseen by another eunuch, *"Shaashgaz,"* supervisor of the *"concubines"* (v. 14). It was a common practice in the ancient world for kings to have harems of concubines. These women did not have the status of wives but were actually servants.[12] They were to provide the king with sexual pleasure and, in some instances, with children.

Once a young woman had spent a night with King Ahasuerus she was virtually banished to the harem: *"She would not go in to the king again unless the king delighted in her and called for her by name"* (v. 14). Since the king entertained a new virgin every night for several years, it was unlikely that he would ever remember one whom he had ravished days, months, or even years before. In reality, the women in Ahasuerus' contest were sentenced to a life of unfulfilled loneliness. (This information also helps the reader later to understand Esther's hesitation in approaching the king unbidden.)

The saga of Esther continues in verse 15, where she is identified by her full name, *"Esther the daughter of Abihail."* When it was time for her to appear before the king, Esther took only what *"Hegai, the king's eunuch, the custodian of the women, advised."* Presumably he knew what would please the king. Once again we see Esther acting wisely as she trusts her adviser—this time, Hegai. Now Esther *"obtained favor in the sight of all who saw her."* While this phrase might imply that "her modesty and humility" earned favor,[13] it probably testifies instead to her outstanding physical beauty.

Esther finally appeared before the king in the *"tenth month"* of the *"seventh year"* of Ahasuerus (approximately 480 B.C.). Since the feast that ended with Vashti's banishment began in the "third year" of the king's reign (1:3), Esther's initial audience with the king took place about four years later. It is likely that Ahasuerus consorted with over 1000 virgins prior to his meeting with Esther. Obviously, the odds for any one virgin to be chosen as queen were not good. But Esther's striking beauty and demeanor won the king's affection. Note, however, that given the character of hedonistic Ahasuerus who had only met Esther the night before, we should not understand *"loved"* in a noble sense here (v. 17).

The author wisely omits the details of Esther's first night with the king, but he does tell us that rather than exiling her to the harem, Ahasuerus placed the *"royal crown"* upon her head, thus identifying her as his new queen. So great was his joy that he sponsored another giant feast, this time in Esther's honor (v. 18). Moreover, he proclaimed a national holiday and gave many gifts with liberality. When Ahasuerus was angry, he raged uncontrollably; when he was glad, he celebrated prodigally!

MORDECAI SAVES THE KING'S LIFE (2:19–23)

19 When virgins were gathered together a second time, Mordecai sat within the king's gate.

20 Now Esther had not revealed her family and her people, just as Mordecai had charged her, for Esther obeyed the command of Mordecai as when she was brought up by him.

21 In those days, while Mordecai sat within the king's gate, two of the king's eunuchs, Bigthan and Teresh, doorkeepers, became furious and sought to lay hands on King Ahasuerus.

22 So the matter became known to Mordecai, who told Queen Esther, and Esther informed the king in Mordecai's name.

23 And when an inquiry was made into the matter, it was confirmed, and both were hanged on a gallows; and it was written in the book of the chronicles in the presence of the king.

Esther 2:19–23

The final section of chapter 2 adds a curious footnote to the story of Esther's promotion. The phrase, *"When virgins were gathered together a second time"* has consistently perplexed commentators (v. 19).[14] It is possible that the word translated as "a second time" reflects a copyist's error and originally meant, "When *various* virgins were gathered together."[15] Yet even with this emendation verses 19 and 20 seem curiously out of place. Perhaps they are best understood as a brief review of the chapter, with particular emphasis on the importance of Mordecai. They remind the reader of the fact that Esther's ascendancy depended not only on her beauty, but also on Mordecai, who gave her sage advice (v. 20). The description, *"Mordecai sat within the king's gate"* is significant of more than his location, because in the ancient world where civic trials took place in the gate, those who "sat at the gate" held the positions of judges or other government officials. Perhaps Esther used her position as queen to have Mordecai appointed to a position of authority within the Persian government. At any rate, his "office," so to speak, was located inside the king's gate.

As the story continues to unfold, verses 21–23 relate a simple but portentous event. As Mordecai sat in his place *"within the king's gate,"* he overheard two of the royal servants plotting to assassinate the king (v. 21). Subsequently, he relayed this information to Queen Esther, who passed it on to the king *"in Mordecai's name"* (v. 22). When an official inquiry confirmed Mordecai's accusation, the two conspirators were hanged (v. 23), and the event was entered into *"the book of the chronicles,"* the Persian royal records.

At this point this brief scene appears to play a minor role in the book of Esther, though it does indicate the growing influence of Mordecai and his continued relationship with Esther. It also testifies to Mordecai's loyalty to the king, as well as to Esther's loyalty both to the king and to her adopted father. However, the reader must wait until chapter 6 to understand the full importance of this episode, including the fact that Mordecai's action was recorded in the official records.

LITERARY ASPECTS OF ESTHER 2:1–23

In Chapter 2 we are introduced to the upstanding characters of the story, Mordecai and Esther. In the brief descriptions that are given, Mordecai appears as responsible, caring, and wise; Esther appears as underprivileged, beautiful, subordinate, quiet, and wise. Both

Mordecai and Esther ride the tide of human affairs with expert skill by making the most of their opportunities for personal advancement. It is noteworthy, too, that although Esther and Mordecai had moved into positions of influence within the Persian government, their ethnicity remained unknown to the king—a detail that makes the rest of the story plausible.

The stylistic device of exaggeration that was used in chapter 1, continues in chapter 2. Notice that *all* the beautiful young virgins gathered in Susa for the king's beauty contest (v. 3) where they underwent a preposterous process of beautification and aromatization (v. 12). According to B. W. Jones, the excessive perfuming of the virgins is a case of "conspicuous consumption" in the extreme.[17] Actually, the reader should laugh at the ridiculous excesses of Ahasuerus and his regime.

Though chapter 2 focuses mainly on plot development, it also begins to portray Esther as a wise woman—representative of positive elements in Wisdom Literature. In Hebrew wisdom, Proverbs admonishes children to listen to their parents:

> My son, hear the instruction of your father,
> And do not forsake the law of your mother;
> For they will be a graceful ornament on your head,
> And chains about your neck.
>
> *Proverbs 1:8–9*

Furthermore, according to the sages, wise children obey their parents: "A fool despises his father's instruction, / But he who receives reproof is prudent" (Prov. 15:5). Thus, Esther's willingness to follow Mordecai's advice demonstrates her exemplary behavior as a wise daughter.

Mordecai had advised Esther to keep her ethnic background a secret, so twice in chapter 2 the author mentions that Esther did not reveal her Jewishness (vv. 10, 20). By keeping silent, she not only obeyed her adopted father but also demonstrated one of the primary traits of wisdom. Wise women know when to keep quiet—unlike their foolish counterparts: "A foolish woman is clamorous; / She is simple and knows nothing" (Prov. 9:13). For both women and men, wisdom depends on the ability to be "silent in the proper way."[18] As David Hubbard notes, "Prudent speech begins with restraint in communication."[19] Note several proverbs that make this point:

> A talebearer reveals secrets,
> But he who is of a faithful spirit conceals a matter.
>
> *Proverbs 11:13*

> A prudent man conceals knowledge,
> But the heart of fools proclaims foolishness.
>
> *Proverbs 12:23*[20]

> He who guards his mouth preserves his life.
> But he who opens wide his lips shall have destruction.
>
> *Proverbs 13:3*[21]

Esther was not only obedient and quiet, she was also loyal. While in the preparatory harem, she continued to be loyal to Mordecai and to her Jewishness (v. 10). This was another trait that was highly valued by Jewish wisdom: "What is desirable in a person is loyalty, / and it is better to be poor than a liar" (Prov. 19:22, NRSV).[22] Once Esther was crowned queen, she managed to remain loyal to Mordecai while also being loyal to the king (vv. 21–23). So we see that, in chapter 2, Esther illustrates several wise maxims—as an obedient child who listens to her father, as a prudent speaker who knows when to keep silent, and as one who remains loyal even in conflicting situations.

The picture of Ahasuerus in chapter 2 is also indicative of wisdom influence. Earlier in chapter 1 he was portrayed as a foolish king who boasted, drank to excess, and let his emotions control his life. His rash anger led to the banishment of Vashti, something he appeared to regret later (v. 1). In chapter 2, when confronted by the beauty and character of Esther, Ahasuerus is equally lavish in his response. He honors Esther by throwing a party in her honor, by declaring a national holiday, and by giving generous gifts. This too fits wisdom's image of the king: "The king's wrath is like the roaring of a lion; / But his favor is like dew on the grass" (Prov. 19:12).[23]

ESTHER 2:1–23 FROM A CHRISTIAN PERSPECTIVE

To God, Beauty is More than Skin Deep

I doubt that any woman could read Esther 2 without cringing. The treatment of women in this chapter is offensive to both women and men, but, for obvious reasons, women tend to feel the offense more deeply. Ahasuerus represents the worst of male chauvinists who not only wants beautiful virgins by the hundreds in his harem, but also forces these women to undergo a year's worth of beautification before he uses them for his pleasure. The harem system of ancient Persia objectified women to an extreme, robbing them of their dignity and freedom. They became mere playthings of the king—most to be discarded after one night of royal ecstasy.

At first glance, the example of Esther does not offer much encouragement for women. Here was a woman who rose from the position of orphaned minority to queen primarily because of her stunning beauty. Esther 2 seems to confirm the opinion that women must be beautiful in order to be successful, or that they will succeed in life only if they happen to be pretty and if they submit to men's designs on their lives.

From the perspective of Jewish wisdom, however, Esther's emerging character is far more significant than her beauty. As a daughter, she obeyed her father, like any wise son or daughter should. As a communicator, Esther demonstrated the first rule of wisdom: Be silent when necessary. Even in a Persian harem Esther distinguished herself as a woman with great potential. Though the text accentuates Esther's physical beauty, it begins to show her outstanding character as well.

The New Testament encourages women to develop the beauty of character valued by Jewish wisdom and modeled by Esther. Two relevant passages stand out:

> [I desire] that the women adorn themselves in modest apparel, with propriety and moderation, not with braided hair or gold or pearls or costly clothing, but, which is proper for women professing godliness, with good works.
>
> *1 Timothy 2:9–10*

> [Wives,] do not let your adornment be merely outward—arranging the hair, wearing gold, or putting on fine apparel—rather let it be the hidden person of the heart, with the incorruptible beauty of a gentle and quiet spirit, which is very precious to God.
>
> *1 Peter 3:3–4*

Both texts encourage women to focus on something other than outward beauty. Timothy highlights the beauty of "good works," while Peter focuses on inner beauty.

I often counsel with women who strive to honor God through good works and who seek to cultivate inner beauty, yet who seem to lack male affection because of their average looks. Too many of these women feel like the beautiful virgins in Ahasuerus' harem. Striving for acceptance they may never receive, they are banished to a life of loneliness. While I can offer no simple solution to the pain these women feel, I can offer the assurance that they are very precious to God and that he has a special plan and purpose for their lives—a plan that has nothing to do with physical appearance. But there is another side to this matter: the all-too-frequent, improper perspective of men. Yet I believe that as we men grow in Christ, we can develop God's perspective on people. We can learn to see and to value women in God's way. Still, without doubt, until Christ returns the objectification and abuse of women as portrayed in Esther 2 will be replayed over and over again. God grant us all an awareness of this reality to help us, Christian women and men, to seek God's ways and to offer a place in the community of faith for women to find healing, support, and genuine love.

Riding the Tide of God's Providence

This chapter began with a quotation from Shakespeare in which Brutus advises Cassius to ride the tide of human affairs to good fortune. I illustrated this advice with the example of Jon's success in business. Anyone who knows Jon, however, would recognize this as an error, for he attributes none of his success to luck or to his own ingenuity—he gives all the credit to God. Jon prays daily for his business, offering the whole enterprise to the Lord. He believes that God is sovereign over his company and he seeks divine guidance for each decision. When he takes a risk, he does so after considerable prayer and consultation with other Christians.

We believe that God directs our lives, and works all things together for good (Rom. 8:28). Therefore, we ride to success not on the tide of human affairs but on the tide of God's Providence. Although the author of Esther may or may not have seen God's hand behind the events of chapter 2, we see the story of Esther from a different perspective: that our task is not to hope for a lucky break but to seek God's direction for our lives and to act in obedience to him.

I am reminded of this when I recall a particular event in my life during graduate school. At the time, I ran a small company that prepared students for standardized exams (SAT, LSAT, GRE, etc.). I offered private tutoring and managed a staff of twenty other instructors. During one summer, I was delighted to leave my job behind for several weeks of vacation in California. To my chagrin, however, it seemed I was not going to be able to escape from my work after all. Following morning worship on my first Sunday of vacation, a young woman approached me and asked if I knew anyone who could tutor her in math. Casually, I queried, "What kind of math?" hoping it would be beyond my level. "For the GRE," she answered. Now I had a tough decision to make because that was a level of tutoring in which I was proficient. My flesh grumbled, "Don't volunteer. You're on vacation!" But my spirit urged, "You are part of the Body of Christ. God wants you to do this." Reluctantly I stepped forward to offer my services, a bit angry with God for putting me in this awkward situation. Out of obedience to God I began to tutor the young woman—and two years later I married her!

With apologies to William Shakespeare, my experience, as well as that of my friend Jon and those of Mordecai and Esther, can best be summarized in these lines:

> There is a tide in the affairs of God,
> Which, taken at the flood, leads on to blessing!

NOTES

1. William Shakespeare, *Julius Caesar*, act 4, scene 3, lines 239–42.
2. Paton, *Book of Esther*, p. 164.
3. Josephus, *Jewish Antiquities*, 11:195.
4. Herodotus, *Histories*, 9:33.
5. LaSor, Hubbard, and Bush, *Old Testament Survey*, p. 626.
6. Daniel, for example, received the Babylonian name, "Belteshazzar" (Dan. 1:7).
7. *Hădassâ* would be a feminine name derived from the Hebrew word for "myrtle," *hădas* (Brown, Driver, and Briggs, *Lexicon*, s.v. "*hădas*").
8. Moore, *Esther*, p. 20.
9. *Babylonian Talmud, Megillâ*, 14b–15a.

10. Herodotus, *Histories*, 3:84.

11. Moore, *Esther*, pp. 16, 23; Baldwin, *Esther*, pp. 68–69.

12. R. de Vaux, *Ancient Israel*, 2 vols. (New York: McGraw-Hill, 1965), 1:115–117.

13. Keil and Delitzsch, *Commentary*, p. 339.

14. Paton, *Book of Esther*, pp. 186–187.

15. Moore, *Esther*, pp. 29–30.

16. Gordis, "Religion," pp. 47–48.

17. Jones, "Two Misconceptions," p. 175.

18. von Rad, *Theology*, 1:431.

19. D. A. Hubbard, *Proverbs*, The Communicator's Commentary (Dallas: Word Books, Publisher, 1989), p. 215.

20. Noted by Talmon, "Wisdom," p. 447.

21. See also Ecclesiastes 5:2–3, and the discussion in Hubbard, *Proverbs*, pp. 214–27.

22. The NRSV translation is better here. See the comment on 19:22 in Hubbard, *Proverbs*, p. 185.

23. Cited by Talmon, "Wisdom," p. 433.

CHAPTER THREE

Haman Issues a Royal Decree to Destroy the Jews

Esther 3:1–15

ARE YOU READY TO JEER?

Each year during the holiday of Purim, Jewish leaders around the world read the Book of Esther to excited crowds in the synagogues. Adults, and especially children, wait eagerly for the reading of chapter 3 because with this chapter their fun begins. Verse 1 introduces Haman, the villain of the story, and each time the reader mentions his name—53 times throughout Esther—the synagogue erupts with raucous noise. Horns blow. Rattles shake. Children shout. Adults jeer. With zealous glee synagogue members try to drown out his name with their uproar. They do so because in the book of Esther he is, without a doubt, the "villain," the archetypal enemy of the Jews. His evil deeds in chapter 3 create the central conflict of the book, which can only be resolved by Queen Esther's courageous acts to save her people.

MORDECAI DEFIES HAMAN (3:1–4)

3:1 After these things King Ahasuerus promoted Haman, the son of Hammedatha the Agagite, and advanced him and set his seat above all the princes who were with him.
2 And all the king's servants who were within the king's gate bowed and paid homage to Haman, for so the king had commanded concerning him. But Mordecai would not bow or pay homage.

> 3 Then the king's servants who were within the
> king's gate said to Mordecai, "Why do you transgress
> the king's command?"
> 4 Now it happened, when they spoke to him
> daily and he would not listen to them, that they told it
> to Haman, to see whether Mordecai's words would
> stand; for Mordecai had told them that he was a Jew.
>
> *Esther 3:1–4*

Verse 1 introduces *"Haman"* as *"the son of Hammedatha,"* whose identity is not known. More importantly, Haman is identified as *"the Agagite,"* a descendant of the Amalekite king, Agag. This pagan king brought about the downfall of King Saul before Agag was dismembered by Samuel (1 Sam. 15:8–33). "The Agagite" label distinguished Haman as an ancestral enemy of the Jews. King Ahasuerus disregarded Haman's non-Persian status and promoted him to a high position within the government, perhaps as "prime minister."[1] Furthermore, the king commanded that all of his servants were to bow down before Haman as a sign of honor (v. 2). Throughout the Ancient Near East people commonly bowed before their rulers as a gesture of respect.

Mordecai, however, *"would not bow or pay homage"* to Haman (v. 2). This act of insubordination, not only to Haman but ultimately to the king, puzzled those who served alongside Mordecai, so they asked him, *"Why do you transgress the king's command?"* (v. 3). Verse 4 suggests that they asked this question not only to discover the reason for Mordecai's behavior, but also to encourage him to bow before Haman. Yet even though they *"spoke to him daily, . . . he would not listen to them."* He did, however, explain his reticence to bow by confessing that he was a Jew.

Now the text does not explain why being Jewish kept Mordecai from bowing down. We know that Jews were forbidden from bowing down before other gods (Exod. 20:5), but they were permitted to bow before human authorities (for example, 2 Sam. 14:4). Perhaps Mordecai's refusal was a reaction to Haman's ethnic background as an Agagite, or perhaps it was simply a result of his pride. While the text of Esther simply reports Mordecai's reason for not bowing, without explicit affirmation or criticism, in retrospect, the reader certainly wonders whether Mordecai should have been more conciliatory, for when the servants could not convince Mordecai to bow, they told Haman about his stubbornness.

HAMAN'S ANGRY RESPONSE TO MORDECAI (3:5–7)

5 When Haman saw that Mordecai did not bow or pay him homage, Haman was filled with wrath.
6 But he disdained to lay hands on Mordecai alone, for they had told him of the people of Mordecai. Instead, Haman sought to destroy all the Jews who were throughout the whole kingdom of Ahasuerus—the people of Mordecai.
7 In the first month, which is the month of Nisan, in the twelfth year of King Ahasuerus, they cast Pur (that is, the lot), before Haman to determine the day and the month, until it fell on the twelfth month, which is the month of Adar.

Esther 3:5–7

After hearing from the servants, Haman noticed Mordecai's insubordination and was *"filled with wrath"* (v. 5). So great was his anger, in fact, that he decided *"to destroy all the Jews who were throughout the whole kingdom"* (v. 6). Punishing Mordecai would not satisfy Haman's anger; he was driven by rage to seek revenge on all of *"the people of Mordecai"* (v. 6).

Verse 7 explains how Haman determined the date for the Jewish extermination. His assistants *"cast Pur (that is, the lot) before Haman to determine the day and the month."* The Babylonian word *"pur"* denotes a lot or cube-shaped die used to make decisions. (See "Esther and Purim" in the introduction for more information.) By using this device, Haman and his servants determined to kill the Jews during the month of Adar (late February, early March in our calendars). Eleven months would pass between the casting of the *pur* in Nisan, the first month, and the murder of the Jews. While verse 7 is a parenthetical note that does not contribute substantially to the development of the plot, it does link the story to the Feast of Purim. Chapter 9 will explain this connection in greater detail.

HAMAN PERSUADES THE KING TO ISSUE A DECREE AGAINST THE JEWS (3:8–15)

8 Then Haman said to King Ahasuerus, "There is a certain people scattered and dispersed among the people in all the provinces of your kingdom; their

laws are different from all other people's, and they do not keep the king's laws. Therefore it is not fitting for the king to let them remain.

9 If it pleases the king, let a decree be written that they be destroyed, and I will pay ten thousand talents of silver into the hands of those who do the work, to bring it into the king's treasuries."

10 So the king took his signet ring from his hand and gave it to Haman, the son of Hammedatha the Agagite, the enemy of the Jews.

11 And the king said to Haman, "The money and the people are given to you, to do with them as seems good to you."

12 Then the king's scribes were called on the thirteenth day of the first month, and a decree was written according to all that Haman commanded—to the king's satraps, to the governors who were over each province, to the officials of all people, to every province according to its script, and to every people in their language. In the name of King Ahasuerus it was written, and sealed with the king's signet ring.

13 And the letters were sent by couriers into all the king's provinces, to destroy, to kill, and to annihilate all the Jews, both young and old, little children and women, in one day, on the thirteenth day of the twelfth month, which is the month of Adar, and to plunder their possessions.

14 A copy of the document was to be issued as law in every province, being published for all people, that they should be ready for that day.

15 The couriers went out, hastened by the king's command; and the decree was proclaimed in Shushan the citadel. So the king and Haman sat down to drink, but the city of Shushan was perplexed.

Esther 3:8–15

After plotting with his associates, Haman approached King Ahasuerus with his plan. His proposal in verses 8–9 reflects Haman's ability to manipulate the king with deceit and bribery. First, he began with a statement that was a slight exaggeration: *"There is a certain people scattered and dispersed among the people in all the provinces of your kingdom"* (v. 8). Undoubtedly, Jews did not live in every province of the vast Persian empire, but Haman exaggerated their dispersion in order to magnify their threat to the king. His second charge further stretched the truth: *"Their laws are different from all other people's"* (v. 8). Certainly some Jewish laws were unique, but many were shared by other ancient people. However, by alleging Jewish strangeness Haman underlined the danger of the Jews to the Persian establishment. With his third charge Haman moved from exaggeration to outright deception: *"They do not keep the king's laws"* (v. 8). In fact, Mordecai had disobeyed the king's command to bow before Haman, but the Jewish people in general had done nothing wrong. Having built his case against the Jews with exaggeration and falsehood, Haman concluded, *"it is not fitting for the king to let them remain"* (v. 8). A widely-dispersed, foreign, law-breaking people spread throughout the empire would certainly pose a threat to the king.

But that was not all. Notice how Haman moved from manipulating the king through falsehood and fear to motivating him by greed. If the king agreed to order the annihilation of the Jews, Haman pledged to fill the king's coffers with *"ten thousand talents of silver"* (v. 9). While the precise value of this prize money cannot be known, it undoubtedly represented a vast sum of money—possibly countless millions of dollars.[2] By implication, either Haman was rich beyond measure, or he expected to become rich by plundering the Jews.

Unfortunately, Haman's ploy worked. The king gave *"his signet ring"* to Haman so that he might issue a decree with the king's own authority. Verse 10 clarifies what the previous verses imply: Haman was *"the enemy of the Jews."*

In verse 11 of the NKJV, Ahasuerus appears to decline Haman's offer of riches: *"The money and the people are given to you, to do with them as seems good to you."* Likewise, the NIV translates the verse: *"'Keep the money,' the king said to Haman, 'and do with the people as you please.'"* But since the Hebrew sentence reads literally, "The money (is) given to you and the people to do with as is pleasing in your eyes," it seems to me that Carey Moore offers a plausible alternative translation that accords with the Hebrew and is more compatible with the personality of the king: *"'Well, it's your money,' said the king to Haman, 'do what you like with the people.'"*[3] In other words, the king was saying, "If you want to spend all of your money that way, go right ahead. I'll gladly accept your money, and you can do whatever you want with the Jewish people."

Continuing on, verses 12 through 15 recount the process by which the royal decree against the Jews was circulated throughout the empire. The royal *"scribes"* drafted a decree for all of the Persian leaders: *"satraps"* (divisional leaders), *"governors"* (leaders of smaller provinces), and *"officials"* (or nobles in general). That such a decree would have been translated into every dialect found within the Persian empire is historically improbable, but from a literary point of view such a project accentuates the zeal of Haman to wipe out all of the Jews. Even though Haman dictated the decree, he did so with the authority of the king, as indicated by the royal seal (v. 12).

Verse 13 underscores the reprehensible thoroughness of Haman's vendetta against the Jews, for the people were not merely encouraged to kill the Jews, they were instructed *"to destroy, to kill, and to annihilate"* their victims. Moreover, *"all the Jews"* were to be eliminated, including *"young and old, little children and women."* Only total genocide would satisfy the wicked wrath of Haman. Finally, the Persians were to *"plunder their possessions,"* either for personal gain or for the king's treasury. This was the dreadful decree the *"couriers"* hastened to take throughout the vast empire so that all the people would *"be ready for that day"* (vv. 13–14).

Verse 15 mentions specifically that the decree was *"proclaimed"* in Susa, the capital city of the empire. Thus the chapter ends abruptly with a pointed contrast between the satisfaction of the conspirators and the confusion of the people, both Jews and others: *"So the king and Haman sat down to drink, but the city of Shushan was perplexed."*

THE LITERARY ASPECTS OF ESTHER 3:1–15

Chapter 3 functions within the story of Esther chiefly to introduce Haman, the arch villain, and the essential conflict of the book. Entertaining stories, especially those that pit good against evil, often include a scoundrel who epitomizes wickedness. The conflict between the villain and the hero propels the story forward to its conclusion. Examples abound in literature, both sacred and secular: David vs. Goliath; Elijah vs. Ahab; Robin Hood vs. the Sheriff of Nottingham; Batman vs. the Joker.

As we noted in previous chapters, the book of Esther emphasizes plot rather than characterization. Thus, although Haman plays the role of the villain, the reader actually learns very little about the nuances of his personality. From the perspective of Jewish wisdom, however, Haman's vileness is readily evident. For instance, notice the personal traits that God hates:

> These six *things* the LORD hates,
> Yes, seven are an abomination to Him:
> A proud look,
> A lying tongue,
> Hands that shed innocent blood,
> A heart that devises wicked plans,
> Feet that are swift in running to evil,
> A false witness who speaks lies,
> And one who sows discord among brethren.
>
> *Proverbs 6:16–19*

Without doubt, Haman exemplifies most of these traits:

- A proud look—Pride implied in his response to Mordecai (see 5:11).
- A lying tongue / A false witness who speaks lies—Haman lied to the king (v. 8).
- Hands that shed innocent blood—Haman intended to kill, not only all Jews, but specifically *"little children and women"* (v. 13).
- A heart that devises wicked plans—Haman plotted to destroy the Jews (v. 6).

Other proverbs also describe the vileness of Haman, for example: "The bloodthirsty hate the blameless, / But the just seek his well-being" (Prov. 29:10). According to Jewish wisdom, Haman's hatred of the Jews classifies him among the bloodthirsty as well as the wicked.

In addition, Haman's fierce anger against Mordecai motivated him to destroy the Jews (vv. 5–6). Proverbial wisdom acknowledges the power of anger to cause harm: "An angry man stirs up strife, / And a furious man abounds in transgression" (Prov. 29:22).[4] Haman's inability to control his anger shows him to be not only evil but also a fool. "A fool vents all his feelings, / But a wise man holds them back" (Prov. 29:11).[5] Mordecai's reticence to express himself in verses 3–4 may or may not identify him as wise, but Haman clearly fulfills the role of the wicked fool whose uncontrolled anger controls him and leads to transgression. Though a casual reader of Esther might identify Haman as "the bad guy," a reader steeped in Jewish wisdom would know exactly why Haman was bad and why he was hated by God.

ESTHER 3:1–15 FROM A CHRISTIAN PERSPECTIVE

Women as Innocent Victims

Women do not appear as active participants in Esther 3; they appear merely as innocent victims. Specifically, Haman decreed the annihilation of all Jews, including *"little children and women"* (v. 13). The fact is that all of the first three chapters of Esther frequently picture women as victims of male impulses: Vashti lost her throne because of Ahasuerus's drunken anger (chap. 1); hundreds of "beautiful young virgins" provided one night of sexual pleasure for the king before being banished to the harem (chap. 2); even Esther's promotion to queen depended upon a male whim (chap. 2). Then in chapter 3 thousands of Jewish women faced death because of one man's pride—which may have been provoked by another man's foolish pride.[6]

Of course we know that the victimization of women is not unique to Esther 1–3. Throughout history women have suffered because of the impulsive, selfish actions and attitudes of men. Today our newspapers tell the tragic tale of thousands of Muslim women in Bosnia who have been raped by their Serbian attackers. The plight of women in the first three chapters of Esther reminds us of a sad reality we often ignore. The ancient story calls attention to what is happening in our world today and challenges us to respond with the love and justice of Christ.

The surprise of Esther comes in the following chapters, where a woman not only stands up for her own rights, but saves an entire nation. The powerlessness of women in Esther 1–3 sets the stage for the stirring drama that follows.

The Spirit of Haman in the Modern World

Sadly, we cannot look upon Haman as an antique from some distant time. No, ethnic prejudice and hatred flourish in our world also. The "spirit of Haman" lives today in Bosnia, in Germany, and on the

370

streets of Los Angeles. Just recently, ethnic hatred emboldened neo-Nazi German youths to attack and kill foreign "guest-workers" while celebrating Hitler's birthday. In April 1992, African-American teenagers in Los Angeles plundered Korean stores, partly as a response to perceived prejudice from Korean merchants. I live in a community populated predominantly by white people, many of whom have moved to "safe" Irvine in order to avoid the multi-ethnic entanglements of larger cities. Residents regularly express fears about "those people" who might ruin our peaceful existence.

Surely as Christians we must recognize the "spirit of Haman"—not only in our world but within ourselves. Yes, unfortunately, ethnic prejudice runs deep even among those of us who believe that in Christ "there is neither Jew nor Greek" (Gal. 3:28). How do we root out the "spirit of Haman"? First, we do so by confessing to God the sin of racism. Only the Holy Spirit can create in us a clean heart that loves all people, regardless of their ethnicity. Second, we can step out in obedience by taking tangible steps to build relationships with people from other races. For example, Christian leaders in Los Angeles have reached across the lines of racial division to experience unity in Christ; they have joined together in a mission of prayer, called "Love L.A. and Pray." On a regular basis, hundreds of people representing all races gather to pray for each other and for God's work in the city. As these people pray against the spirits of racism and violence that tyrannize Los Angeles, they are demonstrating the wisdom of God that defeats the foolish, wicked "spirit of Haman."

NOTES

1. Moore, *Esther*, p. 33.
2. Moore, *Esther*, pp. 39–40.
3. Moore, *Esther*, p. 34.
4. Cited by Talmon, "Wisdom," p. 444.
5. See also Ecclesiastes 7:9.
6. The author of Esther is strangely silent in his estimation of Mordecai's refusal to bow down before Haman. For this reason, S. A. White concludes that "Mordecai's action appears foolish in the extreme,

placing his life and the life of his people in jeopardy" ("Esther," in *The Woman's Bible Commentary*, ed. C. A. Newsom and S. H. Ringe [Louisville: Westminster/John Knox, 1992], p. 128).

CHAPTER FOUR

The Response of Esther and Mordecai to Haman's Plot

Esther 4:1–17

CHOSEN FOR AN UNEXPECTED CALLING

In the spring of 1955, a brilliant twenty-six-year old student received his doctorate from Boston University after completing his thesis: "A Comparison of the Conception of God in the Thinking of Paul Tillich and Henry Nelson Wieman." Although his professors praised his scholarly potential and colleges offered him faculty positions, this young scholar decided to prepare for his teaching career by spending a few years as a pastor. When Dexter Avenue Baptist Church extended an offer, he moved to Montgomery, Alabama for what he expected to be a brief, quiet season of pastoral work. From his position in the church he would soon return to his first love—academia.

But history altered his plans. On December 1, 1955, a black woman named Rosa Parks refused to leave her seat in the "whites only" section of a Montgomery bus. Before the young pastor of Dexter Avenue Baptist knew what had happened, he had been elected President of the Montgomery Improvement Association, an organization of African Americans committed to racial justice. From that platform he was soon catapulted into national leadership. Martin Luther King, Jr. never returned to academic life. The vicissitudes of history would not allow it. Or, as Dr. King believed, God had chosen him for an unexpected calling.

At the close of Esther 2, all seemed well for Esther and Mordecai. She had won the king's beauty contest and had been crowned queen. She had helped Mordecai receive a royal appointment, and he, in turn, had saved the king's life. Events in chapter 3, however, disturbed their peaceful existence. A conflict between Mordecai and the king's chief official, Haman, escalated into a royal decree that called for the extermination of all Jews. Esther was placed in a precarious position. Would she risk her life to save her people? Although she expected to enjoy the benefits of royal life, had she been crowned as queen for an unexpected calling, for some greater purpose? Chapter 4 begins to answer these questions.

MORDECAI AND THE JEWS MOURN (4:1–3)

4:1 When Mordecai learned all that had happened,
he tore his clothes and put on sackcloth and ashes,
and went out into the midst of the city. He cried out
with a loud and bitter cry.
2 He went as far as the front of the king's gate,
for no one might enter the king's gate clothed with
sackcloth.
3 And in every province where the king's
command and decree arrived, there was great
mourning among the Jews, with fasting, weeping,
and wailing; and many lay in sackcloth and ashes.

Esther 4:1–3

The first three verses of chapter 4 describe typical expressions of mourning for ancient Jews. Mordecai *"tore his clothes and put on sackcloth and ashes"* (v. 1). Feeling no compunction to keep his grief private, he *"cried out with a loud and bitter cry"* even *"in the midst of the city"* (v. 1). He carried his mourning to the very gate of the palace, although Persian law prohibited him from entering the palace while wearing sackcloth (v. 2). Though the text does not explain why Mordecai mourned at the palace gate, it suggests that he intended to attract Esther's attention (see v. 4).

Jews throughout the empire joined Mordecai with *"great mourning"* (v. 3). They also engaged in *"fasting, weeping, and wailing,"* while many *"lay in sackcloth and ashes"* (v. 3). Such public expressions of grief may strike us as odd and inappropriate, especially if we have been raised in the Northern European tradition of emotional reticence, however, Middle Eastern cultures encourage much greater freedom in the expression of sadness. (The Wailing Wall in Jerusalem provides a modern example.) Thus, the Jews' behavior in verse 3 reflects their social norms and matches the horror of the decree that had been issued against them.

ESTHER AND MORDECAI DEBATE ESTHER'S RESPONSE (4:4–17)

4 So Esther's maids and eunuchs came and told her, and the queen was deeply distressed. Then she sent garments to clothe Mordecai and take his sackcloth away from him, but he would not accept them.

5 Then Esther called Hathach, one of the king's eunuchs whom he had appointed to attend her, and she gave him a command concerning Mordecai, to learn what and why this was.

6 So Hathach went out to Mordecai in the city square that was in front of the king's gate.

7 And Mordecai told him all that had happened to him, and the sum of money that Haman had promised to pay into the king's treasuries to destroy the Jews.

8 He also gave him a copy of the written decree for their destruction, which was given at Shushan, that he might show it to Esther and explain it to her, and that he might command her to go in to the king to make supplication to him and plead before him for her people.

9 So Hathach returned and told Esther the words of Mordecai.

10 Then Esther spoke to Hathach, and gave him a command for Mordecai:

11 All the king's servants and the people of the king's provinces know that any man or woman who goes into the inner court to the king, who has not been called, he has but one law: put all to death, except the one to whom the king holds out the golden scepter, that he may live. Yet I myself have not been called to go in to the king these thirty days."

12 So they told Mordecai Esther's words.

13 And Mordecai told them to answer Esther: "Do not think in your heart that you will escape in the king's palace any more than all the other Jews.

375

14 For if you remain completely silent at this time, relief and deliverance will arise for the Jews from another place, but you and your father's house will perish. Yet who knows whether you have come to the kingdom for such a time as this?"

15 Then Esther told them to reply to Mordecai:

16 "Go, gather all the Jews who are present in Shushan, and fast for me; neither eat nor drink for three days, night or day. My maids and I will fast likewise. And so I will go to the king, which is against the law; and if I perish, I perish!"

17 So Mordecai went his way and did according to all that Esther commanded him.

Esther 4:4–17

Verses 4–5 imply that Esther did not know about Haman's plot and the king's decree. This seems strange given Esther's position as queen, but verse 11 explains her ignorance: *"I myself have not been called to go in to the king these thirty days."* Sequestered in her quarters, Esther had no idea of what had happened in the last month. Her first hint of the dire situation came when her servants told her of Mordecai's unusual behavior at the palace gate (v. 4).

Esther's first response was to present Mordecai with new clothing to replace his sackcloth, presumably so he could enter the palace and explain his mourning to her.[1] With resoluteness bordering on indignity, he refused her offer (v. 4). At that point she sent *"Hathach, one of the king's eunuchs whom he had appointed to attend her"* to find out the cause of Mordecai's behavior (v. 5). When Hathach found him, Mordecai related the whole story of his encounter with Haman and how that had led to the plan *"to destroy the Jews"* (vv. 6–7). Mordecai also supplied Hathach with *"a copy of the written decree for their destruction,"* insisting that he show it to Esther and *"command her to go in to the king to make supplication to him and plead before him for her people"* (v. 8). Although Esther was the queen, Mordecai continued to relate to her as an authoritative father, commanding her to approach the king.[2]

When Hathach passed along Mordecai's message to Esther she responded with hesitation, citing a royal law that prohibited anyone from approaching the king without prior invitation (v. 11). The penalty for such an intrusion was death, unless the king *"[held] out the golden scepter,*" in which case the uninvited suppliant would live. Esther could not presume to receive this gesture of welcome, however, because she had ceased to be the apple of his eye. In fact, he had not even summoned her for the past *"thirty days."* Although Esther was queen, Ahasuerus had a considerable collection of concubines in his harem and possibly other wives as well. He did not need Esther to fulfill either his desire for companionship or his lustful cravings. Therefore, Esther initially balked at Mordecai's command, wisely fearing for her life. She may have remembered what happened to the last queen who crossed Ahasuerus (chap. 1).

Notice that the text does not criticize Esther's hesitation. Her wariness about going before King Ahasuerus does not show her weakness but her faithful employment of Jewish wisdom. Proverbs 25:6–7 counsels:

> Do not put yourself forward in the king's presence
> or stand in the place of the great;
> for it is better to be told, "Come up here,"
> than to be put lower in the presence of a noble (NRSV).

This general advice would be even more appropriate for someone in the Persian empire, whose uninvited appearance before the king could result in death.

According to verse 12, *"they"* conveyed Esther's wise hesitation to Mordecai. Others besides Hathach entered the scene at this point though the text does not identify them by name. Mordecai responded to Esther, first with a warning that she would not escape the murder of her people: *"Do not think in your heart that you will escape in the king's palace any more than all the other Jews"* (v. 13). No doubt Mordecai realized that Esther hesitated to go before the king because she was afraid that she might be killed. So he reminded her that if she did not approach the king she would certainly be killed as well.

Then he added further incentive for Esther, uttering what is perhaps the most frequently quoted verse from the entire Book of Esther (v. 14):

> "For if you remain completely silent at this time, relief and deliverance will arise for the Jews from another place, but you and your father's house will perish. Yet who knows whether you have come to the kingdom for such a time as this?"

377

We note with surprise Mordecai's new-found confidence that the Jews would be delivered. If Esther failed to do her duty, *"relief and deliverance [would] arise for the Jews from another place."* Mordecai, a man wailing at the palace gate, had become Mordecai, a man of faith. But faith in what? What does the obscure phrase *"from another place"* mean? Both Jewish and Christian commentators on this verse have seen in it a veiled reference to God.[3] While this connotation cannot be derived from the meaning of the Hebrew, it may represent the author's intended message.[4] Even if this is true, however, we must take seriously Mordecai's reticence to mention God explicitly.

Furthermore, Mordecai urged Esther to consider her own destiny: *"Yet who knows whether you have come to the kingdom for such a time as this?"* Again, most commentators see in this line a veiled reference to God: "Yet who knows whether you have come to the kingdom [by God's Providence] for such a time as this?" This religious interpretation may reflect correctly what the author of Esther truly believed, but the actual words of Mordecai conceal the author's religious convictions. The most theologically-profound verse in all of Esther refers to God obliquely at best. If it suggests that God's providence stands behind human affairs, it does so without mentioning either God or providence explicitly.

Mordecai's suggestion that Esther had *"come to the kingdom for such a time as this"* reflects the confession of God's sovereignty in Jewish wisdom.

> The LORD has made everything for its purpose,
> even the wicked for the day of trouble.
>
> *Proverbs 16:4 (NRSV)[5]*

> A man's heart plans his way,
> But the LORD directs his steps.
>
> *Proverbs 16:9*

While Mordecai's vague confession of providence is consistent with Jewish wisdom, his failure to mention God directly cannot be explained entirely by the author's reflection of wisdom since the proverbs cited above clearly speak of God.[6] The author of Esther allows Mordecai to speak in a surprisingly secular tone, perhaps to convey Mordecai's sense of life's ambiguities (or the author's).

Apparently Mordecai's appeal to providence was successful for Esther responded affirmatively. First, she told Mordecai to lead all of the Jews in Susa in a three-day fast on her behalf (v. 16). Although prayer may be implied here, since it frequently accompanied fasting (for example, Neh. 1:4; Ps. 35:13), it is not mentioned specifically—another indication of the secular slant of the book. Second, Esther demonstrated a new willingness to risk her life for the sake of her people: "*And so I will go to the king, which is against the law; and if I perish, I perish!*" Her hesitancy had disappeared, to be replaced by courage; such courage, in fact, that Esther was willing to put her very life on the line.

For the first time in the Book of Esther, a woman has stepped out of the role of victim to become a person of strength, confidence, and courage. Whereas earlier chapters had emphasized her beauty, chapter 4 now shows that Esther is both beautiful and wise. Although the Jewish sages warned young men about the limitations of female beauty: "Like a gold ring in a pig's snout, / is a beautiful woman without good sense" (Prov. 11:22, NRSV), Esther proves herself to be both lovely and full of good sense. From the perspective of wisdom, Esther's beauty may even have been a liability in her quest for virtue, but her wisdom and character certainly earn praise.

Ironically, verse 17 underlines Esther's new strength. Now Mordecai "*did according to all that Esther commanded him.*" Whereas earlier he had commanded her (v. 8), now she commands him, and he obeys (v. 17). Whereas he had been her counselor (2:10), commander (v. 8), and adviser (vv. 13–14), beginning with verse 16 Mordecai takes his cues from the newly empowered Esther.

THE LITERARY ASPECTS OF ESTHER 4:1–17

Chapter 4 focuses on the interaction between Esther and Mordecai—a dialogue that contributes to the story in several ways. First, through a series of suspenseful interactions, it develops the plot. Along the way the reader wonders: Will Mordecai be able to communicate with Esther? Will he convince her to intercede before the king? Will Esther risk her life? Will she perish? Second, the dialogue of chapter 4 also shows Esther's development as a character. Whereas in the earlier parts of the chapter she appeared as someone both ignorant (v. 5) and wisely cautious (v. 11), by the final verses she is decisive, courageous, and authoritative (vv. 16–17). She even commands Mordecai, who promptly obeys.

In addition, while later instances will be more striking, we see in chapter 4 the first suggestions of reversal, a prevalent theme throughout the book. Whereas Mordecai had once taken care of Esther (2:7), in this chapter Esther attempts to return the favor, though he refuses her help (v. 4). Whereas Mordecai had given counsel and commands to Esther, in this passage she begins to give commands to him. Once Esther had typified the weak Persian woman, valued only for her beauty; in chapter 4 she emerges as a person of power and courage. And, of course, with Esther's empowerment, the tide of events began to change in favor of the Jews. She was fundamentally responsible for the reversal of Jewish fortune.[7]

ESTHER 4:1–17 FROM A CHRISTIAN PERSPECTIVE

The Inspiration of Esther

The first three chapters of Esther portrayed women as victims of capricious male power. Even Esther flowed with the current of the king's chauvinism as it carried her to royal dignity. In the first half of chapter 4 Esther remained "out of the loop," dependent upon Mordecai for news and counsel. Yet, when he confessed his faith in providence and suggested that she had come into the kingdom "for such a time as this," something happened to change Esther from victimized to vigorous. She began to assert herself and her authority, even going so far as to give commands to her surrogate father Mordecai. From 4:16 to the end of the book, Esther acts with wisdom and power.

Given the pervasive sexism of the ancient Middle Eastern culture, we marvel at the strength of Esther. The contrast between the powerlessness of women in chapters 1–3 and her assertiveness in chapter 4 highlights Esther's unique genius. She stood alone, above all women and men in the Persian empire. She accepted her providential calling even though this endangered her royal position and her very life. "Do not worry," Esther stated. "If I perish, I perish!"

Throughout the centuries, Esther's sense of providence and her courage have inspired numerous Christian women and men to greatness, but the example of Henrietta Mears is one of the most inspiring. As early as 1945, she had accomplished marvelous works for the kingdom of God. Under her leadership the Sunday school of Hollywood Presbyterian Church had grown to be one of the largest and most effective in the world. Her College Department had introduced hundreds of young men and women to Christ, many of whom went on to serve the Lord in missions and ordained ministry. Dr. Mears' curriculum and inspiration had given birth to Gospel Light Publications, and following the Spirit's guidance, she had founded Forest Home Christian Conference Center in the mountains of Southern California.

Yet, in the aftermath of World War II, Henrietta Mears felt a deep restlessness in her spirit. A visit to Europe in 1947 confirmed her sense of the world's desperation. While in Germany, she observed that "disillusionment and undefined godlessness have taken over. Hardly anyone goes to church. . . . Men are hating culture and religion. They are rebelling against God."[8] Dr. Mears saw similar devastation throughout the world, including the United States:

> But the same processes that brought Germany low are working in the United States today. . . . [I]n America we see divorce and drunkenness increasing. What is happening to our world?— crime, ruthlessness, killing, mass starvation, mass bombing, mass exportation of slaves! And there is no penitence among the nations today![9]

On her return voyage from Europe to America, Henrietta Mears felt a disquieting sense of God's call upon her life. She began to read and to meditate on the story of Esther. In the midst of her despair about the world (which paralleled Jewish desperation in Esther 4), Dr. Mears found new purpose through the counsel of Mordecai and the response of Esther in verses 13–16. Perhaps God had brought Henrietta to her place in his kingdom "for such a time as this"! As it did for Queen Esther, Mordecai's advice emboldened Dr. Mears. She began to believe that she could make a greater difference in a dying world, so she committed herself anew to seeking God's direction and power.

In June of 1947, Henrietta Mears gathered for prayer with four young men. As they sought God's vision for the world, they experienced the presence of God in a way they compared to Pentecost. During their time of supplication, God revealed his plan for their efforts to renew the world. They would focus on college students. College campuses, they believed, held the key to world leadership. Dr. Mears and her partners marched forth from their prayer vigil with renewed vision and power. God would use them to impact the world for Christ!

And indeed, he did! Among those young men praying with Dr. Mears were Richard Halverson (current chaplain of the U. S. Senate), Louis H. Evans, Jr. (leader of renewal in the Presbyterian Church), and Bill Bright (founder of Campus Crusade for Christ). Along with Dr. Mears they launched a new conference to prepare collegians for world evangelization—the College Briefing Conference at Forest Home. Since 1947 God has done amazing things at this conference, leading hundreds to faith in Christ, calling hundreds more into full-time ministry, and empowering thousands to serve as lay disciples. College Briefing has also given birth to world-changing ministries, including that of Billy Graham, who dates the turning point in his ministry to the College Briefing conference of 1949.

The words of Mordecai and the example of Esther inspired Henrietta Mears to even greater works than her amazing accomplishments prior to 1947. Like Dr. Mears, we who read Esther 4 as Christians can see between the lines of Mordecai's reticence to mention God. Like the Jewish sages and the apostle Paul, we know that God "works all things together for good" according to his divine purposes (Rom. 8:28). God has placed us, wherever we are, for his reasons: to do his will and to represent him in our fallen world. The Spirit of God fills us to proclaim Christ in all parts of the globe, starting right where we are—at home, at school, in our neighborhoods, in our places of work.

Our impact upon the world may never be as great as that of Henrietta Mears or Martin Luther King, Jr., yet, who knows what God has planned for us? Our task is not to fret about the scope of our influence, but to make a difference for God right where we are and leave providence to him. Sometimes we will not even be sure of God's specific guidance. We may experience the same ambiguity that Mordecai expressed when looking for deliverance in "another place." Yet in such times of uncertainty we can grasp in faith the promise of God's presence and power to use us for his work in the world (Matt. 28:18–20; Acts 1:8).

This is what has happened to Sherry. She has discovered an unexpected ministry in her local Burger King restaurant. Each week she spends several mornings there preparing Bible studies while enjoying a cup of coffee. Over the past months she has become acquainted with many employees and "the regulars." Increasingly, she has been able to share the love of Christ with these people, even though it means less time for study. A few days ago, Sherry encountered one of the employees in the parking lot. Paul was deeply distraught. When Sherry asked what was wrong, he shared that his sister had just died from a stroke, leaving behind a husband and several children. Right there in the parking lot of Burger King, Sherry ministered to Paul's needs; she listened to his grief and prayed for him and his family.

I couldn't help but think of the words of Mordecai when Sherry told me this story. Without doubt, she had "come to the Burger King for such a time as this"! Indeed, as we offer ourselves to God for his work, he will direct us to unexpected opportunities for service. As we pray, "Lord, use me!" we will discover our rightful place in his kingdom and will experience the joy of being used by God for his providential purposes.

NOTES

1. Paton, *Book of Esther*, p. 216.

2. Some translations soften Mordecai's boldness in sending an order to Esther. For example, "And [Mordecai] told [Hatach] to *urge* her to go into the king's presence to beg for mercy" (v. 8, NIV). But this translation misconstrues the Hebrew verb, ṣāwâ, which means "to command" or "to charge" in an authoritative sense (Brown, Driver, and Briggs, *Lexicon*, s.v. "ṣāwâ").

3. Moore, *Esther*, p. 50.

4. Humphreys, "Esther and Mordecai," p. 111. But see the contrary opinion of Fox, *Character*, p. 63.

5. The NKJV translation in Proverbs 16:4, "for Himself," misinterprets the Hebrew. See Hubbard, *Proverbs*, p. 235.

6. Gordis, "Religion," p. 374.

7. A. Lacocque, *The Feminine Unconventional: Four Subversive Figures in Israel's Tradition* (Minneapolis: Fortress, 1990), p. 72.

8. Quoted in E. M. Baldwin and D. V. Benson, *Henrietta Mears and How She Did It!* (Glendale, CA: Gospel Light Publications [Regal Books], 1966), p. 229.

9. Quoted in Baldwin and Benson, *Henrietta Mears*, pp. 228–29.

CHAPTER FIVE

Esther's Favor and Haman's Pride

Esther 5:1–14

PRIDE GOETH BEFORE A FALL

During my senior year of high school, I applied for several scholarships to finance my college education. When I was chosen as a finalist in the Frank L. Fox Competition, I was informed that I would be interviewed by a panel of judges. Just prior to the interview I received good news from one of the colleges to which I had applied: they had accepted me and had agreed to provided a generous amount of financial aid. Basking in the surety of such lofty endorsements, I went in to my interview for the Fox scholarship with unusual self-confidence—even a touch of conceit. Things had been going so well for me, it was likely the Fox scholarship would fall into my lap as well. Throughout the interview I spoke boldly about myself and my achievements. I even boasted of my recent acceptance to college and of the generous financial package I had been offered. With momentum building in my direction I dabbled in uncharacteristic pride. It felt good, and I was soaring with confidence as I left the interview.

Yet weeks later when the selection was made, I did not receive the Fox scholarship. It went to my friend Roger, even though his high school record was not as strong as mine. During his interview Roger had felt insecure and awkward. He had spoken humbly, with suitable deference to members of the committee. As I discovered later, my pride was the very factor that had alienated the judges. In fact, they completely overlooked my strong resume to choose a student with a more honorable, humble character.

Chapter 5 of Esther presents the reader with a similar contrast between humility and pride. One attitude earns the favor of the king; the other attitude foreshadows an imminent fall.

ESTHER APPROACHES THE KING (5:1–5)

5:1 Now it happened on the third day that Esther
put on her royal robes and stood in the inner court of
the king's palace, across from the king's house, while
the king sat on his royal throne in the royal house,
facing the entrance of the house.
2 So it was, when the king saw Queen Esther
standing in the court, that she found favor in his
sight, and the king held out to Esther the golden
scepter that was in his hand. Then Esther went near
and touched the top of the scepter.
3 And the king said to her, "What do you wish,
Queen Esther? What is your request? It shall be given
to you—up to half the kingdom!"
4 So Esther answered, "If it pleases the king, let
the king and Haman come today to the banquet that I
have prepared for him."
5 Then the king said, "Bring Haman quickly, that
he may do as Esther has said." So the king and
Haman went to the banquet that Esther had prepared.

Esther 5:1–5

At the close of chapter 4 Esther had decided to approach the king
on behalf of her people. She commanded Mordecai to direct all Jewish citizens of Susa to fast for the three days prior to her appearance
before Ahasuerus (4:16). According to Persian law, an uninvited visi-
tor to the king could be put to death at the king's pleasure (4:11). If,
however, the king wished to welcome his unannounced guest he
would extend his golden scepter

Chapter 5 begins *"on the third day"* of the Jewish fast (v. 1). Esther
dressed carefully in her finest royal garb in order to delight the king
and to remind him of her standing as his queen. She stood in *"the inner court of the king's palace"* in a place where he could see her from his
throne (v. 1). When the king saw Esther he did not condemn her to
death, but instead *"she found favor in his sight, and the king held out to
Esther the golden scepter"* (v. 2). She received his gesture of welcome
by touching the top of his scepter.

Obviously pleased with her appearance, Ahasuerus asked Esther
what she wanted. He offered to give her anything, *"up to half the kingdom!"* (v. 3). This apparently magnanimous offer, repeated again in

verse 6, was a common expression that was not meant to be taken literally.[1] It emphasized the king's pleasure in Esther's company and his desire to respond favorably to her need. A modern paraphrase would be: "I will give you anything your heart desires."

Instead of immediately asking the king to spare her people, Esther invited the king and Haman to come to a banquet that she had prepared (v. 4). She phrased her request carefully, using traditional words of honor: "*if it pleases the king.*" Yet, we find Esther's response surprising. This was her golden opportunity. The king would grant her any request. What an opportune time to intercede for her people! Why did she delay? Although the text does not answer this question directly, it is obvious that this loss of opportunity intensifies the suspense of the story.

Another puzzle in this incident is Esther's inclusion of Haman in her invitation. Certainly she could have made her appeal to the king without the risk of Haman's opposition, so why include him in the festivities? For centuries scholars have puzzled over this question without arriving at any consensus.[2] Ancient Jewish rabbis suggested twelve possible reasons for Haman's inclusion without agreeing on any one of them.[3] Although we cannot determine Esther's motivation, we can note how Haman's presence at her banquet added an element of danger and risk and thus heightened the tension of the story. If Esthei dares to ask the king to spare the Jews in the presence of the very man who sought their destruction, will she prevail? By including Haman in Esther's invitation the author raises the "degree-of-difficulty" factor for her intercession, and thus heightens the drama.

ESTHER'S FIRST BANQUET (5:6–8)

6 At the banquet of wine the king said to Esther, "What is your petition? It shall be granted you. What is your request, up to half the kingdom? It shall be done!"

7 Then Esther answered and said, "My petition and request is this:

8 If I have found favor in the sight of the king, and if it pleases the king to grant my petition and fulfill my request, then let the king and Haman come to the banquet which I will prepare for them, and tomorrow I will do as the king has said."

Esther 5:6–8

The last part of verse 5 describes the king and Haman going to Esther's banquet. Verse 6 places the action *"at the banquet of wine."* Typically, in that culture, a time of drinking wine would follow the meal, providing a context for jovial discussion.[4] At that point, Ahasuerus once more asked Esther what she desired, *"up to half the kingdom"* (v. 6). Again Esther began her request with due reverence: *"If I have found favor in the sight of the king, and if it pleases the king to grant my petition"* (v. 8). Even though she knew already that she had won the king's favor and that he had offered her anything she desired, nevertheless, Esther exercised appropriate humility in her request.

As in verse 4, once again Esther chose not to ask the king to spare her people. Instead she invited him and Haman to another banquet (v. 8). And once again the author of the book does not account for her hesitation, but uses it to add suspense. The reader wonders: Is Esther losing her nerve? Why is she procrastinating? Will she ever be bold enough to intercede for her people? What if the king tires of Esther again and chooses not to attend her banquet? From a literary point of view, Esther's delay in making her request successfully builds the level of reader-anxiety and allows the story to develop in the rest of chapter 5 and in 6. If Esther had presented her request in 5:8, the entertaining and educational elements of 5:9–6:14 would have been forfeited.

HAMAN'S PRIDEFUL OBSESSION (5:9–14)

9 So Haman went out that day joyful and with a glad heart; but when Haman saw Mordecai in the king's gate, and that he did not stand or tremble before him, he was filled with indignation against Mordecai.

10 Nevertheless Haman restrained himself and went home, and he sent and called for his friends and his wife Zeresh.

11 Then Haman told them of his great riches, the multitude of his children, everything in which the king had promoted him, and how he had advanced him above the officials and servants of the king.

12 Moreover Haman said, "Besides, Queen Esther invited no one but me to come in with the king to the banquet that she prepared; and tomorrow I am again invited by her, along with the king.

13 Yet all this avails me nothing, so long as I see
Mordecai the Jew sitting at the king's gate."
14 Then his wife Zeresh and all his friends said to him,
"Let a gallows be made, fifty cubits high, and in the
morning suggest to the king that Mordecai be hanged
on it; then go merrily with the king to the banquet." And
the thing pleased Haman; so he had the gallows made.

Esther 5:9–14

Haman's delight over having been included in Esther's banquet
turned sour when he noticed Mordecai's failure to bow before him (v. 9).
The translation *"indignation"* actually gives too much credit to Haman and
avoids the literal sense of the Hebrew.[5] A more accurate translation of
verse 9 would reveal that Haman was "filled with *rage* against Mordecai."

Yet because he knew what awaited Mordecai, Haman was able to
restrain himself from any further action (v. 10). Upon arriving home
he gathered his friends and his wife together in order to brag about
his great achievements (v. 11). This boasting provided solace after his
encounter with Mordecai by quenching Haman's anger in a sea of
pride. Before his friends and his wife, he proceeded to highlight his
many virtues: riches, progeny, royal favors, and promotions (v. 11).
His bravado is ironic, however, in that his audience certainly knew
all of this already. The purpose of his boasting was obviously to bol-
ster his own ego, not to communicate information. However, at this
point, he provided new information for his admirers—he told them
of his privileged status as the only one invited to join the king at
Esther's banquet. The reader, of course, begins to sense the irony of
Haman's boast. That in which he takes such enormous pride will be
the very thing that brings about his shameful downfall.

Yet Haman could not enjoy all of his successes because Mordecai
remained stubbornly insubordinate (v. 13). The Hebrew of verse 13
literally reads, "But all of this, it is not adequate for me." Nothing
could satisfy Haman as long as one man failed to honor him. It is the
description of a man obsessed, driven by his need for approval, and
dissatisfied even with his formidable achievements.

Upon hearing his complaints, Haman's wife and friends attempted to
assuage him by proposing an exaggerated death for Mordecai: he would
be hanged on a gallows that was *"fifty cubits high"* (v. 14). A cubit was the
length of the forearm from elbow to fingertip, ranging from seventeen to
twenty-one inches.[6] Mordecai's gallows, therefore, would rise to the

ridiculous height of approximately seventy-five feet. This literary hyperbole accentuates Haman's maniacal anger with Mordecai, which would be assuaged only by an extravagant execution. So as verse 14 reports, he acted on this suggestion and ordered such a gallows to be made.

The Literary Aspects of Esther 5:1-14

The plot thickens in chapter 5. Just to recap the events: Esther risked her life by approaching the king, who gladly received her and offered to oblige any request. Yet she delayed making her request and invited the king to a private banquet instead, graciously extending her invitation to include Haman. Then, when she had a second chance to help her people, at the banquet, Esther procrastinated once again. Her delay in resolving the problem heightens the drama of the story by enhancing its suspense.[7] Her delay also serves the literary purpose of allowing for the development of further strategic events and circumstances that add to the drama of Haman's fall.

Another literary highlight of chapter 5 is the motif of banquets, which ties the entire book together.[8] Notice how significant events occur and decisions are made during feasts, usually when the participants are drinking wine. The narrative also suggests that the person hosting the banquet holds the balance of power. Thus, whereas the king ruled over his banquets in chapter 1, Esther defined the terms of relationship when she acted as hostess in chapter 5 (and 7).

With regard to character development, chapter 5 contrasts the clever humility of Esther with the uncontrollable pride of Haman. Esther knew how to act humbly before the king and to communicate with suitable deference. As a result, she received favor and opportunity. On the contrary, Haman's pride drove him to the absurdity of boasting before his friends and wife, telling them what they already had known. His pride so obscured his judgment that manifold successes could not balance the insult of one cantankerous Jew.

We also see the influence of Jewish wisdom in this chapter. For example, although Esther's way of approaching the king adds to the suspense of the story, it also reflects her faithfulness to Jewish wisdom. She did not bowl the king over with her request; rather, she approached him patiently, as recommend by the sages: "By long forbearance a ruler is persuaded, / And a gentle tongue breaks a bone" (Prov. 25:15).[9] She shows understanding of one of Jewish wisdom's fundamental doctrines, which Gerhard von Rad calls "The Doctrine of the Proper Time."[10] Ecclesiastes applies this doctrine specifically to the case of approaching a king:

> Where the word of a king is, there is power;
> And who may say to him, "What are you doing?"
> He who keeps his command will experience nothing harmful;
> And a wise man's heart discerns both time and judgment,
> Because for every matter there is a time and judgment. . . .
>
> *Ecclesiastes 8:4–7a*

Even when she had secured the king's favor, Esther continued to communicate graciously: "He who loves purity of heart / And has grace on his lips, / The king will be his friend" (Prov. 22:11). By means of her caution and rhetorical grace Esther earned the king's friendship, thus showing herself to be a paradigm of wisdom.

Equally significant to Jewish wisdom, the portrayal of Haman in chapter 5 expands upon his foolishness, a trait initially conveyed in chapter 3. There, Haman's venting of his anger showed him to be the sort of fool mentioned in Prov. 29:11 (see the commentary on chapter 3). Esther 5:10 confirms and elaborates upon this characterization. Whereas Esther 3 had only hinted at Haman's pride, chapter 5 parades it before his wife, his friends, and the readers of the Book of Esther. According to Jewish wisdom, pride and folly go hand in hand: "Do you see a man wise in his own eyes? / There is more hope for a fool than for him" (Prov. 26:12). The Jewish sages condemn pride as worse than folly. It is an abomination: "Everyone proud in heart is an abomination to the LORD; / Though they join forces, none will go unpunished" (Prov. 16:5). Not only is pride evil, but ruinous: "Pride goes before destruction, / And a haughty spirit before a fall" (Prov. 16:18). Thus, from the perspective of Jewish wisdom, Haman is portrayed as an increasingly boastful fool with the logical implication that his pride foreshadows his fall, which begins in the next chapter.

ESTHER 5:1–14 FROM A CHRISTIAN PERSPECTIVE

The Example of Esther's Pragmatism

In chapter 5 Esther grows in her stature as a woman of wisdom and action. She risked her life by approaching the king unannounced, and once she had earned his favor, she advanced her agenda adroitly, demonstrating a masterful sense of timing and clever rhetorical skills.

Whereas a critic might accuse Esther of playing games, of continuing to be a hesitant pawn in a man's game, from the perspective of Jewish wisdom Esther appears to be in control. Not only did she approach the king with astute caution, but she moved him (and subsequent interaction with him) into her domain so that she could control the action. Yes, Esther played the role of demure wife, but, in fact, she used her position of influence to arrange the game pieces according to her strategy. The checkmate of Haman was drawing near, but Esther was the chess mistress firmly in control of the game.

Carla felt a bit like Esther as she approached the elders of her church. She wanted to teach a Bible study but faced unusual scrutiny because of her gender. Her church, though theoretically supportive of women in ministry, had never before allowed a woman to teach an adult Bible study for men and women. Carla had to "play the game" of approval, including special meetings with the elders in which she submitted her proposed curriculum and answered questions concerning her personal integrity. Yet she responded to the elders with respect and honesty, and ultimately they affirmed her leadership and approved her Bible study. I am sure that many women would have given up on the lengthy, convoluted process, but Carla's determined objective was to teach the Bible rather than to display her frustration. She was a pragmatist who, like Esther, ordered her life by "The Doctrine of the Proper Time." And God honored her wise and humble attitude, as he did Esther's.

Overcoming the Obsession of Haman

I must confess that when reading chapter 5 I relate more to Haman than to Esther. I can understand how privileged he felt after being invited to Esther's private banquet, and I empathize with the depletion of his joy when he saw Mordecai still refusing to bow. I do not expect people to bow down before me, of course, but I do have a disproportionate need to be liked by everybody. On the scales of my ego, one person's disapproval can weigh (disproportionately) as much as the praises of a hundred! Many Christians share my obsession with approval. And while being liked is not a bad thing in and of itself, our need for approval can overwhelm our better judgment and destroy our joy. We can end up like Haman, blessed beyond measure, but coveting the one thing we do not possess—the approval of our "Mordecai."

The first letter of Peter provides an antidote to pride and to the obsessive need for approval:

> Yes, all of you be submissive to one another, and be clothed with humility, for "God resists the proud, But gives grace to the humble." Therefore humble yourselves under the mighty hand of God, that He may exalt you in due time, casting your care upon Him, for He cares for you.
>
> *1 Peter 5:5–7*

Peter calls us to humble ourselves before God, to bow before his majesty. When we submit ourselves to God, when we are overwhelmed by his care for us, then we find that the opinions of others lose their power. Moreover, when we submit our lives to God and seek his pleasure alone, we not only experience freedom, but God actually exalts us in his time. Once I have been lifted up by a God who cares for me, I find human disapproval (or approval, for that matter) growing "strangely dim in the light of God's glory and grace."

Recently, I have been preaching a series on human sexuality. In my sermons I have been blunt about behavior that the Bible regards as sinful. Although the vast majority of church members have been grateful for my sermons, a few have criticized me for being too harsh. At times I have felt my need for approval tempt me to back away from my convictions. In these moments I have turned to the Lord in prayer. By humbling myself before God and casting my care upon him, I have been able to balance my need to be liked with the necessity to share the truth of God's Word even at the expense of "popularity."

NOTES

1. Baldwin, *Esther*, p. 86.
2. See the list of options in Moore, *Esther*, p. 56.
3. Paton, *Book of Esther*, p. 234. He refers to *Babylonian Talmud, Megillâ* 15b.

4. Paton, *Book of Esther*, p. 236.

5. The Hebrew term *ḥēmâ* means "heat, rage, wrath" (Brown, Driver, and Briggs, *Lexicon*, s.v. "*ḥēmâ*").

6. O. R. Sellers, "Weights and Measures," *IDB*. See especially pp. 836–37.

7. Moore, *Esther*, p. 57.

8. Berg, *Esther*, pp. 31–39.

9. Cited by Talmon, "Wisdom," p. 437.

10. von Rad, *Wisdom*, pp. 138–43.

11. Cited by Talmon, "Wisdom," p. 444.

CHAPTER SIX

The King Honors Mordecai
Over Haman

Esther 6:1–14

ESTHER AND THE HARDY BOYS

As a youth I read every one of the Hardy Boys mystery stories. These books, written under the pseudonym of Franklin W. Dixon, relate the adventures of two high-school boys, Frank and Joe Hardy. Inspired by their father, a famous detective, the Hardy boys unwittingly stumble into the middle of criminal conspiracies and unsolved mysteries. Their natural curiosity leads them to follow up clues, to solve riddles, and to send criminals to prison.

The Hardy Boys mysteries are fun to read in part because of "coincidences" that shape the plot. Strangers who "accidentally" run Frank and Joe off the road in the early chapters of a book turn out to be notorious lawbreakers who ultimately meet their doom because of the boys' efforts. Often they "just happen" to get involved in a case that ends up related to their father's own secret investigation. Such coincidences add to the reader's entertainment. In the first chapters one wonders: How will the incidental details of the plot be tied together by the end of the story? The enjoyment of the subsequent chapters is finding out the answer to that question.

The Book of Esther reminds me of the Hardy Boys mysteries because it is replete with apparent "coincidences." Beginning in chapter 6, these coincidences appear one right after another, delighting the reader while subtly underlining the providence of God, who insures that the right things "just happen" to take place.

THE KING'S SLEEPLESS NIGHT (6:1–3)

> 6:1 That night the king could not sleep. So one was commanded to bring the book of the records of the chronicles; and they were read before the king.
>
> 2 And it was found written that Mordecai had told of Bigthana and Teresh, two of the king's eunuchs, the doorkeepers who had sought to lay hands on King Ahasuerus.
>
> 3 Then the king said, "What honor or dignity has been bestowed on Mordecai for this?" And the king's servants who attended him said, "Nothing has been done for him."
>
> *Esther 6:1–3*

"That night," the very night after Haman had constructed a gallows for Mordecai (v.1; see 5:14), the king "just happened" to suffer from insomnia. He commanded one of his servants to read from *"the book of the records of the chronicles."* No doubt such boring reading would certainly help Ahasuerus fall asleep. By some "fluke," however, the servant read the section of the records that documented Mordecai's effort to save the king from assassination (v. 2). The story of Mordecai's faithfulness (described in detail in Esther 2:21–23) had been carefully recorded in "the book of the chronicles." Curiously, at the time when his life had been saved, Ahasuerus had not felt inclined to honor Mordecai for this valuable deed.

In the midst of his sleepless night, however, the king had a change of heart. He asked his servants, *"What honor or dignity has been bestowed on Mordecai for this?"* obviously with the intention of making sure that Mordecai had received a proper reward (v. 3). When the servants responded, *"Nothing has been done for him,"* the stage was set for the dramatic episode to follow.

Several scholars single out this passage as the turning point of Esther.[1] Yet, though events from this point onward do favor the Jews, the reversal of Jewish fortune already had begun with Esther's willingness to appear before the king (4:16). Furthermore, her successful manipulation of the king and Haman in chapter 5 serve to notify the reader of good things to come. However, it is true that in chapter 6 and continuing, reversal of fortune significantly shapes the plot.

HAMAN IS FORCED TO HONOR MORDECAI (6:4–11)

4 So the king said, "Who is in the court?" Now Haman had just entered the outer court of the king's palace to suggest that the king hang Mordecai on the gallows that he had prepared for him.

5 The king's servants said to him, "Haman is there, standing in the court." And the king said, "Let him come in."

6 So Haman came in, and the king asked him, "What shall be done for the man whom the king delights to honor?" Now Haman thought in his heart, "Whom would the king delight to honor more than me?"

7 And Haman answered the king, "For the man whom the king delights to honor,

8 let a royal robe be brought which the king has worn, and a horse on which the king has ridden, which has a royal crest placed on its head.

9 Then let this robe and horse be delivered to the hand of one of the king's most noble princes, that he may array the man whom the king delights to honor. Then parade him on horseback through the city square, and proclaim before him: 'Thus shall it be done to the man whom the king delights to honor!'"

10 Then the king said to Haman, "Hurry, take the robe and the horse, as you have suggested, and do so for Mordecai the Jew who sits within the king's gate! Leave nothing undone of all that you have spoken."

11 So Haman took the robe and the horse, arrayed Mordecai and led him on horseback through the city square, and proclaimed before him, "Thus shall it be done to the man whom the king delights to honor!"

Esther 6:4–11

After learning that Mordecai had not been honored for his loyalty, Ahasuerus asked: *"Who is in the court?"* (v. 4). He sought one of his advisers to suggest a suitable reward for Mordecai. Coincidentally, Haman *"had just entered the outer court of the king's palace"* (v. 4). The reader notes the irony (and coincidence) of Haman's presence, since he had intended to persuade the king to hang Mordecai.

The king invited Haman into his court in order to ask him what should be done for Mordecai. Ahasuerus "happened" to phrase the question without mentioning Mordecai by name: *"'What shall be done for the man whom the king delights to honor?'"* (v. 6). Haman, obsessed as usual with his own pride, could not fathom that the king would intend to honor anyone other than Haman himself, so he proposed an elaborate rite. First, he suggested, *"let a royal robe be brought which the king has worn"* (v. 8). This robe would be placed upon the man to be honored by the king. Notice that Haman asked for not only a royal robe but one that the king actually had worn. In the ancient world there was no greater honor than to wear one of the king's own robes.[2] Moreover, Haman proposed that the honoree be placed on one of the king's own horses, identified by the *"royal crest placed on its head"* (v. 8).[3] The robing would be done by *"one of the king's most noble princes,"* who would then lead the honoree through the city of Susa, proclaiming: *"Thus shall it be done to the man whom the king delights to honor!"* (v. 9). Expecting to be the recipient of the king's esteem, Haman devised a ceremony that would promote him before the people as the king's equal in honor and glory.

But the axe began to fall on Haman's pride (v. 10). The king took his advice but applied it in a way that horrified Haman: *"Hurry, take the robe and the horse, as you have suggested, and do so for Mordecai the Jew who sits within the king's gate!"* Not only would Mordecai escape from Haman's noose, not only would Mordecai receive public adulation, not only would Mordecai receive what Haman had designed for himself, but Haman would be the one to proclaim Mordecai's greatness to the city! Dramatically and ironically the tables had begun to turn on Haman, who had no choice but to obey the king's command. We can only begin to imagine Haman's revulsion and shame as he paraded his archenemy before the people.

HAMAN'S DOWNFALL PREDICTED (6:12–14)

12 Afterward Mordecai went back to the king's gate. But Haman hurried to his house, mourning and with his head covered.
13 When Haman told his wife Zeresh and all his friends everything that had happened to him, his wise men and his wife Zeresh said to him, "If Mordecai, before whom you have begun to fall, is of Jewish descent, you will not prevail against him but will surely fall before him."

14 While they were still talking with him, the
king's eunuchs came, and hastened to bring Haman
to the banquet which Esther had prepared.

Esther 6:12–14

After completing the unwelcome task of honoring his enemy, Haman *"hurried to his house, mourning and with his head covered"* out of shame (v. 12). Quickly he recounted to *"his wife Zeresh and all his friends everything that had happened to him"* (v. 13). What a contrast between this woeful report and his earlier boasting (5:11–12)! After hearing what had transpired, Haman's wife and friends, here ironically called "wise men," passed judgment on his fate: *"If Mordecai, before whom you have begun to fall, is of Jewish descent, you will not prevail against him but will surely fall before him"* (v. 13). Even to his closest friends it was obvious that since Mordecai the Jew had prevailed over Haman in earning the king's favor, surely Haman's plot against the Jews was doomed to fail. His downfall was imminent. After this prophetic remark was uttered, *"the king's eunuchs"* whisked Haman away to Esther's banquet where his fate would be sealed (v. 14). Thus verse 14 serves as a transition between the events of chapter 6 and those of chapter 7.

THE LITERARY ASPECTS OF ESTHER 6:1–14

With the unfolding of chapter six, coincidences build upon coincidences. (1) The king could not sleep on the night just before Haman intended to hang Mordecai. (2) The king's servant happened to read about Mordecai's action that had saved the king. (Now the reader understands why the author of Esther includes the apparently inconsequential account of Mordecai's effort in the last verses of chapter 2.) (3) When Ahasuerus looked for an adviser, Haman had just entered the outer court of the palace. (4) Because of his bad timing and foolish pride, Haman ended up proposing an ostentatious ceremony for someone who turned out to be Mordecai. (5) By his own recommendation Haman became the one to lead his enemy through the city. All of these coincidences add to the pleasure and anticipation of the reader.

The motif of reversal that began in the end of chapter 4 and continued throughout chapter 5 with Esther's empowerment, reaches an apex on the king's sleepless night. With that event in chapter 6 the reversal reaches a complete 180 degrees. From this point on, all aspects of the story now flow in favor of the Jews, especially Mordecai. By the close of chapter 6, Haman's doom appears to be sealed, though the reader does not yet know how that will occur.

Chapter 6 also abounds with irony. When verse 4 states that Haman *"had just entered the outer court . . . to suggest that the king hang Mordecai,"* the reader knows in advance that Haman's plot will be foiled. As Haman presents his elaborate ceremony to honor someone he believes to be himself, the reader "sees" what Haman does not see: all of this will exalt Mordecai, his own archenemy. A further irony is the very detail of Haman's proposal, involving *"one of the king's most noble princes"* (v. 9), that required his own participation as the one who paraded Mordecai around the city.

With regard to the theme of Jewish wisdom, chapter 6 not only reiterates Haman's pride, which was presented in chapter 5, but also shows how this pride actually caused his disgrace. According to Proverbs 11:2: "When pride comes, then comes shame; / But with the humble is wisdom." Pride leads the fool to experience shame. Thus, Haman's excessive pride led him to propose an ostentatious ceremony to honor someone who turned out to be his enemy. His own prideful words led to his shameful exaltation of Mordecai.

That Haman should end up praising Mordecai also fits the mindset of wisdom. Proverbs 14:19 states: "The evil will bow before the good, / And the wicked at the gates of the righteous." Haman, the archetype of evil in Esther, did indeed bow before the good, represented by Mordecai. In his comments on this proverb, David Hubbard could very well be describing Haman's exaltation of Mordecai: "The note of public embarrassment that plagues the foolish is heightened in the picture of utter public subjection that will be their lot."[5] Both of the proverbs illustrated in chapter 6 exemplify the theme of reversal—a comprehensive theme common both to wisdom literature and to the Book of Esther.

ESTHER 6:1–14 FROM A CHRISTIAN PERSPECTIVE

Mutuality Between Esther and Mordecai

Women are almost invisible in chapter 6. We should remember, however, that Mordecai's exaltation in these passages depended on

Esther's earlier action. When he had discovered the plot against the king, Esther made sure to inform the king "in Mordecai's name" (2:22). Had she not been careful to give credit to Mordecai, then the exaltation of Mordecai in chapter 6 would not have occurred. Even as Esther's advancement had once depended upon Mordecai (chap. 2), so now his promotion to honor depended upon her. The Book of Esther continues to reflect a startling level of comfort with Esther's power and influence as a woman. In a small way, the story of Esther foreshadows the kind of mutuality between men and women developed in Paul's writings (1 Cor. 7; 11:11–12; Eph. 5:18–33).

Coincidence or Providence?

Like the author of the Hardy Boys mysteries, the author of Esther uses coincidence to develop the plot and to delight the reader. From a Christian perspective, however, we see these happenstances as a sign of God's providence. While from a human perspective life is full of accidents, from a biblical perspective life is full of events that reflect God's sovereign plan. (For development of this theme, see the comments on Ezra 1.)

So many times we cannot identify the signs of God's providence until after events have unfolded according to his plan. Then, in retrospect, we recognize that seeming flukes were not accidental at all. This was true of the events that led to my coming to Irvine as pastor of the Presbyterian church. Looking back on the process now, I can see how God directed events in a most "coincidental" manner. In September 1990, I began to receive phone calls from the Search Committee at Irvine Presbyterian. At that time I had not the slightest interest in leaving my position in Hollywood. Moreover, progress on my doctoral dissertation had been stalled for six years. Even though I had sent several chapters to my adviser, I had not heard from him at all—a bad sign! Discouraged and perplexed, in the last week of September I travelled to Massachusetts to discuss my work with him. To my utter amazement he praised my work, suggesting only a few changes and predicting for the first time that the thesis would certainly be acceptable.

During my plane flight back to California I felt a profound change in my hopefulness about the future. I could finally imagine completing my dissertation and getting on with my life. The very day after I returned from Cambridge my secretary insisted that I call "that nice man in Irvine." I cannot imagine that I would have been open to God's call if I had not just learned that my dissertation would be accepted. Was this juxtaposition of events just a strange coincidence—or God's providential work in my life?

During the next few months, coincidences piled up one upon another (as they did in Esther 6). The search committee in Irvine followed a carefully prescribed course of selection. From my point of view, however, the process was excruciatingly slow. Waiting upon the Lord has never been my strong point, and during that difficult time of anxiety and tension I decided to go the local Christian bookstore to see if I could find a good book on waiting. I needed help! Sure enough, I found one appropriate for my needs, *Waiting: Finding Hope When God Seems Silent.*[6] This was just the book for me. Then to my amazement, I noticed that the book was written by Ben Patterson—the man who had just finished fourteen years as pastor of Irvine Presbyterian Church! Reading Ben's excellent study of waiting not only helped me to rely more completely upon God, it also prepared me to follow in his footsteps. Was this another strange coincidence—or God's providential work in my life?

As the Master Author of human history, God weaves together the stories of our lives. To surprise us with joy and to accomplish his inscrutable will, God fills our lives with apparent flukes that, upon deeper inspection, reflect his sovereign care. Coincidence or providence? Our answer depends upon seeing with the eyes of faith.

NOTES

1. Y. T. Radday, "Chiasm in Joshua, Judges, and Others," *Linguistica Biblica,* 3 (1973):9; reproduced and reaffirmed by Berg, *Esther,* p. 108.

2. Keil and Delitzsch, *Commentary,* p. 360.

3. For a picture of a horse with a crown on its head, see Moore, *Esther,* plate 4.

4. Moore, *Esther,* p. 66.

5. Hubbard, *Proverbs,* p. 318.

6. Patterson, *Waiting: Finding Hope When God Seems Silent* (Downers Grove: InterVarsity, 1989).

CHAPTER SEVEN

Esther Defeats Haman

Esther 7:1–10

THE CHALLENGE OF EFFECTIVE COMMUNICATION

"Excuse me, sir. Are you saved?" I turned from my quick sprint into the grocery store to face an earnest young man in his early twenties.

"I beg your pardon," I responded, not quite sure that I had heard his question correctly.

"Are you washed in the blood of the Lamb?" was his follow-up question. Before I could answer "yes" the eager evangelist launched into his spiel: a two-minute summary of the gospel, replete with plenty of theological jargon. I finally managed to get a word in edgewise, convincing the young man that he was wasting his words on me.

While I did the marketing, I reflected on that encounter in the parking lot. I admired the man's courage and boldness—he seemed to be without fear of rejection or disapproval—yet, I felt disquieted, even sad. I wondered how many people would be turned off by his approach. Who but born-again Christians would even know what it meant to be "washed in the blood of the Lamb"? Unfortunately, what the young man possessed in zeal he lacked in sensitivity to his intended audience. I feared that his chosen manner of communication, though it might have reached a few people, would perplex or even alienate the vast majority of potential converts.

Ineffective communication can be more than a nuisance, though. In Esther's case it would have been life-threatening—for every Jew in the Persian Empire. Although Jewish herself, Esther needed to persuade a Gentile king to change his official policy concerning the slaughter of all Jews. If she alienated her audience, King Ahasuerus, she would guarantee the murder of the Jews—including herself. As the king and Haman came for their second banquet in the queen's quarters, surely she must have wondered if she would succeed in her delicate rhetorical task. Could she persuade the king to rescind his decree against the Jews? Would Haman defend himself so effectively that her plea would fail? So begins chapter 7 in a climate of dramatic suspense.

ESTHER DEFEATS HAMAN (7:1–10)

7:1 So the king and Haman went to dine with Queen Esther.

2 And on the second day, at the banquet of wine, the king again said to Esther, "What is your petition, Queen Esther? It shall be granted you. And what is your request, up to half the kingdom? It shall be done!"

3 Then Queen Esther answered and said, "If I have found favor in your sight, O king, and if it pleases the king, let my life be given me at my petition, and my people at my request.

4 For we have been sold, my people and I, to be destroyed, to be killed, and to be annihilated. Had we been sold as male and female slaves, I would have held my tongue, although the enemy could never compensate for the king's loss."

5 So King Ahasuerus answered and said to Queen Esther, "Who is he, and where is he, who would dare presume in his heart to do such a thing?"

6 And Esther said, "The adversary and enemy is this wicked Haman!" So Haman was terrified before the king and queen.

7 Then the king arose in his wrath from the banquet of wine and went into the palace garden; but Haman stood before Queen Esther, pleading for his life, for he saw that evil was determined against him by the king.

8 When the king returned from the palace garden to the place of the banquet of wine, Haman had fallen across the couch where Esther was. Then the king said, "Will he also assault the queen while I am in the house?" As the word left the king's mouth, they covered Haman's face.

9 Now Harbonah, one of the eunuchs, said to the king, "Look! The gallows, fifty cubits high, which

Haman made for Mordecai, who spoke good on the
king's behalf, is standing at the house of Haman."
Then the king said, "Hang him on it!"
    10 So they hanged Haman on the gallows that he
had prepared for Mordecai. Then the king's wrath
subsided.

Esther 7:1–10

At the end of chapter 6, the king's eunuchs brought Haman to
Esther's second banquet (6:14), identified as being *"on the second day"*
(v. 2). Verse 2 refers to the *"banquet of wine,"* repeating an expression
used to describe the first banquet (5:6). Again this phrase probably
refers to a period of wine-drinking that followed the meal. As the trio
imbibed, the king repeated his offer to grant any request Esther
wished to make (v. 2; see 5:3, 6).

Finally the time had come for Esther to present her petition. Notice
how she addressed the king with language that acknowledged his
sovereignty and his need for royal recognition: *"If I have found favor in
your sight, O king, and if it pleases the king, let my life be given me at my
petition, and my people at my request"* (v. 3). The last phrase would
more correctly read: "and the life of my people at my request." Notice that Esther did not identify her people as Jewish. She emphasized
only the threat upon her own life—something the king would certainly have taken seriously. Then Esther presented the reason for her
desperate request: *"For we have been sold, my people and I, to be destroyed, to be killed, and to be annihilated"* (v. 4). Actually, she and her
people had been sold by the king when he accepted money from
Haman in exchange for permission to slaughter the Jews (3:9–11), but
Esther wisely omitted this detail. She used the exact language of the
royal decree penned by Haman, which commanded Persians "to destroy, to kill, and to annihilate all the Jews" (3:12).

To emphasize the extreme nature of the plot against her and her
people, Esther added (with some irony), *"Had we been sold as male and
female slaves, I would have held my tongue"* (v. 4). In other words, if the
offense against the Jews had only involved slavery she would not
have bothered the king. Yet, by implication, the plot was so bad that
she was forced to trouble poor Ahasuerus. The last phrase of verse 4 is
exceptionally cryptic because many of the Hebrew words have questionable or wide ranges of meaning.[1] The NKJV reading, *"although the enemy*

could never compensate for the king's loss," would be more accurately rendered, "the enemy (who plotted against the Jews) could not compensate for the king's loss (of his queen, Esther)." I find the NIV translation both consistent with the Hebrew and more appropriate for the context: "If we had merely been sold as male and female slaves, I would have kept quiet, because no such distress would justify disturbing the king."[2]

Esther's revelation stirred the king, who wanted to know who had done such a vile deed. Who would dare to injure the king by killing his queen? (v. 5). The text gives no indication that Ahasuerus remembered having granted permission to Haman to extinguish the Jews. As of verse 5 the king was not aware that an answer to his question would place him in the awkward position of deciding between his wife and his chief adviser. The reader's suspense reaches an apex in this verse. Now the full truth will be told!

Esther answered the king's question by pointing to Haman as the *"wicked"* perpetrator of the murderous plot: her *"adversary and enemy"* (v. 6). Haman reacted with understandable fear. Ahasuerus, on the other hand, responded in a puzzling way: *"Then the king arose in his wrath from the banquet of wine and went into the palace garden"* (v. 7). Commentators have proposed various explanations for the king's exit to the garden. For example: he needed time to think, or he wanted to work off his anger by chopping down trees.[3] Though the text does not explain the king's behavior, his absence allowed Haman to add insult to injury, thereby securing his final defeat.

While the king was out in the garden, Haman pleaded for his life with Esther. (Notice who was in power now!) As she reclined on her couch (the ordinary position for eating and drinking at Persian banquets), Haman fell on his knees before her and touched her couch. At that moment the king returned from the garden, only to find Haman in a compromised position with the queen. Assuming the worst, the king accused Haman of assaulting Esther in an indecent manner (v. 8). The phrase *"while I am in the house"* emphasizes both the outrageous and foolish nature of Haman's action. The NKJV translates the final sentence of verse 8 quite literally: *"As the word left the king's mouth, they covered Haman's face."* Although the translation does not employ common English, it conveys poetically the horror of the scene for Haman. Even his attempt to beg for mercy had failed miserably. His fate was now sealed—a fact that was reflected in his horror-struck expression.

At that very moment, one of the king's eunuchs named *"Harbonah"* noticed the gallows that Haman had made for Mordecai. Ironically, the extreme height of the framework, built to match the level of Haman's pride and wrath, allowed Harbonah to point out the gallows to the king (v. 9). Without a second thought Ahasuerus promptly ordered Haman's death on the gallows. Such an execution would help to assuage the king's wrath (v. 10).

Here we have the greatest irony of the entire book: Haman died by hanging on the very gallows that he had built for Mordecai. His terrifying death, shaped by the author of the book, also illustrates the conviction of Jewish wisdom that those who do evil will be punished by the work of their own hands. In describing what happens to the wicked man, Proverbs 26:27 states: "Whoever digs a pit will fall into it, / and he who rolls a stone will have it roll back on him."[4] Proverbs 21:7 repeats this theme: "The violence of the wicked will destroy them, / Because they refuse to do justice."

Jewish wisdom predicts not only the end of Haman, but also the success of Esther:

> As righteousness leads to life,
> So he who pursues evil pursues it to his own death.
>
> *Proverbs 11:19*

> The wicked is ensnared by the transgression of his lips,
> But the righteous will come through trouble.
>
> *Proverbs 12:13*

The success of Esther, in contrast to the failure of Haman, confirms her standing as a woman of wisdom and righteousness. She appears as the paradigm of the wise person in the king's court: "The king's favor is toward a wise servant, / But his wrath is against him who causes shame" (Prov. 14:35). Haman exemplifies the fool who endangers his life by provoking the king's anger: "The wrath of a king is like the roaring of a lion; / Whoever provokes him to anger sins against his own life" (Prov. 20:2).[5] Esther, on the contrary, shows her superlative wisdom by appeasing the king: "As messengers of death is the king's wrath, / But a wise man will appease it" (Prov. 16:14).[6]

In chapter 7, Esther's apparent procrastination in bringing her petition before the king is vindicated. Twice in chapter 5 she had put off her crucial request. At that time the reader wondered: Will Esther ever intercede for her people? Why is she delaying? Now, however, her approach to the king at the appropriate time proves her wisdom. Indeed, in all her dealings with the king Esther followed the dictates of Proverbs 25:15: "By long forbearance a ruler is persuaded, / And a gentle tongue breaks a bone."[7] In general, Esther illustrates wisdom's counsel to wait for the proper moment to speak, to say no more than is necessary (Eccl. 3:7; Sir. 4:23). In chapter 2 Esther followed Mordecai's advice by keeping her Jewishness a secret. In chapter 5 she kept her true agenda hidden. Even in chapter 7 she never actually mentioned being a Jew. In sum, her controlled communication skills reflect proverbial wisdom, such as found in Proverbs 17:27–28:

> He who has knowledge spares his words,
> And a man of understanding is of a calm spirit.
> Even a fool is counted wise when he holds his peace;
> When he shuts his lips, he is considered perceptive.

By controlling her remarks, Esther controlled her encounter with Ahasuerus and Mordecai. She said no more than was necessary to accomplish her goals and that she said clearly and carefully.

The Literary Aspects of Esther 7:1–10

While the events in chapter 6 placed a literary noose around Haman's neck, events in chapter 7 tightened the noose and completed the hanging. The plot continues to be a cliff-hanger, but in chapter 7 the reader finds moments of resolution. The tension of verses 5–6 melts into the finality of verse 10. Haman, the wicked enemy of the Jews, has met his match in Esther, who vanquishes him with wisdom. Haman's final act in life, approaching the couch of Esther to beg for mercy, shows his foolishness more than his wickedness. Indeed, his ironic death on the very gallows he had prepared for Mordecai seems totally appropriate.

Chapter 7 also elaborates upon and confirms Esther's development as a woman of wisdom and power. Although we wondered in chapter 5 if Esther knew what she was doing, now we see her in full control of the situation. In fact, Esther overshadows all other characters in the book with her confident display of wisdom.[8]

Communicating the Gospel in Our Secular World

In spite of the fact that Esther began life with considerable handicaps (a member of an ethnic minority in an alien land, an orphan, and a woman in a world dominated by men), because of her beauty she was able to reach the pinnacle of feminine success as queen. Yet her beauty alone could not help where she needed help the most—to defeat Haman. No, Esther conquered her opponent because she faithfully followed the dictates of Jewish wisdom. Unlike Haman, she did not stir up the king's wrath but appeased it. She did not rush into the king's presence with her request but exercised a "long forbearance" (Prov. 25:15). She waited for just the right time to speak and then did so with "a gentle tongue" (Prov. 25:15). Even in making her petition she chose her words carefully, avoiding, for example, explicit mention of her Jewishness.

The author of Esther portrayed his heroine in light of the maxims of proverbial wisdom so that her example would teach and encourage Jews living in a foreign land. If an orphaned woman who employed wisdom could succeed in her highly challenging situation, then so could the Jewish readers of *Esther*. They could learn to appease the king who exercised sovereignty over them; they could be patient in their interactions with the royal government; they could wait for the right time to communicate; and they could communicate in the right way.

We who confess Christ as Lord find ourselves in a similar situation to that of the diaspora Jews. We can no longer assume that we live in a nation that shares our language and our values. In his recent book, *The American Religion*, Harold Bloom argues that the American religious spirit resembles ancient Gnosticism more than the Judeo-Christian tradition.[9] America is "post-Christian" rather than authentically Christian, according to Bloom. In practice, this means that we Christians cannot communicate as if our neighbors, our communities, and our institutions were Christian. When we speak of God's absolute truth or moral standards, for example, most people will not understand what we mean and will disagree with us once they do understand. According to a recent survey, sixty-seven percent of Americans agreed with this statement: "There is no such thing as absolute truth; different people can define truth in conflicting ways and still be correct."[10]

There was once a time when Americans could employ biblical imagery with the assurance that common people would understand their meaning. One could assume a common knowledge of the Bible—but no longer. According to George Gallup, Jr. and Jim Castelli, "Americans revere the Bible—but, by and large, they don't read it. And because they don't read it, they have become a nation of biblical illiterates."[11] The majority of Americans do not know that Jesus delivered the Sermon on the Mount, nor can they name the four Gospels.[12] With such widespread ignorance of biblical basics, is it any wonder that so many people today have a hard time understanding even simple biblical truths, like what it means to be saved?

The secularism of our world challenges biblical communicators as never before. How can we convey theological truths to people who do not have a background in the church? How can we teach people who do not know the Bible at all? How can we preach the gospel of Jesus Christ in terms understandable to those who need to be saved? The example of Queen Esther suggests wise and daring answers to these questions.

For instance, Esther succeeded in her communication *because of her sense of timing.* She did not rush immediately to the king with her request, but approached him gradually, with "long forbearance." She waited until just the right time to come forward with her request. In the introduction to this chapter, I told the story of meeting a young evangelist in the parking lot of my local market. He obviously did not share Esther's sense of timing. It did not matter to him that I was in a hurry, nor did it concern him that he did not know me, or my interests, or my needs. I felt more like a victim of his evangelistic zeal than a person with whom he wanted to share the love and truth of Christ.

Sometimes God allows us to lead people to Christ the first time we meet them—God's timing can be spontaneous and quick—but I believe most communicators of the gospel could learn something from Esther. By and large, the secular people in our world will listen to our witness only after we have built a relationship with them—and that takes time. We must learn to speak openly about our relationship with Christ while not foisting it upon those who are not ready. And the keys to finding God's timing are prayer and openness to the Holy Spirit. As we pray and as we allow the Spirit to guide us, God will help us to know when to speak, how to speak, and when to remain quiet.

Another reason Esther succeeded as a communicator was because *she framed her communication in terms of her secular audience*—the king. When she spoke, she used the proverbial "gentle tongue" that breaks bones (Prov. 25:15). She paid attention to his royal position by seeking his "favor" and by endeavoring in her request to "please" him. Moreover, Esther did not blatantly state, "The Jews will be killed," because this would not have moved the king at all. Rather, she appealed to the king's interests by stating that his wife and queen would be "destroyed, killed, and annihilated." She showed wisdom by using words sparingly, saying no more to the king than was necessary. Wisely, she did not expect King Ahasuerus to enter her language world; rather, she entered his. Does Esther's example suggest that Christian communicators living in a secular society might do the same?

Paul's sermon in the Areopagus of Athens is one of the most secular pieces of writing in the entire New Testament. He begins by praising his pagan audience as "very religious" (Acts 17:22), then he builds upon their interests and ideas, even quoting Greek poets (Acts 17:28). He ends his speech, however, by making reference to Christ as "the man whom God has ordained" and by noting his resurrection (Acts 17:31). With wise perceptiveness Paul did not preach the whole gospel before this Athenian crowd. In fact, he did not even mention the cross of Christ, sin, or salvation. Yet in making a vigorous effort to connect with his secular audience, he did not step back from talking about things they found offensive (Acts 17:31–32). To me, Paul's sermon in Athens exemplifies the sort of Christian communication suggested by the example of Esther—one that enters boldly into the world of secular speech in order to convey the good news of God.

Of course, the danger in this approach is the possibility of losing God's truth in watered-down rhetoric. In an effort to communicate inoffensively in our secular culture, some preachers have abandoned biblical concepts such as sin, righteousness, and holiness altogether. They tell us that to preach about sin, for example, just will not work today. On the one hand I agree with them. In my experience, the vast majority of people do not have a correct understanding of sin. Consequently, if I use the word "sin" without further explanation they will not know what I mean. On the other hand, this conclusion does not permit me to drop the *concept* of sin from my preaching. For not only is sin our fundamental problem as people, it is the reason Christ died on the cross. Thus, although I use the word "sin," I am careful to define it regularly and to use synonymous language for clarification. So I preach about sin, and also about missing the mark, failing to do what is right, disobeying God, breaking God's laws, messing up, falling short, blowing it—or whatever communicates most effectively with my listeners.

If we hope to communicate with secular people, especially those who are not Christians, then we must find ways to recognize their perspectives and to connect with their interests. Again, this is a risky path because we may be tempted to compromise God's truth in our zeal to communicate it. Rather than emphasizing the call of Christ to discipleship, for example, we may instead preach that "Christ will fulfill all of your desires if you only believe in him." Our challenge is to convey the full, authentic gospel by reaching into our secular culture for metaphors and illustrations that engage and instruct our listeners.

Yet I find this to be one of the most difficult aspects of preaching and teaching, because in order to find secular metaphors and illustrations I must be "in-but-not-of-the-world." Newspapers, magazines, television, movies, music—all of these provide avenues into the culture of my listeners. In fact, since I preach to many teenagers each week, I even force myself to watch MTV every now and then.[13] Now I know that some Christians would be uncomfortable with my forays into secular and popular culture (and certainly there are limits to what I will experience or mention in a sermon), but I find that most preaching remains so cloistered within acceptable Christian boundaries that it fails to communicate with secular people—the people who desperately need to hear the gospel of Jesus Christ.

As was mentioned earlier in the Introduction to Esther, Christians for centuries have been scandalized by the secularism of the book of Esther. They ask, "How can a book that fails to mention God be accepted in the canon of Scripture?" Yet it seems to me that this discomfort with Esther assumes that godly communication must mention God in a way that meets certain standards. Surely the inclusion of this book in the canon challenges such narrowness. Furthermore, isn't it possible that the author of Esther is demonstrating the same sort of reticence in his writing that Esther demonstrated in her speech? Is he purposely concealing his faith? Is he recommending by example that diaspora Jews develop a more secular means of communication within their alien world? It makes me wonder—did

God inspire the book of Esther and place it in the canon to upset our comfortable assumptions about godly communication and to call us to a new engagement with our secular world?

NOTES

1. See the extensive discussion in Paton, *Book of Esther*, pp. 260–62.
2. Moore concurs with this translation, *Esther*, pp. 68, 70–71.
3. These and other options are listed in Paton, *Book of Esther*, p. 262.
4. Talmon, "Wisdom," p. 446. See also Eccl. 10:8 and Sir. 27:25–27.
5. Talmon, "Wisdom," p. 442.
6. Talmon, "Wisdom," pp. 442–43.
7. Talmon, "Wisdom," p. 437; Jones, "Two Misconceptions," p. 177.
8. Talmon, "Wisdom," p. 449.
9. H. Bloom, *The American Religion: The Emergence of the Post-Christian Nation* (New York: Simon & Schuster, 1992).
10. Cited in G. Barna, *What Americans Believe: An Annual Survey of Values and Religious Views in the United States* (Ventura, CA: Regal Books, 1991), p. 85.
11. G. Gallup, Jr. and J. Castelli, *The People's Religion: American Faith in the 90's* (New York: Macmillan, 1989), p. 60.
12. Gallup and Castelli, *People's Religion*, p. 60.
13. In a recent survey, George Barna found that 36 percent of young adults between the ages of 18 and 26 watched MTV within the last week. (His survey did not include younger teens.) Strangely, 50 percent of adults 65 and older admitted to watching MTV in the last seven days. Distressingly, more born-again Christians watched MTV than non-Christians. See G. Barna, *The Barna Report 1992–1992: An Annual Survey of Life-Styles, Values and Religious Views* (Ventura, CA: Regal Books, 1992), p. 235.

CHAPTER EIGHT

Mordecai Issues a New Royal Decree for Jewish Self-Defense

Esther 8:1–17

REVERSAL OF FORTUNE

The trials of Claus von Bülow captured American attention from 1981 through 1985. Claus, a Danish aristocrat, seemed to have it all— a life of luxury and privilege with his fabulously wealthy wife, Sunny. His fortune began to change, however, in December of 1980 when Sunny fell into a permanent coma. Seven months later, Claus was indicted by a Rhode Island grand jury on two counts of assault with the intent to murder his wife. In March 1982, the jury found him guilty of attempting to murder his wife.

Out on bail pending appeal, Claus employed Harvard Law School Professor Alan Dershowitz as his appellate lawyer. After months of effort, Dershowitz and his team managed to have von Bülow's convictions overturned by the Rhode Island Supreme Court. However, a few months later the state decided to prosecute Claus one more time. But again he was acquitted on both charges against him.

Alan Dershowitz tells the tale of Claus von Bülow in his engaging book, *Reversal of Fortune*,[1] a title that could not be more appropriate, since Claus's fortune reversed direction several times during the early 1980s. Although true, Dershowitz's story reads like a fictional thriller, like a detective story penned by an imaginative author. Without doubt the ups and downs of von Bülow's life make compelling reading.

One might say the same thing for the Book of Esther, which also could be entitled *Reversal of Fortune.* Consider: chapter 2 highlights Esther's reversal from orphaned alien to queen of the Persian empire;

chapters 3 to 7 tell the story of Haman's turnabout from prized royal adviser to executed traitor; and here chapter 8 focuses on the reversal of national Jewish fortune, epitomized by the fate of Mordecai.

ESTHER APPEALS FOR HER PEOPLE (8:1–8)

8:1 On that day King Ahasuerus gave Queen Esther the house of Haman, the enemy of the Jews. And Mordecai came before the king, for Esther had told how he was related to her.

2 So the king took off his signet ring, which he had taken from Haman, and gave it to Mordecai; and Esther appointed Mordecai over the house of Haman.

3 Now Esther spoke again to the king, fell down at his feet, and implored him with tears to counteract the evil of Haman the Agagite, and the scheme which he had devised against the Jews.

4 And the king held out the golden scepter toward Esther. So Esther arose and stood before the king,

5 and said, "If it pleases the king, and if I have found favor in his sight and the thing seems right to the king and I am pleasing in his eyes, let it be written to revoke the letters devised by Haman, the son of Hammedatha the Agagite, which he wrote to annihilate the Jews who are in all the king's provinces.

6 For how can I endure to see the evil that will come to my people? Or how can I endure to see the destruction of my countrymen?"

7 Then King Ahasuerus said to Queen Esther and Mordecai the Jew, "Indeed, I have given Esther the house of Haman, and they have hanged him on the gallows because he tried to lay his hand on the Jews.

8 You yourselves write a decree concerning the Jews, as you please, in the king's name, and seal it with the king's signet ring; for whatever is written in the king's name and sealed with the king's signet ring no one can revoke."

Esther 8:1–8

"On that day," the day of Esther's banquet and Haman's hanging (chap. 7), the king gave to Esther *"the house of Haman, the enemy of the Jews"* (v. 1). Not only did Esther defeat her enemy, she also received title to his house. Given the author's use of wisdom motifs, one could have predicted Haman's loss of property, since "The curse of the LORD is on the house of the wicked" (Prov. 3:33a). In fact, the passing of his house to Esther also fits the promise of Proverbs 13:22: "A good man leaves an inheritance to his children's children, / But the wealth of a sinner is stored up for the righteous."[2]

Further on, we see that Esther used her position of influence with the king to secure an audience for Mordecai (v. 1). Ironically, the king honored Mordecai by giving him the same *"signet ring"* that he had given to Haman earlier (3:10). Recall that possession of this ring had empowered Haman to issue a royal decree against the Jews (3:12). By implication, Mordecai was given the same power that Haman had used against him and his people. Verse 2 adds that *"Esther appointed Mordecai over the house of Haman."* She used her authority—even over her cousin and adopted father—to raise Mordecai's status, to give him power and wealth.

Yet in spite of newly acquired power and wealth, and the defeat of Haman, the decree against the Jews still stood. An emboldened Esther, seizing the opportunity of the moment, approached the king again, falling before him and begging him *"to counteract the evil of Haman the Agagite"* (v. 3). By holding out his *"golden scepter"* once more (see 5:2), Ahasuerus indicated his acceptance of Esther and his openness to her petition. In contrast to her earlier audiences with the king, this time she heaped rhetoric upon rhetoric: *"If it pleases the king, and if I have found favor in his sight and the thing seems right to the king and I am pleasing in his eyes, let it be written to revoke the letters devised by Haman"* (v. 5). Why did Esther, who had seemed so cool in chapters 5–7, resort to such hyperbolic language? The answer would seem to lie in the difficulty of her request. On the one hand, she was asking the king to reverse publicly a decision he had made earlier—an embarrassing change. No leader relishes the prospect of waffling on the issues. On the other hand, as the book of Esther has already clarified, once a piece of legislation was sealed with the king's ring, it was irrevocable (v. 8; see also 1:19). In essence, Esther was asking the king to break the law by revoking Haman's decree. No wonder she went to such lengths to praise the king in her petition!

Verse 7 can be read with different nuances of meaning. At first glance it seems like the king is complaining: "Look, haven't I done enough for you already by getting rid of Haman and giving you his house?" In context, however, Ahasuerus was restating what he had done with Haman to indicate his support for Esther's request. Thus, he gave permission to Esther and Mordecai to *"write a decree concerning the Jews, as you please, in the king's name, and seal it with the king's signet ring"* (v. 8). They received equal authority to that given to Haman. The reminder about the irrevocability of legislation sealed with the king's ring in the latter part of verse 8 functions in two ways: (1) it underscores the authority given to Esther and Mordecai, and (2) it reminds us that they could not simply undo the previous decree. Another solution was required.

A NEW ROYAL DECREE WRITTEN BY MORDECAI (8:9–14)

9 So the king's scribes were called at that time, in the third month, which is the month of Sivan, on the twenty-third day; and it was written, according to all that Mordecai commanded, to the Jews, the satraps, the governors, and the princes of the provinces from India to Ethiopia, one hundred and twenty-seven provinces in all, to every province in its own script, to every people in their own language, and to the Jews in their own script and language.

10 And he wrote in the name of King Ahasuerus, sealed it with the king's signet ring, and sent letters by couriers on horseback, riding on royal horses bred from swift steeds.

11 By these letters the king permitted the Jews who were in every city to gather together and protect their lives—to destroy, kill, and annihilate all the forces of any people or province that would assault them, both little children and women, and to plunder their possessions,

12 on one day in all the provinces of King Ahasuerus, on the thirteenth day of the twelfth month, which is the month of Adar.

13 A copy of the document was to be issued as a decree in every province and published for all people, so that the Jews would be ready on that day to avenge themselves on their enemies.

416

14 The couriers who rode on royal horses went
out, hastened and pressed on by the king's command.
And the decree was issued in Shushan the citadel.

Esther 8:9–14

"The king's scribes" gathered *"in the third month, which is the month of Sivan"* (v. 9; late-May, early-June). This was over eight months prior to the appointed date for the slaughter of the Jews (Adar 13, early in our month of March). Notice that the scribes wrote *"according to all that Mordecai commanded"* (v. 9). Even though the king had granted authority to both Esther and Mordecai (v. 8), at this point Esther disappears from focus until later in chapter 9. Now Mordecai takes center stage—assuming the position of power and authority granted to him through the efforts of Esther. Notice how the description of the formation and announcement of the new royal decree parallels that in chapter 3, where Haman had issued his murderous decree (3:12–15). However, there is one major difference in this instance: Mordecai's decree went to all officials and residents of Persia, including explicitly *"the Jews"* (v. 9).

The content of the new decree explains why the Jews needed to be informed. Although Mordecai could not erase Haman's command for the Jews to be slaughtered, he could permit them *"to gather together and protect their lives"* (v. 11). In language paralleling that of Haman, Mordecai's decree allowed the Jews *"to destroy, kill, and annihilate all the forces of any people or province that would assault them, both little children and women, and to plunder their possessions"* (compare Haman's decree in 3:13). For modern readers this decree seems unduly harsh, even vicious. Certainly the Jews should defend themselves against their attackers, but why should they be permitted to kill children and women? Furthermore, Mordecai seemed to assume that children and women would be among those who attacked the Jews—an unlikely reality.

Two points of clarification are needed here. First, Mordecai's decree used the exact language found in Haman's decree. It was Haman who had demanded the killing of "little children and women" (3:12). Mordecai did not invent a vendetta against innocent people. Indeed, the Persian women and children would be attacked only if they first attacked the Jews. Second, Robert Gordis argues that the translation of verse 11 should reflect a quotation from Haman's decree. According

417

to Gordis, Mordecai allowed the Jews "to destroy, kill, and annihilate all the forces of any people or province that would assault 'them, their children and their wives, with their goods and booty'."[3] In other words, the Jews were not to kill Persian children and women, but were to defend themselves against Persians who attacked the Jews and their children and wives. Indeed, the account of Jewish self-defense in chapter 9 supports Gordis' explanation (see 9:6, 10, 15, 16).

Verse 13 reiterates Mordecai's intention that Jews throughout the Persian empire *"would be ready on that day to avenge themselves on their enemies."* The emphasis is on self-defense against enemies, not aggression against innocent people. Messengers on royal horses delivered the new decree throughout the empire, including the capital of Susa (v. 14).

THE IMPACT OF JEWISH VINDICATION (8:15–17)

15 So Mordecai went out from the presence of the
king in royal apparel of blue and white, with a great
crown of gold and a garment of fine linen and purple;
and the city of Shushan rejoiced and was glad.
16 The Jews had light and gladness, joy and
honor.
17 And in every province and city, wherever the
king's command and decree came, the Jews had joy
and gladness, a feast and a holiday. Then many of the
people of the land became Jews, because fear of the
Jews fell upon them.

Esther 8:15–17

The story of Mordecai's successful audience before the king is actually not complete until verse 15. After dictating a new decree, he left the palace wearing royal garments, including even *"a great crown of gold."* This was not the king's own crown, but, rather, a "turban" that signified Mordecai's authoritative status.[4] The *"city"* of Susa, already accustomed to Mordecai's royal favor (5:11), rejoiced with gladness. Once again the author has shaped his story according to the maxims of the sages. Proverbs 11:10 promises: "When it goes well with the righteous, the city rejoices; / And when the wicked perish, there is jubilation." Mordecai's exaltation over Haman also fits the pattern of Jewish wisdom: "A man's pride will bring him low, / But the humble in spirit will retain honor" (Prov. 29:23). Whereas Haman's pride, which demanded honor, led to his destruction, Mordecai received honor because of his obvious humility.[5]

In verse 16 the Jews are mentioned specifically. Given the victory of their leaders, Esther and Mordecai, and the new decree permitting their self-defense, the Jews naturally celebrated. A distinction is made between verse 16, which refers to Jews in the capital, and verse 17, which includes Jews throughout the empire. They all stopped and celebrated "*a feast and a holiday.*" Notably, even "*the people of the land,*" a Hebrew expression for Gentiles, "*became Jews, because fear of the Jews fell upon them.*" The Hebrew term translated "became Jews" does not clarify whether the Gentiles actually converted to Judaism or simply pretended to be Jews as a matter of safety. They did not, according to the text, convert because they wanted to worship God; rather, they wanted to escape Jewish wrath. The theme of rejoicing over the victories of the righteous in these verses is another reflection of Jewish wisdom: "When the righteous rejoice, there is great glory . . ." (Prov. 28:12). Even the Gentile change of heart in verse 17 finds an antecedent in Proverbs 16:7: "When a man's ways please the LORD, / He makes even his enemies to be at peace with him."

THE LITERARY ASPECTS OF ESTHER 8:1–17

One significant literary feature in this chapter of the saga of Esther is the abundance of reversals. For example, the house once belonging to Haman was given to Esther (v. 1); Esther, formerly under Mordecai's sway, appointed him as steward of her new house (v. 2); the king granted to Mordecai the authority to issue a decree that reversed the decree issued by Haman (vv. 8–12); whereas citizens once bowed before Haman, in chapter 8 they celebrated Mordecai's promotion (v. 15); and finally, many Gentiles who once intended to harm the Jews began to identify themselves as Jews (v. 17).

Another important element in the chapter is the continuing character development of Esther. Whereas once she had wisely hesitated to present her petition to the king (chap. 5), in this chapter she boldly approached him without delay—a confirmation of her courage and sense of timing. Esther was not one to procrastinate when the time was right. At this point, although Esther was responsible for Mordecai's promotion to chief royal adviser, she drops out of the narrative after verse 8. The passage from 8:9 through 9:11 focuses on the actions and greatness of Mordecai.

ESTHER 8:1–17 FROM A CHRISTIAN PERSPECTIVE

God's Reversal of Fortune

Chapter 8 completes the reversal of fortune for Esther and Mordecai. She reigns in authority as queen, and Mordecai reigns as the king's top adviser—one who uses the king's own signet ring to issue royal decrees. Whereas Esther and Mordecai once feared for their lives as Jews, now they have the power to control their own fate and the fate of their people. With Haman finally out of the way and Mordecai living in his house, the tables of fortune have fully turned in favor of the heroes.

The theme of reversal is prominent throughout the Bible. As we have seen, many Proverbs predict the rise of the righteous and the fall of the wicked. The prophet Isaiah looks ahead to a great day of reversal:

> The voice of one crying in the wilderness:
> "Prepare the way of the LORD;
> Make straight in the desert
> A highway for our God.
> Every valley shall be exalted
> And every mountain and hill brought low;
> The crooked places shall be made straight
> And the rough places smooth;
> The glory of the LORD shall be revealed,
> And all flesh shall see it together;
> For the mouth of the LORD has spoken."
>
> *Isaiah 40:3–5*

When the disciples of Jesus debated which of them would be the greatest, Jesus confounded them with the logic of reversal: "If anyone desires to be first, he shall be last of all and servant of all" (Mark 9:35). Paul describes the ministry of Jesus in one of the most dramatic biblical statements of inversion:

> Let this mind be in you which was also in Christ Jesus, who, be-
> ing in the form of God, did not consider it robbery to be equal

420

with God, but made Himself of no reputation, taking the form of a bondservant, and coming in the likeness of men. And being found in appearance as a man, He humbled Himself and became obedient to the point of death, even the death of the cross. Therefore God also has highly exalted Him and given Him the name which is above every name, that at the name of Jesus every knee should bow, of those in heaven, and of those on earth, and of those under the earth, and that every tongue should confess that Jesus Christ is Lord, to the glory of God the Father.

Philippians 2:5–11

The author of Esther does not say, of course, that God caused the reversal in the lives of Esther and Mordecai. He may have believed this and expected his readers to know it, but he did not say it explicitly. As Christian readers, however, we can see in the story of Esther the same principles at work throughout the Bible: the way down is the way up; the first shall be last; the way to glory is the way of the Cross.

Which of us does not wish to be great in one way or another? Who would not enjoy wearing royal robes and being lauded by a whole city? This desire for greatness is not necessarily wrong. After all, we were created to rule over God's creation (Gen. 1:26–30); indeed, some day we will sit alongside Christ in the heavenly places to rule with him (Eph. 2:6; 2 Tim. 2:12). Yet, our desire for greatness also reflects our sinful nature, our prideful desire to be like God (Gen. 3:5–6). The stories of Esther, Mordecai, and Haman illustrate dramatically the reality of Proverbs 29:23: "A man's pride will bring him low, / But the humble in spirit will retain honor."

We who teach and preach in the church must walk a fine line between challenging people to greatness and calling people to humility. We have all heard motivational speakers who encourage us to "do great things for God." Some hear this message as a charge to serve Christ with abandon, while others receive it as an opportunity to nurture prideful ambition. As I spend time with young leaders, I am sometimes distressed by their spirit of pride—one that too frequently has been encouraged by their mentors. Rather than seeking to serve a great God, they want to be great in God's service! The difference is crucial. Many excellent young leaders find themselves on the fast track to greatness, but Scripture warns us that the fast track usually leads to a crushing U-turn. That is why we see around us the wreckage of lives destined for glory but destroyed by the flames of ambition.

The example of Jesus, who took the form of a servant, calls us to a holy ambition—to serve God humbly and to leave our greatness to him. If he chooses to exalt us in this life, so be it; if not, so be it. Perhaps nobody in our modern world demonstrates God's way of reversal more dramatically than Mother Teresa of Calcutta. She has been lauded around the world for her service and faith. She has counseled presidents, bishops, and business leaders. Yet Mother Teresa never aspired to greatness. She simply chose to share the love of Christ with the destitute of Calcutta. I cannot imagine a more humble avenue of service, one with no promise of earthly reward. Of course God does not exalt all of his humble servants in this life as he has Mother Teresa, but the call and promise of Scripture is for us all: "Therefore humble yourselves under the mighty hand of God, that He may exalt you in due time" (1 Pet. 5:6). Perhaps for some Christians that "due time" will occur in this life, but certainly for all Christians it will come when Christ returns in glory.

NOTES

1. A. M. Dershowitz, *Reversal of Fortune: Inside the von Bülow Case* (New York: Pocket Books, 1990).

2. Talmon, "Wisdom," p. 448.

3. R. Gordis, "Studies in the Esther Narrative," *Journal of Biblical Literature* 95 (1976): 51–52.

4. Moore, *Esther*, p. 81.

5. See also Sir. 10:14: "The LORD overthrows the thrones of rulers, / and enthrones the lowly in their place" (NRSV).

CHAPTER NINE

The Jews Defend Themselves

Esther 9:1–19

VENGEANCE IS MINE

My friends in junior high and I greatly loved our Sunday school teacher, Mr. Young. He fascinated us with stories from his unusually rich life. I will never forget the episode he told to illustrate Romans 12:19: "'Vengeance is Mine, I will repay,' says the Lord."

As a young entrepreneur trying to build his printing business, Mr. Young faced stiff competition. One of his rivals, a man named Phillips, regularly stole business from Mr. Young by lying about him. As his anger grew, Mr. Young began to plot ways to get revenge on Phillips. One day as he was reading through Romans, however, Mr. Young discovered God's promise: "Vengeance is Mine, I will repay." So, he began to ask God to retaliate against Phillips. Only one month later, Phillips died of a heart attack. For Mr. Young this proved the truth of Romans 12:19. Although I was fascinated by Mr. Young's story, I was also perplexed. Did God really strike down Phillips because he had wronged Mr. Young? How could this fit with Jesus' commands that we turn the other cheek (Matt. 5:39) and love our enemies (Matt. 5:44)?

I am also perplexed when I read Esther, where under the leadership of Mordecai and Esther the Jews defended themselves against their attackers and in the wake of their success, celebrated with feasting and gladness. How are we as Christians to respond to the events of this chapter? Do we rejoice along with the Jews and find ways to imitate their actions? Or, do we respond with a more critical judgment?

SUCCESSFUL DEFENSE ON ADAR 13 (9:1–10)

9:1 Now in the twelfth month, that is, the month of Adar, on the thirteenth day, the time came for the king's command and his decree to be executed. On the day that the enemies of the Jews had hoped to overpower them, the opposite occurred, in that the Jews themselves overpowered those who hated them.

2 The Jews gathered together in their cities throughout all the provinces of King Ahasuerus to lay hands on those who sought their harm. And no one could withstand them, because fear of them fell upon all people.

3 And all the officials of the provinces, the satraps, the governors, and all those doing the king's work, helped the Jews, because the fear of Mordecai fell upon them.

4 For Mordecai was great in the king's palace, and his fame spread throughout all the provinces; for this man Mordecai became increasingly prominent.

5 Thus the Jews defeated all their enemies with the stroke of the sword, with slaughter and destruction, and did what they pleased with those who hated them.

6 And in Shushan the citadel the Jews killed and destroyed five hundred men.

7 Also Parshandatha, Dalphon, Aspatha,

8 Poratha, Adalia, Aridatha,

9 Parmashta, Arisai, Aridai, and Vajezatha—

10 the ten sons of Haman the son of Hammedatha, the enemy of the Jews—they killed; but they did not lay a hand on the plunder.

Esther 9:1–10

Verse 1 provides an overview of the events in chapter 9. On the day appointed for *"the enemies of the Jews"* to kill them, *"the opposite occurred, in that the Jews themselves overpowered those who hated them"* (v. 1). Verses 2–10 provide additional details of the foray.

For example, verse 2 emphasizes that the Jews prepared *"to lay hands"* only *"on those who sought their harm."* In other words, they did not randomly attack whomever they pleased; they only fought defensively. The text attributes the Jews' victory to the fact that *"all people"* feared the Jews, and it is possible that widespread fear of the Jews meant that relatively few people actually attacked them. Or, in light of 8:17, it is also possible that those who had claimed to be Jews out of fear added significant numbers to the ranks of the Jewish defense forces. Verse 3 reveals that many Persian officials *"helped the Jews,"* not because of fear of the Jews in general, but because they feared Mordecai. Obviously, in the months since Mordecai's appointment as a royal adviser he had increased in power and prominence (v. 4). Persian officials helped the Jews because Mordecai had become their superior.

Verse 5 elaborates upon the Jews' victory, adding that they *"did what they pleased with those who hated them."* Although the text does not provide additional details on what *"pleased"* the Jews, it implies that something more than self-defense occurred. Verse 6 mentions specifically that *"five hundred men"* were killed in the capital, which signifies that women and children were not killed. This fact supports the thesis of Robert Gordis that Mordecai's decree only permitted the Jews to kill the men who attacked them, not innocent victims.[1]

A noteworthy detail is mentioned in verse 10: *"but they* [the Jews] *did not lay a hand on the plunder."* Again, this supports the interpretation of 8:11 by Gordis, who understands Mordecai's decree to grant permission to Jews to defend themselves against those who would plunder Jewish possessions, but not to plunder the possessions of their attackers. The fact that the Jews did not take the goods of those whom they killed in self-defense underlines the integrity of their motivation: they sought only to protect their lives and their property. The author clarifies this point by repeating it three times within seven verses (vv. 10, 15, 16).

ADDITIONAL DEFENSE ON ADAR 14 (9:11–15)

11 On that day the number of those who were
killed in Shushan the citadel was brought to the king.
12 And the king said to Queen Esther, "The Jews
have killed and destroyed five hundred men in
Shushan the citadel, and the ten sons of Haman. What
have they done in the rest of the king's provinces?
Now what is your petition? It shall be granted to you.
Or what is your further request? It shall be done."

13 Then Esther said, "If it pleases the king, let it be granted to the Jews who are in Shushan to do again tomorrow according to today's decree, and let Haman's ten sons be hanged on the gallows."

14 So the king commanded this to be done; the decree was issued in Shushan, and they hanged Haman's ten sons.

15 And the Jews who were in Shushan gathered together again on the fourteenth day of the month of Adar and killed three hundred men at Shushan; but they did not lay a hand on the plunder.

Esther 9:11–15

Continuing on through the passage, verses 11–15 describe how the Jews in Susa happened to spend another day killing their enemies. After King Ahasuerus heard about the killing of five hundred in Susa (v. 11, see v. 6), he asked Esther if she had a *"further request"* (v. 12). In reply, she asked the king to approve two additional events: (1) hanging Haman's dead sons; and (2) a second Jewish defense (or attack?) on the next day, Adar 14.

Why did Esther want to have Haman's sons hanged if they had already been killed (vv. 7–10)? According to Paton, this request shows Esther's vengeance and desire to degrade the house of Haman completely.[2] Moore counters that Esther may have wanted to display Haman's sons as a deterrent to others in Susa who might attack the Jews.[3] Unfortunately, the text does not explain Esther's motivation. It also fails to account for why she would have wanted an additional day for Jews *"to do again according to today's decree"* (v. 13). Did she want permission for the Jews to move offensively against their potential enemies?[4] Or, did she simply want the Jews to be able to defend themselves against any attack that spilled over onto the following day? If we take the language of Esther's request literally, then she asked only for permission *"*to do again according to today's decree," that is, for the Jews to defend themselves against those who might attack them on Adar 14.

Good to his word, the king granted Esther's two requests by hanging the bodies of Haman's sons and issuing a decree (v. 14). On the following day, Adar 14, the Jews in Susa *"gathered together again"* and *"killed three hundred men"* (v. 15). Although it is not clear in the text, they may have gone on the offensive in order to root out their enemies, or they may have defended themselves against three hundred foolish residents of Susa who once more attempted to defeat the Jews. Again the text mentions that the Jews did not take any of the possessions of those they defeated in battle. Whether they used an offensive or a defensive strategy, we do know that the Jews were not motivated by material gain.

OVERLAPPING DAYS FOR FIGHTING AND FEASTING (9:16–19)

16 The remainder of the Jews in the king's provinces gathered together and protected their lives, had rest from their enemies, and killed seventy-five thousand of their enemies; but they did not lay a hand on the plunder.
17 This was on the thirteenth day of the month of Adar. And on the fourteenth of the month they rested and made it a day of feasting and gladness.
18 But the Jews who were at Shushan assembled together on the thirteenth day, as well as on the fourteenth; and on the fifteenth of the month they rested, and made it a day of feasting and gladness.
19 Therefore the Jews of the villages who dwelt in the unwalled towns celebrated the fourteenth day of the month of Adar with gladness and feasting, as a holiday, and for sending presents to one another.

Esther 9:16–19

In verse 16 the author backtracks from the events of verse 15, which occurred on Adar 14, to recount what happened in the rest of the empire outside of Susa on Adar 13. There the Jews defended themselves successfully against those who attacked them, killing *"seventy-five thousand of their enemies"* (v. 16). Again, the author confirms that the victorious Jews did not take any of the plunder. Since they had completed their self-defense on Adar 13, the Jews outside of Susa celebrated their victory on Adar 14: *"they rested and made it a day of feasting and gladness"* (v. 17). Since the Jews in Susa fought on two days, Adar 13 and 14, they celebrated on Adar 15 (v. 18). Verse 19 reiterates the fact that Jews outside of the capital celebrated on "the fourteenth day of the month of Adar," adding that they used the day "for sending presents to one another." Thus while the details of dating

427

complicate the story, they do help to explain why the festival of Purim later was celebrated on two days (see 9:20–32), and why sending presents figures prominently in the celebration (9:22)

THE LITERARY ASPECTS OF ESTHER 9:1–19

The theme of reversal continues dramatically in 9:1–19 as the Jews defeat their enemies. With regard to character development in this section, Mordecai grows in importance to such an extent that Persian officials actually side with the Jews out of fear of him (vv. 3–4). In contrast, this passage may introduce aspects of Esther's character that are less than flattering, depending on how one interprets verse 13. Either Esther is a careful strategist whose caution prohibits the killing of Jews, or she is a vindictive avenger who punishes her enemies even after their death. The author of the book provides two clues that favor the first option. First, Esther asked the king to allow the Jews to do on another day only what was allowed by his previous decree (v. 13). She sought permission for added self-defense, not revenge. Second, the Jews only killed men on the second day; they neither hurt women and children, nor plundered their enemies' property (v. 15). This sounds more like self-defense than revenge.

Furthermore, the author of Esther has consistently portrayed his heroine as a paragon of wisdom, a portrayal that supports the view that her request in verse 13 was motivated by a desire to help the Jews, not to get revenge on their enemies. Then in keeping with the wisdom theme, several proverbs suggest that if Esther was truly wise she would not pursue revenge beyond self-defense:

> My son, if sinners entice you,
> Do not consent.
> If they say, "Come with us,
> Let us lie in wait to shed blood;
> Let us lurk secretly for the innocent without cause; . . .
> We shall find all kinds of precious possessions,
> We shall fill our houses with spoil.
>
> *Proverbs 1:10–11, 13*

> The soul of the wicked desires evil;
> His neighbor finds no favor in his eyes.
>
> *Proverbs 21:10*

It is a joy for the just to do justice,
But destruction will come to the workers of iniquity.

Proverbs 21:15

If your enemy is hungry, give him bread to eat;
And if he is thirsty, give him water to drink;
For so you will heap coals of fire on his head,
And the LORD will reward you.

Proverbs 25:21–22

Since the first eight chapters have established Esther's wisdom, one would not expect her to seek innocent blood, to desire evil against her neighbors, or to seek revenge against her enemies. Only the pursuit of justice fits Esther's character. Thus, although her request for an additional day of fighting raises the possibility that Esther was vindictive, the combination of textual evidence and wisdom input suggests another interpretation. It should be noted, however, that the author does not explore the moral dimensions of Esther's additional request. Rather, he uses it to account for the unusual two-day celebration of Purim. (See commentary on 9:20–10:3).

ESTHER 9:1–19 FROM A CHRISTIAN PERSPECTIVE

Transformation of a Vengeful Heart

At first glance, Esther 9:1–19 seems to applaud the vengeance of the Jews against their enemies. Verse 5 underlines the fact that the Jews not only *"defeated their enemies with the stroke of the sword,"* but also *"did what they pleased with those who hated them."* Such wording implies an attitude of revenge, if not the outright brutal treatment of the enemies. Other aspects of the chapter, however, emphasize that the Jewish response was primarily defensive. In Susa they killed only men, not women and children (vv. 12, 15); they never took plunder (vv. 10, 15, 16); and Esther sought permission for one additional day of defense, not for a wanton attack on Jewish enemies (v. 13). It would be strange indeed if the author of Esther, who has shown how Jews can succeed in a Gentile land through cooperating with Gentiles, would turn around and celebrate unwarranted Jewish attacks against non-Jews. It would be doubly strange for him to paint Esther, previously a paradigm of wisdom, as someone whose vengeful actions betrayed her wisdom. Therefore, the most feasible interpretation is that Esther 9:1–19 portrays Jewish self-defense—not vengeance. In this chapter we see vindication primarily, not vindictiveness.[5]

Nevertheless, nowhere does the book of Esther hint that God secures justice for his people. Vengeance, even if just, is a human affair in Esther.[6] Does this mean we should seek vindication against our enemies? Earlier in this commentary I made a distinction between descriptive and prescriptive sections of the Bible.[7] That distinction must come into play again here. Esther 9 certainly describes people attacking and defeating their enemies, but this does not mean that we should imitate their behavior. As Christians we must view the events of Esther through the lens of Jesus, who called us to forgive 490 times (Matt. 18:22), to turn the other cheek (Matt. 5:39), and to love our enemies (Matt. 5:43). Even if the Jews simply responded to their enemies according to the principle of "an eye for an eye," we are called to a different standard:

> Repay no one evil for evil. Have regard for good things in the sight of all men. If it is possible, as much as depends on you, live peaceably with all men. Beloved, do not avenge yourselves, but rather give place to wrath; for it is written, "Vengeance is Mine, I will repay," says the LORD. Therefore "If your enemy hungers, feed him; If he thirsts, give him a drink; For in so doing you will heap coals of fire on his head." Do not be overcome by evil, but overcome evil with good.
>
> *Romans 12:17–21*

Then too, it is easy for us whose lives are in no danger to cast aspersions on the Jews who defended themselves against their enemies. We can talk about turning the other cheek cheaply enough when our own cheeks are safely protected from enemy blows, but surely such our protestations sound hollow and self-righteous. Furthermore, when we criticize the Jews in this way we miss the opportunity to confront the shallowness, even the vengefulness of our own hearts.

I was challenged by my own shallowness while leading a Bible study at Los Angeles City College. One afternoon the discussion focused on the passage in Matthew 5 where Jesus instructs us to turn the other cheek and to love our enemies. I mentioned how hard it is for me to know if I could truly love an enemy who threatened my life. A young man in the group named Roberto suggested that the Holy Spirit gives us strength to love our enemies in hard times. Assuming that he was offering an easy Christian truism, I challenged him, saying: "Have you ever had to love real enemies?" "Yes," he answered, and then proceeded to tell an amazing story.

Roberto grew up in a Central American country. As a teenager he became active in an evangelical Christian group that shared a hunger for evangelism and Bible study. The group began to make an impact on their village as dozens of young people received Christ and started to attend Christian youth gatherings. The success of Roberto's group threatened the local government, however, which saw any growing movement as politically dangerous. One evening the local police stormed the meeting and killed all of the leaders except Roberto. Shortly thereafter he sought political asylum in the United States.

Roberto shared how once he had hated the men who had killed his friends. But he had asked God to change his heart—to give him love for his enemies—and, slowly, the Holy Spirit had transformed his hatred into compassion. Because of how God had changed his heart, Roberto decided to study medicine in the United States so that he could return to his village as a doctor. He believed that the authorities would not kill a doctor, even if he were an active Christian.

Jesus calls us to love our enemies, to bless those who curse us, to do good to those who hate us, and to pray for those who spitefully use us (Matt. 5:44). From this perspective we may critique any spirit of vengeance in Esther 9 and even question the validity of Jewish self-defense. Yet most of us must realize that our ability to love our enemies has never been tested. To be truthful, we even have a difficult time loving fellow-Christians with whom we disagree. And how do we respond to those who barely rank on the scale of enemies: people whose dishonesty hurts our business, or people who cut in front of us on the highway, or people who criticize us behind our backs?

An empathic reading of Esther 9 allows us to confront the vengeful, unforgiving spirit within our hearts. Rather than standing back and judging the Jews, we should let the story lead us to discover that we are actually no different from those whom we would blithely condemn. Certainly, we all stand in need of a Savior whose self-sacrifice earned our salvation. Like Roberto, we all need the Holy Spirit to transform our judgmental, unforgiving hearts. And when we leave vengeance to God, we often find that God uses us to bring his love to the very persons who have wronged us.

NOTES

1. R. Gordis, "Esther Narrative," pp. 51–52. See also the discussion of 8:11, above.
2. Paton, *Book of Esther*, p. 287.
3. Moore, *Esther*, pp. 90–91.
4. Moore, *Esther*, p. 91.
5. See the helpful discussion in Baldwin, *Esther*, pp. 100–102.
6. Moore, *Esther*, p. 91.
7. See "Reflections on Ezra 9:1–10:44."

CHAPTER TEN

Mordecai and Esther
Establish Purim

Esther 9:20–10:3

WHAT THEY NEVER TOLD ME IN SUNDAY SCHOOL

Growing up in Glendale, California, I had only two Jewish friends. Thus my knowledge of Judaism came almost entirely from Sunday School. Actually I learned quite a bit about God's chosen people: their laws, their history, and their hopes. Bible stories came to life through drama, film strips, and elaborate puppet shows. During my years in Sunday School I became familiar with the major Jewish holidays: Passover, The Day of Atonement, The Feast of Tabernacles, and even Hanukkah.

It came as a surprise, therefore, when my Jewish roommate in college first told me about Purim. Even though I remembered Sunday school lessons on Queen Esther, these had neglected to mention Purim. I listened with fascination to my roommate's account. He told of people dressing in costume for the reading of the Scroll of Esther, shouting with disapproval whenever Haman's name was heard, and yelling with joy at the mention of Mordecai. I was even more amazed to learn that one ancient rabbi recommended that on Purim Jews drink wine until they cannot tell the difference between "Cursed by Haman" and "Blessed be Mordecai."[1] No wonder the Sunday school teachers neglected to tell us about Purim!

As discussed in the "Introduction to Esther," the relationship between the Book of Esther and the development of Purim probably secured its place in the Hebrew canon of sacred writings. For Christians, however, this connection has posed a problem. H. A. Ironside criticizes the celebration of Purim as "a season of godless merry-making" that is "more patriotic than devotional in character."[2] So unless we choose to ignore them altogether, Christian communicators must face the challenge of understanding and applying the closing verses of the book. We need to consider what difference, if any, the establishment and celebration of Purim makes for Christian readers.

MORDECAI'S LETTER INSTITUTES PURIM (9:20–28)

20 And Mordecai wrote these things and sent letters to all the Jews, near and far, who were in all the provinces of King Ahasuerus,

21 to establish among them that they should celebrate yearly the fourteenth and fifteenth days of the month of Adar,

22 as the days on which the Jews had rest from their enemies, as the month which was turned from sorrow to joy for them, and from mourning to a holiday; that they should make them days of feasting and joy, of sending presents to one another and gifts to the poor.

23 So the Jews accepted the custom which they had begun, as Mordecai had written to them,

24 because Haman, the son of Hammedatha the Agagite, the enemy of all the Jews, had plotted against the Jews to annihilate them, and had cast Pur (that is, the lot), to consume them and destroy them;

25 but when Esther came before the king, he commanded by letter that this wicked plot which Haman had devised against the Jews should return on his own head, and that he and his sons should be hanged on the gallows.

26 So they called these days Purim, after the name Pur. Therefore, because of all the words of this letter, what they had seen concerning this matter, and what had happened to them,

27 the Jews established and imposed it upon themselves and their descendants and all who would join them, that without fail they should celebrate these two days every year, according to the written instructions and according to the prescribed time,

28 that these days should be remembered and kept throughout every generation, every family,

> every province, and every city, that these days of
> Purim should not fail to be observed among the Jews,
> and that the memory of them should not perish
> among their descendants.
>
> *Esther 9:20–28*

According to verse 20, *"Mordecai wrote these things and sent letters to all the Jews." "These things"* refers to the earlier events of chapter 9, in which the Jews defended themselves against attacks from their enemies. Making use of his authority and popularity (8:8; 9:4), Mordecai wrote *"to establish among them"* a celebration on Adar 14 and 15 (v. 21; Adar covers the middle of February to the middle of March in our calendar). Specifically, Mordecai established these two days of Adar as *"days of feasting and joy, of sending presents to one another and gifts to the poor"* (v. 22). These actions reminded the Jews of how their sorrow had turned to joy when they defeated their enemies (v. 22).

Verses 23–25 provide a brief synopsis of the story of Esther, focusing on Haman's evil plot to annihilate the Jews, specifically as it related to his use of *"Pur (that is, the lot)"* (v. 24). The summary also notes Esther's appearance before the king, after which *"he commanded by letter that this wicked plot which Haman had devised against the Jews should return on his own head, and that he and his sons should be hanged on the gallows"* (v. 25). This synopsis of events tells a slightly different story than the earlier chapters of Esther. For example, no letter of the king appears in the longer version of the story. The reader should not be concerned by inconsequential contradictions, however, since verse 25 involves considerable telescoping of events.[3] The point is that Esther's coming before the king led to justice for Haman, who was killed, and to celebration for the Jews, who were spared. Notice that Mordecai does not appear at all in this version of the story, while Esther returns to her starring role.

The first part of verse 26 explains that Purim was named after the word *"Pur,"* which is Babylonian for "lot."[4] The remainder of verse 26 and verses 27–28 reiterate that the Jews established the celebration of Purim because of the events that had transpired and because of Mordecai's letter (v. 26). Notice how the repetition in these verses emphasizes the importance and the permanence of Purim: *"the Jews established and imposed"* (v. 27); *"without fail . . . these days of Purim should not fail . . . the memory of them should not perish"* (vv. 27–28); *"these days should be remembered and kept throughout every generation, every family, every province, and every city"* (v. 28). Within the literary structure of Esther, verses 20–28 intend to prove that Mordecai established Purim.

QUEEN ESTHER JOINS MORDECAI IN SUPPORT OF PURIM (9:29–32)

29 Then Queen Esther, the daughter of Abihail,
with Mordecai the Jew, wrote with full authority to
confirm this second letter about Purim.
30 And Mordecai sent letters to all the Jews, to the
one hundred and twenty-seven provinces of the
kingdom of Ahasuerus, with words of peace and truth,
31 to confirm these days of Purim at their
appointed time, as Mordecai the Jew and Queen
Esther had prescribed for them, and as they had
decreed for themselves and their descendants
concerning matters of their fasting and lamenting.
32 So the decree of Esther confirmed these matters
of Purim, and it was written in the book.

Esther 9:29–32

Verses 29–32 add Queen Esther's authority to the establishment of Purim. Along with Mordecai, she *"wrote with full authority to confirm this second letter about Purim"* (v. 29). Though an awkward phrase, *"this second letter,"* probably refers to Esther's own letter (mentioned in this verse), which was in addition to Mordecai's earlier letter (v. 20).[5] The fact that Esther wrote *"with full authority"* validates, once again, the celebration of Purim. She did not simply give her personal opinion, but wrote *ex cathedra*—from her royal throne. Verse 30 appears to relate that yet another collection of letters was dispatched from Mordecai to the Jews throughout the Persian empire. This time he wrote *"with words of peace and truth"* (v. 30). Although not stated clearly, the text implies that Mordecai's earlier effort to establish Purim had not been completely successful. Perhaps some Jews resented his imperious attitude. This time, however, he wrote in a more irenic fashion. Verse 31 again brings in the dual authority of *"Mordecai the Jew and Queen Esther"* in support for the founding of Purim.

The mention of *"matters of fasting and lamenting"* at the end of verse 31 is unexpected. In fact, the phrase appears as a parenthetical remark in the Hebrew. At some point in the history of Purim, Jews began to fast on Adar 13 in expectation of the celebrations to come on Adar 14 and 15. Thus, the odd phrase at the end of verse 31 may refer to this type of ritual, though the text provides no explanation.

In verse 32 Esther is mentioned for the last time in the book. Not only her letter but also her *"decree"* confirmed the establishment of Purim. This fact was written in a book, perhaps "the book of the chronicles of the kings of Media and Persia" mentioned in 10:2.

Epilogue in Praise of Mordecai (10:1–3)

10:1 And King Ahasuerus imposed tribute on the land and on the islands of the sea.
2 Now all the acts of his power and his might, and the account of the greatness of Mordecai, to which the king advanced him, are they not written in the book of the chronicles of the kings of Media and Persia?
3 For Mordecai the Jew was second to King Ahasuerus, and was great among the Jews and well received by the multitude of his brethren, seeking the good of his people and speaking peace to all his countrymen.

Esther 10:1–3

The concluding epilogue of Esther begins, as did the prologue in chapter 1, by noting the wealth and power of King Ahasuerus, who levied taxes on land and sea (v. 1) and whose *"acts of his power and his might"* were recorded in *"the book of the chronicles of the kings of Media and Persia"* (v. 2). We do not know whether this book actually existed as one of the sources used by the author of Esther, or whether he invented the book as part of his literary fiction. No historical record by this name has been found to date.

Unlike the prologue of Esther, however, in this epilogue another man shares the spotlight with the king. The royal records also include *"the account of the greatness of Mordecai"* (v. 2). Verse 3 summarizes his stature: he was second only to the king; he was great and well-liked among the Jews; and he sought good for his people, both in deed and in word.

THE LITERARY ASPECTS OF ESTHER 9:20–10:3

Most scholars treat 9:20–10:3 as a separate unit of the book. Some even treat it as a composition by a writer other than the author of the bulk of Esther.[6] Whether or not this is true, 9:20–10:3 serves a distinctive purpose within the book. It makes abundantly clear, through repetition that verges on redundancy, that Mordecai and Esther established Purim for all Jews. It is likely that the author of Esther wrote his story, in part, to support the celebration of Purim at a time when it was not accepted by all Jews.

After playing a starring role in the story, Esther appears only briefly in the final verses of the book. Chapters 9 and 10 focus instead upon the greatness of Mordecai. Oddly enough, Esther does not even appear in the epilogue, though her wisdom saved the Jewish people (whose lives had been threatened because of Mordecai's action) and her influence with the king earned Mordecai's promotion. It almost seems as if the author suddenly became uncomfortable with his exaltation of Esther and, to counteract that, strove to reestablish the importance of Mordecai in the closing chapters of his work, especially in chapter 10 (see also 8:8–9; 9:3–4; 9:29–30). Perhaps he knew that his audience would accept his work more enthusiastically if he subordinated Esther's achievements to those of Mordecai. The actual story, however, leaves no question about Esther's superiority even over Mordecai.

ESTHER 9:20–10:3 FROM A CHRISTIAN PERSPECTIVE

The Message of Purim for Christians

Probably the closest most American (non-Jewish) Christians will come to celebrating Purim is the Fourth of July, when once a year we become unabashedly patriotic. We celebrate our national freedom and independence much as the Jews celebrate their deliverance from the evil plot of Haman. Of course though both are celebrations, we who are not Jewish by birth still find it difficult to relate to Purim, even as those who are not American scarcely celebrate the Fourth of July. Indeed, the fact that Purim appears in the Old Testament does not necessarily commend its celebration to New Testament believers.

We should pause, nevertheless, to consider the implications of its inclusion in Christian Bibles. If, as I believe, God both inspired the writing of Esther and directed the process of its canonization, then we must not act as if our Bibles did not mention Purim. The book of Esther, a work notable for its secularism, was written to support the establishment of Purim, a holiday noted for its secularism. As I have mentioned previously in this commentary, God appears to be much more comfortable with secularism in communication and in celebration than we are. That is not to say that God approves of sinful behavior that is often associated with worldly merrymaking, for we know that Christians are not to engage in "filthiness, nor foolish talking, nor coarse jesting, which are not fitting" (Eph. 5:4). Paul urges his Ephesian readers not to "be drunk with wine," but to "be filled with the Spirit" (Eph. 5:18). And to the Romans he advises: "Let us walk properly, as in the day, not in revelry and drunkenness, not in lewdness and lust, not in strife and envy" (Rom. 13:13).

Christians walk a fine line when it comes to the world. On the one hand, John charges: "Do not love the world or the things in the world" (1 John 2:15). Similarly, Paul calls us not to be "conformed to this world" (Rom 12:2). On the other hand, Jesus sends his disciples *into the world* as his representatives (John 17:15–18). Jesus himself confounded his Jewish critics by living in a way they considered too worldly. His association with questionable people in questionable contexts led them to complain: "'Look, a glutton and a winebibber, a friend of tax collectors and sinners!'" (Matt. 11:19). According to his critics, Jesus compromised his holiness by touching a leper (Mark 1:40–41) and by allowing himself to be touched by a prostitute (Luke 7:36–38).

There is a world of difference between the celebration of Purim and the ministry of Jesus, but both of these canonical facets challenge us to reconsider our relationship to the world. I believe that God is calling us to be both less and more secular at the same time. Most of us need to repent of our love for the things in the world. We need to have our minds transformed so that our thinking is no longer conformed to this world. Yet, at the same time, we need to engage the world more creatively for the sake of the gospel. As God's holy people we need to permeate the world.

An example might help to explain what I mean. Two members of Irvine Presbyterian Church serve on the local Board of Education. They do so as an outgrowth of their Christian faith even though they do not make evangelistic speeches at board meetings. Sadly, both of these men have been poorly supported in some quarters of the Christian community. One received criticism within our church for "being on the school board instead of serving as a deacon." The other has been faulted for not devoting enough time to "church work." How sad and short-sighted! If Christians are to be salt and light in the world, what better place for them to season and to enlighten than on the Board of Education! Like the example of Jesus, the story of Esther encourages Christians to risk living in a holy secularism.

The Book of Esther, with its many peculiarities including the establishment of Purim, leaves Christian readers unsettled, and perhaps that is why God included it within our canon—for it continually challenges us to consider our relationship to a world of people that are loved by God in a world-system that we are not to love (John 3:16; 1 John 2:15). Moreover, we who accept the canonicity of Esther should be particularly careful not to minimize the riddles it poses for Christian interpreters. The Book of Esther stands as a warning for those of us who take too much pride in our neatly-formulated doctrines of Scripture. Just when we think we have it all figured out, the reality of Esther challenges our ability to domesticate the Bible. The puzzles of Esther keep us in a position of humbly seeking God's truth rather than pretending to control it with complacency and presumption.

NOTES

1. *Babylonian Talmud, Megillâ* 7b.
2. Ironside, *Joshua • Ezra • Nehemiah • Esther*, p. 115.
3. Moore, *Esther*, p. 94.
4. For further discussion, see "Esther and Purim" in the "Introduction to Esther."
5. Moore, *Esther*, p. 96.
6. See for example, Paton, *Book of Esther*, pp. 57–60.

Bibliography

Ezra-Nehemiah

Ackroyd, P. R. *Exile and Restoration*. Philadelphia: The Westminster Press, 1968.

Blenkinsopp, J. *Ezra-Nehemiah*. Old Testament Library. Philadelphia: The Westminster Press, 1988.

Bright, J. *A History of Israel*. Third edition. Philadelphia: The Westminster Press, 1981.

Brockington, L. H. *Ezra, Nehemiah, and Esther*. New Century Bible. Greenwood, SC: The Attic Press, Inc., 1969.

Fensham, F. C. *The Books of Ezra and Nehemiah*. The New International Commentary on the Old Testament. Grand Rapids: Eerdmans Pub. Co., 1982.

Keil, C.F. and Delitzsch, F. *Commentary on the Old Testament*. 10 vols. Peabody, MA: Hendrickson Pub., 1989.

Kidner, D. *Ezra & Nehemiah*. Tyndale Old Testament Commentaries. Downers Grove: InterVarsity Press, 1979.

Klein, R.W. "The Books of Ezra-Nehemiah." In *The Anchor Bible Dictionary*, ed. D. N. Freedman. 6 vols. New York: Doubleday, 1992.

LaSor, W. S., Hubbard, D. A., and Bush, F. W. *Old Testament Survey*. Grand Rapids: Eerdmans Pub. Co., 1982.

Myers, J. M. *Ezra • Nehemiah*. Anchor Bible. Garden City, NY: Doubleday & Co., Inc., 1965.

Pfeiffer, R. H. "The Books of Ezra and Nehemiah." In *Interpreter's Dictionary of the Bible, Supplementary Volume*, ed. K. Crim. Nashville: Abingdon Press, 1976.

Throntveit, M. A. *Ezra-Nehemiah*. Interpretation. Louiseville: John Knox Press, 1992.

Williamson, H. G. M. *Ezra, Nehemiah*. Word Biblical Commentary. Waco, TX: Word Books, Pub., 1985.

————. *Ezra and Nehemiah*. Sheffield, England:JSOT Press, 1987.

Esther

Baldwin, J. G. *Esther*. Tyndale Old Testament Commentaries. Downers Grove, IL.: InterVarsity Press, 1984.

Berg, S. B. *The Book of Esther: Motifs, Themes and Structure*. Missoula, MT: Scholars Press, 1979.

Brockington, L. H. *Ezra, Nehemiah, and Esther*. New Century Bible. Greenwood, SC: The Attic Press, Inc., 1969.

Clines, D. J. A. *The Esther Scroll: The Story of the Story*. Sheffield, England: JSOT Press, 1984.

Crenshaw, J. L. "Methods in Determining Wisdom Influence Upon Historical Literature." *Journal of Biblical Literature* 88 (1969): 129–42.

Fox, M. V. *Character and Ideology in the Book of Esther*. Columbia, SC: University of South Carolina Press, 1991.

Gordis, R. "Religion, Wisdom and History in the Book of Esther—A New Solution to an Ancient Crux." *Journal of Biblical Literature* 100 (1981): 359–88.

————. "Studies in the Esther Narrative." *Journal of Biblical Literature* 95 (1976): 43–58.

Humphreys, W. L. "Novella." In *Saga, Legend, Tale, Novella, Fable: Narrative Forms in Old Testament Literature*, pp. 82–96. Ed. G. W. Coats. Sheffield, England: JSOT Press, 1985.

————. "The Story of Esther and Mordecai: An Early Jewish Novella." In *Saga, Legend, Tale, Novella, Fable: Narrative Forms in Old Testament Literature*, pp. 97–113. Ed. G. W. Coats. Sheffield, England: JSOT Press, 1985.

————."The Book of Esther." In *Interpreter's Dictionary of the Bible, Supplementary Volume*. Ed. K. Crim. Nashville: Abingdon Press, 1976.

Keil, C. F. and Delitzsch, F. *Commentary on the Old Testament*. 10 vols. Peabody, MS: Hendrickson Publishers, 1989. Volume 3 includes "Ezra, Nehemiah, Esther." Translated by S. Taylor.

LaSor, W. S., Hubbard, D. A., and Bush, F. W. *Old Testament Survey*. Grand Rapids, MI: Wm. B. Eerdmans, 1982.

Moore, C. A. "The Book of Esther." In *Anchor Bible Dictionary*. Ed. D. N. Freedman. 6 vols. New York: Doubleday, 1992.

————. *Esther*. Anchor Bible. Garden City, NY: Doubleday & Co., Inc., 1971.

Paton, L. B. *The Book of Esther*. International Critical Commentary. Edinburgh: T. & T. Clark, 1908.

Talmon, S. "Wisdom in the Book of Esther." *Vetus Testamentum* 13 (1963): 419–55.